D1245482

PENGUIN CLASSICS

NINETEENTH-CENTURY AMERICAN POETRY

William Spengemann, Professor of English at Dartmouth College, is the author of five books, most recently *A New World of Words: Redefining Early American Literature* (Yale, 1994), as well as the editor of two other volumes of Penguin Classics: Henry James's *The American* and Herman Melville's *Pierre*.

Jessica Roberts is an undergraduate English major and a Presidential Scholar at Dartmouth College, Class of 1997. For her senior honors thesis, she is planning an edition of the poems of Sarah Morgan Piatt.

NINETEENTH-CENTURY AMERICAN POETRY

EDITED WITH
AN INTRODUCTION AND NOTES BY

WILLIAM C. SPENGEMANN
WITH
JESSICA F. ROBERTS

PENGUIN BOOKS

PENGUIN BOOKS

Published by the Penguin Group

Penguin Group (USA) Inc., 375 Hudson Street, New York, New York 10014, U.S.A.

Penguin Books Ltd, 80 Strand, London WC2R 0RL, England

Penguin Books Australia Ltd, 250 Camberwell Road, Camberwell, Victoria 3124, Australia

Penguin Books Canada Ltd, 10 Alcorn Avenue, Toronto, Ontario, Canada M4V 3B2

Penguin Books India (P) Ltd, 11 Community Centre, Panchsheel Park, New Delhi – 110 017, India

Penguin Group (NZ), cnr Airborne and Rosedale Roads, Albany, Auckland 1310, New Zealand

Penguin Books (South Africa) (Pty) Ltd, 24 Sturdee Avenue,
Rosebank, Johannesburg 2196, South Africa

Penguin Books Ltd, Registered Offices: 80 Strand, London WC2R 0RL, England

First published in Penguin Books 1996

9 10 8

Copyright © William C. Spengemann, 1996

Grateful acknowledgment is made for permission to reprint copyrighted selections from the following volumes:

Collected Poems of Henry David Thoreau, edited by Carl Bode, 1966. Reprinted by permission of the Johns Hopkins University Press.

Collected Poems of Herman Melville, edited by Howard Vincent. By permission of Hendricks House, Inc., Publishers, Putney, Vt.

Clarel: A Poem and Pilgrimage in the Holy Land by Herman Melville, edited by Walter Bezanson. By permission of Hendricks House, Inc., Publishers, Putney, Vt.

The Complete Poems of Frederick Goddard Tuckerman, edited by N. Scott Momaday. Copyright © 1965, 1993 by Oxford University Press, Inc.; renewed 1993 by N. Scott Momaday. Reprinted by permission.

The Complete Poems of Emily Dickinson, edited by Thomas H. Johnson. Copyright 1929, 1935 by Martha Dickinson Bianchi; copyright © renewed 1957, 1963 by Mary L. Hampson. By permission of Little, Brown and Company.

The Poems of Emily Dickinson, Thomas H. Johnson, ed., Cambridge, Mass.: The Belknap Press of Harvard University Press. Copyright © 1951, 1955, 1979, 1983 by the President and Fellows of Harvard College. Reprinted by permission of the publishers and the Trustees of Amherst College.

LIBRARY OF CONGRESS CATALOGING-IN-PUBLICATION DATA
Nineteenth-century American poetry / edited with an introduction and
notes by William C. Spengemann with Jessica F. Roberts.
p. cm.
ISBN 0 14 04.3587 5 (pbk.)
1. American poetry—19th century. I. Spengemann, William C.
II. Roberts, Jessica F.
PS607.N56 1996
811'.308—dc20 96-3466

Printed in the United States of America
Set in Sabon
Designed by Kate Nichols

CONTENTS

SARAH MORGAN BRYAN PIATT *(1836–1919)*

INTRODUCTION

The title of this anthology, *Nineteenth-Century American Poetry*, rests on a number of unspoken assumptions that need a hearing. There is, first of all, the idea of a century, a stretch of time with a beginning, an end, and a character of its own. "Funny—to be a Century," said one of the very greatest poets of hers,

> And see the People—going by—
> I—should die of the Oddity—
> But then—I'm not so staid as He.

Here, as usual, Emily Dickinson manages to grasp firmly, in a few words, a problem that taxed some of the best philosophical minds of her day: because we exist inevitably in time, we cannot see time from an unmoving point above it. Our view of history, of the past, is itself historical, conditioned by our present, ever-changing circumstances. To know the world the way staid, old "He" does would be, in effect, to die.

Rather than a real segment of history that we discover and describe, a century is a construction we place upon historical data according to our own interests and intentions. Indeed, it is only quite recently, as the world goes, that historians began to think in terms of centuries at all or that people in general started thinking of themselves, the way we do, as living in one. Before 1800, history tended to come in other packages: reigns, ages, eras, millennia, and the like. The "Nineteenth Century," in other words, is itself a nineteenth-century idea; and like all timely notions, this one has changed over time. The nineteenth century is not the same thing to us as it was to those who lived in it. It was not even the same thing to all of them, any more than it is to all of us—as it would be if we could all see it from outside history rather than from our various historical situations.

The fact is that, far from occurring in a single century that begins in 1800 and ends in 1900, any event we may choose from those years actually lies in 100 different centuries: the one that begins in that year, the one that ends there, and the ninety-eight in between. Herman Melville wrote poetry in the same century as Alexander Pope but also in the same century as Adrienne Rich. To call Melville a nineteenth-century poet, consequently, is to divorce him from both of these flanking coevals and to associate the poems he wrote in, say, 1890 more closely with those that William Cullen Bryant wrote seventy years earlier than with those Ezra Pound wrote fifteen years later. Any historical idea that is as blinkering as this one is needs a lot of justifying.

There is, second, the assumption that poetry, like the nineteenth century, is a single, recognizable entity: in the case of this anthology, a form of writing that differs from prose by virtue of being broken into lines. Poetry in this sense is verse. The word, however, is also commonly used to designate writing of especial eloquence, suggestiveness, emotional effect, and the like. In that sense, poetry and verse may be very different things. To William Cullen Bryant, poetry had to be verse. Ralph Waldo Emerson, however, distinguished sharply between versifiers and poets. Edgar Allan Poe called his cosmological essay *Eureka: A Prose Poem*. To Walt Whitman, versification got in the way of poetry. He moved passages back and forth between his poems and prefaces without alteration. Comparing the jagged rhythms of *Battle-Pieces* and *Clarel* to the perfect blank-verse passages of *Moby-Dick*, more than one critic has opined that Melville was a poet only in prose.

The meaning of the word "poetry," clearly, changed markedly between 1800 and 1900 and has changed just as much if not more since then. As a result, much of what the nineteenth century called poetry seems to us merely verse, while what we think of as poetry, few if any poets and readers of the nineteenth century would even recognize as such. What, then, is nineteenth-century poetry: the verse written then that seems poetry now, or that which seemed poetry at the time but, owing to changes in the meaning of the word, no longer seems so?

The third assumption underlying the title of this volume is that American poetry is a distinct subcategory of poetry as a whole, a readily identifiable set of poems ready for collection and study. Asked to define American poetry, most people would say, "Poetry written by Americans." That answer, however, merely raises harder questions. How does the adjective "American" get transferred from the poets, where it denotes citizenship, to the poetry, where it seems to denote a peculiar way of writing? Whitman, Dickinson, Melville, and Poe were all Americans, to be sure. But what do their poems have in common that we could agree to call American? Often thought of as the most American poets of their time, they differ from one another as much as they do from their contemporaries elsewhere in the English-speaking world. They all wrote as they did, no doubt, at least partly because they lived in America, rather than somewhere else, and thought of themselves as Americans. These conditioning factors, however, surely influenced these poets far less than did the (mostly non-American) poetry they read and admired. And even if their nationality conditioned their writing more than did all other factors put together, it takes so many different forms in their work that the word "American" ends up denoting little more than whatever certain American poets happen, for whatever reasons, to have done.

The difficulty of connecting the words "American" and "poetry" illustrates a more general problem: an apparently fundamental conflict between history and poetry—a conflict that frustrates any effort to recover the past through poetry or to explain poems historically. Whitman's *Drum-Taps* and Melville's *Battle-Pieces* are, by present standards, the very best poems to come out of the Civil War. They tell us far less about the conflict itself, however, than do the doggerel verses preserved in the letters and journals written by soldiers in the field. By the same token, we could know everything about the Civil War and about Whitman's and Melville's involvement in it and still not be able to explain how they came to write the poems they did or how those poems alone have managed to survive the passing of the circumstances that produced them.

American literary historians have apparently resigned themselves to the incompatibility of history and poetry. In surveying the various trends and movements thought to have characterized American culture in the nineteenth century, *The Columbia Literary History of the United States* (1988) relies almost entirely on prose for its sources and illustrations. The discussion of nineteenth-century poetry is restricted to such presently esteemed figures as Whitman and Dickinson, who inhabit their own isolated chapters, well outside the currents of cultural history. As if to confirm this separation of verse and state, a companion volume calls itself *The Columbia History of American Poetry* (1994), supplanting *the United States* with *Poetry* as the object of historical attention now that verse alone supplies the documentation. Prose, it appears, will reflect or reveal a history of something else—of America, for example. Poetry, however, has a history of its own.

This is not to say what many nineteenth-century poets themselves believed: that true poetry is timeless. On the contrary, poems, like everything else, arise out of specific historical situations and are received amidst circumstances equally historical. What enables certain poems to escape their original occasions and to be read with pleasure and interest at later, very different times—to remain poems—is not timelessness but timeliness, an appearance of being as true and as pertinent to the world in which they are read as to the one in which they were written. Indeed, poetry may be said to be historically determined, insofar as only time will tell which poems will outlive their originating moment and how long they will do so.

Poetry, then, is historical through and through. Because poetry is made entirely of words, however, the poetry written in any language has its history—its causes, its being, and its effects—in that language, wherever it is written and read. When the language in question is not unique to some nation, as English is not unique to America, the poems written there cannot provide an adequate history of poetry in that language. When, in addition, that language is not common to all the poets of the country, as English is not common to all American poets, poems written there in that tongue will represent that country and its poetry as imperfectly as they do the poetry written in that language. No selection of poems written in English by Americans can be assumed to tell us anything conclusive either about poetry in English or about poetry in America.

What, the reader may well be asking at this point, is going on here? If every year belongs to a hundred different centuries, not just to one; if verse can be poetry at one time and not at another, and vice versa; if poetry is an unreliable source of historical information; and if the poetry that Americans have written in English can adequately represent neither poetry by Americans nor poetry in English, what possible excuse can there be for a collection of poems written in English by Americans between 1800 and 1900 or for our calling it *Nineteenth-Century American Poetry*? What justifies the construction of that particular century, the selection of poems to represent it, and the designation of these poems as American?

In the first place, the century carved out here has a beginning and an ending that are at once poetic and American. The period opens with a revolution in the way English poetry was written—or at least with the emergence of a sort of poetry so unfamiliar that many readers refused to call it poetry at all. Known to us as Romantic, this poetic revolution is usually said to have erupted in 1798, with the publication of Wordsworth's and Coleridge's *Lyrical Ballads*, including that Romantic *locus classicus*, Coleridge's "Rime of the Ancient Mariner," the story of one man's complete change of being as a result of his voyage from the Old World to the New. Our century then closes with a second, equally momentous poetic revolution, that triggered by the migration of the Americans Ezra Pound and T. S. Eliot to London and the publication of

Pound's *Personae* (1908) and Eliot's *Prufrock and Other Observations* (1917).

Among its many consequences, this second, Modernist, revolution had two linked effects of particular importance to our subject. It upset prevailing attitudes concerning the relative worth of British and American poets and their relative importance in the development of English poetry, leading Americans in particular to review the poetry of their earlier compatriots and to find there, rather than in England, the nineteenth-century origins of twentieth-century poetry in English. As a result, current anthologies of modern poetry often arrange their writers chronologically instead of dividing them by nationality, include more Americans than Britons, and begin their historical surveys with Whitman and Dickinson.

This revision of America's perceived role in the evolution of English poetry has had, in turn, an effect on established ideas concerning the earlier, Romantic, revolution as a distinctly British phenomenon. Even if the poetic symptoms of upheaval first appeared in England and spread to the United States, their root causes have come to seem more and more American, first as scholars like John Livingstone Lowes unearthed the devotion of the young Wordsworth and Coleridge to narratives of New-World exploration, and more recently as literary historians have begun to think about the wholesale changes undergone by the English language as a result of its rapidly expanding presence in America and of America in the language, after 1500—a reciprocal development at once vividly displayed in writings of the sort that charmed the authors of *Lyrical Ballads* and largely responsible for the linguistic changes that seemed to them to demand a new poetry.

Seen from the vantage point of poetic Modernism, in sum, America has come to seem a prime catalyst of English literary history since 1500, triggering in succession the literary epochs known as the Renaissance, which extends from the English discovery of America, at the beginning of the sixteenth century, to the first permanent British settlements, at the beginning of the seventeenth; the Enlightenment, which coincides with the period of British colonization and ends with the American Revolution; the variously designated nineteenth century, which extends to America's entry into the First World War; and the Modern period, in which we still find ourselves.

This American history of English poetry takes a crucial turn during the nineteenth century. Prior to 1800, the poets whom English Modernism has identified as its important forerunners were all non-Americans—poets, like Shakespeare, Milton, and Blake, who were especially sensitive to what America was doing to their world of English words. With the planting of the first British colonies in the New World, however, the English-speaking world began to expand westward. By the time of the American Revolution, Philadelphia was the second-largest anglophone city in the world. By the later nineteenth century, there were more English-speakers in North America than in Great Britain; and as a result of this demographic shift, Boston and New York began to compete with London as the stylistic capital of the English-speaking world, the place where changes in the language were legislated and approved. Progressive Americans and Britons alike came to see the United States not as a rude province of the language, far removed from its elegant center, but as its advancing frontier, the place where things happened and the future came first into view. It is this feeling of newly won linguistic authority that pervades Emerson's essay "The Poet" (1844) and Whitman's original preface to *Leaves of Grass* (1855) and would lead Matthew Arnold, in 1883, to rank Emerson with Wordsworth as one of the century's two most important writers of English.

Like all historical constructions, this one necessarily views the past in the light of the present—something that no historian can escape. Whether one emphasizes the differences or the similarities between the past and the present, it is always the present that identifies the important data and dictates their treatment. In electing to emphasize certain past events that, however unimportant they may have seemed at the time, take on great significance when viewed in the light of the twentieth century, the history constructed here is unblushingly modern. In seeking especially to explain why some poems written in the nineteenth century still seem poems (although, perhaps, poems of a very different sort) while others seem trapped in the past and are hence useful only as sources for a history of vanished poetic tastes—in this respect, our history is also poetic. And, insofar as it locates that ever-changing thing called America and a small cadre of American poets squarely at the center of its explanations regarding the emergence of the present from the past, this history is American. As Whitman never tired of saying, America is at once potentially the greatest poem and the threshold of the modern; to be modern, poetry must be American; and to be truly American, everyone must become a modern poet. Poetic, Modern, American: the three adjectives are virtually synonymous.

An anthology of nineteenth-century American poetry compiled, as this one is, to suggest what nineteenth-century America contributed to the history of poetry, rather than what poetry may contribute to a history of nineteenth-century America, will necessarily emphasize those poets who have survived the Modernist revolution over those whom this upheaval in poetic practices and tastes has left behind, consigned to the history of changing poetic values. And yet, a collection that included only those nineteenth-century poets most agreeable to present ideas of poetry would fail to show how truly unusual they were in their own time. The poems of Whitman, Dickinson, and Melville can come so close to current ideas of what poetry is and does that they may seem quite conventional, even natural, the way Hemingway's prose and Marlon Brando's acting do, now that their once revolutionary styles have become virtual commonplaces. Only when we read these poetic innovators alongside the recognized giants of their day do we begin to see how truly extraordinary they are; why they remained either undervalued, unread, or altogether unknown in their own time; and, not least, how much any apparent resemblances among them consist in their differences from everyone else. What Whitman, Dickinson, and Melville manage to do depends heavily on what they decided not to do, on the ideas and methods of poetry they rejected.

For these reasons, this anthology includes selections from some of the most widely read, financially successful, and technically skilled poets of nineteenth-century America. To readers accustomed to such modern poetic values as informality, colloquialism, compactness, concreteness, ambiguity, and difficulty, the poems of Bryant, Longfellow, Lowell, Whittier, and Holmes are apt to seem rhetorically inflated, formally contrived, and morally simplistic—in a word, artificial. No one who reads much in the verse of these poets, never mind that of their less able contemporaries, will wonder at the feelings of suffocation that would send the Modernists screaming for the exits in search of unbreathed air—only to find Whitman, Dickinson, and Melville there before them.

The effects of including the so-called Fireside Poets are by no means entirely negative, however. Their poems may seem to us unnatural—which is to say, unlike our own. But who is to say that ours are natural, rather than obedient to a set of conventions just as artificial and hence just as apt to disappear in time? Merely by asking that question, we see our ideas as no less conditioned by our historical situation than were those of, say, Oliver Wendell Holmes by his. At the same time, we can see something that neither he nor the Modernists who rejected him could. To Holmes, his way of writing poetry was the only way. To Pound, Holmes's was no way to write poetry at all. To us, Pound's and Holmes's are simply different ways of writing poetry, equally conventional, equally capable of being well or ill done. We cannot rise entirely above our own poetic values; they reflect and reinforce our notions of reality. By reading poems constructed on very different principles, however, we become conscious of our own notions of poetry as notions, ideas conditioned by our own peculiar circumstances. If twentieth-century poetic tastes devalue those of the nineteenth century, theirs historicize ours.

It is Whitman, Dickinson, and Melville, however, who occupy the center of this anthology and command the bulk of its pages. These are the poets in whose ability to speak directly to our ears, modern poetry has recognized its forebears. They stand almost alone among poets of their time in regarding poetry as a necessary medium of knowledge concerning matters of ultimate importance, rather than as a haven for religious sentiment in an increasingly secular world or as an innocent pastime for the leisure hours of otherwise busy and useful people. Whereas Bryant, Longfellow, and Lowell entertain such troubling problems as religious doubt, personal loss, and social change, as a rule, to prepare the way for consoling reassurances of the most acceptable sort, Whitman, Dickinson, and Melville stare the hard questions of their day straight in the face and force them to deliver their own answers without the assistance of unexamined pieties or moral cant. If this deadly seriousness leads them, at times, into obscurity, irregularity, or inconclusiveness, these are the costs of framing a new language for a new world. Above all, while the Fireside Poets are masters at generating such sentiments as nostalgia, melancholy, wistful longing, and, when the occasion calls, righteous indignation, their verse generally lacks what has always been considered the essence of poetry, that aura of mystery that surrounds poems like Emerson's "Days," Poe's "Eldorado," Whitman's "Out of the Cradle Endlessly Rocking," and Melville's "Pebbles," rendering them impervious to paraphrase or final explication.

The result of all these considerations is a quite various collection of nineteenth-century American poets: some of them, like Longfellow, Lowell, and Whittier, hugely celebrated in their own time but little appreciated now; some, like Whitman, Dickinson, and Melville, either notorious or hardly known in their day but greatly admired now, both for the quality of their poems and for the historical importance that has been retroactively conferred upon them; some, like Frederick Goddard Tuckerman and Jones Very, taken more or less for granted then but made the objects of considerable critical and scholarly attention in this century; and some, like Emerson and Poe, who have survived the wholesale changes in poetic taste that lie between them and us largely, it seems, by virtue of their willful eccentricities. Although concentrating on nineteenth-century poets, the collection includes part of a late poem by Joel Barlow, who died in 1812, that looks back to the styles and forms of the previous century, as well as selections from the poems of Edwin Arlington Robinson, whose career lies mainly in the twentieth century but whose earliest writings foreshadow the formal and stylistic revolution just ahead.

The one poet included who fits none of these categories is Sarah Morgan Bryan Piatt, who turned up quite unexpectedly in the survey of nineteenth-century publications that led to the selections for this anthology. The author of eighteen volumes of verse, Sarah Piatt had something of a following in her day, largely, it seems, among women who found in her poems agreeable renditions of familiar domestic themes. This reputation has allowed twentieth-century literary historians either to ignore her altogether or to dismiss her poems as "conventional" without taking the trouble to read them. Enough to say at this point, that anyone who does read them will find them unusually fresh, free of the poetic boilerplate that enabled countless nineteenth-century hacks and poetasters to produce versified sentiments and pieties by the yard, without much thought, effort, or skill. She is no Emily Dickinson, but then neither is anyone else. Like Dickinson, however, she has the gift, indispensable to poetry, of making even the most commonplace themes and forms her very own, the most conventional sentiments believable. Very much a poet of her time both in matter and manner, she has failed so far to attract critical attention. And yet, her poems remain alive in ways that those of her far more famous contemporaries simply do not, providing the reader with that mysterious sensation of listening to a present voice from the vanished past.

The inclusion of Sarah Piatt raises one or two additional points regarding the contents of this anthology. No effort has been made here to represent the great majority of poems written by Americans during the nineteenth century. Then as always, the average was, by any poetic standard one might wish to apply, mediocre and is hence of potential interest to cultural historians but little or none to readers of poetry. As a result, many sorts and degrees of nineteenth-century Americans who wrote verse at one time or another, but none that measures up to the poetic standards of either that time or this, find a place in this volume. The amount of verse written by nineteenth-century Americans is astonishing. It was a common parlance of the age, and virtually every literate American seems to have employed it on some special occasions: personal, social, or civic. As a result, even the most moribund verse can offer the cultural historian a unique window on the past. The fact remains, however, that while poetry includes some verse, the two things are by no means synonymous; and there is no point in calling some versifier a poet in order to affirm his or her right to our attention if doing so strips the word "poet" of all value.

This collection, then, concentrates entirely on poets, writers who produced a significant body of work recognizable as poetry either by nineteenth-century lights or by today's. Consequently, it omits a number of esteemed figures, like Nathaniel Hawthorne, who wrote only a few verses, as well as a much larger number of poets, like Edwin Markham, who wrote a great deal of verse but only one or two pieces that can still be called poetry. One aim of this volume is to introduce readers to poets whose entire writings will repay investigation. A select poem or two by a William Dean Howells or a Rose Terry Cooke would only whet an appetite that the rest of their verse cannot satisfy.

Also excluded from this volume are translations from non-English poetry, although that was at the time, as it still is, a widely practiced and much respected literary exercise; although translations can provide important information about the poetic habitudes of an era; and although nineteenth-century Americans like Longfellow and Lowell learned their craft by translating poetry from the Classical and modern languages. Translations, however, deliver their unique information only to readers who know the originals or are at least in a position to compare different translations of the same source—Bryant's rendering of Homer, say, with those of Chapman, Pope, and Fitzgerald; or Longfellow's Dante with those of Ciardi and Pinsky. In the case of nineteenth-century translations from Native American chants and songs, such comparisons are impossible, since no written texts exist to validate their English versions or to have produced different translations of any one piece. Although a potentially fascinating and important subject, poetic as well as historical, nineteenth-century verse translation is too large and complex a matter to be decently represented here.

The poems chosen for each author included in this collection aim to represent as fairly as possible within the space allowed the full range and variety of his or her themes and verse forms, as well as any significant changes in matter or manner during that career. The selections aim in addition to include some of the most prevalent poetic topics, forms, and styles of the time—poems about the losses and gains attendant upon historical change; sonnets, elegies, and narratives; poems in formal, colloquial, and vernacular English—in order to permit comparisons among these poets and to underscore the stunning differences between conventional treatments and those by the great poetic innovators of the age.

The poems chosen to represent each included writer are arranged chronologically according to their dates of initial publication in any form, or, in the case of poems not published in the poet's lifetime, according to the dates of composition that have been assigned them by scholars. The poets themselves appear in the order of their births. Between them, these two sets of dates should help readers to identify and compare poems written by different poets at about the same time—the outbreak of the Civil War, say—and to locate the career of any one poet in relation to those of his or her compatriots, as well as to the world of English-language poetry at large. It is worth noting, for example, that William Cullen Bryant was born in the second administration of George Washington and died one year before the birth of Wallace Stevens. When he wrote "Thanatopsis," in 1810, Wordsworth, Scott, and Coleridge were flourishing. The poems he wrote in mid-career appeared alongside those of Tennyson, Browning, and Dickinson, his last poems alongside those of Hopkins and Hardy.

The picture drawn by this assembly of poems is one of poetry gradually coming to terms with a new world by divesting itself of inherited methods and fashioning altogether different ones. The road from Bryant's "Thanatopsis" to T. S. Eliot's "The Waste Land" is very long, but it can be seen to pass through the metrical irregularities of Emerson, Poe's symbolisms, Whitman's free-verse evocations of the modern city, Dickinson's densely impacted style, Melville's self-sufficient images, Tuckerman's obscurely personal allusions, and Robinson's psychological themes. This picture of unilinear change is, of course, illusory in that the nineteenth-century American poetry on offer here is an editorial construction, not an organism or a biological species capable of evolution. A different selection of poems written in English by Americans between 1800 and 1900 might describe an altogether different development, or none at all. There were more poets like Bryant writing in the last quarter of the century than there were in the first, owing to the growing popularity during those years of his once innovative Wordsworthian style. There were, on the other hand, not many more poets like Melville or Robinson writing at the end of the century than there were a half century earlier, in the days of Emerson and Poe.

The subject is better understood as a debate among a number of very different ideas regarding the nature and function of poetry itself in a time of rapid, bewildering change. If anything unites nineteenth-century poets as a group and distinguishes them from those who came before and after, it is their shared consciousness of living in a time of thoroughgoing and unprecedented change in every arrangement of life—

social, political, intellectual, economic, material, and demographic—changes that would, in the view of Henry Adams, put the year 1800 closer to the Middle Ages than to the turn of the twentieth century. The overthrow of authoritarian regimes and the institution of democracies throughout Europe and the Americas; rapid industrialization and the explosion of technology; the mass migration of long-settled populations from farms and villages to cities, from the Old World to the New, and from the eastern United States to the western territories; the steep rise in literacy and in the production of printed materials to supply the new market; the infinite extension of the known universe both spatially and temporally, thanks to modern science; the desanctification of nature by Darwin, of culture by Marx, and of the mind by Freud and the delivery of these former habitations of God over to what Melville called "the eternal tides of time and fate"—these upheavals and a thousand others like them conspired to detach the present utterly from the past and set it adrift toward an unknown destination.

Like every other department of knowledge, poetry responded in different ways to this dizzying panoply of change. Bryant, Longfellow, Lowell, Whittier, and Holmes labored mightily to explain the present in past terms. Emerson saw the decline of past authorities as an opportunity to rediscover in the present those timeless truths that had become buried in time. Poe considered the loss irretrievable and made poetry its only mitigation and constant reminder. Jones Very fled the changing present to an ever-present God, Thoreau to the transcendent self. Tuckerman set his sonnets the task of finding some consolation for his unforgettable loss. Whitman sought to make the present, in all its variety and instability, explain the past anew and reveal the future. Dickinson wrote poem after poem in an attempt to reach that state of timeless being that Very reported and Emerson envisioned. Melville wedded seriousness and irony in a poetic idiom capable of confronting the present without either pointless regret or groundless hope.

Although this collection of poets constitutes less a development than a very mixed bag—one fairly representative of all poetic responses to the changing world of the nineteenth century—there does emerge in the course of the century an increasingly intimate connection between poetry as a distinct mode of expression and the poet as a peculiar, unrepresentative figure. To trace this poetic development within the wide variety of nineteenth-century forms and styles is to understand one of the bases on which the twentieth century has found its poetic forebears where it has.

For Barlow (that is, for the poet implied by his poems), poetry is a largely public act, the exposition in an approved poetic form of views deemed worthy of general adoption. Indeed, since these views are seldom argued or explained, the readers addressed seem already to hold them, at least in general outline. Their enunciation, therefore, serves not so much to bring the reader to the speaker's way of thinking as to proclaim the speaker someone much like his audience. The poems have about them an air of ritual performance, like that of a commencement address, whose purpose is to tighten the communal bonds between the speaker and his readers. Except, perhaps, for his ability to array commonly held values in especially witty, eloquent, or original figures, and to set these easily in recognized verse-forms, nothing distinguishes the poet from his audience or singles him out as an authority for the things said.

Barlow's, of course, was not the only sort of poetry being written at the turn of the nineteenth century. In 1798, the *Lyrical Ballads* of Wordsworth and Coleridge introduced a poetry so unusual as to be hardly recognizable, prompting Wordsworth to argue in his preface to the second edition that poetry is not what readers suppose but what poets do, while poets are not just producers of what poetry is supposed to be but individuals of exceptional sensitivity and insight, capable of apprehending and expressing the supernatural atmosphere in which ordinary life unconsciously proceeds. Instead of confirming what readers already know, poetry of this sort puts them in touch with dimensions of existence previously unrealized but immediately recognizable when displayed in the movements of the poet's uniquely responsive soul.

Among American writers, this new, poet-centered poetry took several forms. Bryant, Longfellow, Whittier, and Lowell owed their enormous popularity to their gift for making the poet deeply feel and eloquently express what his readers were already feeling, consciously or otherwise: nostalgia for the disappearing past, anxiety or optimism regarding the uncertain future, weariness with the busy routines of modern life, religious uncertainty. While these poets abandoned the hortatory didacticism of Enlightenment verse for Wordsworth's rhetoric of solitary musing, they retained the idea of poetry as a communal act, enlisting the language of personal experience in the service of public exhortation and reassurance. The moral lesson that Oliver Wendell Holmes learns from privately contemplating the chambered nautilus is clearly aimed at his readers, who seem already to believe in moral progress but are glad to have their intuitions affirmed.

If these poets took care to stay within the reader's sight and avoid all moves likely to frighten the horses, others looked more seriously upon Romantic ideas of the poet as a seer and of poetry as a medium of extraordinary revelation. Distinguishing poetry from verse and identifying it with Truth, Emerson sought to recover a poetic language unheard since biblical times, a language of "original relation" with the divine, fearless, though never unconcerned, that this primal idiom might violate the rules of prosody or the expectations of his readers. For him, as for William Blake and Coleridge, poetry was a serious business, the most serious of all. Rather than recreation for idle hours or a source of balm for the troubled soul, poetry took over the function of an increasingly discredited scripture; and like the Books of Job and Isaiah and the Gospel of Saint Matthew, its purpose was to disturb all habitual relations and unexamined ideas. If that entailed an initial estrangement of the poet from his readers, the risk was unavoidable. Once readers learned the sound of true poetry and its way of moving, they, too, could become poets and, by going their individual ways, arrive at last at the same place: that absolute ground of complete being and true community from which poetry springs and to which it unerringly returns.

For Emerson, then, as for the Fireside Poets and their Enlightenment forebears, poetry retained at bottom its public function of strengthening the bonds of community. The difference is that, whereas they tended to ground that community in its common feelings and experiences, Emerson planted the community's foundations squarely in the independent self, thus removing the poet a step farther from the audience, behind a screen of words that mean everything to him but may strike the reader as gnomically obscure.

Writing at the same time, Poe took a giant step farther yet in the direction of poetic privacy by turning Emerson's method on its head. Ostensibly renouncing all pretenses to poetic inspiration or privileged vision that gives the poet moral authority, Poe declared poetry a pure artifice, completely detached from truth, whether personal or communal, and dedicated entirely to the creation of beauty, which he associated with the melancholy recollection of an unrecoverable loss. With no truth to impart except the utter unavailability of truth, he wrote a language at once transparent and insincere, behind whose glittering façade the despairing poet all but vanished.

It is in Poe's desperate aestheticism and Emerson's idealistic unconventionality that we see the earliest stirrings of Modernist poetry. Emerson's efforts to attain beatitude by way of concrete experience colloquially expressed would be validated repeatedly, albeit variously, in the poetry of Whitman, Dickinson, and Robert Frost, while the fin de siècle aesthetes and such of their Modernist progeny as Wallace Stevens would find in Poe's blatant artifices and darkly portentous symbolisms their spiritual antecedents. These two proto-Modernists could not have been more different. Emerson strove to still the jingle of conventional prosody in order to hear the true music of the spheres. Poe elaborated the properties of versification to the brink of self-parody in order at once to veil and disclose the void that lay behind them. Both, however, distinguished themselves from their poetic contemporaries and immediate forebears and aligned themselves proleptically with their Modernist heirs in regarding poetry not as the versification of received opinions or common feelings but as a unique mode of human action, the only one at all capable of plotting the course for a mind adrift in a sea of change, with no fixed points on earth or in the heavens by which to steer.

The sonnets of Frederick Goddard Tuckerman approach a degree of self-absorption that Longfellow and Whittier, Emerson and Poe would have all thought inappropriate to the larger designs of poetry. Whereas Tuckerman seems to speak solely to himself about his own griefs and religious doubts, seldom arriving at conclusions that might solace readers similarly afflicted, Longfellow would not publish "Mezzo Cammin" because it seemed to him too personal to be of general use. To readers schooled in the self-displays of Sylvia Plath and Theodore Roethke, Longfellow's scruples must seem over-nice, his poem elastic enough to fit almost any middle-aged foot. Until at least 1900, however, private disclosures of the sort that we tend to expect and even demand of poets remained off limits, and anything smacking of the merely personal required elaborate apologies in advance, along with assurances that anything seemingly too private was intended to serve a public good.

To read Tuckerman in this light is to wonder at his audacity in publishing the sonnets. As the great poem "In Memoriam," by his friend Tennyson, would have reminded him, personal grief is socially isolating; consolation alone will return the mourner to the world. Instead of venting his private sorrows in order to reaffirm the powers of religious consolation, however, Tuckerman explores his losses in hopes of arriving at consolation through them alone, without calling in the religious cavalry to rescue him. Only in the final sonnet of the First Series does he despair of grief-driven poetry as a means of overcoming grief and decide instead to fly directly to God on the silent wings of faith. But even that decision does not quite settle the problem, insofar as silence does not permit him to escape his isolation by explaining how faith restored his spiritual well-being and, even more, since, instead of resting in his silent faith, he wrote four more series of sonnets on the same melancholy theme of unrelieved personal loss.

Given this interdict against unimproving displays of personal experience, it is no wonder that Emily Dickinson disdained to publish. Even more than Tuckerman, she seems to speak entirely to herself, for while he composes his private musings in complete sentences as if addressing another person, she regularly omits syntactical elements, logical transitions, and even the name of the things under consideration—much as we do when talking to ourselves. To read Longfellow, we need only sit back and let the poet span the gulf between himself and us with bridges of explicitness. To read Dickinson, we must do the work, supply the missing elements. Seldom accommodating or ingratiating, her poems demand that we abandon our own standpoint and take up hers. Seeking answers to her own persistent questions, her poems can no more stop to explain themselves to us than can the rapid calculations of a mathematical thinker in pursuit of a solution. With their eyes fixed firmly on their subjects, and a reader at best peripherally in sight, her poems have virtually abandoned the public purposes that were the be-all and end-all of Barlow's verse, as well as the ultimate justification for poetry in general in her day. Once a way of focusing and clarifying common issues for a literate community, poetry has become an altogether private matter, a mode of thinking, like music, painting, or dance, that records its own motions less for the reader's sake than to facilitate still further thought.

This is not to suggest, by any means, that Dickinson's poems make themselves altogether unavailable to readers. On the contrary, once we catch their peculiar way of moving and learn to move with them, they expose us to a world of thought and sensation that is as unforgettable as it is breathtaking. No one who has heard her refer to the human body as "that pink stranger we call dust" will ever again contemplate the image in the bathroom mirror without a gasp. The point is that, in reading her poems, we enter a mind that is utterly unique, if not in its concerns with familiar problems like mortality, then certainly in its metaphoric construction of those problems. There is, simply, no one like her.

When we come to Whitman, the debate between relative publicity and privacy takes a peculiar turn. Whereas the Fireside Poets shunned the personal except as it conformed to general experience, and Dickinson shunned every form of publicity in order to pursue her private inquiries, Whitman set himself the grandiose task of making his own, highly idiosyncratic voice the common parlance of his place and time, of America in particular and of the modern world in general. Not even his mentor Emerson adopted so unreservedly the Romantic idea of the poet as the new legislator of the world, supplanting the kings and priests of the old order, or the idea of poetry as a new scripture with all the authority of those elder bibles that history had made obsolete. What the modern world needed was a brand-new testament to reconcile the political conflict, inherent in democracies, between potentially anarchic individualism and potentially tyrannical collectivism, the way the Gospels had reconciled the ontological division between the human and the divine—that is to say, by means of an incarnation, a miraculous embodiment of the two logically irreconcilable principles. Whitman's answer to this perceived modern need was the invented figure of the poet "Walt Whitman," a persona at once absolutely unique and universally representative, unmistakably identifiable and indistinguishable from everyone else, of whatever gender, race, or social condition.

Different as they are from each other in their poetic intentions and methods, Whitman and Dickinson stand together and apart from their contemporaries on one historical promontory: both fashioned voices so distinct as to speak their own names, and theirs alone. Poetry here ceases to be a furnished room that new poets enter in order to keep company with their illustrious forebears and becomes a unique costume that poets assemble from conventional remnants to identify and distinguish themselves. Confined to subject matter in Tuckerman's sonnets, the personal here takes on form, prosodic and stylistic, making the poems of Whitman and Dickinson enactions of their unmistakable personalities first of all, and treatments of the announced subjects by the way.

Whitman and Dickinson opened still wider the door to the poet's private life by introducing into their poems the theme of sexuality, the very darkest secret of their day. For both of them, sexual appetite in all its forms—autoerotic, homoerotic, connubial, orgiastic—offered a powerful metaphor for the problem of individual isolation, whether from the rest of humankind or from God, and also for its imagined solution, the opening of an intercourse with the desired entity. In the popular imagination, Whitman survives as the Good Gray Poet who heard America singing, Dickinson as the Belle of Amherst who liked to see the choo-choo lap the miles—a bachelor and a nun. Carefully read, however, their poems prove them crafty encoders of their own sexual energies, those desires for ecstatic communion that they sought neither to flaunt nor to deny but to sublimate—to make sublime.

The final stage in this poetic movement from publicity to privacy arrives with the poems of Herman Melville. Of all the nineteenth-century American poets, he comes closest to T. S. Eliot's ideal of poetry as an escape from personality to self-possession by way of impersonation. Having concluded, in *Moby-Dick* and *Pierre*, that he had no unitary, substantial self to discover or reveal, Melville abandoned fiction and took up poetry as a medium of expression that permitted him to be whatever a particular subject, occasion, and mood might demand, without requiring him to be always one person or to know who that was.

The resulting poems speak in many voices, sometimes one per poem (a Confederate, a Yankee, an Englishman of the old order, a utilitarian), sometimes two in a single poem (an enthusiast and a cynic, a man and a woman, youth and age, a human being and the sea or a wood). All together, these assumed masks, perhaps mutually contradictory but equally sincere, enable Melville to dramatize his conflicted convictions, his ambivalences, his abiding sense of unresolvable ambiguities—his several selves in differing guises. At once self-effacing and self-revealing, the poet inhabits every line of his poetry, everywhere present and everywhere hidden. Poetry here has ceased to versify public opinion or to search for undiscovered truth and has come to do all that Robert Frost said it can do: provide the writer and the reader "a momentary stay against confusion."

From publicity to privacy: that is one change described by the poems in this collection. There are others: a change in the locus of authority for the statements made, from the community of readers, to the poet, to the poem itself; a progressive blurring of the distinction between poetry and prose, owing to the muting of such elements of versification as rhyme, regular meter, measured lines, and the stanza; the renunciation of prescribed forms, like the epic, for piecemeal composition in the construction of longer poems; a shift from satire, to sentiment, to irony as the dominant moral tone; a marked shrinkage in the size of the audience being addressed and a corresponding increase in the obscurity of allusions, intentions, even subjects. The possibilities for spotting trends, developments, are manifold, and the poems in this collection have been selected and arranged to encourage such inquiries.

Were the contents of the volume differently chosen and arranged, once again, the subject might look altogether different, inviting different generalizations regarding the character and development of nineteenth-century American poetry. An editor might, for example, take a more historical view of the subject and concentrate on the most, rather than the least, typical poems of the period; or on poems that address events of a particular moment in American history: abolition, the Civil War, Reconstruction. One might seek to represent the wide variety of verse written by Americans during the century, including work songs, popular ditties, patriotic effusions, and verse epistles; or the equally wide variety of Americans who wrote it: shopkeepers, housewives, social reformers, immigrants, cowboys, freed slaves; or the countless places it was published: commercially and privately printed chapbooks and volumes, newspapers, magazines, gift books, annuals, keepsakes, advertisements. The possibilities here are endless, and each has its justifications.

None of these alternative approaches, however, would produce an anthology of poetry, of writing that present readers interested particularly in this profoundly resourceful, terribly difficult, and ultimately mysterious art would be apt to grace with that name. There are times and places in human history that have produced more poetry than nineteenth-century America did. It produced its share, however, including some that meets Emily Dickinson's acid test for the genuine article: "If I feel physically as if the top of my head were taken off," she said, "I know *that* is poetry." The American past has come in for a good deal of retroactive scolding recently, on account of its mistreatment of the powerless and the despised among its citizens. If, like most cultures, nineteenth-century America has little to offer in the way of mitigation except its art, the portion on display here may do for a saving remnant.

One last word: this anthology is conceived as a place for the reader to begin, not to conclude, the study of the several subjects it touches upon: poetry written by Americans, poetry written in English, nineteenth-century America, the nineteenth century in general, and, above all, poetry. If the volume succeeds at all, the reader will peruse it with deepening pleasure and finish it hungry for more. Poetry is a unique form of human utterance, calling upon all the resources of the language to grasp and express things otherwise unsayable. That is why every culture has produced it and why it goes on being written in an age preoccupied with technology, politics, and commerce. Poetry is also unique among the verbal discourses in its primary allegiance to pleasure, rather than to duty. As Robert Frost said, the poem "begins in delight." Pursuing this impulse in search of words that will suffice, it ends in a sort of wisdom that is delight hugely magnified and transfigured. If wisdom of one sort or another is the object of all our studies, artistic and scientific alike, poetry ranks high among the most pleasurable means to that desideratum; and the poems collected in this volume are as good a place as any to begin.

SUGGESTIONS
FOR FURTHER READING

Topical Collections

Witherbee, Sidney (ed.). *Spanish-American War Songs*. Detroit: Sidney Witherbee, 1898.

Steinmetz, Lee (ed.). *The Poetry of the American Civil War*. East Lansing: Michigan State University Press, 1960.

Cronyn, George William (ed.). *American Indian Poetry: An Anthology of Songs and Chants*. New York: Liveright, 1962.

Cooke, George Willis (ed.). *The Poets of Transcendentalism: An Anthology*. Hartford, Conn.: Transcendental Books, 1971.

Emrich, Duncan (ed.). *American Folk Poetry: An Anthology*. Boston: Little, Brown, 1974.

Sherman, Joan R. (ed.). *African-American Poetry of the Nineteenth Century: An Anthology*. Urbana and Chicago: University of Illinois Press, 1992.

Walker, Cheryl (ed.). *American Women Poets of the Nineteenth Century: An Anthology*. New Brunswick, N.J.: Rutgers University Press, 1992.

Contemporary Anthologies

[Teft, Israel K. (comp.)]. *Specimens of the American Poets; with Critical Notices and a Preface*. London: T. and J. Allman, 1822.

Bryant, William Cullen (ed.). *Selections from the American Poets*. New York: Harper & Brothers, 1841.

Griswold, Rufus W. (ed.). *The Poets and Poetry of America*. Philadelphia: Carey and Hart, 1842.

Stedman, Edmund Clarence (ed.). *An American Anthology, 1787–1900*. Boston and New York: Houghton Mifflin & Co., 1900.

History and Criticism

Allen, Gay Wilson. *American Prosody*. New York: American Book Co., 1935.

Pearce, Roy Harvey. *The Continuity of American Poetry*. Princeton, N.J.: Princeton University Press, 1961.

Waggoner, Hyatt H. *American Poets from the Puritans to the Present*. Boston: Houghton Mifflin & Co., 1968.

Gelpi, Albert J. *The Tenth Muse: The Psyche of the American Poet*. Cambridge, Mass.: Harvard University Press, 1975.

Duffe, Bernard I. *Poetry in America: Expression and Its Values in the Times of Bryant, Whitman, and Pound*. Durham, N.C.: Duke University Press, 1978.

Blasing, Mutlu Konuk. *American Poetry: The Rhetoric of Its Forms*. New Haven, Conn.: Yale University Press, 1987.

New, Elisa. *The Regenerate Lyric: Theology and Innovation in American Poetry*. Cambridge: Cambridge University Press, 1993.

Parini, Jay (ed.). *The Columbia History of American Poetry*. New York: Columbia University Press, 1993.

Reference

Jason, Philip K. (comp.). *Nineteenth-Century American Poetry: An Annotated Bibliography*. Pasadena, Calif.: Salem Press, 1989.

A NOTE
ON THE TEXTS

The texts reprinted here of poems by Bryant, Emerson, Longfellow, Whittier, Poe, Holmes, Very, Lowell, Whitman, Piatt, and Robinson are based on the latest editions supervised (or corrected) by the poets themselves. The texts of poems by Thoreau, Melville, Tuckerman, and Dickinson, respectively, are taken from the following editions:

Collected Poems of Henry David Thoreau, ed. Carl Bode. Baltimore: Johns Hopkins University Press, 1966.

Collected Poems of Herman Melville, ed. Howard Vincent. Chicago: Packard and Company; Hendricks House, 1947.

Clarel: A Poem and Pilgrimage in the Holy Land, by Herman Melville, ed. Walter Bezanson. New York: Hendricks House, 1960.

The Complete Poems of Frederick Goddard Tuckerman, ed. N. Scott Momaday. New York: Oxford University Press, 1965.

The Complete Poems of Emily Dickinson, ed. Thomas H. Johnson: Boston: Little, Brown & Co., 1960.

The date following each poem is that of its first printing in any form, or, in the case of poems not printed during the poet's lifetime, the date of composition (in parentheses). In the few cases where that has not been determined, the parentheses enclose a question mark.

One consequence of selecting poems attractive to today's reader is a reduced need for explanatory notes, which unavoidably interrupt the pleasures of the text. Even where special knowledge of some sort is required, the notes have been kept to a minimum, glossing only such items as do not ordinarily appear in a good desk dictionary or reader's encyclopedia. The notes aim to help the reader find things, not to remove the necessity of looking things up. For biblical and common literary allusions (Shakespeare, Dante, and the like), the notes cite only chapter and verse, inviting the reader to examine the relevant passages, as the poets themselves did, in context.

NINETEENTH-CENTURY
AMERICAN POETRY

JOEL BARLOW

(1754–1812)

From Noah Webster to Napoléon, Barlow traveled in illustrious company all his life. At Yale from 1776 to 1778, he studied with Timothy Dwight alongside his friend Webster. After graduation, some school-teaching, further study at Yale, and three years as a chaplain in the Continental Army during the Revolutionary War, he set up a publishing house in Hartford, Connecticut, where he joined the group of Federalist poets known as the Connecticut Wits, including Dwight, John Trumbull, David Humphreys, and Lemuel Hopkins. Together, they published *The Anarchiad* (1786–87), a verse satire. On his own, Barlow published the first version of his epic *The Vision of Columbus* (1787), listing George Washington, Benjamin Franklin, Thomas Paine, and the Marquis de Lafayette among its subscribers. In 1788, business took him to Paris, where, under the influence of Thomas Jefferson and Lafayette he underwent a political conversion and became a supporter of the French Revolution. Moving to London in 1791, he associated with such progressive thinkers as Mary Wollstonecraft and William Godwin and wrote defenses of the Revolution that won him honorary French citizenship. During the Reign of Terror, Barlow wrote his best-known poem, the nostalgic mock-epic *Hasty Pudding* (1793), and arranged for the publication of Paine's *The Age of Reason* following the arrest of the author. After a year in Hamburg, studying German literature in the company of the poet Friedrich Klopstock, he returned to Paris and formed a friendship with James Monroe that led to his appointment as U.S. consul at Algiers and, after long negotiations, to a treaty freeing American seamen who were enslaved there. Back in Paris, he wrote a series of attacks on American dealings with France that damaged his reputation at home. At the same time, he collaborated with Robert Fulton, inventor of the steamboat, on a long scientific poem called "The Canal," which was never finished. In 1804, Barlow returned to America for the first time since 1788, settling initially in Washington, then in Philadelphia, where he revised his epic and published it anew under the title of *The Columbiad* (1807). Four years later, James Madison appointed Barlow to negotiate a trade agreement with Napoléon, then conducting his military campaign in Russia. Barlow's attempts to reach the emperor embroiled him in the retreat of the French army from Moscow. Stranded in Poland, he contracted a lung infection and died.

In the following excerpt from *The Columbiad*, the poet's remarks to his fellow Americans are interrupted by Atlas, a personification of Africa, who addresses his brother Hesper, the spirit of the New World. At the end of Atlas's tirade, the poet again speaks to his compatriots.

from THE COLUMBIAD: BOOK THE EIGHTH

My friends, I love your fame; I joy to raise
The high toned anthem of my country's praise;
To sing her victories, virtues, wisdom, weal,
Boast with loud voice the patriot pride I feel;
5   Warm wild I sing; and, to her failings blind,
Mislead myself, perhaps mislead mankind.
Land that I love! is this the whole we owe?
Thy pride to pamper, thy fair face to show;
Dwells there no blemish where such glories shine?
10   And lurks no spot in that bright sun of thine?
Hark! a dread voice, with heaven-astounding strain,
Swells like a thousand thunders o'er the main,
Rolls and reverberates around thy hills,
And Hesper's heart with pangs paternal fills.
15   Thou hearst him not; tis Atlas, throned sublime,
Great brother guardian of old Afric's clime;
High o'er his coast he rears his frowning form,
O'erlooks and calms his sky-borne fields of storm,
Flings off the clouds that round his shoulders hung
20   And breaks from clogs of ice his trembling tongue;
While far thro space with rage and grief he glares,
Heaves his hoar head and shakes the heaven he bears;
—Son of my sire! Oh latest brightest birth
That sprang from his fair spouse, prolific earth!
25   Great Hesper, say what sordid ceaseless hate
Impels thee thus to mar my elder state?
Our sire assign'd thee thy more glorious reign,
Secured and bounded by our laboring main;
That main (tho still my birthright name it bear)
30   Thy sails o'ershadow, thy brave children share;

I grant it thus; while air surrounds the ball,
Let breezes blow, let oceans roll for all.
But thy proud sons, a strange ungenerous race,
Enslave my tribes, and each fair world disgrace,
35 Provoke wide vengeance on their lawless land,
The bolt ill placed in thy forbearing hand.—
Enslave my tribes! then boast their cantons free,
Preach faith and justice, bend the sainted knee,
Invite all men their liberty to share,
40 Seek public peace, defy the assaults of war,
Plant, reap, consume, enjoy their fearless toil,
Tame their wild floods to fatten still their soil,
Enrich all nations with their nurturing store
And rake with venturous fluke each wondering shore.—
45 Enslave my tribes! what, half mankind imban,
Then read, expound, enforce the rights of man!
Prove plain and clear how nature's hand of old
Cast all men equal in her human mold!
Their fibres, feelings, reasoning powers the same,
50 Like wants await them, like desires inflame.
Thro former times with learned book they tread,
Revise past ages and rejudge the dead,
Write, speak, avenge, for ancient sufferings feel,
Impale each tyrant on their pens of steel,
55 Declare how freemen can a world create,
And slaves and masters ruin every state.—
Enslave my tribes! and think, with dumb disdain,
To scape this arm and prove my vengeance vain!
But look! methinks beneath my foot I ken
60 A few chain'd things that seem no longer men;
Thy sons perchance! whom Barbary's coast can tell
The sweets of that loved scourge they wield so well.
Link'd in a line, beneath the driver's goad,
See how they stagger with their lifted load;
65 The shoulder'd rock, just wrencht from off my hill
And wet with drops their straining orbs distil,
Galls, grinds them sore, along the rampart led,
And the chain clanking counts the steps they tread.
By night close bolted in the bagnio's gloom,
70 Think how they ponder on their dreadful doom,
Recal the tender sire, the weeping bride,

The home, far sunder'd by a waste of tide,
Brood all the ties that once endear'd them there,
But now, strung stronger, edge their keen despair.
75   Till here a fouler fiend arrests their pace:
Plague, with his burning breath and bloated face,
With saffron eyes that thro the dungeon shine,
And the black tumors bursting from the groin,
Stalks o'er the slave; who, cowering on the sod,
80   Shrinks from the Demon and invokes his God,
Sucks hot contagion with his quivering breath
And rackt with rending torture sinks in death.
     Nor shall these pangs atone the nation's crime;
Far heavier vengeance, in the march of time,
85   Attends them still; if still they dare debase
And hold inthrall'd the millions of my race;
A vengeance that shall shake the world's deep frame,
That heaven abhors and hell might shrink to name.
Nature, long outraged, delves the crusted sphere
90   And molds the mining mischief dark and drear;
Europa too the penal shock shall find,
The rude soul-selling monsters of mankind.
Where Alps and Andes at their bases meet,
In earth's mid caves to lock their granite feet,
95   Heave their broad spines, expand each breathing lobe
And with their massy members rib the globe,
Her cauldron'd floods of fire their blast prepare;
Her wallowing womb of subterranean war
Waits but the fissure that my wave shall find,
100   To force the foldings of the rocky rind,
Crash your curst continent, and whirl on high
The vast avulsion vaulting thro the sky,
Fling far the bursting fragments, scattering wide
Rocks, mountains, nations o'er the swallowing tide.
105   Plunging and surging with alternate sweep,
They storm the day-vault and lay bare the deep,
Toss, tumble, plow their place, then slow subside,
And swell each ocean as their bulk they hide;
Two oceans dasht in one! that climbs and roars,
110   And seeks in vain the exterminated shores,
The deep drencht hemisphere. Far sunk from day,
It crumbles, rolls, it churns the settling sea,

Turns up each prominence, heaves every side,
To pierce once more the landless length of tide;
115 Till some poised Pambamarca[1] looms at last
A dim lone island in the watery waste,
Mourns all his minor mountains wreckt and hurl'd,
Stands the sad relic of a ruin'd world,
Attests the wrath our mother kept in store
120 And rues her judgments on the race she bore.
No saving Ark around him rides the main,
Nor Dove weak-wing'd her footing finds again;
His own bald eagle skims alone the sky,
Darts from all points of heaven her searching eye,
125 Kens thro the gloom her ancient rock of rest
And finds her cavern'd crag, her solitary nest.
        Thus toned the Titan his tremendous knell
And lasht his ocean to a loftier swell;
Earth groans responsive and with laboring woes
130 Leans o'er the surge and stills the storm he throws.
        Fathers and friends, I know the boding fears
Of angry genii and of rending spheres
Assail not souls like yours; whom science bright
Thro shadowy nature leads with surer light;
135 For whom she strips the heavens of love and hate,
Strikes from Jove's hand the brandisht bolt of fate,
Gives each effect its own indubious cause,
Divides her moral from her physic laws,
Shows where the virtues find their nurturing food,
140 And men their motives to be just and good.
You scorn the Titan's threat; nor shall I strain
The powers of pathos in a task so vain
As Afric's wrongs to sing; for what avails
To harp for you these known familiar tales;
145 To tongue mute misery, and re-rack the soul
With crimes oft copied from that bloody scroll
Where Slavery pens her woes? tho tis but there
We learn the weight that mortal life can bear.
The tale might startle still the accustom'd ear
150 Still shake the nerve that pumps the pearly tear,
Melt every heart and thro the nation gain
Full many a voice to break the barbarous chain.
But why to sympathy for guidance fly,

(Her aids uncertain and of scant supply)
155 When your own self-excited sense affords
A guide more sure, and every sense accords?
Where strong self-interest join'd with duty lies,
Where doing right demands no sacrifice,
Where profit, pleasure, life-expanding fame
160 League their allurements to support the claim,
Tis safest there the impleaded cause to trust;
Men well instructed will be always just.
  From slavery then your rising realms to save,
Regard the master, notice not the slave;
165 Consult alone for freemen, and bestow
Your best, your only cares to keep them so.
Tyrants are never free; and small and great,
All masters must be tyrants soon or late;
So nature works; and oft the lordling knave
170 Turns out at once a tyrant and a slave,
Struts, cringes, bullies, begs, as courtiers must,
Makes one a god, another treads in dust,
Fears all alike and filches whom he can,
But knows no equal, finds no friend in man.
175 Ah, would you not be slaves, with lords and kings,
Then be not masters; there the danger springs.
The whole crude system that torments this earth,
Of rank, privation, privilege of birth,
False honor, fraud, corruption, civil jars,
180 The rage of conquest and the curse of wars,
Pandora's total shower, all ills combined
That erst o'erwhelm'd and still distress mankind,
Boxt up secure in your deliberate hand,
Wait your behest to fix or fly this land.
185 Equality of Right is nature's plan;
And following nature is the march of man.
Whene'er he deviates in the least degree,
When, free himself, he would be more than free,
The baseless column, rear'd to bear his bust,
190 Falls as he mounts and whelms him in the dust.
  See Rome's rude sires, with autocratic gait,
Tread down their tyrant and erect their state;
Their state secured, they deem it wise and brave
That every freeman should command a slave,

195 And, flusht with franchise of his camp and town,
Rove thro the world and hunt the nations down;
Master and man the same vile spirit gains,
Rome chains the world and wears herself the chains.
Mark modern Europe with her feudal codes,
200 Serfs, villains, vassals, nobles, kings and gods,
All slaves of different grades, corrupt and curst
With high and low, for senseless rank athirst,
Wage endless wars; not fighting to be free,
But *cujum pecus*,[2] whose base herd they'll be.
205 Too much of Europe, here transplanted o'er,
Nursed feudal feelings on your tented shore,
Brought sable serfs from Afric, call'd it gain,
And urged your sires to forge the fatal chain.
But now, the tents o'erturn'd, the war dogs fled,
210 Now fearless Freedom rears at last her head
Matcht with celestial Peace,—my friends, beware
To shade the splendors of so bright a pair;
Complete their triumph, fix their firm abode,
Purge all privations from your liberal code,
215 Restore their souls to men, give earth repose
And save your sons from slavery, wars and woes.
Based on its rock of right your empire lies,
On walls of wisdom let the fabric rise;
Preserve your principles, their force unfold,
220 Let nations prove them and let kings behold.
EQUALITY, your first firm-grounded stand;
Then FREE ELECTION; then your FEDERAL BAND;
This holy Triad should for ever shine
The great compendium of all rights divine,
225 Creed of all schools, whence youths by millions draw
Their themes of right, their decalogues of law;
Till men shall wonder (in these codes inured)
How wars were made, how tyrants were endured.
Then shall your works of art superior rise,
230 Your fruits perfume a larger length of skies,
Canals careering climb your sunbright hills,
Vein the green slopes and strow their nurturing rills,
Thro tunnel'd heights and sundering ridges glide,
Rob the rich west of half Kenhawa's[3] tide,
235 Mix your wide climates, all their stores confound

And plant new ports in every midland mound.
Your lawless Mississippi, now who slimes
And drowns and desolates his waste of climes,
Ribb'd with your dikes, his torrent shall restrain
240   And ask your leave to travel to the main;
Won from his wave while rising cantons smile,
Rear their glad nations and reward their toil.

1807

WILLIAM CULLEN BRYANT

(1794–1878)

Poetry may be said to have done more for Bryant than he ever managed to do for it. Born in rural Massachusetts to cultured descendants of the earliest New England settlers, he displayed a precocious capacity for learning and a passion for the outdoors that, together, would equip him superbly for poetry of the sort just then emerging. Reading Pope in his father's large library, he conceived the desire to become a poet and, in 1808, wrote a verse satire on Thomas Jefferson, called "The Embargo," which his father had published along with several other pieces by the thirteen-year-old boy. In 1810, Bryant entered Williams College as a sophomore, planning to transfer to Yale the next year. His father's meager income as a country doctor, however, forced him to leave college and begin the study of law. At this juncture, he wrote "Thanatopsis" under the influence of William Cowper and the so-called Graveyard Poets but did not seek to have it published. Upon his admission to the bar in 1815, he wrote "To a Waterfowl," signaling the transfer of his poetic allegiances to Wordsworth, where they would largely remain. That poem, too, lay unpublished on his desk at home, while Bryant went off to practice law in a neighboring village. Then, in 1817, when an editor of the *North American Review* arrived soliciting contributions, Bryant's father gave him both poems, which appeared in subsequent issues of the magazine to great acclaim. By 1821, Bryant had become sufficiently successful in the law to marry and sufficiently admired as a poet to deliver the Phi Beta Kappa poem at Harvard. The publication of his first book of poems, in the same year, landed him a contract to write poetry for a New York newspaper. That connection, in turn, enabled him to give up the law for a career in editing, first with a magazine and, in 1829, at the New York *Evening Post,* where he would remain for nearly fifty years.

Editorial duties conspired with the responsibilities of increasing ownership of the paper to leave Bryant financially secure but with little time for poetry. When his second volume of *Poems* appeared, in 1832, it contained very little written after 1829 and nearly a third of the poems he would ever write. Enthusiastically received, both in the United States and in England, the volume earned him the reputation, as the premier

American poet, that would follow him throughout his life. Although he would publish two more collections, *The Fountain and Other Poems* (1842) and *The White-Footed Deer and Other Poems* (1844), and, over the five years following the death of his wife in 1865, a complete blank-verse translation of Homer, his long career with the *Evening Post* would be distinguished largely by his progressive editorial positions. Not even when profits from his ownership of the newspaper allowed him time for extensive travel, as well as for improving his country estate on Long Island, did he produce poems in anything like the quantity and quality of those written before he was thirty. Nonetheless, he went to his death with his laurels intact, the very image of the benign, bewhiskered patriarch of the American schoolroom.

THANATOPSIS

     To him who in the love of Nature holds
Communion with her visible forms, she speaks
A various language; for his gayer hours
She has a voice of gladness, and a smile
5   And eloquence of beauty, and she glides
Into his darker musings, with a mild
And healing sympathy, that steals away
Their sharpness, ere he is aware. When thoughts
Of the last bitter hour come like a blight
10 Over thy spirit, and sad images
Of the stern agony, and shroud, and pall,
And breathless darkness, and the narrow house,
Make thee to shudder, and grow sick at heart;—
Go forth, under the open sky, and list
15 To Nature's teachings, while from all around—
Earth and her waters, and the depths of air—
Comes a still voice—Yet a few days, and thee
The all-beholding sun shall see no more
In all his course; nor yet in the cold ground,
20 Where thy pale form was laid, with many tears,
Nor in the embrace of ocean, shall exist
Thy image. Earth, that nourished thee, shall claim
Thy growth, to be resolved to earth again,

And, lost each human trace, surrendering up
25   Thine individual being, shalt thou go
To mix for ever with the elements,
To be a brother to the insensible rock
And to the sluggish clod, which the rude swain
Turns with his share, and treads upon. The oak
30   Shall send his roots abroad, and pierce thy mould.

Yet not to thine eternal resting-place
Shalt thou retire alone, nor couldst thou wish
Couch more magnificent. Thou shalt lie down
With patriarchs of the infant world—with kings,
35   The powerful of the earth—the wise, the good,
Fair forms, and hoary seers of ages past,
All in one mighty sepulchre. The hills
Rock-ribbed and ancient as the sun,—the vales
Stretching in pensive quietness between;
40   The venerable woods—rivers that move
In majesty, and the complaining brooks
That make the meadows green; and, poured round all,
Old Ocean's gray and melancholy waste,—
Are but the solemn decorations all
45   Of the great tomb of man. The golden sun,
The planets, all the infinite host of heaven,
Are shining on the sad abodes of death,
Through the still lapse of ages. All that tread
The globe are but a handful to the tribes
50   That slumber in its bosom.—Take the wings
Of morning, pierce the Barcan wilderness,
Or lose thyself in the continuous woods
Where rolls the Oregon, and hears no sound,
Save his own dashings—yet the dead are there:
55   And millions in those solitudes, since first
The flight of years began, have laid them down
In their last sleep—the dead reign there alone.
So shalt thou rest, and what if thou withdraw
In silence from the living, and no friend
60   Take note of thy departure? All that breathe
Will share thy destiny. The gay will laugh
When thou art gone, the solemn brood of care

Plod on, and each one as before will chase
His favorite phantom; yet all these shall leave
65   Their mirth and their employments, and shall come
And make their bed with thee. As the long train
Of ages glide away, the sons of men,
The youth in life's green spring, and he who goes
In the full strength of years, matron and maid,
70   The speechless babe, and the gray-headed man—
Shall one by one be gathered to thy side,
By those, who in their turn shall follow them.

So live, that when thy summons comes to join
The innumerable caravan, which moves
75   To that mysterious realm, where each shall take
His chamber in the silent halls of death,
Thou go not, like the quarry-slave at night,
Scourged to his dungeon, but, sustained and soothed
By an unfaltering trust, approach thy grave,
80   Like one who wraps the drapery of his couch
About him, and lies down to pleasant dreams.

                                        1817

TO A WATERFOWL

    Whither, midst falling dew,
While glow the heavens with the last steps of day,
Far, through their rosy depths, dost thou pursue
    Thy solitary way?

5   Vainly the fowler's eye
Might mark thy distant flight to do thee wrong,
As, darkly seen against the crimson sky,
    Thy figure floats along.

    Seek'st thou the plashy brink
10   Of weedy lake, or marge of river wide,
Or where the rocking billows rise and sink
    On the chafed ocean-side?

There is a Power whose care
Teaches thy way along that pathless coast—
15   The desert and illimitable air—
       Lone wandering, but not lost.

All day thy wings have fanned,
At that far height, the cold, thin atmosphere,
Yet stoop not, weary, to the welcome land,
20   Though the dark night is near.

And soon that toil shall end;
Soon shalt thou find a summer home, and rest,
And scream among thy fellows; reeds shall bend,
       Soon, o'er thy sheltered nest.

25   Thou'rt gone, the abyss of heaven
Hath swallowed up thy form; yet, on my heart
Deeply hath sunk the lesson thou hast given,
       And shall not soon depart.

He who, from zone to zone,
30   Guides through the boundless sky thy certain flight,
In the long way that I must tread alone,
       Will lead my steps aright.

                     1818

MUTATION

They talk of short-lived pleasure—be it so—
    Pain dies as quickly: stern, hard-featured pain
Expires, and lets her weary prisoner go.
    The fiercest agonies have shortest reign;
5   And after dreams of horror, comes again
The welcome morning with its rays of peace.
    Oblivion, softly wiping out the stain,
Makes the strong secret pangs of shame to cease:
Remorse is virtue's root; its fair increase
10   Are fruits of innocence and blessedness:

Thus joy, o'erborne and bound, doth still release
   His young limbs from the chains that round him press.
Weep not that the world changes—did it keep
A stable, changeless state, 'twere cause indeed to weep.

1824

HYMN TO THE NORTH STAR

   The sad and solemn night
Hath yet her multitude of cheerful fires;
   The glorious hosts of light
Walk the dark hemisphere till she retires;
All through her silent watches, gliding slow,
Her constellations come, and climb the heavens, and go.

   Day, too, hath many a star
To grace his gorgeous reign, as bright as they:
   Through the blue fields afar,
Unseen, they follow in his flaming way:
Many a bright lingerer, as the eve grows dim,
Tells what a radiant troop arose and set with him.

   And thou dost see them rise,
Star of the Pole! and thou dost see them set.
   Alone, in thy cold skies,
Thou keep'st thy old unmoving station yet,
Nor join'st the dances of that glittering train,
Nor dipp'st thy virgin orb in the blue western main.

   There, at morn's rosy birth,
Thou lookest meekly through the kindling air,
   And eve, that round the earth
Chases the day, beholds thee watching there;
There noontide finds thee, and the hour that calls
The shapes of polar flame to scale heaven's azure walls.

   Alike, beneath thine eye,
The deeds of darkness and of light are done;
   High toward the starlit sky

Towns blaze, the smoke of battle blots the sun,
The night storm on a thousand hills is loud,
30   And the strong wind of day doth mingle sea and cloud.

On thy unaltering blaze
The half-wrecked mariner, his compass lost,
Fixes his steady gaze,
And steers, undoubting, to the friendly coast;
35 And they who stray in perilous wastes, by night,
Are glad when thou dost shine to guide their footsteps right.

And, therefore, bards of old,
Sages and hermits of the solemn wood,
Did in thy beams behold
40 A beauteous type of that unchanging good,
That bright eternal beacon, by whose ray
The voyager of time should shape his heedful way.

1825

TO A MOSQUITO

Fair insect! that, with threadlike legs spread out,
And blood-extracting bill and filmy wing,
Dost murmur, as thou slowly sail'st about,
In pitiless ears full many a plaintive thing,
5 And tell how little our large veins would bleed,
Would we but yield them to thy bitter need.

Unwillingly, I own, and, what is worse,
Full angrily men hearken to thy plaint;
Thou gettest many a brush, and many a curse,
10 For saying thou art gaunt, and starved, and faint;
Even the old beggar, while he asks for food,
Would kill thee, hapless stranger, if he could.

I call thee stranger, for the town, I ween,
Has not the honor of so proud a birth,—
15 Thou com'st from Jersey meadows, fresh and green,
The offspring of the gods, though born on earth;

For Titan was thy sire, and fair was she,
The ocean-nymph that nursed thy infancy.

Beneath the rushes was thy cradle swung,
20   And when at length thy gauzy wings grew strong,
Abroad to gentle airs their folds were flung,
      Rose in the sky and bore thee soft along;
The south wind breathed to waft thee on the way,
And danced and shone beneath the billowy bay.

25 Calm rose afar the city spires, and thence
      Came the deep murmur of its throng of men,
And as its grateful odors met thy sense,
      They seemed the perfumes of thy native fen.
Fair lay its crowded streets, and at the sight
30 Thy tiny song grew shriller with delight.

At length thy pinions fluttered in Broadway—
      Ah, there were fairy steps, and white necks kissed
By wanton airs, and eyes whose killing ray
      Shone through the snowy veils like stars through mist;
35 And fresh as morn, on many a cheek and chin,
Bloomed the bright blood through the transparent skin.

Sure these were sights to touch an anchorite!
      What! do I hear thy slender voice complain?
Thou wailest when I talk of beauty's light,
40   As if it brought the memory of pain:
Thou art a wayward being—well—come near,
And pour thy tale of sorrow in my ear.

What sayest thou—slanderer!—rouge makes thee sick?
      And China bloom at best is sorry food?
45 And Rowland's Kalydor,[4] if laid on thick,
      Poisons the thirsty wretch that bores for blood?
Go! 'twas a just reward that met thy crime—
But shun the sacrilege another time.

That bloom was made to look at, not to touch;
50   To worship, not approach, that radiant white;
And well might sudden vengeance light on such

As dared, like thee, most impiously to bite.
Thou shouldst have gazed at distance and admired,
Murmured thy adoration, and retired.

55 Thou'rt welcome to the town; but why come here
        To bleed a brother poet, gaunt like thee?
    Alas! the little blood I have is dear,
        And thin will be the banquet drawn from me.
    Look round—the pale-eyed sisters in my cell,
60 Thy old acquaintance, Song and Famine, dwell.

    Try some plump alderman, and suck the blood
        Enriched by generous wine and costly meat;
    On well-filled skins, sleek as thy native mud,
        Fix thy light pump and press thy freckled feet.
65 Go to the men for whom, in ocean's halls,
    The oyster breeds, and the green turtle sprawls.

    There corks are drawn, and the red vintage flows
        To fill the swelling veins for thee, and now
    The ruddy cheek and now the ruddier nose
70   Shall tempt thee, as thou flittest round the brow;
    And when the hour of sleep its quiet brings,
    No angry hands shall rise to brush thy wings.

                                            1825

A MEDITATION ON
RHODE ISLAND COAL

> "Decolor, obscurus, vilis, non ille repexam
>   Cesariem regum, non candida virginis ornat
>   Colla, nec insigni splendet per cingula morsu
>   Sed nova si nigri videas miracula saxi,
>   Tune superat pulchros cultus et quicquid Eois
>   Indus litoribus rubra scrutatur in alga."
>   CLAUDIAN.[5]

I sat beside the glowing grate, fresh heaped
    With Newport coal, and as the flame grew bright

—The many-colored flame—and played and leaped,
   I thought of rainbows, and the northern light,
5   Moore's Lalla Rookh, the Treasury Report,[6]
And other brilliant matters of the sort.

And last I thought of that fair isle which sent
   The mineral fuel; on a summer day
I saw it once, with heat and travel spent,
10   And scratched by dwarf-oaks in the hollow way.
Now dragged through sand, now jolted over stone—
A rugged road through rugged Tiverton.

And hotter grew the air, and hollower grew
   The deep-worn path, and horror-struck, I thought,
15   Where will this dreary passage lead me to?
   This long dull road, so narrow, deep, and hot?
I looked to see it dive in earth outright;
I looked—but saw a far more welcome sight.

Like a soft mist upon the evening shore,
20   At once a lovely isle before me lay,
Smooth, and with tender verdure covered o'er,
   As if just risen from its calm inland bay;
Sloped each way gently to the grassy edge,
And the small waves that dallied with the sedge.

25   The barley was just reaped; the heavy sheaves
   Lay on the stubble-field; the tall maize stood
Dark in its summer growth, and shook its leaves,
   And bright the sunlight played on the young wood—
For fifty years ago, the old men say,
30   The Briton hewed their ancient groves away.

I saw where fountains freshened the green land,
   And where the pleasant road, from door to door,
With rows of cherry-trees on either hand,
   Went wandering all that fertile region o'er—
35   Rogue's Island once[7]—but when the rogues were dead,
Rhode Island was the name it took instead.

Beautiful island! then it only seemed
   A lovely stranger; it has grown a friend.

I gazed on its smooth slopes, but never dreamed
40   How soon that green and quiet isle would send
The treasures of its womb across the sea,
To warm a poet's room and boil his tea.

Dark anthracite! that reddenest on my hearth,
    Thou in those island mines didst slumber long;
45 But now thou art come forth to move the earth,
    And put to shame the men that mean thee wrong:
Thou shalt be coals of fire to those that hate thee,
And warm the shins of all that underrate thee.

Yea, they did wrong thee foully—they who mocked
50   Thy honest face, and said thou wouldst not burn;
Of hewing thee to chimney-pieces talked,
    And grew profane, and swore, in bitter scorn,
That men might to thy inner caves retire,
And there, unsinged, abide the day of fire.

55 Yet is thy greatness nigh. I pause to state,
    That I too have seen greatness—even I—
Shook hands with Adams, stared at La Fayette,[8]
    When, barehead, in the hot noon of July,
He would not let the umbrella be held o'er him,
60 For which three cheers burst from the mob before him.

And I have seen—not many months ago—
    An eastern Governor in chapeau bras[9]
And military coat, a glorious show!
    Ride forth to visit the reviews, and ah!
65 How oft he smiled and bowed to Jonathan!
How many hands were shook and votes were won!

'Twas a great Governor; thou too shalt be
    Great in thy turn, and wide shall spread thy fame
And swiftly; furthest Maine shall hear of thee,
70   And cold New Brunswick gladden at thy name;
And, faintly through its sleets, the weeping isle
That sends the Boston folks their cod shall smile.

For thou shalt forge vast railways, and shalt heat
    The hissing rivers into steam, and drive

75   Huge masses from thy mines, on iron feet,
           Walking their steady way, as if alive,
       Northward, till everlasting ice besets thee,
       And South as far as the grim Spaniard lets thee.

       Thou shalt make mighty engines swim the sea,
80   Like its own monsters—boats that for a guinea
       Will take a man to Havre—and shalt be
           The moving soul of many a spinning-jenny,
       And ply thy shuttles, till a bard can wear
       As good a suit of broadcloth as the mayor.

85   Then we will laugh at winter when we hear
           The grim old churl about our dwellings rave:
       Thou, from that "ruler of the inverted year,"[10]
           Shalt pluck the knotty sceptre Cowper gave,
       And pull him from his sledge, and drag him in,
90   And melt the icicles from off his chin.

                                            1826

       THE PRAIRIES

           These are the Gardens of the Desert, these
       The unshorn fields, boundless and beautiful,
       And fresh as the young earth, ere man had sinned—
       The Prairies. I behold them for the first,
5   And my heart swells, while the dilated sight
       Takes in the encircling vastness. Lo! they stretch
       In airy undulations, far away,
       As if the ocean, in his gentlest swell,
       Stood still, with all his rounded billows fixed,
10   And motionless for ever.—Motionless?—
       No—they are all unchained again. The clouds
       Sweep over with their shadows, and beneath
       The surface rolls and fluctuates to the eye;
       Dark hollows seem to glide along and chase
15   The sunny ridges. Breezes of the South!
       Who toss the golden and the flame-like flowers,

And pass the prairie-hawk that, poised on high,
Flaps his broad wings, yet moves not—ye have played
Among the palms of Mexico and vines
20   Of Texas, and have crisped the limpid brooks
That from the fountains of Sonora glide
Into the calm Pacific—have ye fanned
A nobler or a lovelier scene than this?
Man hath no part in all this glorious work:
25   The hand that built the firmament hath heaved
And smoothed these verdant swells, and sown their slopes
With herbage, planted them with island groves,
And hedged them round with forests. Fitting floor
For this magnificent temple of the sky—
30   With flowers whose glory and whose multitude
Rival the constellations! The great heavens
Seem to stoop down upon the scene in love,—
A nearer vault, and of a tenderer blue,
Than that which bends above the eastern hills.

35   As o'er the verdant waste I guide my steed,
Among the high rank grass that sweeps his sides,
The hollow beating of his footstep seems
A sacrilegious sound. I think of those
Upon whose rest he tramples. Are they here—
40   The dead of other days!—and did the dust
Of these fair solitudes once stir with life
And burn with passion? Let the mighty mounds
That overlook the rivers, or that rise
In the dim forest crowded with old oaks,
45   Answer. A race, that long has passed away,
Built them;—a disciplined and populous race
Heaped, with long toil, the earth, while yet the Greek
Was hewing the Pentelicus to forms
Of symmetry, and rearing on its rock
50   The glittering Parthenon. These ample fields
Nourished their harvests, here their herds were fed,
When haply by their stalls the bison lowed,
And bowed his maned shoulder to the yoke.
All day this desert murmured with their toils,
55   Till twilight blushed and lovers walked, and wooed

In a forgotten language, and old tunes,
From instruments of unremembered form,
Gave the soft winds a voice. The red man came—
The roaming hunter tribes, warlike and fierce,
60   And the mound-builders vanished from the earth.
The solitude of centuries untold
Has settled where they dwelt. The prairie wolf
Hunts in their meadows, and his fresh dug den
Yawns by my path. The gopher mines the ground
65   Where stood their swarming cities. All is gone—
All—save the piles of earth that hold their bones—
The platforms where they worshipped unknown gods—
The barriers which they builded from the soil
To keep the foe at bay—till o'er the walls
70   The wild beleaguerers broke, and, one by one,
The strong holds of the plain were forced, and heaped
With corpses. The brown vultures of the wood
Flocked to those vast uncovered sepulchres,
And sat, unscared and silent, at their feast.
75   Haply some solitary fugitive,
Lurking in marsh and forest, till the sense
Of desolation and of fear became
Bitterer than death, yielded himself to die.
Man's better nature triumphed. Kindly words
80   Welcomed and soothed him; the rude conquerors
Seated the captive with their chiefs. He chose
A bride among their maidens. And at length
Seemed to forget,—yet ne'er forgot,—the wife
Of his first love, and her sweet little ones
85   Butchered, amid their shrieks, with all his race.

Thus change the forms of being. Thus arise
Races of living things, glorious in strength,
And perish, as the quickening breath of God
Fills them, or is withdrawn. The red man too—
90   Has left the blooming wilds he ranged so long,
And, nearer to the Rocky Mountains, sought
A wider hunting ground. The beaver builds
No longer by these streams, but far away,
On waters whose blue surface ne'er gave back
95   The white man's face—among Missouri's springs,

And pools whose issues swell the Oregon,
He rears his little Venice. In these plains
The bison feeds no more. Twice twenty leagues
Beyond remotest smoke of hunter's camp,
100   Roams the majestic brute, in herds that shake
The earth with thundering steps—yet here I meet
His ancient footprints stamped beside the pool.

     Still this great solitude is quick with life.
Myriads of insects, gaudy as the flowers
105   They flutter over, gentle quadrupeds,
And birds, that scarce have learned the fear of man
Are here, and sliding reptiles of the ground,
Startlingly beautiful. The graceful deer
Bounds to the wood at my approach. The bee,
110   A more adventurous colonist than man,
With whom he came across the eastern deep,
Fills the savannas with his murmurings,
And hides his sweets, as in the golden age,
Within the hollow oak. I listen long
115   To his domestic hum, and think I hear
The sound of that advancing multitude
Which soon shall fill these deserts. From the ground
Comes up the laugh of children, the soft voice
Of maidens, and the sweet and solemn hymn
120   Of Sabbath worshippers. The low of herds
Blends with the rustling of the heavy grain
Over the dark-brown furrows. All at once
A fresher wind sweeps by, and breaks my dream,
And I am in the wilderness alone.

1833

THE CROWDED STREET

Let me move slowly through the street,
   Filled with an ever-shifting train,
Amid the sound of steps that beat
   The murmuring walks like autumn rain.

5   How fast the flitting figures come!
           The mild, the fierce, the stony face;
       Some bright with thoughtless smiles, and some
           Where secret tears have left their trace.

       They pass—to toil, to strife, to rest;
10   To halls in which the feast is spread;
       To chambers where the funeral guest
           In silence sits beside the dead.

       And some to happy homes repair,
           Where children, pressing cheek to cheek,
15   With mute caresses shall declare
           The tenderness they cannot speak.

       And some, who walk in calmness here,
           Shall shudder as they reach the door
       Where one who made their dwelling dear,
20   Its flower, its light, is seen no more.

       Youth, with pale cheek and slender frame,
           And dreams of greatness in thine eye!
       Go'st thou to build an early name,
           Or early in the task to die?

25   Keen son of trade, with eager brow!
           Who is now fluttering in thy snare?
       Thy golden fortunes, tower they now,
           Or melt the glittering spires in air?

       Who of this crowd to-night shall tread
30   The dance till daylight gleam again?
       Who sorrow o'er the untimely dead?
           Who writhe in throes of mortal pain?

       Some, famine-struck, shall think how long
           The cold dark hours, how slow the light;

35   And some, who flaunt amid the throng,
           Shall hide in dens of shame to-night.

Each, where his tasks or pleasures call,
    They pass, and heed each other not.
There is who heeds, who holds them all,
40   In His large love and boundless thought.

These struggling tides of life that seem
    In wayward, aimless course to tend,
Are eddies of the mighty stream
    That rolls to its appointed end.

                        1843

NOT YET

Oh country, marvel of the earth!
    Oh realm to sudden greatness grown!
The age that gloried in thy birth,
    Shall it behold thee overthrown?
5   Shall traitors lay that greatness low?
No, land of Hope and Blessing, No!

And we, who wear thy glorious name,
    Shall we, like cravens, stand apart,
When those whom thou hast trusted aim
10   The death-blow at thy generous heart?
Forth goes the battle-cry, and lo!
Hosts rise in harness, shouting, No!

And they who founded, in our land,
    The power that rules from sea to sea,
15   Bled they in vain, or vainly planned
    To leave their country great and free?
Their sleeping ashes, from below,
Send up the thrilling murmur, No!

Knit they the gentle ties which long
20   These sister States were proud to wear,
And forged the kindly links so strong
    For idle hands in sport to tear?

For scornful hands aside to throw?
No, by our fathers' memory, No!

25   Our humming marts, our iron ways,
            Our wind-tossed woods on mountain-crest,
The hoarse Atlantic, with its bays,
            The calm, broad Ocean of the West,
And Mississippi's torrent-flow,
30   The loud Niagara, answer, No!

Not yet the hour is nigh when they
            Who deep in Eld's dim twilight sit,
Earth's ancient kings, shall rise and say,
            "Proud country, welcome to the pit!
35   So soon art thou, like us, brought low!"
No, sullen group of shadows, No!

For now, behold, the arm that gave
            The victory in our fathers' day,
Strong, as of old, to guard and save—
40   That mighty arm which none can stay—
On clouds above and fields below,
Writes, in men's sight, the answer, No!

                                        1861

THE POET

Thou, who wouldst wear the name
            Of poet mid thy brethren of mankind,
And clothe in words of flame
            Thoughts that shall live within the general mind!
5   Deem not the framing of a deathless lay
The pastime of a drowsy summer day.

But gather all thy powers,
            And wreak them on the verse that thou dost weave,
And in thy lonely hours,
10   At silent morning or at wakeful eve,
While the warm current tingles through thy veins,
Set forth the burning words in fluent strains.

No smooth array of phrase,
    Artfully sought and ordered though it be,
15 Which the cold rhymer lays
    Upon his page with languid industry,
Can wake the listless pulse to livelier speed,
Or fill with sudden tears the eyes that read.

The secret wouldst thou know
20   To touch the heart or fire the blood at will?
Let thine own eyes o'erflow;
    Let thy lips quiver with the passionate thrill;
Seize the great thought, ere yet its power be past,
And bind, in words, the fleet emotion fast.

25 Then, should thy verse appear
    Halting and harsh, and all unaptly wrought,
Touch the crude line with fear,
    Save in the moment of impassioned thought;
Then summon back the original glow, and mend
30 The strain with rapture that with fire was penned.

Yet let no empty gust
    Of passion find an utterance in thy lay,
A blast that whirls the dust
    Along the howling street and dies away;
35 But feelings of calm power and mighty sweep,
Like currents journeying through the windless deep.

Seek'st thou, in living lays,
    To limn the beauty of the earth and sky?
Before thine inner gaze
40   Let all that beauty in clear vision lie;
Look on it with exceeding love, and write
The words inspired by wonder and delight.

Of tempests wouldst thou sing,
    Or tell of battles—make thyself a part
45 Of the great tumult; cling
    To the tossed wreck with terror in thy heart;
Scale, with the assaulting host, the rampart's height,
And strike and struggle in the thickest fight.

So shalt thou frame a lay
50   That haply may endure from age to age,
And they who read shall say:
   "What witchery hangs upon this poet's page!
What art is his the written spells to find
That sway from mood to mood the willing mind!"

      1864

THE DEATH OF LINCOLN

Oh, slow to smite and swift to spare,
   Gentle and merciful and just!
Who, in the fear of God, didst bear
   The sword of power, a nation's trust!

5 In sorrow by thy bier we stand,
   Amid the awe that hushes all,
And speak the anguish of a land
   That shook with horror at thy fall.

Thy task is done; the bond are free:
10   We bear thee to an honored grave,
Whose proudest monument shall be
   The broken fetters of the slave.

Pure was thy life; its bloody close
   Hath placed thee with the sons of light,
15 Among the noble host of those
   Who perished in the cause of Right.

      1866

RALPH WALDO EMERSON

(1803–1882)

Although he published only three volumes of his own poetry, Emerson wrote verse continually from the time he was nine and always referred to himself as a poet, by which he meant a sayer of truths. Descended on his father's side from early settlers of the Massachusetts Bay colony, he was born in Boston, the third of eight children, only three of whom would survive their twenties. By the time Emerson finished school and entered Harvard, at fourteen, his father had also died, forcing him to earn his own keep until he graduated in 1821, as class poet. After four years spent teaching in his brother's school for young ladies, he enrolled in the Harvard Divinity School to prepare himself for the Unitarian ministry. Although persistent ill health interrupted his studies, he was licensed to preach in 1826, only to leave his pulpit for the South, in search of a healthier climate. In 1828, Emerson became engaged to Ellen Tucker, who was desperately ill with tuberculosis. When he was elected a minister of Boston's Second Church, a year later, they married. Within seventeen months, she was dead. Before another year was out, he had resigned his pastorate on account of personal reservations regarding the administration of the sacraments and the institution of the ministry as a whole.

With nothing to keep him in Boston, he sailed for Europe, intending to make the acquaintance and take the measure of poets and thinkers like Coleridge, Wordsworth, and Carlyle, who shared his concern with the despiritualization of modern life. Happy to find himself the equal of these luminaries, he returned to Boston, where he supported himself by occasional preaching and, increasingly, by public lecturing on literary and historical topics. In 1835, he married Lydia Jackson and settled in Concord, the village outside Boston that, thanks largely to Emerson, would soon appear on the intellectual map of the transatlantic world. Within five years of his arrival, he had made himself known throughout New England. In 1836, he published his first book, *Nature,* and helped form the association of radical thinkers that would become the Transcendental Club. At Harvard in 1837, he delivered his lecture "The American Scholar," which Oliver Wendell Holmes would call "our intellectual Declaration of Independence." In 1838, he addressed the Harvard Divinity School with an attack on institutional religion that would make him unwelcome at the university for the next thirty years. In 1840, he helped found and edit *The Dial,* the journal that would publish writings by members of the Transcendental circle, including Emerson's young friends Henry David Thoreau and Jones Very.

The publication of his *Essays* in 1841 and of a *Second Series* in 1844 spread Emerson's name throughout America and England, bringing him invitations to lecture everywhere from the Mississippi valley to London. From then on, any intellectual or literary movement would have to reckon, somehow, with him. In 1847, popular demand led to the publication of his first collection of poems. In 1855, he gave Walt Whitman visibility by professing to find in *Leaves of Grass* the American poet for whom he had long been searching. Although reluctant to involve himself in controversial matters ever since the Divinity School address, he lent respectability to the abolitionist movement by speaking out against slavery, defying the Fugitive Slave Law, and befriending John Brown, at the same time that he was connected, through the *Atlantic Monthly* and Boston's Saturday Club, with such literary eminences as Lowell, Longfellow, Holmes, and Whittier.

By 1866, Harvard had changed enough, partly under the influence of Emerson himself, to end their long mutual estrangement with the award of an honorary degree, followed by an invitation to teach there. As it happened, this tardy recognition came just at the moment that he felt the waning of his own powers, as recorded in the poem "Terminus." Although he remained active throughout the decade, publishing a second collection of poems in 1867, teaching at Harvard, and lecturing widely, by 1871 he was drifting toward senility. From then on, his publications, including his *Selected Poems* (1876), comprised earlier writings prepared with the help of his wife and friends. In the spring of 1882, he attended the funeral of Longfellow, unable to remember who that was. Within a month, he was dead himself.

EACH AND ALL

Little thinks, in the field, yon red-cloaked clown,
Of thee from the hill-top looking down;
The heifer that lows in the upland farm,
Far-heard, lows not thine ear to charm;
5   The sexton, tolling his bell at noon,
Deems not that great Napoleon

Stops his horse, and lists with delight,
Whilst his files sweep round yon Alpine height;
Nor knowest thou what argument
10   Thy life to thy neighbor's creed has lent.
All are needed by each one;
Nothing is fair or good alone.
I thought the sparrow's note from heaven,
Singing at dawn on the alder bough;
15   I brought him home, in his nest, at even;
He sings the song, but it pleases not now,
For I did not bring home the river and sky;—
He sang to my ear,—they sang to my eye.
The delicate shells lay on the shore;
20   The bubbles of the latest wave
Fresh pearls to their enamel gave;
And the bellowing of the savage sea
Greeted their safe escape to me.
I wiped away the weeds and foam,
25   I fetched my sea-born treasures home;
But the poor, unsightly, noisome things
Had left their beauty on the shore,
With the sun, and the sand, and the wild uproar.
The lover watched his graceful maid,
30   As 'mid the virgin train she strayed,
Nor knew her beauty's best attire
Was woven still by the snow-white choir.
At last she came to his hermitage,
Like the bird from the woodlands to the cage;—
35   The gay enchantment was undone,
A gentle wife, but fairy none.
Then I said, "I covet truth;
Beauty is unripe childhood's cheat;
I leave it behind with the games of youth."—
40   As I spoke, beneath my feet
The ground-pine curled its pretty wreath,
Running over the club-moss burrs;
I inhaled the violet's breath;
Around me stood the oaks and firs;
45   Pine-cones and acorns lay on the ground,
Over me soared the eternal sky,
Full of light and of deity;

Again I saw, again I heard,
The rolling river, the morning bird;—
50   Beauty through my senses stole;
I yielded myself to the perfect whole.

1839

THE HUMBLE-BEE

Burly, dozing, humble-bee,
Where thou art is clime for me.
Let them sail for Porto Rique,
Far-off heats through seas to seek;
5   I will follow thee alone,
Thou animated torrid-zone!
Zigzag steerer, desert cheerer,
Let me chase thy waving lines;
Keep me nearer, me thy hearer,
10   Singing over shrubs and vines.

Insect lover of the sun,
Joy of thy dominion!
Sailor of the atmosphere;
Swimmer through the waves of air;
15   Voyager of light and noon;
Epicurean of June;
Wait, I prithee, till I come
Within earshot of thy hum,—
All without is martyrdom.

20   When the south wind, in May days,
With a net of shining haze
Silvers the horizon wall,
And, with softness touching all,
Tints the human countenance
25   With a color of romance,
And, infusing subtle heats,
Turns the sod to violets,
Thou, in sunny solitudes,
Rover of the underwoods,

30   The green silence dost displace
        With thy mellow, breezy bass.

        Hot midsummer's petted crone,
        Sweet to me thy drowsy tone
        Tells of countless sunny hours,
35   Long days, and solid banks of flowers;
        Of gulfs of sweetness without bound
        In Indian wildernesses found;
        Of Syrian peace, immortal leisure,
        Firmest cheer, and bird-like pleasure.

40   Aught unsavory or unclean
        Hath my insect never seen;
        But violets and bilberry bells,
        Maple-sap, and daffodels,
        Grass with green flag half-mast high,
45   Succory to match the sky,
        Columbine with horn of honey,
        Scented fern, and agrimony,
        Clover, catchfly, adder's tongue,
        And brier roses, dwelt among;
50   All beside was unknown waste,
        All was picture as he passed.

        Wiser far than human seer,
        Yellow-breeched philosopher!
        Seeing only what is fair,
55   Sipping only what is sweet,
        Thou dost mock at fate and care,
        Leave the chaff, and take the wheat.
        When the fierce north-western blast
        Cools sea and land so far and fast,
60   Thou already slumberest deep;
        Woe and want thou canst outsleep;
        Want and woe, which torture us,
        Thy sleep makes ridiculous.

                        1839

THE SNOW-STORM

Announced by all the trumpets of the sky,
Arrives the snow, and, driving o'er the fields,
Seems nowhere to alight: the whited air
Hides hills and woods, the river, and the heaven,
5   And veils the farm-house at the garden's end.
The sled and traveller stopped, the courier's feet
Delayed, all friends shut out, the housemates sit
Around the radiant fireplace, enclosed
In a tumultuous privacy of storm.

10   Come see the north wind's masonry.
Out of an unseen quarry evermore
Furnished with tile, the fierce artificer
Curves his white bastions with projected roof
Round every windward stake, or tree, or door.
15   Speeding, the myriad-handed, his wild work
So fanciful, so savage, nought cares he
For number or proportion. Mockingly,
On coop or kennel he hangs Parian wreaths;
A swan-like form invests the hidden thorn;
20   Fills up the farmer's lane from wall to wall,
Maugre the farmer's sighs; and, at the gate,
A tapering turret overtops the work.
And when his hours are numbered, and the world
Is all his own, retiring, as he were not,
25   Leaves, when the sun appears, astonished Art
To mimic in slow structures, stone by stone,
Built in an age, the mad wind's night-work,
The frolic architecture of the snow.

                                        1841

GRACE

How much, Preventing God! how much I owe
To the defences thou hast round me set:
Example, custom, fear, occasion slow,—
These scorned bondmen were my parapet.

5   I dare not peep over this parapet
       To guage with glance the roaring gulf below,
       The depths of sin to which I had descended,
       Had not these me against myself defended.

                                              1842

BLIGHT

                       Give me truths;
       For I am weary of the surfaces,
       And die of inanition. If I knew
       Only the herbs and simples of the wood,
5   Rue, cinquefoil, gill, vervain, and agrimony,
       Blue-vetch, and trillium, hawkweed, sassafras,
       Milkweeds, and murky brakes, quaint pipes, and sundew,
       And rare and virtuous roots, which in these woods
       Draw untold juices from the common earth,
10   Untold, unknown, and I could surely spell
       Their fragrance, and their chemistry apply
       By sweet affinities to human flesh,
       Driving the foe and stablishing the friend,—
       O, that were much, and I could be a part
15   Of the round day, related to the sun
       And planted world, and full executor
       Of their imperfect functions.
       But these young scholars, who invade our hills,
       Bold as the engineer who fells the wood,
20   And travelling often in the cut he makes,
       Love not the flower they pluck, and know it not,
       And all their botany is Latin names.
       The old men studied magic in the flowers,
       And human fortunes in astronomy,
25   And an omnipotence in chemistry,
       Preferring things to names, for these were men,
       Were unitarians of the united world,
       And, wheresoever their clear eye-beams fell,
       They caught the footsteps of the SAME. Our eyes
30   Are armed, but we are strangers to the stars,
       And strangers to the mystic beast and bird,

And strangers to the plant and to the mine.
The injured elements say, "Not in us;"
And night and day, ocean and continent,
35   Fire, plant, and mineral say, "Not in us,"
And haughtily return us stare for stare.
For we invade them impiously for gain;
We devastate them unreligiously,
And coldly ask their pottage, not their love.
40   Therefore they shove us from them, yield to us
Only what to our griping toil is due;
But the sweet affluence of love and song,
The rich results of the divine consents
Of man and earth, of world beloved and lover,
45   The nectar and ambrosia, are withheld;
And in the midst of spoils and slaves, we thieves
And pirates of the universe, shut out
Daily to a more thin and outward rind,
Turn pale and starve. Therefore, to our sick eyes,
50   The stunted trees look sick, the summer short,
Clouds shade the sun, which will not tan our hay,
And nothing thrives to reach its natural term;
And life, shorn of its venerable length,
Even at its greatest space is a defeat,
55   And dies in anger that it was a dupe;
And, in its highest noon and wantonness,
Is early frugal, like a beggar's child;
With most unhandsome calculation taught,
Even in the hot pursuit of the best aims
60   And prizes of ambition, checks its hand,
Like Alpine cataracts frozen as they leaped,
Chilled with a miserly comparison
Of the toy's purchase with the length of life.

                                        1844

MOTTO TO "THE POET"

A moody child and wildly wise
Pursued the game with joyful eyes,
Which chose, like meteors, their way,
And rived the dark with private ray:

5   They overleapt the horizon's edge,
       Searched with Apollo's privilege;[11]
       Through man, and woman, and sea, and star,
       Saw the dance of nature forward far;
       Through worlds, and races, and terms, and times,
10   Saw musical order, and pairing rhymes.

                                              1844

THE WORLD-SOUL

       Thanks to the morning light,
          Thanks to the foaming sea,
       To the uplands of New Hampshire,
          To the green-haired forest free;
5   Thanks to each man of courage,
          To the maids of holy mind;
       To the boy with his games undaunted,
          Who never looks behind.

       Cities of proud hotels,
10   Houses of rich and great,
       Vice nestles in your chambers,
          Beneath your roofs of slate.
       It cannot conquer folly,
          Time-and-space-conquering steam;
15   And the light-outspeeding telegraph
          Bears nothing on its beam.

       The politics are base;
          The letters do not cheer;
       And 'tis far in the deeps of history,
20   The voice that speaketh clear.
       Trade and the streets ensnare us,
          Our bodies are weak and worn;
       We plot and corrupt each other,
          And we despoil the unborn.

25   Yet there in the parlor sits
          Some figure of noble guise,—

Our angel, in a stranger's form,
  Or woman's pleading eyes;
Or only a flashing sunbeam
30   In at the window-pane;
Or Music pours on mortals
  Its beautiful disdain.

The inevitable morning
  Finds them who in cellars be;
35 And be sure the all-loving Nature
  Will smile in a factory.
Yon ridge of purple landscape,
  Yon sky between the walls,
Hold all the hidden wonders,
40   In scanty intervals.

Alas! the Sprite that haunts us
  Deceives our rash desire;
It whispers of the glorious gods,
  And leaves us in the mire.
45 We cannot learn the cipher
  That's writ upon our cell;
Stars help us by a mystery
  Which we could never spell.

If but one hero knew it,
50   The world would blush in flame;
The sage, till he hit the secret,
  Would hang his head for shame.
But our brothers have not read it,
  Not one has found the key;
55 And henceforth we are comforted,—
  We are but such as they.

Still, still the secret presses,
  The nearing clouds draw down;
The crimson morning flames into
60   The fopperies of the town.
Within, without the idle earth,
  Stars weave eternal rings;

The sun himself shines heartily,
    And shares the joy he brings.

65 And what if Trade sow cities
        Like shells along the shore,
    And thatch with towns the prairie broad,
        With railways ironed o'er?—
    They are but sailing foam-bells
70   Along Thought's causing stream,
    And take their shape and sun-color
        From him that sends the dream.

    For Destiny does not like
        To yield to men the helm;
75 And shoots his thought, by hidden nerves,
        Throughout the solid realm.
    The patient Dæmon sits,
        With roses and a shroud;
    He has his way, and deals his gifts,—
80   But ours is not allowed.

    He is no churl nor trifler,
        And his viceroy is none,—
    Love-without-weakness,—
        Of Genius sire and son.
85 And his will is not thwarted;
        The seeds of land and sea
    Are the atoms of his body bright,
        And his behest obey.

    He serveth the servant,
90   The brave he loves amain;
    He kills the cripple and the sick,
        And straight begins again.
    For gods delight in gods,
        And thrust the weak aside;
95 To him who scorns their charities,
        Their arms fly open wide.

    When the old world is sterile,
        And the ages are effete,

He will from wrecks and sediment
100   The fairer world complete.
He forbids to despair;
     His cheeks mantle with mirth;
And the unimagined good of men
     Is yeaning at the birth.

105   Spring still makes spring in the mind,
     When sixty years are told;
Love wakes anew this throbbing heart,
     And we are never old.
Over the winter glaciers,
110   I see the summer glow,
And, through the wild-piled snowdrift,
     The warm rosebuds below.

                        1847

MITHRIDATES

I cannot spare water or wine,
     Tobacco-leaf, or poppy, or rose;
From the earth-poles to the line,
     All between that works or grows,
5   Every thing is kin of mine.

Give me agates for my meat;
Give me cantharids to eat;
From air and ocean bring me foods,
From all zones and altitudes;—

10   From all natures, sharp and slimy,
     Salt and basalt, wild and tame:
Tree and lichen, ape, sea-lion,
     Bird, and reptile, be my game.

Ivy for my fillet band;
15   Blinding dog-wood in my hand;
Hemlock for my sherbet cull me,

And the prussic juice to lull me;
Swing me in the upas boughs,
Vampyre-fanned, when I carouse.

20   Too long shut in strait and few,
Thinly dieted on dew,
I will use the world, and sift it,
To a thousand humors shift it,
As you spin a cherry.
25   O doleful ghosts, and goblins merry!
O all you virtues, methods, mights,
Means, appliances, delights,
Reputed wrongs and braggart rights,
Smug routine, and things allowed,
30   Minorities, things under cloud!
Hither! take me, use me, fill me,
Vein and artery, though ye kill me!
God! I will not be an owl,
But sun me in the Capitol.

            1847

HAMATREYA[12]

Minott, Lee, Willard, Hosmer, Meriam, Flint
Possessed the land which rendered to their toil
Hay, corn, roots, hemp, flax, apples, wool, and wood.
Each of these landlords walked amidst his farm,
5   Saying, " 'Tis mine, my children's, and my name's:
How sweet the west wind sounds in my own trees!
How graceful climb those shadows on my hill!
I fancy these pure waters and the flags
Know me, as does my dog: we sympathize;
10   And, I affirm, my actions smack of the soil."
Where are these men? Asleep beneath their grounds;
And strangers, fond as they, their furrows plough.
Earth laughs in flowers, to see her boastful boys
Earth-proud, proud of the earth which is not theirs;
15   Who steer the plough, but cannot steer their feet

Clear of the grave.
They added ridge to valley, brook to pond,
And sighed for all that bounded their domain.
"This suits me for a pasture; that's my park;
20 We must have clay, lime, gravel, granite-ledge,
And misty lowland, where to go for peat.
The land is well,—lies fairly to the south.
'Tis good, when you have crossed the sea and back,
To find the sitfast acres where you left them."
25 Ah! the hot owner sees not Death, who adds
Him to his land, a lump of mould the more.
Hear what the Earth says:—

EARTH-SONG

"Mine and yours;
Mine, not yours.
30 Earth endures;
Stars abide—
Shine down in the old sea;
Old are the shores;
But where are old men?
35 I who have seen much,
Such have I never seen.

"The lawyer's deed
Ran sure,
In tail,[13]
40 To them, and to their heirs
Who shall succeed,
Without fail,
Forevermore.

"Here is the land,
45 Shaggy with wood,
With its old valley,
Mound, and flood.
But the heritors?
Fled like the flood's foam,—
50 The lawyer, and the laws,

And the kingdom,
Clean swept herefrom.

"They called me theirs,
Who so controlled me;
55   Yet every one
Wished to stay, and is gone.
How am I theirs,
If they cannot hold me,
But I hold them?"

60   When I heard the Earth-song,
I was no longer brave;
My avarice cooled
Like lust in the chill of the grave.

                                        1847

ODE,
        Inscribed to W. H. Channing

Though loath to grieve
The evil time's sole patriot,
I cannot leave
My honied thought
5   For the priest's cant,
Or statesman's rant.

If I refuse
My study for their politique,
Which at the best is trick,
10   The angry Muse
Puts confusion in my brain.

But who is he that prates
Of the culture of mankind,
Of better arts and life?
15   Go, blindworm, go,
Behold the famous States

Harrying Mexico
With rifle and with knife!

Or who, with accent bolder,
20 Dare praise the freedom-loving mountaineer?
I found by thee, O rushing Contoocook!
And in thy valleys, Agiochook![14]
The jackals of the negro-holder.

The God who made New Hampshire
25 Taunted the lofty land
With little men;—
Small bat and wren
House in the oak:—
If earth-fire cleave
30 The upheaved land, and bury the folk,
The southern crocodile would grieve.

Virtue palters; Right is hence;
Freedom praised, but hid;
Funeral eloquence
35 Rattles the coffin-lid.

What boots thy zeal,
O glowing friend,
That would indignant rend
The northland from the south?
40 Wherefore? to what good end?
Boston Bay and Bunker Hill
Would serve things still;—
Things are of the snake.

The horseman serves the horse,
45 The neatherd serves the neat,
The merchant serves the purse,
The eater serves his meat;
'Tis the day of the chattel,
Web to weave, and corn to grind;
50 Things are in the saddle,
And ride mankind.

There are two laws discrete,
Not reconciled,—
Law for man, and law for thing;
55 The last builds town and fleet,
But it runs wild,
And doth the man unking.

'Tis fit the forest fall,
The steep be graded,
60 The mountain tunnelled,
The sand shaded,
The orchard planted,
The glebe tilled,
The prairie granted,
65 The steamer built.

Let man serve law for man;
Live for friendship, live for love,
For truth's and harmony's behoof;
The state may follow how it can,
70 As Olympus follows Jove.

    Yet do not I invite
The wrinkled shopman to my sounding woods,
Nor bid the unwilling senator
Ask votes of thrushes in the solitudes.
75 Every one to his chosen work;—
Foolish hands may mix and mar;
Wise and sure the issues are.
Round they roll till dark is light,
Sex to sex, and even to odd;—
80 The over-god
Who marries Right to Might,
Who peoples, unpeoples,—
He who exterminates
Races by stronger races,
85 Black by white faces,—
Knows to bring honey
Out of the lion;[15]
Grafts gentlest scion
On pirate and Turk.

90   The Cossack eats Poland,
        Like stolen fruit;
        Her last noble is ruined,
        Her last poet mute:
        Straight, into double band
95   The victors divide;
        Half for freedom strike and stand;—
        The astonished Muse finds thousands at her side.

                                                        1847

MERLIN I

        Thy trivial harp will never please
        Or fill my craving ear;
        Its chords should ring as blows the breeze,
        Free, peremptory, clear.
5   No jingling serenader's art,
        Nor tinkle of piano strings,
        Can make the wild blood start
        In its mystic springs.
        The kingly bard
10   Must smite the chords rudely and hard,
        As with hammer or with mace;
        That they may render back
        Artful thunder, which conveys
        Secrets of the solar track,
15   Sparks of the supersolar blaze.
        Merlin's blows are strokes of fate,
        Chiming with the forest tone,
        When boughs buffet boughs in the wood;
        Chiming with the gasp and moan
20   Of the ice-imprisoned flood;
        With the pulse of manly hearts;
        With the voice of orators;
        With the din of city arts;
        With the cannonade of wars;
25   With the marches of the brave;
        And prayers of might from martyrs' cave.

Great is the art,
Great be the manners, of the bard.
He shall not his brain encumber
30   With the coil of rhythm and number;
But, leaving rule and pale forethought,
He shall aye climb
For his rhyme.
"Pass in, pass in," the angels say,
35   "In to the upper doors,
Nor count compartments of the floors,
But mount to paradise
By the stairway of surprise."

Blameless master of the games,
40   King of sport that never shames,
He shall daily joy dispense
Hid in song's sweet influence.
Things more cheerly live and go,
What time the subtle mind
45   Sings aloud the tune whereto
Their pulses beat,
And march their feet,
And their members are combined.

By Sybarites beguiled,
50   He shall no task decline;
Merlin's mighty line
Extremes of nature reconciled,—
Bereaved a tyrant of his will,
And made the lion mild.
55   Songs can the tempest still,
Scattered on the stormy air,
Mould the year to fair increase,
And bring in poetic peace.

He shall not seek to weave,
60   In weak, unhappy times,
Efficacious rhymes;
Wait his returning strength.
Bird, that from the nadir's floor
To the zenith's top can soar,

65 The soaring orbit of the muse exceeds that journey's length.
    Nor profane affect to hit
    Or compass that, by meddling wit,
    Which only the propitious mind
    Publishes when 'tis inclined.
70 There are open hours
    When the God's will sallies free,
    And the dull idiot might see
    The flowing fortunes of a thousand years;—
    Sudden, at unawares,
75 Self-moved, fly-to the doors,
    Nor sword of angels could reveal
    What they conceal.

                              1847

MOTTO TO "NATURE"

    A subtle chain of countless rings
    The next unto the farthest brings;
    The eye reads omens where it goes,
    And speaks all languages the rose;
5   And, striving to be man, the worm
    Mounts through all the spires of form.

                              1849

DAYS

    Daughters of Time, the hypocritic Days,
    Muffled and dumb like barefoot dervishes,
    And marching single in an endless file,
    Bring diadems and fagots in their hands.
5   To each they offer gifts after his will,
    Bread, kingdoms, stars, and sky that holds them all.
    I, in my pleached garden, watched the pomp,
    Forgot my morning wishes, hastily

Took a few herbs and apples, and the Day
10   Turned and departed silent. I, too late,
Under her solemn fillet saw the scorn.

                                                    1857

THE CHARTIST'S COMPLAINT

Day! hast thou two faces,
Making one place two places?
One, by humble farmer seen,
Chill and wet, unlighted, mean,
5   Useful only, triste and damp,
Serving for a laborer's lamp?
Have the same mists another side,
To be the appanage of pride,
Gracing the rich man's wood and lake,
10   His park where amber mornings break,
And treacherously bright to show
His planted isle where roses glow?
O Day! and is your mightiness
A sycophant to smug success?
15   Will the sweet sky and ocean broad
Be fine accomplices to fraud?
O Sun! I curse thy cruel ray:
Back, back to chaos, harlot Day!

                                                    1857

TWO RIVERS

Thy summer voice, Musketaquit,[16]
Repeats the music of the rain;
But sweeter rivers pulsing flit
Through thee, as thou through Concord Plain.

5   Thou in thy narrow banks art pent:
The stream I love unbounded goes

Through flood and sea and firmament;
Through light, through life, it forward flows.

I see the inundation sweet,
10   I hear the spending of the stream
Through years, through men, through nature fleet,
Through passion, thought, through power and dream.

Musketaquit, a goblin strong,
Of shard and flint makes jewels gay;
15   They lose their grief who hear his song,
And where he winds is the day of day.

So forth and brighter fares my stream,—
Who drink it shall not thirst again;
No darkness stains its equal gleam,
20   And ages drop in it like rain.

                              1858

MOTTO TO "ILLUSIONS"

Flow, flow the waves hated,
Accursed, adored,
The waves of mutation:
No anchorage is.
5   Sleep is not, death is not;
Who seem to die live.
House you were born in,
Friends of your spring-time,
Old man and young maid,
10   Day's toil and its guerdon,
They are all vanishing,
Fleeing to fables,
Cannot be moored.
See the stars through them,
15   Through treacherous marbles.
Know, the stars yonder,
The stars everlasting,
Are fugitive also,

And emulate, vaulted,
20 The lambent heat-lightning,
And fire-fly's flight.

When thou dost return
On the wave's circulation,
Beholding the shimmer,
25 The wild dissipation,
And, out of endeavor
To change and to flow,
The gas become solid,
And phantoms and nothings
30 Return to be things,
And endless imbroglio
Is law and the world,—
Then first shalt thou know,
That in the wild turmoil,
35 Horsed on the Proteus,
Thou ridest to power,
And to endurance.

1860

TERMINUS

It is time to be old,
To take in sail:—
The god of bounds,
Who sets to seas a shore,
5 Came to me in his fatal rounds,
And said: 'No more!
No farther shoot
Thy broad ambitious branches, and thy root.
Fancy departs: no more invent;
10 Contract thy firmament
To compass of a tent.
There's not enough for this and that,
Make thy option which of two;
Economize the failing river,
15 Not the less revere the Giver,

Leave the many and hold the few.
Timely wise accept the terms,
Soften the fall with wary foot;
A little while
20   Still plan and smile,
And,—fault of novel germs,—
Mature the unfallen fruit.
Curse, if thou wilt, thy sires,
Bad husbands of their fires,
25   Who, when they gave thee breath,
Failed to bequeath
The needful sinew stark as once,
The Baresark marrow to thy bones,
But left a legacy of ebbing veins,
30   Inconstant heat and nerveless reins,—
Amid the Muses, left thee deaf and dumb,
Amid the gladiators, halt and numb.'

      As the bird trims her to the gale,
I trim myself to the storm of time,
35   I man the rudder, reef the sail,
Obey the voice at eve obeyed at prime:
"Lowly faithful, banish fear,
Right onward drive unharmed;
The port, well worth the cruise, is near,
40   And every wave is charmed."
                              1867

HENRY WADSWORTH LONGFELLOW

(1807–1882)

In any competition for the title of Most Famous Nineteenth-Century Poet, Longfellow's only rivals would be Goethe, Tennyson, and Victor Hugo. Longfellow was born in Portland, Maine, a direct descendant of John Alden and Priscilla Mullens, and, like Herman Melville, the grandson of a Revolutionary War general. Beginning at the age of thirteen, he had published a substantial number of poems by the time he graduated from Bowdoin College at eighteen, in the same class with Nathaniel Hawthorne. His plan to continue his studies at Harvard changed with the offer of a professorship at Bowdoin in the new subject of modern languages, conditional upon his studying abroad before assuming his post. After three years in France, Spain, Italy, and Germany, he returned to Bowdoin to find his promised position reduced to an instructorship. When he refused to comply, the authorities relented, and for the next six years he served as professor and college librarian. In 1831, he married, and in 1835, the year he published his first book of prose, he accepted the position of professor of modern languages and belles lettres at Harvard. To prepare for his new duties, he traveled to Scandinavia and Germany; during a stopover in Rotterdam, his wife died suddenly. Back at Harvard, a widower, he divided his time among irksome professorial duties, European travel, and writing. In 1839, he published *Hyperion*, a quasi-autobiographical romance peppered with translated German poems, and *Voices of the Night*, his first book of poetry. Two further collections appeared in 1842: *Poems on Slavery* and *Ballads and Other Poems*. The following year, he married Frances Elizabeth Appleton, who would bear him six children. Two more volumes of poetry, in 1845, preceded the verse narratives for which he is best known: *Evangeline* (1847), *Hiawatha* (1855), and *The Courtship of Miles Standish* (1858), the last two appearing after he had resigned his professorship. In 1861, Elizabeth set fire to her dress while heating a stick of sealing wax and died of her burns, sinking Longfellow in a swamp of grief from which he never fully recovered. To relieve his depression, he set himself to translating Dante's *Divine Comedy* (published 1865–67) and composing the verse narratives for *Tales of a Wayside Inn* (collected 1886). The closing two decades of his life found him world famous, with collections of poems appearing regularly, honorary degrees from both Oxford and Cambridge, an audience with Queen Victoria, and, after 1879, celebrations of his birthday in public schools throughout America. Two years after his death in 1882, his monument joined those of Chaucer, Shakespeare, and Milton in poets' corner of Westminster Abbey.

MEZZO CAMMIN[17]

Half of my life is gone, and I have let
   The years slip from me and have not fulfilled
   The aspiration of my youth, to build
   Some tower of song with lofty parapet.
Not indolence, nor pleasure, nor the fret
   Of restless passions that would not be stilled,
   But sorrow, and a care that almost killed,
   Kept me from what I may accomplish yet;
Though, half-way up the hill, I see the Past
   Lying beneath me with its sounds and sights,—
   A city in the twilight dim and vast,
With smoking roofs, soft bells, and gleaming lights,—
   And hear above me on the autumnal blast
   The cataract of Death far thundering from the heights.

                                                        (1842)

THE WARNING

Beware! The Israelite of old, who tore
   The lion in his path,—when, poor and blind,
He saw the blessed light of heaven no more,
   Shorn of his noble strength and forced to grind
In prison, and at last led forth to be
A pander to Philistine revelry,—

Upon the pillars of the temple laid
   His desperate hands, and in its overthrow
Destroyed himself, and with him those who made

10   A cruel mockery of his sightless woe;
        The poor, blind Slave, the scoff and jest of all,
        Expired, and thousands perished in the fall!

        There is a poor, blind Samson in this land,
            Shorn of his strength, and bound in bonds of steel,
15   Who may, in some grim revel, raise his hand,
            And shake the pillars of this Commonweal,
        Till the vast Temple of our liberties
        A shapeless mass of wreck and rubbish lies.

                                                        1842

THE DAY IS DONE

        The day is done, and the darkness
            Falls from the wings of Night,
        As a feather is wafted downward
            From an eagle in his flight.

5   I see the lights of the village
            Gleam through the rain and the mist,
        And a feeling of sadness comes o'er me
            That my soul cannot resist:

        A feeling of sadness and longing,
10   That is not akin to pain,
        And resembles sorrow only
            As the mist resembles the rain.

        Come, read to me some poem,
            Some simple and heartfelt lay,
15   That shall soothe this restless feeling,
            And banish the thoughts of day.

        Not from the grand old masters,
            Not from the bards sublime,
        Whose distant footsteps echo
20   Through the corridors of Time.

For, like strains of martial music,
    Their mighty thoughts suggest
Life's endless toil and endeavor;
    And to-night I long for rest.

25 Read from some humbler poet,
    Whose songs gushed from his heart,
As showers from the clouds of summer,
    Or tears from the eyelids start;

Who, through long days of labor,
30   And nights devoid of ease,
Still heard in his soul the music
    Of wonderful melodies.

Such songs have power to quiet
    The restless pulse of care,
35 And come like the benediction
    That follows after prayer.

Then read from the treasured volume
    The poem of thy choice,
And lend to the rhyme of the poet
40   The beauty of thy voice.

And the night shall be filled with music,
    And the cares, that infest the day,
Shall fold their tents, like the Arabs,
    And as silently steal away.

                    1844

DANTE

Tuscan, that wanderest through the realms of gloom,
    With thoughtful pace, and sad, majestic eyes,
    Stern thoughts and awful from thy soul arise,
    Like Farinata from his fiery tomb.[18]
5 Thy sacred song is like the trump of doom;
    Yet in thy heart what human sympathies,

What soft compassion glows, as in the skies
    The tender stars their clouded lamps relume!
Methinks I see thee stand, with pallid cheeks,
10   By Fra Hilario in his diocese,[19]
    As up the convent-walls, in golden streaks,
The ascending sunbeams mark the day's decrease;
    And, as he asks what there the stranger seeks,
Thy voice along the cloister whispers, "Peace!"

                               1845

SAND OF THE DESERT IN AN HOUR-GLASS

A handful of red sand, from the hot clime
    Of Arab deserts brought,
Within this glass becomes the spy of Time,
    The minister of Thought.

5 How many weary centuries has it been
    About those deserts blown!
How many strange vicissitudes has seen,
    How many histories known!

Perhaps the camels of the Ishmaelite
10   Trampled and passed it o'er,
When into Egypt from the patriarch's sight
    His favorite son they bore.

Perhaps the feet of Moses, burnt and bare,
    Crushed it beneath their tread;
15 Or Pharaoh's flashing wheels into the air
    Scattered it as they sped;

Or Mary, with the Christ of Nazareth
    Held close in her caress,
Whose pilgrimage of hope and love and faith
20   Illumed the wilderness;

Or anchorites beneath Engaddi's[20] palms
    Pacing the Dead Sea beach,

And singing slow their old Armenian psalms
   In half-articulate speech;

25   Or caravans, that from Bassora's[21] gate
     With westward steps depart;
Or Mecca's pilgrims, confident of Fate,
     And resolute in heart!

These have passed over it, or may have passed!
30   Now in this crystal tower
Imprisoned by some curious hand at last,
     It counts the passing hour.

And as I gaze, these narrow walls expand;
     Before my dreamy eye
35   Stretches the desert with its shifting sand,
     Its unimpeded sky.

And borne aloft by the sustaining blast,
     This little golden thread
Dilates into a column high and vast,
40   A form of fear and dread.

And onward, and across the setting sun,
     Across the boundless plain,
The column and its broader shadow run,
     Till thought pursues in vain.

45   The vision vanishes! These walls again
     Shut out the lurid sun,
Shut out the hot, immeasurable plain;
     The half-hour's sand is run!

               1848

THE FIRE OF DRIFT-WOOD

Devereux Farm, Near Marblehead

We sat within the farm-house old,
    Whose windows, looking o'er the bay,
Gave to the sea-breeze, damp and cold,
    An easy entrance, night and day.

5   Not far away we saw the port,
    The strange, old-fashioned, silent town,
The lighthouse, the dismantled fort,
    The wooden houses, quaint and brown.

We sat and talked until the night,
10   Descending, filled the little room;
Our faces faded from the sight,
    Our voices only broke the gloom.

We spake of many a vanished scene,
    Of what we once had thought and said,
15   Of what had been, and might have been,
    And who was changed, and who was dead;

And all that fills the hearts of friends,
    When first they feel, with secret pain,
Their lives thenceforth have separate ends,
20   And never can be one again;

The first slight swerving of the heart,
    That words are powerless to express,
And leave it still unsaid in part,
    Or say it in too great excess.

25   The very tones in which we spake
    Had something strange, I could but mark;
The leaves of memory seemed to make
    A mournful rustling in the dark.

Oft died the words upon our lips,
30   As suddenly, from out the fire

Built of the wreck of stranded ships,
   The flames would leap and then expire.

And, as their splendor flashed and failed,
   We thought of wrecks upon the main,
35   Of ships dismasted, that were hailed
     And sent no answer back again.

The windows, rattling in their frames,
   The ocean, roaring up the beach,
The gusty blast, the bickering flames,
40   All mingled vaguely in our speech;

Until they made themselves a part
   Of fancies floating through the brain,
The long-lost ventures of the heart,
   That send no answers back again.

45   O flames that glowed! O hearts that yearned!
   They were indeed too much akin,
The drift-wood fire without that burned,
   The thoughts that burned and glowed within.

                1849

THE JEWISH CEMETERY AT NEWPORT

How strange it seems! These Hebrews in their graves,
   Close by the street of this fair seaport town,
Silent beside the never-silent waves,
   At rest in all this moving up and down!

5   The trees are white with dust, that o'er their sleep
   Wave their broad curtains in the south-wind's breath,
While underneath these leafy tents they keep
   The long, mysterious Exodus of Death.

And these sepulchral stones, so old and brown,
10   That pave with level flags their burial-place,

Seem like the tablets of the Law, thrown down
　　And broken by Moses at the mountain's base.

The very names recorded here are strange,
　　Of foreign accent, and of different climes;
15　Alvares and Rivera interchange
　　With Abraham and Jacob of old times.

"Blessed be God! for he created Death!"
　　The mourners said, "and Death is rest and peace";
Then added, in the certainty of faith,
20　　"And giveth Life that never more shall cease."

Closed are the portals of their Synagogue,
　　No Psalms of David now the silence break,
No Rabbi reads the ancient Decalogue
　　In the grand dialect the Prophets spake.

25　Gone are the living, but the dead remain,
　　And not neglected; for a hand unseen,
Scattering its bounty, like a summer rain,
　　Still keeps their graves and their remembrance green.

How came they here? What burst of Christian hate,
30　　What persecution, merciless and blind,
Drove o'er the sea—that desert desolate—
　　These Ishmaels and Hagars of mankind?

They lived in narrow streets and lanes obscure,
　　Ghetto and Judenstrass,[22] in mirk and mire;
35　Taught in the school of patience to endure
　　The life of anguish and the death of fire.

All their lives long, with the unleavened bread
　　And bitter herbs of exile and its fears,
The wasting famine of the heart they fed,
40　　And slaked its thirst with marah[23] of their tears.

Anathema maranatha![24] was the cry
　　That rang from town to town, from street to street;

At every gate the accursed Mordecai
    Was mocked and jeered, and spurned by Christian feet.

45   Pride and humiliation hand in hand
    Walked with them through the world where'er they went;
Trampled and beaten were they as the sand,
    And yet unshaken as the continent.

For in the background figures vague and vast
50   Of patriarchs and of prophets rose sublime,
And all the great traditions of the Past
    They saw reflected in the coming time.

And thus forever with reverted look
    The mystic volume of the world they read,
55   Spelling it backward, like a Hebrew book,
    Till life became a Legend of the Dead.

But ah! what once has been shall be no more!
    The groaning earth in travail and in pain
Brings forth its races, but does not restore,
60   And the dead nations never rise again.

                             1852

THE ROPEWALK

In that building, long and low,
With its windows all a-row,
    Like the port-holes of a hulk,
Human spiders spin and spin,
5   Backward down their threads so thin
    Dropping, each a hempen bulk.

At the end, an open door;
Squares of sunshine on the floor
    Light the long and dusky lane;
10   And the whirring of a wheel,
Dull and drowsy, makes me feel
    All its spokes are in my brain.

As the spinners to the end
Downward go and reascend,
15   Gleam the long threads in the sun;
While within this brain of mine
Cobwebs brighter and more fine
      By the busy wheel are spun.

Two fair maidens in a swing,
20   Like white doves upon the wing,
      First before my vision pass;
Laughing, as their gentle hands
Closely clasp the twisted strands,
      At their shadow on the grass.

25   Then a booth of mountebanks,
With its smell of tan and planks,
      And a girl poised high in air
On a cord, in spangled dress,
With a faded loveliness,
30   And a weary look of care.

Then a homestead among farms,
And a woman with bare arms
      Drawing water from a well;
As the bucket mounts apace,
35   With it mounts her own fair face,
      As at some magician's spell.

Then an old man in a tower,
Ringing loud the noontide hour,
      While the rope coils round and round
40   Like a serpent at his feet,
And again, in swift retreat,
      Nearly lifts him from the ground.

Then within a prison-yard,
Faces fixed, and stern, and hard,
45   Laughter and indecent mirth;
Ah! it is the gallows-tree!
Breath of Christian charity,
      Blow, and sweep it from the earth!

Then a school-boy, with his kite
50   Gleaming in a sky of light,
          And an eager, upward look;
Steeds pursued through lane and field;
Fowlers with their snares concealed;
          And an angler by a brook.

55   Ships rejoicing in the breeze,
Wrecks that float o'er unknown seas,
          Anchors dragged through faithless sand;
Sea-fog drifting overhead,
And, with lessening line and lead,
60   Sailors feeling for the land.

All these scenes do I behold,
These, and many left untold,
          In that building long and low;
While the wheel goes round and round,
65   With a drowsy, dreamy sound,
          And the spinners backward go.

                                        1854

THE GOLDEN MILE-STONE

Leafless are the trees; their purple branches
Spread themselves abroad, like reefs of coral,
          Rising silent
In the Red Sea of the winter sunset.

5   From the hundred chimneys of the village,
Like the Afreet in the Arabian story,
          Smoky columns
Tower aloft into the air of amber.

At the window winks the flickering fire-light;
10   Here and there the lamps of evening glimmer,
          Social watch-fires
Answering one another through the darkness.

On the hearth the lighted logs are glowing,
And like Ariel in the cloven pine-tree
15   For its freedom
Groans and sighs the air imprisoned in them.

By the fireside there are old men seated,
Seeing ruined cities in the ashes,
          Asking sadly
20 Of the Past what it can ne'er restore them.

By the fireside there are youthful dreamers,
Building castles fair, with stately stairways,
          Asking blindly
Of the Future what it cannot give them.

25 By the fireside tragedies are acted
In whose scenes appear two actors only,
          Wife and husband,
And above them God the sole spectator.

By the fireside there are peace and comfort,
30 Wives and children, with fair, thoughtful faces,
          Waiting, watching
For a well-known footstep in the passage.

Each man's chimney is his Golden Mile-stone;
Is the central point, from which he measures
35   Every distance
Through the gateways of the world around him.

In his farthest wanderings still he sees it;
Hears the talking flame, the answering night-wind,
          As he heard them
40 When he sat with those who were, but are not.

Happy he whom neither wealth nor fashion,
Nor the march of the encroaching city,
          Drives an exile
From the hearth of his ancestral homestead.

45 We may build more splendid habitations,
Fill our rooms with paintings and with sculptures,
      But we cannot
Buy with gold the old associations!

                1854

from HIAWATHA:
THE WHITE MAN'S FOOT

    From his wanderings far to eastward,
From the regions of the morning,
From the shining land of Wabun,
Homeward now returned Iagoo,
5 The great traveller, the great boaster,
Full of new and strange adventures,
Marvels many and many wonders.
    And the people of the village
Listened to him as he told them
10 Of his marvellous adventures,
Laughing answered him in this wise:
"Ugh! it is indeed Iagoo!
No one else beholds such wonders!"
    He had seen, he said, a water
15 Bigger than the Big-Sea-Water,
Broader than the Gitche Gumee,
Bitter so that none could drink it!
At each other looked the warriors,
Looked the women at each other,
20 Smiled, and said, "It cannot be so!
Kaw!" they said, "it cannot be so!"
    O'er it, said he, o'er this water
Came a great canoe with pinions,
A canoe with wings came flying,
25 Bigger than a grove of pine-trees,
Taller than the tallest tree-tops!
And the old men and the women
Looked and tittered at each other;
"Kaw!" they said, "we don't believe it!"
30   From its mouth, he said, to greet him,

Came Waywassimo, the lightning,
Came the thunder, Annemeekee!
And the warriors and the women
Laughed aloud at poor Iagoo;
35   "Kaw!" they said, "what tales you tell us!"
In it, said he, came a people,
In the great canoe with pinions
Came, he said, a hundred warriors;
Painted white were all their faces,
40   And with hair their chins were covered!
And the warriors and the women
Laughed and shouted in derision,
Like the ravens on the tree-tops,
Like the crows upon the hemlocks.
45   "Kaw!" they said, "what lies you tell us!
Do not think that we believe them!"
Only Hiawatha laughed not,
But he gravely spake and answered
To their jeering and their jesting:
50   "True is all Iagoo tells us;
I have seen it in a vision,
Seen the great canoe with pinions,
Seen the people with white faces,
Seen the coming of this bearded
55   People of the wooden vessel
From the regions of the morning,
From the shining land of Wabun.
"Gitche Manito the Mighty,
The Great Spirit, the Creator,
60   Sends them hither on his errand,
Sends them to us with his message.
Wheresoe'er they move, before them
Swarms the stinging fly, the Ahmo.
Swarms the bee, the honey-maker;
65   Wheresoe'er they tread, beneath them
Springs a flower unknown among us,
Springs the White-man's Foot in blossom.
"Let us welcome, then, the strangers,
Hail them as our friends and brothers,
70   And the heart's right hand of friendship
Give them when they come to see us.

Gitche Manito, the Mighty,
Said this to me in my vision.
    "I beheld, too, in that vision
75 All the secrets of the future,
Of the distant days that shall be.
I beheld the westward marches
Of the unknown, crowded nations.
All the land was full of people,
80 Restless, struggling, toiling, striving,
Speaking many tongues, yet feeling
But one heart-beat in their bosoms.
In the woodlands rang their axes,
Smoked their towns in all the valleys,
85 Over all the lakes and rivers
Rushed their great canoes of thunder.
    "Then a darker, drearier vision
Passed before me, vague and cloud-like:
I beheld our nation scattered,
90 All forgetful of my counsels,
Weakened, warring with each other;
Saw the remnants of our people
Sweeping westward, wild and woful,
Like the cloud-rack of a tempest,
95 Like the withered leaves of Autumn!"

                                        1855

SNOW-FLAKES

Out of the bosom of the Air,
    Out of the cloud-folds of her garments shaken,
Over the woodlands brown and bare
    Over the harvest-fields forsaken,
5   Silent, and soft, and slow
        Descends the snow.

Even as our cloudy fancies take
    Suddenly shape in some divine expression,
Even as the troubled heart doth make

10   In the white countenance confession,
            The troubled sky reveals
            The grief it feels.

        This is the poem of the air,
            Slowly in silent syllables recorded;
15   This is the secret of despair,
            Long in its cloudy bosom hoarded,
                Now whispered and revealed
                To wood and field.

                            1863

THE LEGEND OF RABBI BEN LEVI

        Rabbi Ben Levi, on the Sabbath, read
        A volume of the Law, in which it said,
        "No man shall look upon my face and live."
        And as he read, he prayed that God would give
5   His faithful servant grace with mortal eye
        To look upon His face and yet not die.

        Then fell a sudden shadow on the page,
        And, lifting up his eyes, grown dim with age,
        He saw the Angel of Death before him stand,
10   Holding a naked sword in his right hand.
        Rabbi Ben Levi was a righteous man,
        Yet through his veins a chill of terror ran.
        With trembling voice he said, "What wilt thou here?"
        The angel answered, "Lo! the time draws near
15   When thou must die; yet first, by God's decree,
        Whate'er thou askest shall be granted thee."
        Replied the Rabbi, "Let these living eyes
        First look upon my place in Paradise."

        Then said the Angel, "Come with me and look."
20   Rabbi Ben Levi closed the sacred book,
        And rising, and uplifting his gray head,

"Give me thy sword," he to the Angel said,
"Lest thou shouldst fall upon me by the way."
The Angel smiled and hastened to obey,
25   Then led him forth to the Celestial Town,
And set him on the wall, whence, gazing down,
Rabbi Ben Levi, with his living eyes,
Might look upon his place in Paradise.

Then straight into the city of the Lord
30   The Rabbi leaped with the Death-Angel's sword,
And through the streets there swept a sudden breath
Of something there unknown, which men call death.
Meanwhile the Angel stayed without, and cried,
"Come back!" To which the Rabbi's voice replied,
35   "No! in the name of God, whom I adore,
I swear that hence I will depart no more!"

Then all the Angels cried, "O Holy One,
See what the son of Levi here hath done!
The kingdom of Heaven he takes by violence,
40   And in Thy name refuses to go hence!"
The Lord replied, "My Angels, be not wroth;
Did e'er the son of Levi break his oath?
Let him remain; for he with mortal eye
Shall look upon my face and yet not die."

45   Beyond the outer wall the Angel of Death
Heard the great voice, and said, with panting breath,
"Give back the sword, and let me go my way."
Whereat the Rabbi paused, and answered, "Nay!
Anguish enough already has it caused
50   Among the sons of men." And while he paused
He heard the awful mandate of the Lord
Resounding through the air, "Give back the sword!"

The Rabbi bowed his head in silent prayer;
Then said he to the dreadful Angel, "Swear,
55   No human eye shall look on it again;
But when thou takest away the souls of men,

Thyself unseen, and with an unseen sword,
Thou wilt perform the bidding of the Lord."

The Angel took the sword again, and swore,
60 And walks on earth unseen forevermore.

                                          1863

THE RHYME OF SIR CHRISTOPHER

It was Sir Christopher Gardiner,
Knight of the Holy Sepulchre,
From Merry England over the sea,
Who stepped upon this continent
5   As if his august presence lent
A glory to the colony.

You should have seen him in the street
Of the little Boston of Winthrop's[25] time,
His rapier dangling at his feet,
10 Doublet and hose and boots complete,
Prince Rupert hat with ostrich plume,
Gloves that exhaled a faint perfume,
Luxuriant curls and air sublime,
And superior manners now obsolete!

15 He had a way of saying things
That made one think of courts and kings,
And lords and ladies of high degree;
So that not having been at court
Seemed something very little short
20 Of treason or lese-majesty,
Such an accomplished knight was he.

His dwelling was just beyond the town,
At what he called his country-seat;
For, careless of Fortune's smile or frown,
25 And weary grown of the world and its ways,
He wished to pass the rest of his days
In a private life and a calm retreat.

But a double life was the life he led,
And, while professing to be in search
30 Of a godly course, and willing, he said,
Nay, anxious to join the Puritan church,
He made of all this but small account,
And passed his idle hours instead
With roystering Morton of Merry Mount,[26]
35 That pettifogger from Furnival's Inn,
Lord of misrule and riot and sin,
Who looked on the wine when it was red.

This country-seat was little more
Than a cabin of logs; but in front of the door
40 A modest flower-bed thickly sown
With sweet alyssum and columbine
Made those who saw it at once divine
The touch of some other hand than his own.
And first it was whispered, and then it was known,
45 That he in secret was harboring there
A little lady with golden hair,
Whom he called his cousin, but whom he had wed
In the Italian manner,[27] as men said,
And great was the scandal everywhere.
50 But worse than this was the vague surmise,
Though none could vouch for it or aver,
That the Knight of the Holy Sepulchre
Was only a Papist in disguise;
And the more to embitter their bitter lives,
55 And the more to trouble the public mind,
Came letters from England, from two other wives,
Whom he had carelessly left behind;
Both of them letters of such a kind
As made the governor hold his breath;
60 The one imploring him straight to send
The husband home, that he might amend;
The other asking his instant death,
As the only way to make an end.

The wary governor deemed it right,
65 When all this wickedness was revealed,
To send his warrant signed and sealed,

And take the body of the knight.
Armed with this mighty instrument,
The marshal, mounting his gallant steed,
70 Rode forth from town at the top of his speed,
And followed by all his bailiffs bold,
As if on high achievement bent,
To storm some castle or stronghold,
Challenge the warders on the wall,
75 And seize in his ancestral hall
A robber-baron grim and old.
But when through all the dust and heat
He came to Sir Christopher's country seat,
No knight he found, nor warder there,
80 But the little lady with golden hair,
Who was gathering in the bright sunshine
The sweet alyssum and columbine;
While gallant Sir Christopher, all so gay,
Being forewarned, through the postern gate
85 Of his castle wall had tripped away,
And was keeping a little holiday
In the forests that bounded his estate.
Then as a trusty squire and true
The marshal searched the castle through,
90 Not crediting what the lady said;
Searched from cellar to garret in vain,
And, finding no knight, came out again
And arrested the golden damsel instead,
And bore her in triumph into the town,
95 While from her eyes the tears rolled down
On the sweet alyssum and columbine,
That she held in her fingers white and fine.

The governor's heart was moved to see
So fair a creature caught within
100 The snares of Satan and of sin,
And read her a little homily
On the folly and wickedness of the lives
Of women, half cousins and half wives;
But, seeing that naught his words availed,
105 He sent her away in a ship that sailed
For Merry England over the sea,

To the other two wives in the old countree,
To search her further, since he had failed
To come at the heart of the mystery.

110   Meanwhile Sir Christopher wandered away
Through pathless woods for a month and a day,
Shooting pigeons, and sleeping at night
With the noble savage, who took delight
In his feathered hat and his velvet vest,
115   His gun and his rapier and the rest.
But as soon as the noble savage heard
That a bounty was offered for this gay bird,
He wanted to slay him out of hand,
And bring in his beautiful scalp for a show,
120   Like the glossy head of a kite or crow,
Until he was made to understand
They wanted the bird alive, not dead;
Then he followed him whithersoever he fled,
Through forest and field, and hunted him down,
125   And brought him prisoner into the town.

Alas! it was a rueful sight,
To see this melancholy knight
In such a dismal and hapless case;
His hat deformed by stain and dent,
130   His plumage broken, his doublet rent,
His beard and flowing locks forlorn,
Matted, dishevelled, and unshorn,
His boots with dust and mire besprent;
But dignified in his disgrace,
135   And wearing an unblushing face.
And thus before the magistrate
He stood to hear the doom of fate.
In vain he strove with wonted ease
To modify and extenuate
140   His evil deeds in church and state,
For gone was now his power to please;
And his pompous words had no more weight
Than feathers flying in the breeze.

With suavity equal to his own
145 The governor lent a patient ear
To the speech evasive and highflown,
In which he endeavored to make clear
That colonial laws were too severe
When applied to a gallant cavalier,
150 A gentleman born, and so well known,
And accustomed to move in a higher sphere.

All this the Puritan governor heard,
And deigned in answer never a word;
But in summary manner shipped away
155 In a vessel that sailed from Salem bay,
This splendid and famous cavalier,
With his Rupert hat and his popery,
To Merry England over the sea,
As being unmeet to inhabit here.

160 Thus endeth the Rhyme of Sir Christopher,
Knight of the Holy Sepulchre,
The first who furnished this barren land
With apples of Sodom[28] and ropes of sand.

1874

JOHN GREENLEAF WHITTIER

(1807–1892)

Pulled this way and that by politics and poetry, Whittier managed to couple this ill-matched pair only in the harness of his Quaker humanitarianism. He was born in Haverhill, Massachusetts, a descendant of two old and established Quaker families. Forced to leave school very early, he worked on the family farm and began to write poetry in the manner of Robert Burns. In 1829, he assumed the first of several editorial positions on political journals that would lead him initially to elective office in the Massachusetts legislature in 1835 and then to active participation in the abolition movement. Over the next twenty-five years, his publications alternated between poems about the local past (*Legends of New England*, 1831; *Moll Pitcher*, 1832; *Mogg Megone*, 1836; *Lays of My Home*, 1843; *Poems*, 1849; *The Chapel of the Hermits*, 1853) and anti-slavery verse (*Poems Written During the Progress of the Abolition Question*, 1837 and 1838; *Voices of Freedom*, 1846). With the founding of the *Atlantic Monthly* in 1857, Whittier made his way into the Boston literary establishment; and with the coming of the Civil War, he was able at last to give his full attention to poetry. Following collections of his poems in 1860 and 1863, the publication of *Snow-Bound*, in 1866, and of *Tent on the Beach*, a year later, enabled him to retire in comfort to an estate in Danvers, Massachusetts, where he went on publishing verse until his death. By then, he had over twenty volumes of poetry to his name and had become a national icon, his birthdays celebrated in the public schools.

THE CITIES OF THE PLAIN[29]

"Get ye up from the wrath of God's terrible day!
Ungirded, unsandalled, arise and away!
'T is the vintage of blood, 't is the fulness of time,
And vengeance shall gather the harvest of crime!"

5   The warning was spoken—the righteous had gone,
And the proud ones of Sodom were feasting alone;

All gay was the banquet—the revel was long,
With the pouring of wine and the breathing of song.

'T was an evening of beauty; the air was perfume,
10 The earth was all greenness, the trees were all bloom;
And softly the delicate viol was heard,
Like the murmur of love or the notes of a bird.

And beautiful maidens moved down in the dance,
With the magic of motion and sunshine of glance;
15 And white arms wreathed lightly, and tresses fell free
As the plumage of birds in some tropical tree.

Where the shrines of foul idols were lighted on high,
And wantonness tempted the lust of the eye;
Midst rites of obsceneness, strange, loathsome, abhorred,
20 The blasphemer scoffed at the name of the Lord.

Hark! the growl of the thunder,—the quaking of earth!
Woe, woe to the worship, and woe to the mirth!
The black sky has opened; there's flame in the air;
The red arm of vengeance is lifted and bare!

25 Then the shriek of the dying rose wild where the song
And the low tone of love had been whispered along;
For the fierce flames went lightly o'er palace and bower,
Like the red tongues of demons, to blast and devour!

Down, down on the fallen the red ruin rained,
30 And the reveller sank with his wine-cup undrained;
The foot of the dancer, the music's loved thrill,
And the shout and the laughter grew suddenly still.

The last throb of anguish was fearfully given;
The last eye glared forth in its madness on Heaven!
35 The last groan of horror rose wildly and vain,
And death brooded over the pride of the Plain!

1831

THE FAREWELL

of a Virginia Slave Mother to Her Daughters
Sold into Southern Bondage

    Gone, gone,—sold and gone,
      To the rice-swamp dank and lone.
Where the slave-whip ceaseless swings,
Where the noisome insect stings,
Where the fever demon strews
Poison with the falling dews,
Where the sickly sunbeams glare
Through the hot and misty air;
    Gone, gone,—sold and gone,
      To the rice-swamp dank and lone,
      From Virginia's hills and waters;
      Woe is me, my stolen daughters!

    Gone, gone,—sold and gone,
      To the rice-swamp dank and lone.
There no mother's eye is near them,
There no mother's ear can hear them;
Never, when the torturing lash
Seams their back with many a gash,
Shall a mother's kindness bless them,
Or a mother's arms caress them.
    Gone, gone,—sold and gone,
      To the rice-swamp dank and lone,
      From Virginia's hills and waters;
      Woe is me, my stolen daughters!

    Gone, gone,—sold and gone,
      To the rice-swamp dank and lone.
Oh, when weary, sad, and slow,
From the fields at night they go,
Faint with toil, and racked with pain,
To their cheerless homes again,
There no brother's voice shall greet them;
There no father's welcome meet them.
    Gone, gone,—sold and gone,

To the rice-swamp dank and lone,
35   From Virginia's hills and waters;
Woe is me, my stolen daughters!

Gone, gone,—sold and gone,
To the rice-swamp dank and lone.
From the tree whose shadow lay
40   On their childhood's place of play;
From the cool spring where they drank;
Rock, and hill, and rivulet bank;
From the solemn house of prayer,
And the holy counsels there;
45   Gone, gone,—sold and gone,
To the rice-swamp dank and lone,
From Virginia's hills and waters;
Woe is me, my stolen daughters!

Gone, gone,—sold and gone,
50   To the rice-swamp dank and lone;
Toiling through the weary day,
And at night the spoiler's prey.
Oh, that they had earlier died,
Sleeping calmly, side by side,
55   Where the tyrant's power is o'er,
And the fetter galls no more!
Gone, gone,—sold and gone,
To the rice-swamp dank and lone,
From Virginia's hills and waters;
60   Woe is me, my stolen daughters!

Gone, gone,—sold and gone,
To the rice-swamp dank and lone.
By the holy love He beareth;
By the bruisëd reed He spareth;
65   Oh, may He, to whom alone
All their cruel wrongs are known,
Still their hope and refuge prove,
With a more than mother's love.

Gone, gone,—sold and gone,
70   To the rice-swamp dank and lone,
From Virginia's hills and waters;
Woe is me, my stolen daughters!

                                        1838

OFFICIAL PIETY

Suggested by reading a state paper, wherein the higher
law is invoked to sustain the lower one.

A pious magistrate! sound his praise throughout
The wondering churches. Who shall henceforth doubt
That the long-wished millennium draweth nigh?
Sin in high places has become devout,
5   Tithes mint, goes painful-faced, and prays its lie
Straight up to Heaven, and calls it piety!

The pirate, watching from his bloody deck
The weltering galleon, heavy with the gold
Of Acapulco, holding death in check
10   While prayers are said, brows crossed, and beads are told;
The robber, kneeling where the wayside cross
On dark Abruzzo[30] tells of life's dread loss
From his own carbine, glancing still abroad
For some new victim, offering thanks to God!
15   Rome, listening at her altars to the cry
Of midnight Murder, while her hounds of hell
Scour France, from baptized cannon and holy bell
And thousand-throated priesthood, loud and high,
Pealing Te Deums to the shuddering sky,
20   "Thanks to the Lord, who giveth victory!"
What prove these, but that crime was ne'er so black
As ghostly cheer and pious thanks to lack?
Satan is modest. At Heaven's door he lays
His evil offspring, and, in Scriptural phrase
25   And saintly posture, gives to God the praise
And honor of the monstrous progeny.
What marvel, then, in our own time to see
His old devices, smoothly acted o'er,—

Official piety, locking fast the door
30   Of Hope against three million souls of men,—
Brothers, God's children, Christ's redeemed,—and then,
With uprolled eyeballs and on bended knee,
Whining a prayer for help to hide the key!

                                          1853

THE HASCHISH[31]

Of all that Orient lands can vaunt
    Of marvels with our own competing,
The strangest is the Haschish plant,
    And what will follow on its eating.

5   What pictures to the taster rise,
    Of Dervish or of Almeh dances!
Of Eblis, or of Paradise,
    Set all aglow with Houri glances!

The poppy visions of Cathay,
10   The heavy beer-trance of the Suabian;[32]
The wizard lights and demon play
    Of nights Walpurgis and Arabian!

The Mollah and the Christian dog
    Change place in mad metempsychosis;
15   The Muezzin climbs the synagogue,
    The Rabbi shakes his beard at Moses!

The Arab by his desert well
    Sits choosing from some Caliph's daughters,
And hears his single camel's bell
20   Sound welcome to his regal quarters.

The Koran's reader makes complaint
    Of Shitan[33] dancing on and off it;
The robber offers alms, the saint
    Drinks Tokay and blasphemes the Prophet.

25   Such scenes that Eastern plant awakes;
          But we have one ordained to beat it,
      The Haschish of the West, which makes
          Or fools or knaves of all who eat it.

      The preacher eats, and straight appears
30   His Bible in a new translation;
      Its angels negro overseers,
          And Heaven itself a snug plantation!

      The man of peace, about whose dreams
          The sweet millennial angels cluster,
35   Tastes the mad weed, and plots and schemes,
          A raving Cuban filibuster!

      The noisiest Democrat, with ease,
          It turns to Slavery's parish beadle;
      The shrewdest statesman eats and sees
40   Due southward point the polar needle.

      The Judge partakes, and sits erelong
          Upon his bench a railing blackguard;
      Decides off-hand that right is wrong,
          And reads the ten commandments backward.

45   O potent plant! so rare a taste
          Has never Turk or Gentoo gotten;
      The hempen Haschish of the East
          Is powerless to our Western Cotton!

                                              1854

SKIPPER IRESON'S RIDE

      Of all the rides since the birth of time,
      Told in story or sung in rhyme,—
      On Apuleius's Golden Ass,
      Or one-eyed Calendar's horse of brass,[34]
5   Witch astride of a human back,
      Islam's prophet on Al-Borák,—[35]

The strangest ride that ever was sped
Was Ireson's, out from Marblehead!
  Old Floyd Ireson, for his hard heart,
10   Tarred and feathered and carried in a cart
    By the women of Marblehead!

Body of turkey, head of owl,
Wings a-droop like a rained-on fowl,
Feathered and ruffled in every part,
15 Skipper Ireson stood in the cart.
Scores of women, old and young,
Strong of muscle, and glib of tongue,
Pushed and pulled up the rocky lane,
Shouting and singing the shrill refrain:
20   "Here's Flud Oirson, fur his horrd horrt,
    Torr'd an' futherr'd an' corr'd in a corrt
    By the women o' Morble'ead!"

Wrinkled scolds with hands on hips,
Girls in bloom of cheek and lips,
25 Wild-eyed, free-limbed, such as chase
Bacchus round some antique vase,
Brief of skirt, with ankles bare,
Loose of kerchief and loose of hair,
With conch-shells blowing and fish-horns' twang,
30 Over and over the Mænads sang:
   "Here's Flud Oirson, fur his horrd horrt,
    Torr'd an' futherr'd an' corr'd in a corrt
    By the women o' Morble'ead!"

Small pity for him!—He sailed away
35 From a leaking ship in Chaleur Bay,—[36]
Sailed away from a sinking wreck,
With his own town's-people on her deck!
"Lay by! lay by!" they called to him.
Back he answered, "Sink or swim!
40 Brag of your catch of fish again!"
And off he sailed through the fog and rain!
  Old Floyd Ireson, for his hard heart,
    Tarred and feathered and carried in a cart
    By the women of Marblehead!

45 Fathoms deep in dark Chaleur
That wreck shall lie forevermore.
Mother and sister, wife and maid,
Looked from the rocks of Marblehead
Over the moaning and rainy sea,—
50 Looked for the coming that might not be!
What did the winds and the sea-birds say
Of the cruel captain who sailed away?—
    Old Floyd Ireson, for his hard heart,
    Tarred and feathered and carried in a cart
55   By the women of Marblehead!

Through the street, on either side,
Up flew windows, doors swung wide;
Sharp-tongued spinsters, old wives gray,
Treble lent the fish-horn's bray.
60 Sea-worn grandsires, cripple-bound,
Hulks of old sailors run aground,
Shook head, and fist, and hat, and cane,
And cracked with curses the hoarse refrain:
    "Here's Flud Oirson, fur his horrd horrt,
65   Torr'd an' futherr'd an' corr'd in a corrt
    By the women o' Morble'ead!"

Sweetly along the Salem road
·Bloom of orchard and lilac showed.
Little the wicked skipper knew
70 Of the fields so green and the sky so blue.
Riding there in his sorry trim,
Like an Indian idol glum and grim,
Scarcely he seemed the sound to hear
Of voices shouting, far and near:
75   "Here's Flud Oirson, fur his horrd horrt,
    Torr'd an' futherr'd an' corr'd in a corrt
    By the women o' Morble'ead!"

"Hear me, neighbors!" at last he cried,—
"What to me is this noisy ride?
80 What is the shame that clothes the skin
To the nameless horror that lives within?

Waking or sleeping, I see a wreck,
And hear a cry from a reeling deck!
Hate me and curse me,—I only dread
85　The hand of God and the face of the dead!"
　　Said old Floyd Ireson, for his hard heart,
　　Tarred and feathered and carried in a cart
　　By the women of Marblehead!

Then the wife of the skipper lost at sea
90　Said, "God has touched him! why should we!"
Said an old wife mourning her only son,
"Cut the rogue's tether and let him run!"
So with soft relentings and rude excuse,
Half scorn, half pity, they cut him loose,
95　And gave him a cloak to hide him in,
And left him alone with his shame and sin.
　　Poor Floyd Ireson, for his hard heart,
　　Tarred and feathered and carried in a cart
　　By the women of Marblehead!

                                        1857

THE PALM-TREE

Is it the palm, the cocoa-palm,
On the Indian Sea, by the isles of balm?
Or is it a ship in the breezeless calm?

A ship whose keel is of palm beneath,
5　Whose ribs of palm have a palm-bark sheath,
And a rudder of palm it steereth with.

Branches of palm are its spars and rails,
Fibres of palm are its woven sails,
And the rope is of palm that idly trails!

10　What does the good ship bear so well?
The cocoa-nut with its stony shell,
And the milky sap of its inner cell.

What are its jars, so smooth and fine,
But hollowed nuts, filled with oil and wine,
15 And the cabbage that ripens under the Line?

Who smokes his nargileh, cool and calm?
The master, whose cunning and skill could charm
Cargo and ship from the bounteous palm.

In the cabin he sits on a palm-mat soft,
20 From a beaker of palm his drink is quaffed,
And a palm-thatch shields from the sun aloft!

His dress is woven of palmy strands,
And he holds a palm-leaf scroll in his hands,
Traced with the Prophet's wise commands!

25 The turban folded about his head
Was daintily wrought of the palm-leaf braid,
And the fan that cools him of palm was made.

Of threads of palm was the carpet spun
Whereon he kneels when the day is done,
30 And the foreheads of Islam are bowed as one!

To him the palm is a gift divine,
Wherein all uses of man combine,—
House, and raiment, and food, and wine!

And, in the hour of his great release,
35 His need of the palm shall only cease
With the shroud wherein he lieth in peace.

"Allah il Allah!" he sings his psalm,
On the Indian Sea, by the isles of balm;
"Thanks to Allah who gives the palm!"

1858

BROWN OF OSSAWATOMIE[37]

John Brown of Ossawatomie spake on his dying day:
"I will not have to shrive my soul a priest in Slavery's pay.
But let some poor slave-mother whom I have striven to free,
With her children, from the gallows-stair put up a prayer
    for me!"

5   John Brown of Ossawatomie, they led him out to die;
And lo! a poor slave-mother with her little child pressed nigh.
Then the bold, blue eye grew tender, and the old harsh face
    grew mild,
As he stooped between the jeering ranks and kissed the negro's
    child!

The shadows of his stormy life that moment fell apart;
10   And they who blamed the bloody hand forgave the loving
    heart.
That kiss from all its guilty means redeemed the good intent,
And round the grisly fighter's hair the martyr's aureole bent!

Perish with him the folly that seeks through evil good!
Long live the generous purpose unstained with human blood!
15   Not the raid of midnight terror, but the thought which
    underlies;
Not the borderer's pride of daring, but the Christian's sacrifice.

Nevermore may yon Blue Ridges the Northern rifle hear,
Nor see the light of blazing homes flash on the negro's spear.
But let the free-winged angel Truth their guarded passes scale,
20   To teach that right is more than might, and justice more than
    mail!

So vainly shall Virginia set her battle in array;
In vain her trampling squadrons knead the winter snow with
    clay.
She may strike the pouncing eagle, but she dares not harm the
    dove;
And every gate she bars to Hate shall open wide to Love!

                             1859

A WORD FOR THE HOUR

The firmament breaks up. In black eclipse
Light after light goes out. One evil star,
Luridly glaring through the smoke of war,
As in the dream of the Apocalypse,
5   Drags others down. Let us not weakly weep
Nor rashly threaten. Give us grace to keep
Our faith and patience; wherefore should we leap
On one hand into fratricidal fight,
Or, on the other, yield eternal right,
10   Frame lies of law, and good and ill confound?
What fear we? Safe on freedom's vantage-ground
Our feet are planted: let us there remain
In unrevengeful calm, no means untried
Which truth can sanction, no just claim denied,
15   The sad spectators of a suicide!
They break the links of Union: shall we light
The fires of hell to weld anew the chain
On that red anvil where each blow is pain?
Draw we not even now a freer breath,
20   As from our shoulders falls a load of death
Loathsome as that the Tuscan's victim bore
When keen with life to a dead horror bound?[38]
Why take we up the accursed thing again?
Pity, forgive, but urge them back no more
25   Who, drunk with passion, flaunt disunion's rag
With its vile reptile-blazon. Let us press
The golden cluster on our brave old flag
In closer union, and, if numbering less,
Brighter shall shine the stars which still remain.

                                                    1861

BARBARA FRIETCHIE

Up from the meadows rich with corn,
Clear in the cool September morn,

The clustered spires of Frederick stand
Green-walled by the hills of Maryland.

5   Round about them orchards sweep,
Apple and peach tree fruited deep,

Fair as the garden of the Lord
To the eyes of the famished rebel horde,

On that pleasant morn of the early fall
10   When Lee marched over the mountain-wall;

Over the mountains winding down,
Horse and foot, into Frederick town.

Forty flags with their silver stars,
Forty flags with their crimson bars,

15   Flapped in the morning wind: the sun
Of noon looked down, and saw not one.

Up rose old Barbara Frietchie then,
Bowed with her fourscore years and ten;

Bravest of all in Frederick town,
20   She took up the flag the men hauled down;

In her attic window the staff she set,
To show that one heart was loyal yet.

Up the street came the rebel tread,
Stonewall Jackson riding ahead.

25   Under his slouched hat left and right
He glanced; the old flag met his sight.

"Halt!"—the dust-brown ranks stood fast.
"Fire!"—out blazed the rifle-blast.

It shivered the window, pane and sash;
30   It rent the banner with seam and gash.

Quick, as it fell, from the broken staff
Dame Barbara snatched the silken scarf.

She leaned far out on the window-sill,
And shook it forth with a royal will.

35   "Shoot, if you must, this old gray head,
But spare your country's flag," she said.

A shade of sadness, a blush of shame,
Over the face of the leader came;

The nobler nature within him stirred
40   To life at that woman's deed and word;

"Who touches a hair of yon gray head
Dies like a dog! March on!" he said.

All day long through Frederick street
Sounded the tread of marching feet:

45   All day long that free flag tost
Over the heads of the rebel host.

Ever its torn folds rose and fell
On the loyal winds that loved it well;

And through the hill-gaps sunset light
50   Shone over it with a warm good-night.

Barbara Frietchie's work is o'er,
And the Rebel rides on his raids no more.

Honor to her! and let a tear
Fall, for her sake, on Stonewall's bier.

55   Over Barbara Frietchie's grave,
        Flag of Freedom and Union, wave!

        Peace and order and beauty draw
        Round thy symbol of light and law;

        And ever the stars above look down
60   On thy stars below in Frederick town!

                                        1863

from TENT ON THE BEACH:
[THE DREAMER]

        And one there was, a dreamer born,
            Who, with a mission to fulfil,
        Had left the Muses' haunts to turn
            The crank of an opinion-mill,
5   Making his rustic reed of song
        A weapon in the war with wrong,
        Yoking his fancy to the breaking-plough
        That beam-deep turned the soil for truth to spring and grow.

        Too quiet seemed the man to ride
10   The wingèd Hippogriff Reform;
        Was his a voice from side to side
            To pierce the tumult of the storm?
        A silent, shy, peace-loving man,
        He seemed no fiery partisan
15   To hold his way against the public frown,
        The ban of Church and State, the fierce mob's hounding down.

        For while he wrought with strenuous will
            The work his hands had found to do,
        He heard the fitful music still
20   Of winds that out of dream-land blew.
        The din about him could not drown
        What the strange voices whispered down;
        Along his task-field weird processions swept,
        The visionary pomp of stately phantoms stepped.

25   The common air was thick with dreams,—
              He told them to the toiling crowd;
          Such music as the woods and streams
              Sang in his ear he sang aloud;
          In still, shut bays, on windy capes,
30   He heard the call of beckoning shapes,
    And, as the gray old shadows prompted him,
    To homely moulds of rhyme he shaped their legends grim.

          He rested now his weary hands,
              And lightly moralized and laughed,
35   As, tracing on the shifting sands
              A burlesque of his paper-craft,
          He saw the careless waves o'errun
              His words, as time before had done,
    Each day's tide-water washing clean away,
40   Like letters from the sand, the work of yesterday.

                                                    1867

OVERRULED

    The threads our hands in blindness spin
    No self-determined plan weaves in;
    The shuttle of the unseen powers
    Works out a pattern not as ours.

5   Ah! small the choice of him who sings
    What sound shall leave the smitten strings;
    Fate holds and guides the hand of art;
    The singer's is the servant's part.

    The wind-harp chooses not the tone
10   That through its trembling threads is blown;
    The patient organ cannot guess
    What hand its passive keys shall press.

    Through wish, resolve, and act, our will
    Is moved by undreamed forces still;

15 And no man measures in advance
His strength with untried circumstance.

As streams take hue from shade and sun,
As runs the life the song must run;
But, glad or sad, to His good end
20 God grant the varying notes may tend!

1859–78

EDGAR ALLAN POE

(1809–1849)

Poe's life is a parade of losses brought on by ill fortune and his own penchant for self-destruction. He was born in Boston to a pair of traveling actors, both of whom died before he was three, leaving him, a brother, and a sister to reside in separate foster homes. Young Edgar lived in Richmond, Virginia, with John Allan, a local merchant, and his wife, who sent the child to schools in Richmond and then, when the family went abroad on business for five years, in Scotland and England. Back in Richmond, Poe completed his schooling and, when Allan came into a large inheritance, entered the University of Virginia, only to withdraw after one term because of gambling debts and unpaid bills.

Refusing Allan's demand that he now turn to the study of law, Poe left for Boston to begin his literary career in poverty under an assumed name. In 1827, he published privately his first book of verse, *Tamerlane and Other Poems, By a Bostonian* and enlisted in the army under yet another pseudonym. After some eighteen months of creditable service, Poe and his foster father were partially reconciled in accordance with Mrs. Allan's dying wish. With Allan's help, he secured an honorable discharge and an appointment to the U.S. Military Academy, effective the following year. Meanwhile, he lived in Baltimore with members of his long-estranged family, including his father's widowed sister, Maria Clemm, and her seven-year-old daughter, Virginia. There, he published his second book, *Al Araaf, Tamerlane, and Minor Poems* (1829).

Hoping to ingratiate himself with his now wealthy guardian, Poe enrolled at West Point in 1830. But when further quarrels and Allan's remarriage divided them absolutely, he shirked his duties and was dismissed. Now entirely on his own, he set out to make his living as a writer, shuttling endlessly between Baltimore, Philadelphia, New York, and Richmond; publishing whatever he could, wherever he could; and holding one editorship after another, only to find himself repeatedly fired for intransigence or drunkenness. Starting out in New York, he published *Poems of Edgar A. Poe* (1831), which went unnoticed, then returned to Mrs. Clemm and Virginia in Baltimore. The next year, he published his first story, "Metzengerstein," and the year after that, "MS. Found in a Bottle," the first of his writings to attract the attention of reviewers. In 1835, he left the Clemms for Richmond, to become an editor on the *Southern Literary Messenger*. Although successful in increasing the circulation of the magazine, he soon lost his post because of drinking, returned to Baltimore, and took out a license to marry his cousin Virginia, now thirteen years old. Reinstated by the *Messenger*, Poe moved with his bride and her mother to Richmond. In the next year, he wrote countless reviews, articles, poems, and stories (including *The Narrative of Arthur Gordon Pym*) for that magazine, then departed for New York, where *Pym* was published in book form, and Poe did freelance writing in an effort to keep his family from starving. In 1838, the three vagabonds moved to Philadelphia. After months of hack writing, Poe was made an editor of *Burton's Gentleman's Magazine;* published his first collection of stories, *Tales of the Grotesque and Arabesque* (1840), which did not sell; then became literary editor of *Graham Lady's and Gentleman's Magazine,* helping to make it the most successful periodical of its kind in the country before misbehavior once again forced his departure.

By 1842, Poe had become a person of some consequence in the literary world, owing to his truculent reviews, brainy essays, and his first tale of detection, "The Murders in the Rue Morgue" (1841). As his literary fortunes rose, however, his spirits and income declined, subjecting him to bouts of drinking and his family to destitution. In 1844, with Virginia in the advanced stages of tuberculosis, the three removed once again to New York, where Poe published "The Raven," at first anonymously, then signed. In 1845, he joined the *New York Mirror* as an editor and began a series of attacks on Longfellow that would make him notorious in New England and famous in Manhattan. Moving to the *Broadway Journal,* which he supplied with pieces old and new, Poe found himself at the top of his career, with no way to go but down. After publishing a third collection of tales, as well as *The Raven and Other Poems* (both in 1845), he withdrew from the *Journal* in order to pursue his long-cherished aim of founding his own magazine.

Two years of freelance writing brought him only utter destitution and ended with the death of Virginia. Soon thereafter, he began a series of frenzied, simultaneous alliances with female admirers in New York, Massachusetts, Rhode Island, and Virginia, interspersed with binges, arrests, at least one attempt at suicide, periodic returns to the care of Mrs. Clemm, and the publication of his cosmological prose poem *Eureka* (1848). This mad marathon came to an end when, on his way to New York from Richmond, Poe stopped off in Baltimore, fell among thieves, and was found, days later, in a state of delirium. Four days later, he was dead, his losses complete.

DREAMS

Oh that my young life were a lasting dream,
My spirit not awakening till the beam
Of an eternity should bring the morrow!
Yes, though that long dream were of hopeless sorrow,
'T were better than the cold reality
Of waking life to him whose heart must be,
And hath been still, upon the lovely earth,
A chaos of deep passion from his birth.
But should it be—that dream eternally
Continuing, as dreams have been to me
In my young boyhood—should it thus be given,
'T were folly still to hope for higher heaven.
For I have revelled, when the sun was bright
I' the summer sky, in dreams of living light
And loveliness; have left my very heart
In climes of mine imagining, apart
From mine own home, with beings that have been
Of mine own thought—what more could I have seen?
'T was once, and only once, and the wild hour
From my remembrance shall not pass—some power
Or spell had bound me—'t was the chilly wind
Came o'er me in the night and left behind
Its image on my spirit, or the moon
Shone on my slumbers in her lofty noon
Too coldly, or the stars—howe'er it was,
That dream was as that night-wind—let it pass.

I have been happy, though but in a dream.
I have been happy, and I love the theme;
Dreams! in their vivid coloring of life,
As in that fleeting, shadowy, misty strife
Of semblance with reality which brings
To the delirious eye more lovely things
Of paradise and love—and all our own!—
Than young Hope in his sunniest hour hath known.

1827

SONNET: TO SCIENCE

Science! true daughter of old Time thou art,
   Who alterest all things with thy peering eyes.
Why preyest thou thus upon the poet's heart,
   Vulture, whose wings are dull realities?
5 How should he love thee, or how deem thee wise,
   Who wouldst not leave him in his wandering
To seek for treasure in the jewelled skies,
   Albeit he soared with an undaunted wing?
Hast thou not dragged Diana from her car,
10 And driven the hamadryad from the wood
To seek a shelter in some happier star?
   Hast thou not torn the naiad from her flood,
The elfin from the green grass, and from me
The summer dream beneath the tamarind tree?

1829

ROMANCE

Romance, who loves to nod and sing,
   With drowsy head and folded wing,
   Among the green leaves as they shake
Far down within some shadowy lake,
5   To me a painted paroquet
Hath been—a most familiar bird;
   Taught me my alphabet to say,
To lisp my very earliest word
While in the wild wood I did lie,
10 A child, with a most knowing eye.

Of late, eternal condor years
   So shake the very heaven on high
   With tumult as they thunder by,
I have no time for idle cares
15   Through gazing on the unquiet sky.
And when an hour with calmer wings
Its down upon my spirit flings,

That little time with lyre and rhyme
    To while away—forbidden things!
20   My heart would feel to be a crime
    Unless it trembled with the strings.

                                    1829

A DREAM WITHIN A DREAM

Take this kiss upon the brow!
And, in parting from you now,
Thus much let me avow:
You are not wrong who deem
5   That my days have been a dream;
Yet if hope has flown away
In a night, or in a day,
In a vision, or in none,
Is it therefore the less gone?
10   All that we see or seem
Is but a dream within a dream.

I stand amid the roar
Of a surf-tormented shore,
And I hold within my hand
15   Grains of the golden sand—
How few! yet how they creep
Through my fingers to the deep,
While I weep—while I weep!
O God! can I not grasp
20   Them with a tighter clasp?
O God! can I not save
One from the pitiless wave?
Is *all* that we see or seem
But a dream within a dream?

                                    1829

THE CITY IN THE SEA

Lo! Death has reared himself a throne
In a strange city lying alone
Far down within the dim west
Where the good and the bad and the worst and the best
5   Have gone to their eternal rest.
There shrines and palaces and towers
(Time-eaten towers that tremble not!)
Resemble nothing that is ours.
Around, by lifting winds forgot,
10   Resignedly beneath the sky
The melancholy waters lie.

No rays from the holy heaven come down
On the long night-time of that town;
But light from out the lurid sea
15   Streams up the turrets silently,
Gleams up the pinnacles far and free,
Up domes, up spires, up kingly halls,
Up fanes, up Babylon-like walls,
Up shadowy long-forgotten bowers
20   Of sculptured ivy and stone flowers,
Up many and many a marvellous shrine
Whose wreathèd friezes intertwine
The viol, the violet, and the vine.
Resignedly beneath the sky
25   The melancholy waters lie.
So blend the turrets and shadows there
That all seem pendulous in air,
While from a proud tower in the town
Death looks gigantically down.

30   There open fanes and gaping graves
Yawn level with the luminous waves;
But not the riches there that lie
In each idol's diamond eye,
Not the gayly-jewelled dead
35   Tempt the waters from their bed;
For no ripples curl, alas!
Along that wilderness of glass;

No swellings tell that winds may be
Upon some far-off happier sea;
40   No heavings hint that winds have been
On seas less hideously serene.

But lo, a stir is in the air!
The wave—there is a movement there!
As if the towers had thrust aside,
45   In slightly sinking, the dull tide;
As if their tops had feebly given
A void within the filmy heaven.
The waves have now a redder glow;
The hours are breathing faint and low;
50   And when, amid no earthly moans,
Down, down that town shall settle hence,
Hell, rising from a thousand thrones,
Shall do it reverence.

1831

TO ONE IN PARADISE

Thou wast that all to me, love,
   For which my soul did pine—
A green isle in the sea, love,
   A fountain and a shrine,
5   All wreathed with fairy fruits and flowers,
   And all the flowers were mine.

Ah, dream too bright to last!
   Ah, starry hope, that didst arise
But to be overcast!
10   A voice from out the future cries,
   "On! on!" but o'er the past
   (Dim gulf!) my spirit hovering lies
Mute, motionless, aghast!

For, alas! alas! with me
15   The light of life is o'er!
   "No more—no more—no more—"
(Such language holds the solemn sea

          To the sands upon the shore)
        Shall bloom the thunder-blasted tree,
20   Or the stricken eagle soar!

        And all my days are trances,
          And all my nightly dreams
        Are where thy dark eye glances,
          And where thy footstep gleams,
25   In what ethereal dances,
          By what eternal streams.

                                        1834

SILENCE

There are some qualities, some incorporate things,
    That have a double life, which thus is made
A type of that twin entity which springs
    From matter and light, evinced in solid and shade.
5   There is a twofold Silence—sea and shore—
    Body and soul. One dwells in lonely places,
        Newly with grass o'ergrown; some solemn graces,
Some human memories and tearful lore,
Render him terrorless: his name 's "No More."
10 He is the corporate Silence: dread him not!
        No power hath he of evil in himself;
But should some urgent fate (untimely lot!)
        Bring thee to meet his shadow (nameless elf,
That haunteth the lone regions where hath trod
15 No foot of man), commend thyself to God!

                                        1840

THE SLEEPER

At midnight, in the month of June,
I stand beneath the mystic moon.
An opiate vapor, dewy, dim,
Exhales from out her golden rim,

5   And, softly dripping, drop by drop,
Upon the quiet mountain-top,
Steals drowsily and musically
Into the universal valley.
The rosemary nods upon the grave;
10   The lily lolls upon the wave;
Wrapping the fog about its breast,
The ruin moulders into rest;
Looking like Lethe, see! the lake
A conscious slumber seems to take,
15   And would not, for the world, awake.
All beauty sleeps!—and lo! where lies
Irene, with her destinies!

O lady bright! can it be right,
This window open to the night?
20   The wanton airs, from the tree-top,
Laughingly through the lattice drop;
The bodiless airs, a wizard rout,
Flit through thy chamber in and out,
And wave the curtain canopy
25   So fitfully, so fearfully,
Above the closed and fringèd lid
'Neath which thy slumb'ring soul lies hid,
That, o'er the floor and down the wall,
Like ghosts the shadows rise and fall.
30   O lady dear, hast thou no fear?
Why and what art thou dreaming here?
Sure thou art come o'er far-off seas,
A wonder to these garden trees!
Strange is thy pallor: strange thy dress:
35   Strange, above all, thy length of tress,
And this all solemn silentness!

The lady sleeps. Oh, may her sleep,
Which is enduring, so be deep!
Heaven have her in its sacred keep!
40   This chamber changed for one more holy,
This bed for one more melancholy,
I pray to God that she may lie

Forever with unopened eye,
While the pale sheeted ghosts go by.

45 My love, she sleeps. Oh, may her sleep,
As it is lasting, so be deep!
Soft may the worms about her creep!
Far in the forest, dim and old,
For her may some tall vault unfold:
50 Some vault that oft hath flung its black
And wingèd panels fluttering back,
Triumphant, o'er the crested palls
Of her grand family funerals:
Some sepulchre, remote, alone,
55 Against whose portal she hath thrown,
In childhood, many an idle stone:
Some tomb from out whose sounding door
She ne'er shall force an echo more,
Thrilling to think, poor child of sin,
60 It was the dead who groaned within!

                                   1841

THE CONQUEROR WORM

Lo! 't is a gala night
    Within the lonesome latter years!
An angel throng, bewinged, bedight
    In veils, and drowned in tears,
5 Sit in a theatre, to see
    A play of hopes and fears,
While the orchestra breathes fitfully
    The music of the spheres.

Mimes, in the form of God on high,
10   Mutter and mumble low,
And hither and thither fly;
    Mere puppets they, who come and go
At bidding of vast formless things
    That shift the scenery to and fro,

15   Flapping from out their condor wings
          Invisible woe!

      That motley drama—oh, be sure
          It shall not be forgot!
      With its phantom chased for evermore,
20   By a crowd that seize it not,
      Through a circle that ever returneth in
          To the self-same spot,
      And much of madness, and more of sin,
          And horror the soul of the plot.

25   But see, amid the mimic rout
          A crawling shape intrude!
      A blood-red thing that writhes from out
          The scenic solitude!
      It writhes! it writhes! with mortal pangs
30   The mimes become its food,
      And the angels sob at vermin fangs
          In human gore imbued.

      Out, out are the lights, out all!
          And, over each quivering form,
35   The curtain, a funeral pall,
          Comes down with the rush of a storm,
      And the angels, all pallid and wan,
          Uprising, unveiling, affirm
      That the play is the tragedy "Man,"
40   And its hero the Conqueror Worm.

                                        1843

      DREAMLAND

      By a route obscure and lonely,
      Haunted by ill angels only,
      Where an Eidolon, named Night,
      On a black throne reigns upright,
5   I have reached these lands but newly
      From an ultimate dim Thule—

From a wild weird clime that lieth, sublime,
   Out of Space, out of Time.

      Bottomless vales and boundless floods,
10   And chasms and caves and Titan woods,
      With forms that no man can discover
      For the dews that drip all over;
      Mountains toppling evermore
      Into seas without a shore;
15   Seas that restlessly aspire,
      Surging, unto skies of fire;
      Lakes that endlessly outspread
      Their lone waters lone and dead,
      Their still waters—still and chilly
20   With the snows of the lolling lily.

      By the lakes that thus outspread
      Their lone waters, lone and dead,
      Their sad waters, sad and chilly
      With the snows of the lolling lily,
25   By the mountains, near the river
      Murmuring lowly, murmuring ever,
      By the gray woods, by the swamp
      Where the toad and the newt encamp,
      By the dismal tarns and pools
30   Where dwell the Ghouls,
      By each spot the most unholy,
      In each nook most melancholy,
      There the traveller meets aghast
      Sheeted memories of the past—
35   Shrouded forms that start and sigh
      As they pass the wanderer by—
      White-robed forms of friends long given,
      In agony, to the earth—and heaven.

      For the heart whose woes are legion
40   'T is a peaceful, soothing region;
      For the spirit that walks in shadow
      'T is—oh, 't is an Eldorado!
      But the traveller, travelling through it,
      May not, dare not openly view it;

45 Never its mysteries are exposed
To the weak human eye unclosed;
So wills its king, who hath forbid
The uplifting of the fringed lid;
And thus the sad soul that here passes
50 Beholds it but through darkened glasses.

By a route obscure and lonely,
Haunted by ill angels only,
Where an Eidolon, named Night,
On a black throne reigns upright,
55 I have wandered home but newly
From this ultimate dim Thule.

                                        1844

STANZAS

Lady! I would that verse of mine
    Could fling, all lavishly and free,
Prophetic tones from every line,
    Of health, joy, peace, in store for thee.

5 Thine should be length of happy days,
    Enduring joys and fleeting cares,
Virtues that challenge envy's praise,
    By rivals loved, and mourned by heirs.

Thy life's free course should ever roam
10   Beyond this bounded earthly clime,
No billow breaking into foam
    Upon the rock-girt shore of Time.

The gladness of a gentle heart,
    Pure as the wishes breathed in prayer,
15 Which has in others' joys a part,
    While in its own all others share.

The fullness of a cultured mind,
    Stored with the wealth of bard and sage,

Which Error's glitter cannot blind,
20   Lustrous in youth, undimmed in age;

The grandeur of a guileless soul,
    With wisdom, virtue, feeling fraught,
Gliding serenely to its goal,
    Beneath the eternal sky of Thought:—

25 These should be thine, to guard and shield,
        And this the life thy spirit live,
Blest with all bliss that earth can yield,
    Bright with all hopes that Heaven can give.

                                        1845

THE RAVEN

Once upon a midnight dreary, while I pondered, weak and
        weary,
Over many a quaint and curious volume of forgotten lore,
While I nodded, nearly napping, suddenly there came a
        tapping,
As of some one gently rapping, rapping at my chamber door.
5   " 'T is some visitor," I muttered, "tapping at my chamber
        door,
                        Only this and nothing more."

Ah, distinctly I remember it was in the bleak December,
And each separate dying ember wrought its ghost upon the
        floor.
Eagerly I wished the morrow; vainly I had sought to borrow
10 From my books surcease of sorrow—sorrow for the lost
        Lenore,
For the rare and radiant maiden whom the angels name
        Lenore,
                        Nameless here for evermore.

And the silken sad uncertain rustling of each purple curtain
Thrilled me, filled me with fantastic terrors never felt before;
15 So that now, to still the beating of my heart, I stood repeating:

" 'T is some visitor entreating entrance at my chamber door—
Some late visitor entreating entrance at my chamber door;
                                        This it is and nothing more."

Presently my soul grew stronger; hesitating then no longer,
20   "Sir," said I, "or Madam, truly your forgiveness I implore;
But the fact is I was napping, and so gently you came rapping,
And so faintly you came tapping, tapping at my chamber
        door,
That I scarce was sure I heard you"—here I opened wide the
        door;
                                        Darkness there and nothing more.

25   Deep into that darkness peering, long I stood there wondering,
        fearing,
Doubting, dreaming dreams no mortals ever dared to dream
        before;
But the silence was unbroken, and the stillness gave no token,
And the only word there spoken was the whispered word,
        "Lenore!"
This I whispered, and an echo murmured back the word,
        "Lenore!"
30   Merely this and nothing more.

Back into the chamber turning, all my soul within me burning,
Soon again I heard a tapping something louder than before.
"Surely," said I, "surely that is something at my window
        lattice;
Let me see, then, what thereat is, and this mystery explore;
35   Let my heart be still a moment, and this mystery explore;
                                        'T is the wind and nothing more."

Open here I flung the shutter, when, with many a flirt and
        flutter,
In there stepped a stately Raven of the saintly days of yore.
Not the least obeisance made he; not a minute stopped or
        stayed he,
40   But, with mien of lord or lady, perched above my chamber
        door,
Perched upon a bust of Pallas just above my chamber door,
                                        Perched, and sat, and nothing more.

Then this ebony bird beguiling my sad fancy into smiling,
By the grave and stern decorum of the countenance it wore,
45   "Though thy crest be shorn and shaven, thou," I said, "art
     sure no craven,
Ghastly grim and ancient Raven wandering from the Nightly
     shore;
Tell me what thy lordly name is on the Night's Plutonian
     shore!"
                 Quoth the Raven, "Nevermore."

Much I marvelled this ungainly fowl to hear discourse so
     plainly,
50   Though its answer little meaning, little relevancy bore;
For we cannot help agreeing that no living human being
Ever yet was blessed with seeing bird above his chamber
     door—
Bird or beast upon the sculptured bust above his chamber
     door,
              With such name as "Nevermore."

55   But the Raven, sitting lonely on that placid bust, spoke only
That one word, as if his soul in that one word he did outpour.
Nothing further then he uttered; not a feather then he
     fluttered;
Till I scarcely more than muttered: "Other friends have flown
     before;
On the morrow *he* will leave me as my hopes have flown
     before."
60   Then the bird said, "Nevermore."

Startled at the stillness broken by reply so aptly spoken,
"Doubtless," said I, "what it utters is its only stock and store,
Caught from some unhappy master whom unmerciful disaster
Followed fast and followed faster till his songs one burden
     bore,
65   Till the dirges of his hope that melancholy burden bore
            Of 'Never—nevermore.' "

But the Raven still beguiling all my sad soul into smiling,
Straight I wheeled a cushioned seat in front of bird and bust
     and door;

Then, upon the velvet sinking, I betook myself to linking
70 Fancy unto fancy, thinking what this ominous bird of yore,
What this grim, ungainly, ghastly, gaunt, and ominous bird of
    yore
                    Meant in croaking "Nevermore."

This I sat engaged in guessing, but no syllable expressing
To the fowl whose fiery eyes now burned into my bosom's
    core;
75 This and more I sat divining, with my head at ease reclining
On the cushion's velvet lining that the lamp-light gloated o'er,
But whose velvet violet lining with the lamp-light gloating o'er
                    She shall press, ah, nevermore!

Then, methought, the air grew denser, perfumed from an
    unseen censer
80 Swung by seraphim whose foot-falls tinkled on the tufted
    floor.
"Wretch," I cried, "thy God hath lent thee—by these angels he
    hath sent thee
Respite, respite and nepenthe from thy memories of Lenore!
Quaff, oh quaff this kind nepenthe and forget this lost
    Lenore!"
                    Quoth the Raven, "Nevermore."

85 "Prophet!" said I, "thing of evil! prophet still, if bird or devil!
Whether Tempter sent or whether tempest tossed thee here
    ashore,
Desolate, yet all undaunted, on this desert land enchanted,
On this home by Horror haunted, tell me truly, I implore,
Is there, is there balm in Gilead?³⁹ tell me, tell me, I implore!"
90   Quoth the Raven, "Nevermore."

"Prophet!" said I, "thing of evil! prophet still, if bird or devil!
By that heaven that bends above us, by that God we both
    adore,
Tell this soul with sorrow laden if, within the distant Aidenn,⁴⁰
It shall clasp a sainted maiden whom the angels name Lenore,
95 Clasp a rare and radiant maiden whom the angels name
    Lenore."
                    Quoth the Raven, "Nevermore."

"Be that word our sign of parting, bird or fiend!" I shrieked,
    upstarting;
"Get thee back into the tempest and the night's Plutonian
    shore!
Leave no black plume as a token of that lie thy soul hath
    spoken!
100 Leave my loneliness unbroken! quit the bust above my door!
Take thy beak from out my heart, and take thy form from off
    my door!"
                      Quoth the Raven, "Nevermore."

And the Raven, never flitting, still is sitting, still is sitting
On the pallid bust of Pallas just above my chamber door;
105 And his eyes have all the seeming of a demon's that is
    dreaming,
And the lamp-light o'er him streaming throws his shadow on
    the floor;
And my soul from out that shadow that lies floating on the
    floor
                    Shall be lifted—nevermore!
                        1845

A VALENTINE

For her this rhyme is penned, whose luminous eyes,
    Brightly expressive as the twins of Leda,[41]
Shall find her own sweet name, that, nestling lies
    Upon the page, enwrapped from every reader.
5 Search narrowly the lines!—they hold a treasure
    Divine, a talisman, an amulet
That must be worn at heart. Search well the measure,
    The words, the syllables! Do not forget
The trivialest point, or you may lose your labor!
10   And yet there is in this no Gordian knot
Which one might not undo without a sabre,
    If one could merely comprehend the plot.
Enwritten upon the leaf where now are peering
    Eyes' scintillating soul, there lie *perdus*[42]
15 Three eloquent words oft uttered in the hearing

Of poets, by poets, as the name is a poet's too.
  Its letters, although naturally lying
    Like the knight Pinto—Mendez Ferdinando—[43]
  Still form a synonym for Truth. Cease trying!
20   You will not read the riddle, though you do the best you
        can do.

[To translate the address, read the first letter of the first line in connection with the second letter of the second line, the third letter of the third line, the fourth of the fourth, and so on to the end. The name will thus appear.]

1846

ULALUME

The skies they were ashen and sober,
    The leaves they were crispèd and sere,
    The leaves they were withering and sere;
  It was night in the lonesome October
5   Of my most immemorial year;
  It was hard by the dim lake of Auber,
    In the misty mid region of Weir,
  It was down by the dank tarn of Auber,
    In the ghoul-haunted woodland of Weir.

10 Here once, through an alley Titanic,
      Of cypress, I roamed with my Soul,
      Of cypress, with Psyche, my Soul.
    These were days when my heart was volcanic
      As the scoriac[44] rivers that roll,
15   As the lavas that restlessly roll
    Their sulphurous currents down Yaanek
      In the ultimate climes of the pole,
    That groan as they roll down Mount Yaanek
      In the realms of the boreal pole.

20 Our talk had been serious and sober,
      But our thoughts they were palsied and sere,
      Our memories were treacherous and sere,

For we knew not the month was October,
  And we marked not the night of the year
25   (Ah, night of all nights in the year!);
We noted not the dim lake of Auber
  (Though once we had journeyed down here),
Remembered not the dank tarn of Auber,
  Nor the ghoul-haunted woodland of Weir.

30 And now, as the night was senescent
    And star-dials pointed to morn,
    As the star-dials hinted of morn,
  At the end of our path a liquescent
    And nebulous lustre was born,
35 Out of which a miraculous crescent
    Arose with a duplicate horn,
  Astarte's bediamonded crescent
    Distinct with its duplicate horn.
  And I said: "She is warmer than Dian;
40   She rolls through an ether of sighs,
    She revels in a region of sighs:

  She has seen that the tears are not dry on
    These cheeks, where the worm never dies,
  And has come past the stars of the Lion[45]
45   To point us the path to the skies,
    To the Lethean peace of the skies;
  Come up, in despite of the Lion,
    To shine on us with her bright eyes,
  Come up through the lair of the Lion,
50   With love in her luminous eyes."

  But Psyche, uplifting her finger,
    Said: "Sadly this star I mistrust,
    Her pallor I strangely mistrust;
  Oh, hasten! oh, let us not linger!
55   Oh, fly! let us fly! for we must."
  In terror she spoke, letting sink her
    Wings until they trailed in the dust;
  In agony sobbed, letting sink her
    Plumes till they trailed in the dust,
60   Till they sorrowfully trailed in the dust.

I replied: "This is nothing but dreaming:
    Let us on by this tremulous light!
    Let us bathe in this crystalline light!
Its sibyllic splendor is beaming
65   With hope and in beauty to-night!
    See, it flickers up the sky through the night!
Ah, we safely may trust to its gleaming,
    And be sure it will lead us aright;
We safely may trust to a gleaming
70   That cannot but guide us aright,
    Since it flickers up to heaven through the night."

Thus I pacified Psyche and kissed her,
    And tempted her out of her gloom,
    And conquered her scruples and gloom;
75 And we passed to the end of the vista,
    But were stopped by the door of a tomb,
    By the door of a legended tomb;
And I said: "What is written, sweet sister,
    On the door of this legended tomb?"
80   She replied: "Ulalume! Ulalume!
    'T is the vault of thy lost Ulalume!"

Then my heart it grew ashen and sober
    As the leaves that were crispèd and sere,
    As the leaves that were withering and sere,
85 And I cried: "It was surely October
    On this very night of last year
    That I journeyed, I journeyed down here,
    That I brought a dread burden down here,
    On this night of all nights in the year,
90   Ah, what demon has tempted me here?
Well I know, now, this dim lake of Auber,
    This misty mid region of Weir,
Well I know, now, this dank tarn of Auber,
    This ghoul-haunted woodland of Weir."

1847

ANNABEL LEE

It was many and many a year ago,
   In a kingdom by the sea,
That a maiden there lived whom you may know
   By the name of Annabel Lee;
5   And this maiden she lived with no other thought
   Than to love and be loved by me.

I was a child and she was a child,
   In this kingdom by the sea:
But we loved with a love that was more than love—
10   I and my Annabel Lee;
With a love that the winged seraphs of heaven
   Coveted her and me.

And this was the reason that, long ago,
   In this kingdom by the sea,
15   A wind blew out of a cloud, chilling
   My beautiful Annabel Lee;
So that her high-born kinsmen came
   And bore her away from me,
To shut her up in a sepulchre
20   In this kingdom by the sea.

The angels, not half so happy in heaven,
   Went envying her and me;
Yes, that was the reason (as all men know,
   In this kingdom by the sea)
25   That the wind came out of the cloud by night,
   Chilling and killing my Annabel Lee.

But our love it was stronger by far than the love
   Of those who were older than we,
   Of many far wiser than we;
30   And neither the angels in heaven above
   Nor the demons down under the sea
Can ever dissever my soul from the soul
   Of the beautiful Annabel Lee;

For the moon never beams without bringing me dreams
35   Of the beautiful Annabel Lee;
And the stars never rise but I feel the bright eyes
       Of the beautiful Annabel Lee;
And so, all the night-tide, I lie down by the side
Of my darling, my darling, my life and my bride,
40   In the sepulchre there by the sea,
       In her tomb by the sounding sea.

                                        1849

ELDORADO

       Gaily bedight,
       A gallant knight,
In sunshine and in shadow,
       Had journeyed long,
5   Singing a song,
In search of Eldorado.

       But he grew old,
       This knight so bold,
And o'er his heart a shadow
10   Fell as he found
       No spot of ground
That looked like Eldorado.

       And, as his strength
       Failed him at length,
15 He met a pilgrim shadow;
       "Shadow," said he,
       "Where can it be,
This land of Eldorado?"

       "Over the mountains
20   Of the moon,
Down the valley of the shadow,
       Ride, boldly ride,"
       The shade replied,—
"If you seek for Eldorado!"

                                        1849

OLIVER WENDELL HOLMES

(1809–1894)

In his own lifetime and, albeit decreasingly, until the early decades of this century, Holmes enjoyed a place in the nation's literary affections that is now almost impossible to revisit. Descended from pedigreed clerical and mercantile families, Harvard educated, intellectually liberal, morally conservative, socially decorous, resolutely provincial, and altogether self-satisfied, he was the very type of the Boston Brahmin, a caste he himself identified and named. He was born in Cambridge, Massachusetts, to Abiel Holmes, pastor of Boston's First Church and pioneer historian of the United States, and his second wife, Sarah (Wendell) Holmes, daughter of a prominent Boston merchant. Following school at Phillips Academy, Andover, and graduation from Harvard in 1829, Holmes studied law for one year, then switched to medicine, his life-long profession. In 1831, the *Boston Daily Advertiser* published his poem "Old Ironsides," which received widespread attention and led to the preservation of the U.S. man-of-war *Constitution*, slated for destruction. In the next two years, the *New England Magazine* published two pieces called "The Autocrat of the Breakfast Table," essays sprinkled with verse that would make him famous when they were resumed, decades later. The intervening years he devoted primarily to medicine, beginning with two years of study in Paris, followed by two in private practice in Boston, and two more on the medical faculty of Dartmouth College. That appointment ended with his marriage, in 1840, to Amelia Lee Jackson, the daughter of a state supreme court justice (alongside the future father-in-law of Herman Melville), and, in time, the mother of Oliver Wendell Holmes, Jr., future justice of the U.S. Supreme Court. That same year, Holmes returned to Harvard, first as a lecturer in anatomy and then, thanks to his pioneering research in puerperal fever, as Parkman Professor, a chair he would hold until his death.

By 1857, over twenty years had passed since the publication of his first book of poems. In that year, solicitations from his friend James Russell Lowell, founding editor of the *Atlantic Monthly*, led to the resumption of "The Autocrat of the Breakfast Table." The collection of these essays in 1858 initiated a series of volumes that would continue for over thirty years: *The Professor at the Breakfast Table* (1860), *The*

Poet at the Breakfast Table (1872), and *Over the Teacups* (1891). During these years, Holmes also published three novels: *Elsie Venner* (1861), *The Guardian Angel* (1867), and *A Moral Antipathy* (1885), as well as volumes of essays and travel writing and a biography of Emerson. Four more collections of poems, in 1862, 1875, 1880, and 1887, reflect his emergence as a man of letters and his recognition as the poet laureate of public occasions, social, civic, and academic. All together, these writings made him so well known throughout the English-speaking world that, during his only visit to Europe since he had studied there, a half century earlier, both Oxford and Cambridge granted him honorary degrees. A complete edition of his poems appeared in 1895, the year following his death.

OLD IRONSIDES

Ay, tear her tattered ensign down!
    Long has it waved on high,
And many an eye has danced to see
    That banner in the sky;
5   Beneath it rung the battle shout,
    And burst the cannon's roar;—
The meteor of the ocean air
    Shall sweep the clouds no more.

Her deck, once red with heroes' blood,
10   Where knelt the vanquished foe,
When winds were hurrying o'er the flood,
    And waves were white below,
No more shall feel the victor's tread,
    Or know the conquered knee;—
15 The harpies of the shore shall pluck
    The eagle of the sea!

Oh, better that her shattered hulk
    Should sink beneath the wave;
Her thunders shook the mighty deep,
20   And there should be her grave;

Nail to the mast her holy flag,
    Set every threadbare sail,
And give her to the god of storms,
    The lightning and the gale!

                                    1830

OUR LIMITATIONS

    We trust and fear, we question and believe,
From life's dark threads a trembling faith to weave,
Frail as the web that misty night has spun,
Whose dew-gemmed awnings glitter in the sun.
5   While the calm centuries spell their lessons out,
Each truth we conquer spreads the realm of doubt;
When Sinai's summit was Jehovah's throne,
The chosen Prophet knew his voice alone;
When Pilate's hall that awful question heard,
10 The Heavenly Captive answered not a word.

    Eternal Truth! beyond our hopes and fears
Sweep the vast orbits of thy myriad spheres!
From age to age, while History carves sublime
On her waste rock the flaming curves of time,
15 How the wild swayings of our planet show
That worlds unseen surround the world we know.

                                    1850

LATTER-DAY WARNINGS

I should have felt more nervous about the late comet, if I had
thought the world was ripe. But it is very green yet, if I am not
mistaken; and besides, there is a great deal of coal to use up,
which I cannot bring myself to think was made for nothing. If
certain things, which seem to me essential to a millennium, had
come to pass, I should have been frightened; but they have n't.

When legislators keep the law,
    When banks dispense with bolts and locks,
When berries—whortle, rasp, and straw—
    Grow bigger *downwards* through the box,—

5   When he that selleth house or land
    Shows leak in roof or flaw in right,—
When haberdashers choose the stand
    Whose window hath the broadest light,—

When preachers tell us all they think,
10   And party leaders all they mean,—
When what we pay for, that we drink,
    From real grape and coffee-bean,—

When lawyers take what they would give,
    And doctors give what they would take,—
15   When city fathers eat to live,
    Save when they fast for conscience' sake,—

When one that hath a horse on sale
    Shall bring his merit to the proof,
Without a lie for every nail
20   That holds the iron on the hoof,—

When in the usual place for rips
    Our gloves are stitched with special care,
And guarded well the whalebone tips
    Where first umbrellas need repair,—

25   When Cuba's weeds have quite forgot
    The power of suction to resist,
And claret-bottles harbor not
    Such dimples as would hold your fist,—

When publishers no longer steal,
30   And pay for what they stole before,—
When the first locomotive's wheel
    Rolls through the Hoosac Tunnel's[46] bore;—

Till then let Cumming blaze away,
    And Miller's[47] saints blow up the globe;
35 But when you see that blessed day,
    Then order your ascension robe!

                   1857

THE CHAMBERED NAUTILUS

This is the ship of pearl, which, poets feign,
    Sails the unshadowed main,—
    The venturous bark that flings
On the sweet summer wind its purpled wings
5 In gulfs enchanted, where the Siren sings,
    And coral reefs lie bare,
Where the cold sea-maids rise to sun their streaming hair.

Its webs of living gauze no more unfurl;
    Wrecked is the ship of pearl!
10   And every chambered cell,
Where its dim dreaming life was wont to dwell,
As the frail tenant shaped his growing shell,
    Before thee lies revealed,—
Its irised ceiling rent, its sunless crypt unsealed!

15 Year after year beheld the silent toil
    That spread his lustrous coil;
    Still, as the spiral grew,
He left the past year's dwelling for the new,
Stole with soft step its shining archway through,
20   Built up its idle door,
Stretched in his last-found home, and knew the old no more.

Thanks for the heavenly message brought by thee,
    Child of the wandering sea,
    Cast from her lap, forlorn!
25 From thy dead lips a clearer note is born
Than ever Triton blew from wreathèd horn!
    While on mine ear it rings,
Through the deep caves of thought I hear a voice that sings:—

Build thee more stately mansions, O my soul,
30   As the swift seasons roll!
        Leave thy low-vaulted past!
Let each new temple, nobler than the last,
Shut thee from heaven with a dome more vast,
        Till thou at length art free,
35   Leaving thine outgrown shell by life's unresting sea!

                                                          1858

IRIS, HER BOOK

I pray thee by the soul of her that bore thee,
By thine own sister's spirit I implore thee,
Deal gently with the leaves that lie before thee!

For Iris had no mother to infold her,
5   Nor ever leaned upon a sister's shoulder,
Telling the twilight thoughts that Nature told her.

She had not learned the mystery of awaking
Those chorded keys that soothe a sorrow's aching,
Giving the dumb heart voice, that else were breaking.

10   Yet lived, wrought, suffered. Lo, the pictured token!
Why should her fleeting day-dreams fade unspoken,
Like daffodils that die with sheaths unbroken?

She knew not love, yet lived in maiden fancies,—
Walked simply clad, a queen of high romances,
15   And talked strange tongues with angels in her trances.

Twin-souled she seemed, a twofold nature wearing:
Sometimes a flashing falcon in her daring,
Then a poor mateless dove that droops despairing.

Questioning all things: Why her Lord had sent her?
20   What were these torturing gifts, and wherefore lent her?
Scornful as spirit fallen, its own tormentor.

And then all tears and anguish: Queen of Heaven,
Sweet Saints, and Thou by mortal sorrows riven,
Save me! Oh, save me! Shall I die forgiven?

25   And then— Ah, God! But nay, it little matters:
Look at the wasted seeds that autumn scatters,
The myriad germs that Nature shapes and shatters!

If she had— Well! She longed, and knew not wherefore.
Had the world nothing she might live to care for?
30   No second self to say her evening prayer for?

She knew the marble shapes that set men dreaming,
Yet with her shoulders bare and tresses streaming
Showed not unlovely to her simple seeming.

Vain? Let it be so! Nature was her teacher.
35   What if a lonely and unsistered creature
Loved her own harmless gift of pleasing feature,

Saying, unsaddened,—This shall soon be faded,
And double-hued the shining tresses braided,
And all the sunlight of the morning shaded?

40   This her poor book is full of saddest follies,
Of tearful smiles and laughing melancholies,
With summer roses twined and wintry hollies.

In the strange crossing of uncertain chances,
Somewhere, beneath some maiden's tear-dimmed glances
45   May fall her little book of dreams and fancies.

Sweet sister! Iris, who shall never name thee,
Trembling for fear her open heart may shame thee,
Speaks from this vision-haunted page to claim thee.

Spare her, I pray thee! If the maid is sleeping,
50   Peace with her! she has had her hour of weeping.
No more! She leaves her memory in thy keeping.

1859

PROLOGUE

The piping of our slender, peaceful reeds
Whispers uncared for while the trumpets bray;
Song is thin air; our hearts' exulting play
Beats time but to the tread of marching deeds,
5   Following the mighty van that Freedom leads,
Her glorious standard flaming to the day!
The crimsoned pavement where a hero bleeds
Breathes nobler lessons than the poet's lay.
Strong arms, broad breasts, brave hearts, are better worth
10   Than strains that sing the ravished echoes dumb.
Hark! 't is the loud reverberating drum
Rolls o'er the prairied West, the rock-bound North:
The myriad-handed Future stretches forth
Its shadowy palms. Behold, we come,—we come!

15   Turn o'er these idle leaves. Such toys as these
Were not unsought for, as, in languid dreams,
We lay beside our lotus-feeding streams,
And nursed our fancies in forgetful ease.
It matters little if they pall or please,
20   Dropping untimely, while the sudden gleams
Glare from the mustering clouds whose blackness seems
Too swollen to hold its lightning from the trees.
Yet, in some lull of passion, when at last
These calm revolving moons that come and go—
25   Turning our months to years, they creep so slow—
Have brought us rest, the not unwelcome past
May flutter to thee through these leaflets, cast
On the wild winds that all around us blow.

                                                 1861

TARTARUS

While in my simple gospel creed
That "God is Love" so plain I read,
Shall dreams of heathen birth affright
My pathway through the coming night?

5   Ah, Lord of life, though spectres pale
Fill with their threats the shadowy vale,
With Thee my faltering steps to aid,
How can I dare to be afraid?

Shall mouldering page or fading scroll
10   Outface the charter of the soul?
Shall priesthood's palsied arm protect
The wrong our human hearts reject,
And smite the lips whose shuddering cry
Proclaims a cruel creed a lie?
15   The wizard's rope we disallow
Was justice once,—is murder now!

Is there a world of blank despair,
And dwells the Omnipresent there?
Does He behold with smile serene
20   The shows of that unending scene,
Where sleepless, hopeless anguish lies,
And, ever dying, never dies?
Say, does He hear the sufferer's groan,
And is that child of wrath his own?

25   O mortal, wavering in thy trust,
Lift thy pale forehead from the dust!
The mists that cloud thy darkened eyes
Fade ere they reach the o'erarching skies!
When the blind heralds of despair
30   Would bid thee doubt a Father's care,
Look up from earth, and read above
On heaven's blue tablet, GOD IS LOVE!

                      1890

JONES VERY

(1813–1880)

Very's poetic life was brief but intense; the poems for which he is remembered were all written over a period of eighteen months, in his mid-twenties. Born in Salem, Massachusetts, to a sea captain and his first cousin, Very entered Harvard in 1833. There, he wrote verses of an ordinary sort for college publications, for local newspapers, and for one national magazine. Sometime prior to graduating with unprecedented honors in 1837, he underwent a profound religious upheaval and began a spiritual regimen aimed at supplanting his own will with that of God. Upon graduation he was appointed a tutor in Greek at the College and developed a loyal following among his students, including Frederick Goddard Tuckerman. In his second year as a tutor, he came to the notice of Emerson, who, greatly impressed by the young man's intelligence, learning, and gravity, introduced him to the Transcendental Club. At the beginning of his third year, Very's religious life reached a crisis, leading to erratic behavior that got him fired from Harvard and then institutionalized for one month in a local asylum. Shortly after his release, he published the first of his ecstatic poems, "The New Birth," in the *Salem Observer*; and in the next year and a half he wrote some three hundred sonnets, about a third of all the poems he would produce in the course of fifty years. These sonnets he attributed to the Holy Ghost, speaking directly to and through him. During these months, Very behaved in ways that some Transcendentalists found exemplary, others considered mad and embarrassing to the movement, and everyone else thought no more than might be expected. In 1839, Emerson helped Very publish a collection entitled *Essays and Poems*, including his writings on Shakespeare but omitting those sonnets whose speaker is the divinity in *propria persona*. Eventually, Very's enthusiasm waned, and from 1840 on he lived in semiretirement in Salem, earning his living as an unordained Unitarian preacher throughout New England, meeting occasionally with his former associates in Concord and Boston, and once again writing poetry of no particular distinction.

During his lifetime, Very's poems appeared in various periodicals, newspapers, anthologies, and hymnbooks, in addition to the Emerson collection of 1839. In the decade following his death, there appeared two further collections, both drawn from Emerson's. Then, except for occasional appearances in anthologies, Very pretty much disappeared for fifty years, to be revived in the 1940s and treated thereafter to growing critical and scholarly attention.

THE NEW BIRTH

'Tis a new life—thoughts move not as they did
With slow uncertain steps across my mind,
In thronging haste fast pressing on they bid
The portals open to the viewless wind;
5   That comes not, save when in the dust is laid
The crown of pride that gilds each mortal brow,
And from before man's vision melting fade
The heavens and earth—Their walls are falling now—
Fast crowding on each thought claims utterance strong,
10 Storm-lifted waves swift rushing to the shore
On from the sea they send their shouts along,
Back through the cave-worn rocks their thunders roar,
And I a child of God by Christ made free
Start from death's slumbers to eternity.

                                        1838

THE SON

Father! I wait thy word—the sun doth stand,
Beneath the mingling line of night and day,
A listening servant waiting thy command
To roll rejoycing on its silent way;
5   The tongue of time abides the appointed hour,
Till on our ear its solemn warnings fall;
The heavy cloud withholds the pelting shower,
Then every drop speeds onward at thy call;
The bird reposes on the yielding bough
10 With breast unswollen by the tide of song;

So does my spirit wait thy presence now
To pour thy praise in quickening life along
Chiding with voice divine man's lengthened sleep,
While round the Unuttered Word and Love their vigils keep.

1838

THE WORD

The Word! it cannot fail; it ever speaks;
Unheard by all save by the sons of heaven,
It waits, while time counts on the appointed weeks,
The purpose to fulfill for which 'twas given;
5   Unchangeable its ever-fixed command;
When human feet would from its precepts stray
It points their pathway with its flaming hand,
And bids them keep the strait and narrow way;
And when by its unerring counsels led
10   The child would seek again his Father's face,
Upon its stores of heavenly manna fed
He gains at length through grief his resting place;
And hears its praise from angels' countless throng,
And joins forever in the new-raised song.

1838

THE SPIRIT

I would not breathe, when blows thy mighty wind
O'er desolate hill and winter-blasted plain,
But stand in waiting hope if I may find
Each flower recalled to newer life again;
5   That now unsightly hide themselves from Thee,
Amid the leaves or rustling grasses dry,
With ice-cased rock and snowy-mantled tree
Ashamed lest Thou their nakedness should spy;
But Thou shalt breathe and every rattling bough
10   Shall gather leaves; each rock with rivers flow;

And they that hide them from thy presence now
In new found robes along thy path shall glow,
And meadows at thy coming fall and rise,
Their green waves sprinkled with a thousand eyes.

                                                1838

THE SERPENT

They knew that they were naked, and ashamed
From Him who formed them stole themselves away,
And when He spoke they each the other blamed,
And death speaks living in each word they say;
5   The serpent grows, a liar born within,
Self-slaughter speaks in every uttered word,
And earth is filled with temples built in sin,
Where the foul tempter's praise is sung and heard;
But soon the truth shall gain the listening ear,
10   And from the lips in sacred utterance speak,
And weary souls of Christ's own word shall hear,
And in the living bread salvation seek,
And Satan's reign on earth forever cease,
And the new dawn begin of the eternal peace.

                                                1838

THE ROBE

Each naked branch, the yellow leaf or brown,
The rugged rock, and death-deformed plain
Lies white beneath the winter's feathery down,
Nor doth a spot unsightly now remain;
5   On sheltering roof, on man himself it falls;
But him no robe, not spotless snow makes clean;
For 'neath his corse-like spirit ever calls,
That on it too may fall the heavenly screen;
But all in vain, its guilt can never hide
10   From the quick spirit's heart-deep searching eye,

There barren plains, and caverns yawning wide
Must e'er lay naked to the passer by;
Nor can one thought deformed its presence shun,
But to the spirit's gaze stands bright as in the sun.

                                                    1839

THE WINTER RAIN

The rain comes down, it comes without our call;
Each pattering drop knows well its destined place,
And soon the fields whereon the blessings fall,
Shall change their frosty look for Spring's sweet face;
5   So fall the words thy Holy Spirit sends,
Upon the heart where Winter's robe is flung;
They shall go forth as certain of their ends,
As the wet drops from out thy vapors wrung;
Spring will not tarry, though more late its rose
10   Shall bud and bloom upon the sinful heart;
Yet when it buds, forever there it blows,
And hears no Winter bid its bloom depart;
It strengthens with his storms, and grows more bright,
When o'er the earth is cast his mantle white.

                                                    1839

THE CROSS

I must go on, till in my tearful line
Walks the full spirit's love as I on earth;
Till I can all Thou giv'st again resign,
And he be formed in me who gave me birth;
5   Wilt Thou within me bruise the serpent's heel,[48]
That I through Christ the victory may win;
Then shall the peace the blessed in him must feel,
Within my bosom here on earth begin;
Help me to grasp through him eternal life,
10   That must by conflict here by me be wrought;

With all his faith still aid me in the strife,
Till I through blood like him the prize have bought;
And I shall hang upon the accursed tree,
Pierced through with many spears that all may see.

                                                    1839

THE MOUNTAIN

Thou shalt the mountain move; be strong in me,
And I will pluck it from its rocky base,
And cast it headlong in the rolling sea,
And men shall seek but shall not find its place;
5   Be strong; thou shalt throw down the numerous host,
That rises now against thee o'er the earth;
Against thy Father's arm they shall not boast,
In sorrow shall grow dark their day of mirth;
Lift up the banner, bid the trumpets sound,
10   Gather ye nations on the opposing hill!
I will your wisest councils now confound,
And all your ranks with death and slaughter fill;
I come for judgment, and for victory now,
Bow down ye nations! at my footstool bow!

                                                    1839

THE PROMISE

I come the rushing wind that shook the place
Where those once sat who spake with tongues of fire[49]
O'er thee to shed the freely given grace
And bid them speak while I thy verse inspire
5   The world shall hear and know that thou art sent
To preach glad tidings to the needy poor
And witness that by me the power is lent
That wakes the dead, the halt and lame can cure
Thy words shall breathe refreshment to the mind
10   That long has borne the heavy yoke of pain

For thou art to the will of Him who lives resigned
And from thy sorrows reap the promised gain
And gather fruits with Him who with thee sows
Nor can men steal thy goods, for none thy treasure knows

                                                            1839

THE BIRDS OF PASSAGE

Whence comes those many-colored birds,
    That fill with songs each field and bower;
When Winter's blasts their force have spent,
    And spring to summer brings her dower.

5   I've watched them, but I know not whence
    With voices all-attuned they fly;
'Tis from some distant, unknown land,
    Some sunnier clime and fairer sky.

And these the notes they bring to tell,
10   Of that unseen and distant home;
To tempt us who are living here,
    With them when winter comes to roam.

Had I but wings I would not stay,
    When chilling cold I feel him near;
15 But with them journeying there I'd fly,
    That unknown land of which I hear.

                                                    1839

THE SILENT

There is a sighing in the wood,
A murmur in the beating wave,
The heart has never understood
To tell in words the thoughts they gave.

5   Yet oft it feels an answering tone,
     When wandering on the lonely shore;
     And could the lips its voice make known,
     'Twould sound as does the ocean's roar.

     And oft beneath the wind swept pine,
10   Some chord is struck the strain to swell;
     Nor sounds nor language can define,
     'Tis not for words or sounds to tell.

     'Tis all unheard; that Silent Voice,
     Whose goings forth, unknown to all,
15   Bids bending reed and bird rejoice,
     And fills with music nature's hall.

     And in the speechless human heart
     It speaks, where'er man's feet have trod;
     Beyond the lip's deceitful art,
20   To tell of Him, the Unseen God.

                              1839

THE INDIAN'S RETORT

     The white man's soul, it thirsts for gain,
         He makes himself the slave of gold!
     The Indian's free and boundless lands,
         Once all his own, are bought and sold.

5   An Indian to the forest went,
         To strip the birch for his canoe;
     His father's fathers' was that wood,
         Before the White his country knew.

     A weary journey he must take
10   Along a hot, and dusty road;
     And to his distant wigwam bring,
         Upon his back, the heavy load.

Long searched he for a fitting tree,
    Where once they easy were to find;
15 The white man's axe had laid them low,
    The white man's fire left few behind.

At length 'twas found; he stripped its bark,
    He raised his bundle from the ground;
A white man stood beside him there,
20   And on the Indian sternly frowned.

"Thou steal'st!" "Thou art a thief!" he cried;—
    The Indian threw his bundle down,
And proudly answered; as he turned
    To meet the white man's angry frown;

25 "God made the woods, and to his sons,
    The Indians, gave them long ago;
The Indian never was a thief,
    I speak the truth, as thou dost know."

"The White man came! he stole the woods,
30   The hills, the streams, the fields, the game;
The Indian never was a thief!
    The white man steals, his is the name!"

                                        1847

SLAVERY

Not by the railing tongues of angry men,
Who have not learned their passions to control;
Not by the scornful words of press and pen,
That now ill-omened fly from pole to pole;
5   Not by fierce party cries; nor e'en by blood,
Can this our Country's guilt be washed away;
In vain for this would flow the crimson flood,
In vain for this would man his brother slay.
Not by such means; but by the power of prayer;
10 Of faith in God, joined with a sense of sin;

These, these alone can save us from despair,
And o'er the mighty wrong a victory win;
These, these alone can make us free from all
That doth ourselves, our Country still inthral.

                                              1851

THE FIRST ATLANTIC TELEGRAPH

With outward signs, as well as inward life,
The world is hastening onward to its end!
With higher purposes our Age is rife,
Than those to which with grovelling minds we tend.
5   For lo! beneath the Atlantic's stormy breast
Is laid, from shore to shore, the Electric Wire;
And words, with speed of thought, from east to west
Dart to and fro on wings that never tire.
May never man, to higher objects blind,
10   Forget by whom this miracle was wrought;
But worship and adore the Eternal Mind,
Which gave at length to man the wondrous thought;
And on wise-hearted men bestowed the skill
His Providential Purpose to fulfill.

                                              1858

THE SLOWNESS OF BELIEF IN
A SPIRITUAL WORLD

The astronomer with patient, searching gaze
Doth with his tube the depths of space explore;
Shows Neptune's orb, or, 'neath the solar blaze,
Reveals a world by man unseen before.
5   Justly the world rewards his arduous toil,
And claims to share the glory of his fame;
Beyond the boundaries of his native soil
From land to land the breezes bear his name.
But he who doth a Spirit-world reveal,
10   Not far in space, but near to every soul;

Which naught but mists of sense and sin conceal,
(would from men's sight those mists at length might roll!)
He is with incredulity received,
Or with a slow, reluctant faith believed.

1860

FOREVERMORE

A sad refrain I heard, from poet sad,
Which on my soul with deadening weight did fall;
But quick another word, which made me glad,
Did from the heavens above me seem to call.
5 The first was Nevermore: which, like a knell,
Struck on my ear with dull, funereal sound;
The last was Evermore; which like a bell,
In waves of music filled the air around.
Forevermore with loved and lost to be,
10 No more to suffer change, nor grief, nor pain,
From partings sad to be forever free,—
Such was that sweet bell's music; its refrain
Blended with voices from the heavenly shore,
Each whispering to my heart Forevermore.

1871

HENRY DAVID THOREAU

(1817–1862)

Thoreau's first biographer, his friend William Ellery Channing, called him the Poet Naturalist by way of denoting his lifelong efforts to reconcile in written words the divided worlds of spirit and science in which he moved. Born in Concord, Massachusetts, where his father kept a store and manufactured pencils, Thoreau prepared for college at the local academy and entered Harvard in 1833. There, he came under the influence of Edward Tyrell Channing, who taught him English composition, and his classmate Jones Very, who introduced him to the seventeenth-century English poets. There, too, he began the journals that, maintained throughout his life, are the source of all of his published writings as well as the repository of virtually all of his surviving poetry.

After graduating well down in his class in 1837, Thoreau taught school in Concord until his refusal to cane his pupils forced him to resign. For a time, he helped his father make pencils, then opened a private school in Concord with his brother John. In 1839, the two brothers undertook the boating expedition recorded in Thoreau's first book, *A Week on the Concord and Merrimack Rivers* (1849), written during his stay at Walden Pond, six years later. In 1841, the school closed, owing to John's poor health, and Henry moved into Emerson's home as a sort of disciple cum handyman. During his two years there, Thoreau moved in the intellectual circle that centered on the Transcendental Club and its magazine *The Dial,* to which he contributed and which he helped edit. In the same period, John died, and Thoreau underwent a brief infatuation with Ellen Sewall, the recipient of the poem called "Sic Vita." The following year he lived on Staten Island as tutor to the children of Emerson's brother William, the longest time he would spend away from Concord. On his return, he prepared to take up residence at Walden, moving there on Independence Day, 1845. It was in this year that he spent a night in jail for refusing, in protest against slavery and the war with Mexico, to pay his poll tax, an experience that would lead, in 1849, to his most famous essay, "Civil Disobedience."

By 1847, he was back in his father's house, with the completed manuscript of *A Week* in hand, along with the journals that would become *Walden.* After another year at the Emersons', while they were abroad,

Thoreau returned home for the last time, to spend the rest of his life among his surviving brothers and sisters, none of whom ever married or moved away. In 1849, he published at his own expense one thousand copies of *A Week*, only two hundred of which had sold by the time the remainder came back in 1853. The ten years leading up to the Civil War, he divided between walking tours in Cape Cod, Canada, and Maine and increasing involvement in the anti-slavery movement. The former produced the journals that would appear in book form shortly after his death: *Excursions* (1863), *The Maine Woods* (1864), *Cape Cod* (1865), and *A Yankee in Canada* (1866). The latter included active protests against the Fugitive Slave Law and support for John Brown, in addition to speeches and essays that would come to adorn his posthumous reputation: "Life Without Principle," "Slavery in Massachusetts," and "A Plea for Captain John Brown."

The bulk of that reputation, however, would come to rest on *Walden*, which Thoreau distilled from the journals of 1845–47 and published, unsuccessfully, in 1853. In that volume, more than in any of his writings, he managed to reconcile his conflicting allegiances to radical individualism and social justice, to spirituality and naturalism, to sedentary domesticity and moral adventure. Only the second book he saw published, it was also the last. After a trip to Minnesota, undertaken to restore his rapidly declining health, he died of tuberculosis in 1862.

SIC VITA[50]

> I am a parcel of vain strivings tied
>   By a chance bond together,
>   Dangling this way and that, their links
>   Were made so loose and wide,
> 5   Methinks,
>   For milder weather.
>
> A bunch of violets without their roots,
>   And sorrel intermixed,
>   Encircled by a wisp of straw
> 10   Once coiled about their shoots,
>   The law
>   By which I'm fixed.

A nosegay which Time clutched from out
　　Those fair Elysian fields,
15　　　With weeds and broken stems, in haste,
　　　Doth make the rabble rout
　　　　That waste
　　　The day he yields.

And here I bloom for a short hour unseen,
20　　　Drinking my juices up,
　　With no root in the land
　　　To keep my branches green,
　　　　But stand
　　　In a bare cup.

25　Some tender buds were left upon my stem
　　　In mimicry of life,
　　But ah! the children will not know,
　　　Till time has withered them,
　　　　The woe
30　　　With which they're rife.

But now I see I was not plucked for naught,
　　　And after in life's vase
　　Of glass set while I might survive,
　　　But by a kind hand brought
35　　　　Alive
　　To a strange place.

That stock thus thinned will soon redeem its hours,
　　　And by another year,
　　Such as God knows, with freer air,
40　　　More fruits and fairer flowers
　　　　Will bear,
　　While I droop here.

1841

BROTHER WHERE DOST THOU DWELL

Brother where dost thou dwell?
   What sun shines for thee now?
Dost thou indeed farewell?
   As we wished here below.

5   What season didst thou find?
   'Twas winter here.
Are not the fates more kind
   Than they appear?

Is thy brow clear again
10   As in thy youthful years?
And was that ugly pain
   The summit of thy fears?

Yet thou wast cheery still,
   They could not quench thy fire,
15   Thou dids't abide their will,
   And then retire.

Where chiefly shall I look
   To feel thy presence near?
Along the neighboring brook
20   May I thy voice still hear?

Dost thou still haunt the brink
   Of yonder river's tide?
And may I ever think
   That thou art at my side?

25   What bird wilt thou employ
   To bring me word of thee?
For it would give them joy,
   'Twould give them liberty,
   To serve their former lord
30   With wing and minstrelsy.

A sadder strain has mixed with their song,
   They've slowlier built their nests,

Since thou art gone
    Their lively labor rests.

35 Where is the finch—the thrush,
        I used to hear?
    Ah! they could well abide
        The dying year.

    Now they no more return,
40   I hear them not;
    They have remained to mourn,
        Or else forgot.

                            (1843)

ON PONKAWTASSET,⁵¹ SINCE, WE TOOK OUR WAY

On Ponkawtasset, since, we took our way,
Down this still stream to far Billericay,⁵²
A poet wise has settled, whose fine ray
Doth often shine on Concord's twilight day.

5   Like those first stars, whose silver beams on high,
    Shining more brightly as the day goes by,
    Most travellers cannot at first descry,
    But eyes that wont to range the evening sky,

    And know celestial lights, do plainly see,
10 And gladly hail them, numbering two or three;
    For lore that's deep must deeply studied be,
    As from deep wells men read star-poetry.

    These stars are never paled, though out of sight,
    But like the sun they shine forever bright;
15 Ay, *they* are suns, though earth must in its flight
    Put out its eyes that it may see their light.

Who would neglect the least celestial sound,
Or faintest light that falls on earthly ground,
If he could know it one day would be found
20 That star in Cygnus whither we are bound,
And pale our sun with heavenly radiance round?

1849

LOW-ANCHORED CLOUD

Low-anchored cloud,
Newfoundland air,
Fountain-head and source of rivers,
Dew-cloth, dream drapery,
5 And napkin spread by fays;
Drifting meadow of the air,
Where bloom the daisied banks and violets,
And in whose fenny labyrinth
The bittern booms and heron wades;
10 Spirit of lakes and seas and rivers,
Bear only perfumes and the scent
Of healing herbs to just men's fields!

1849

WOOF OF THE SUN, ETHEREAL GAUZE

Woof of the sun, ethereal gauze,
Woven of Nature's richest stuffs,
Visible heat, air-water, and dry sea,
Last conquest of the eye;
5 Toil of the day displayed, sun-dust,
Aerial surf upon the shores of earth,
Ethereal estuary, frith of light,
Breakers of air, billows of heat,
Fine summer spray on inland seas;
10 Bird of the sun, transparent-winged
Owlet of noon, soft-pinioned,
From heath or stubble rising without song;
Establish thy serenity o'er the fields.

1849

MY LIFE HAS BEEN THE POEM
I WOULD HAVE WRIT

My life has been the poem I would have writ,
But I could not both live and utter it.

1849

INSPIRATION

Whate'er we leave to God, God does,
    And blesses us;
The work we choose should be our own,
    God lets alone.

5   If with light head erect I sing,
    Though all the muses lend their force,
From my poor love of anything,
    The verse is weak and shallow as its source.

But if with bended neck I grope,
10   Listening behind me for my wit,
With faith superior to hope,
    More anxious to keep back than forward it,

Making my soul accomplice there
    Unto the flame my heart hath lit,
15 Then will the verse forever wear,—
    Time cannot bend the line which God hath writ.

Always the general show of things
    Floats in review before my mind,
And such true love and reverence brings,
20   That sometimes I forget that I am blind.

But now there comes unsought, unseen,
    Some clear, divine electuary,
And I who had but sensual been,
    Grow sensible, and as God is, am wary.

25 I hearing get who had but ears,
    And sight, who had but eyes before,

I moments live who lived but years,
    And truth discern who knew but learning's lore.

I hear beyond the range of sound,
30   I see beyond the range of sight,
New earths and skies and seas around,
    And in my day the sun doth pale his light.

A clear and ancient harmony
    Pierces my soul through all its din,
35   As through its utmost melody,—
    Farther behind than they—farther within.

More swift its bolt than lightning is,
    Its voice than thunder is more loud,
It doth expand my privacies
40   To all, and leave me single in the crowd.

It speaks with such authority,
    With so serene and lofty tone,
That idle Time runs gadding by,
    And leaves me with Eternity alone.

45   Then chiefly is my natal hour,
    And only then my prime of life,
Of manhood's strength it is the flower,
    'Tis peace's end and war's beginning strife.

'T hath come in summer's broadest noon,
50   By a grey wall or some chance place,
Unseasoned time, insulted June,
    And vexed the day with its presuming face.

Such fragrance round my couch it makes,
    More rich than are Arabian drugs,
55   That my soul scents its life and wakes
    The body up beneath its perfumed rugs.

Such is the Muse—the heavenly maid,
    The star that guides our mortal course,

Which shows where life's true kernel's laid,
60 Its wheat's fine flower, and its undying force.

She with one breath attunes the spheres,
    And also my poor human heart,
With one impulse propels the years
    Around, and gives my throbbing pulse its start.

65 I will not doubt forever more,
    Nor falter from a steadfast faith,
For though the system be turned o'er,
    God takes not back the word which once he saith.

I will then trust the love untold
70 Which not my worth nor want has bought,
Which wooed me young and woos me old,
    And to this evening hath me brought.

My memory I'll educate
    To know the one historic truth,
75 Remembering to the latest date
    The only true and sole immortal youth.

Be but thy inspiration given,
    No matter through what danger sought,
I'll fathom hell or climb to heaven,
80 And yet esteem that cheap which love has bought.

———

Fame cannot tempt the bard
    Who's famous with his God,
Nor laurel him reward
    Who hath his Maker's nod.

1849

FOR THOUGH THE EAVES WERE RABBETED

For though the eaves were rabbeted,
 And the well sweeps were slanted,
Each house seemed not inhabited
 But haunted.

5 The pensive traveller held his way,
 Silent & melancholy,
For every man an ideot was,
 And every house a folly.

       (c. 1860)

PRAY TO WHAT EARTH DOES THIS
SWEET COLD BELONG

 Pray to what earth does this sweet cold belong,
Which asks no duties and no conscience?
The moon goes up by leaps her cheerful path
In some far summer stratum of the sky,
5 While stars with their cold shine bedot her way.
The fields gleam mildly back upon the sky,
And far and near upon the leafless shrubs
The snow dust still emits a silvery light.
Under the hedge, where drift banks are their screen,
10 The titmice now pursue their downy dreams,
As often in the sweltering summer nights
The bee doth drop asleep in the flower cup,
When evening overtakes him with his load.
By the brooksides, in the still genial night,
15 The more adventurous wanderer may hear
The crystals shoot and form, and winter slow
Increase his rule by gentlest summer means.

       (?)

A WINTER AND SPRING SCENE

The willows droop,
The alders stoop,
The pheasants group
   Beneath the snow;
5   The fishes glide
From side to side,
In the clear tide,
   The ice below.

The ferret weeps,
10   The marmot sleeps,
The owlet keeps
   In his snug nook.
The rabbit leaps,
The mouse out-creeps,
15   The flag out-peeps,
   Beside the brook.

The snow-dust falls,
The otter crawls,
The partridge calls
20   Far in the wood;
The traveller dreams,
The tree-ice gleams,
The blue jay screams
   In angry mood.

25   The apples thaw,
The ravens caw,
The squirrels gnaw
   The frozen fruit;
To their retreat
30   I track the feet
Of mice that eat
   The apple's root.

The axe resounds,
And bay of hounds,
35   And tinkling sounds

      Of wintry fame;
The hunter's horn
Awakes the dawn
On field forlorn,
40   And frights the game.

The tinkling air
Doth echo bear
To rabbit's lair,
      With dreadful din;
45 She scents the air,
And far doth fare,
Returning where
      She did begin.

The fox stands still
50 Upon the hill
Not fearing ill
      From trackless wind.
But to his foes
The still wind shows
55 In treacherous snows
      His tracks behind.

Now melts the snow
In the warm sun.
The meadows flow,
60 The streamlets run.
The spring is born,
The wild bees bum,
The insects hum,
And trees drop gum.
65 And winter's gone,
And summer's come.

The chic-a-dee
Lisps in the tree,
The winter bee
70   Not fearing frost;
The small nuthatch
The bark doth scratch

Some worm to catch
   At any cost.

75 The catkins green
Cast o'er the scene
A summer sheen,
A genial glow.

I melt, I flow,
80   And rippling run,
Like melting snow
   In this warm sun.

(?)

JAMES RUSSELL LOWELL

(1819–1891)

Although Lowell is remembered mainly for a handful of his poems, poetry actually ranked on his own professional agenda somewhere below essay writing, magazine editing, and college teaching. Like Longfellow and Holmes a descendant of the earliest New England settlers, Lowell was born in Cambridge, Massachusetts. After private schooling, he went on to Harvard, where he was elected class poet in 1838, and from there to the Law School, graduating in 1840. Rather than practice law, he began to write essays and poems for the periodicals in hopes of earning enough to marry Maria White, a poet and devoted abolitionist to whom he had become engaged. Four years of this work, including collections of his poems in 1841 and 1844, enabled him to marry and brought him the first in a long series of editorial positions that would constitute, in many respects, his most important contributions to the nation's letters. As a founding editor of *The Pioneer,* he published writings by Poe, Jones Very, and Whittier. As a corresponding editor for abolitionist newspapers in Philadelphia and New York, he vented the hatred of slavery that his wife had instilled in him.

Lowell's life in the next ten years stuns the imagination. Between 1847 and 1853, he lost three of his four infant children and then his wife. In 1848, he published his third collection of poems, the first volume of *The Biglow Papers*, and *The Vision of Sir Launfall*. The next year, he published a two-volume collection of poems. In 1855, he published *The Poems of Maria Lowell* and succeeded Longfellow as professor of modern languages and belles lettres at Harvard, a position he would retain, with only one interruption, to the end of his life. After a year in Europe preparing his classes and a first year of teaching at Harvard, he became the founding editor of the *Atlantic Monthly,* soliciting contributions successfully from Emerson, Whittier, Holmes, and Longfellow, but fruitlessly from Melville. In that same year, 1857, he married Frances Dunlap, who had cared for his surviving daughter during his stay in Europe.

With professorial duties at Harvard and editorial duties first at the *Atlantic* and then at the *North American Review,* Lowell's poetic output had declined sharply since the *Poems* of 1849. The later 1860s saw

something of a resurgence, in his ode commemorating Harvard students
who had served in the Civil War (1865), the second volume of *The
Biglow Papers* (collected in 1867), a volume entitled *Under the Willows*
(1869), and *The Cathedral* (1870), touching the widespread problem of
religious doubt. From then on, however, Lowell gave himself mainly to
critical prose, publishing only one volume of verse each decade. The
first of these appeared in 1877, the year he was appointed minister to
Spain; the second in 1888, three years following his subsequent appoint-
ment as ambassador to the Court of St. James; the last in 1895, four
years after his death in the Cambridge house where he was born.

A CONTRAST

Thy love thou sentest oft to me,
    And still as oft I thrust it back;
Thy messengers I could not see
    In those who everything did lack,
5   The poor, the outcast and the black.

Pride held his hand before mine eyes,
    The world with flattery stuffed mine ears;
I looked to see a monarch's guise,
    Nor dreamed thy love would knock for years,
10   Poor, naked, fettered, full of tears.

Yet, when I sent my love to thee,
    Thou with a smile didst take it in,
And entertain'dst it royally,
    Though grimed with earth, with hunger thin,
15   And leprous with the taint of sin.

Now every day thy love I meet,
    As o'er the earth it wanders wide,
With weary step and bleeding feet,
    Still knocking at the heart of pride
20   And offering grace, though still denied.

                                           1845

from A FABLE FOR CRITICS

"There comes Emerson first, whose rich words, every one,
Are like gold nails in temples to hang trophies on,
Whose prose is grand verse, while his verse, the Lord knows,
Is some of it pr— No, 't is not even prose;
5   I 'm speaking of metres; some poems have welled
From those rare depths of soul that have ne'er been excelled;
They 're not epics, but that does n't matter a pin,
In creating, the only hard thing 's to begin;
A grass-blade 's no easier to make than an oak;
10   If you 've once found the way, you 've achieved the grand
          stroke;
In the worst of his poems are mines of rich matter,
But thrown in a heap with a crash and a clatter;
Now it is not one thing nor another alone
Makes a poem, but rather the general tone,
15   The something pervading, uniting the whole,
The before unconceived, unconceivable soul,
So that just in removing this trifle or that, you
Take away, as it were, a chief limb of the statue;
Roots, wood, bark, and leaves singly perfect may be,
20   But, clapt hodge-podge together, they don't make a tree.

"But, to come back to Emerson (whom, by the way,
I believe we left waiting),—his is, we may say,
A Greek head on right Yankee shoulders, whose range
Has Olympus for one pole, for t' other the Exchange;
25   He seems, to my thinking (although I 'm afraid
The comparison must, long ere this, have been made),
A Plotinus-Montaigne, where the Egyptian's gold mist
And the Gascon's shrewd wit cheek-by-jowl coexist;
All admire, and yet scarcely six converts he 's got
30   To I don't (nor they either) exactly know what;
For though he builds glorious temples, 't is odd
He leaves never a doorway to get in a god.
'T is refreshing to old-fashioned people like me
To meet such a primitive Pagan as he,
35   In whose mind all creation is duly respected
As parts of himself—just a little projected;
And who 's willing to worship the stars and the sun,

A convert to—nothing but Emerson.
So perfect a balance there is in his head,
40   That he talks of things sometimes as if they were dead;
Life, nature, love, God, and affairs of that sort,
He looks at as merely ideas; in short,
As if they were fossils stuck round in a cabinet,
Of such vast extent that our earth 's a mere dab in it;
45   Composed just as he is inclined to conjecture her,
Namely, one part pure earth, ninety-nine parts pure lecturer;
You are filled with delight at his clear demonstration,
Each figure, word, gesture, just fits the occasion,
With the quiet precision of science he 'll sort 'em,
50   But you can't help suspecting the whole a *post mortem*.

                    .   .   .

     "He has imitators in scores, who omit
No part of the man but his wisdom and wit,—
Who go carefully o'er the sky-blue of his brain,
And when he has skimmed it once, skim it again;
55   If at all they resemble him, you may be sure it is
Because their shoals mirror his mists and obscurities,
As a mud-puddle seems deep as heaven for a minute,
While a cloud that floats o'er is reflected within it.

                    .   .   .

     "There is Bryant, as quiet, as cool, and as dignified,
60   As a smooth, silent iceberg, that never is ignified,
Save when by reflection 't is kindled o' nights
With a semblance of flame by the chill Northern Lights.
He may rank (Griswold[53] says so) first bard of your nation
(There 's no doubt that he stands in supreme iceolation),
65   Your topmost Parnassus he may set his heel on,
But no warm applauses come, peal following peal on,—
He 's too smooth and too polished to hang any zeal on:
Unqualified merits, I 'll grant, if you choose, he has 'em,
But he lacks the one merit of kindling enthusiasm;
70   If he stir you at all, it is just, on my soul,
Like being stirred up with the very North Pole.

     "He is very nice reading in summer, but *inter
Nos*, we don't want *extra* freezing in winter;

       Take him up in the depth of July, my advice is,
75   When you feel an Egyptian devotion to ices.
       But, deduct all you can, there 's enough that 's right good
          in him,
       He has a true soul for field, river, and wood in him;
       And his heart, in the midst of brick walls, or where'er it is,
       Glows, softens, and thrills with the tenderest charities—
80   To you mortals that delve in this trade-ridden planet?
       No, to old Berkshire's hills, with their limestone and granite.
       If you 're one who *in loco* (add *foco* here) *desipis*,[54]
       You will get of his outermost heart (as I guess) a piece;
       But you 'd get deeper down if you came as a precipice,
85   And would break the last seal of its inwardest fountain,
       If you only could palm yourself off for a mountain.

                         . . .

          "There is Whittier, whose swelling and vehement heart
       Strains the strait-breasted drab of the Quaker apart,
       And reveals the live Man, still supreme and erect,
90   Underneath the bemummying wrappers of sect;
       There was ne'er a man born who had more of the swing
       Of the true lyric bard and all that kind of thing;
       And his failures arise (though he seem not to know it)
       From the very same cause that has made him a poet,—
95   A fervor of mind which knows no separation
       'Twixt simple excitement and pure inspiration,
       As my Pythoness erst sometimes erred from not knowing
       If 't were I or mere wind through her tripod was blowing;[55]
       Let his mind once get head in its favorite direction
100   And the torrent of verse bursts the dams of reflection,
       While, borne with the rush of the metre along,
       The poet may chance to go right or go wrong,
       Content with the whirl and delirium of song;
       Then his grammar 's not always correct, nor his rhymes,
105   And he 's prone to repeat his own lyrics sometimes,
       Not his best, though, for those are struck off at white-heats
       When the heart in his breast like a trip-hammer beats,
       And can ne'er be repeated again any more
       Than they could have been carefully plotted before:
110   Like old what 's-his-name there at the battle of Hastings[56]
       (Who, however, gave more than mere rhythmical bastings),

Our Quaker leads off metaphorical fights
For reform and whatever they call human rights,
Both singing and striking in front of the war,
115 And hitting his foes with the mallet of Thor;
Anne haec, one exclaims, on beholding his knocks,
Vestis filii tui, O leather-clad Fox?[57]
Can that be thy son, in the battle's mid din,
Preaching brotherly love and then driving it in
120 To the brain of the tough old Goliath of sin,
With the smoothest of pebbles from Castaly's spring[58]
Impressed on his hard moral sense with a sling?

· · ·

"There comes Poe, with his raven, like Barnaby Rudge,
Three fifths of him genius and two fifths sheer fudge,
125 Who talks like a book of iambs and pentameters,
In a way to make people of common sense damn metres,
Who has written some things quite the best of their kind,
But the heart somehow seems all squeezed out by the mind,
Who— But hey-day! What 's this? Messieurs Mathews[59]
and Poe,
130 You must n't fling mud-balls at Longfellow so,
Does it make a man worse that his character's such
As to make his friends love him (as you think) too much?
Why, there is not a bard at this moment alive
More willing than he that his fellows should thrive;
135 While you are abusing him thus, even now
He would help either one of you out of a slough;
You may say that he 's smooth and all that till you 're hoarse,
But remember that elegance also is force;
After polishing granite as much as you will,
140 The heart keeps its tough old persistency still;
Deduct all you can, *that* still keeps you at bay;
Why, he 'll live till men weary of Collins and Gray.[60]
I 'm not over-fond of Greek metres in English,[61]
To me rhyme 's a gain, so it be not too jinglish,
145 And your modern hexameter verses are no more
Like Greek ones than sleek Mr. Pope is like Homer;[62]
As the roar of the sea to the coo of a pigeon is,
So, compared to your moderns, sounds old Melesigenes;[63]
I may be too partial, the reason, perhaps, o't is

150   That I 've heard the old blind man[64] recite his own rhapsodies,
      And my ear with that music impregnate may be,
      Like the poor exiled shell with the soul of the sea,
      Or as one can't bear Strauss[65] when his nature is cloven
      To its deeps within deeps by the stroke of Beethoven;
155   But, set that aside, and 't is truth that I speak,
      Had Theocritus written in English, not Greek,
      I believe that his exquisite sense would scarce change a line
      In that rare, tender, virgin-like pastoral Evangeline.
      That 's not ancient nor modern, its place is apart
160   Where time has no sway, in the realm of pure Art,
      'T is a shrine of retreat from Earth's hubbub and strife
      As quiet and chaste as the author's own life.

                    .   .   .

      "There 's Holmes, who is matchless among you for wit;
      A Leyden-jar always full-charged, from which flit
165   The electrical tingles of hit after hit;
      In long poems 't is painful sometimes, and invites
      A thought of the way the new Telegraph writes,
      Which pricks down its little sharp sentences spitefully
      As if you got more than you 'd title to rightfully,
170   And you find yourself hoping its wild father Lightning
      Would flame in for a second and give you a fright'ning.
      He has perfect sway of what I call a sham metre,
      But many admire it, the English pentameter,
      And Campbell,[66] I think, wrote most commonly worse,
175   With less nerve, swing, and fire in the same kind of verse,
      Nor e'er achieved aught in 't so worthy of praise
      As the tribute of Holmes to the grand *Marseillaise*.[67]
      You went crazy last year over Bulwer's New Timon;—[68]
      Why, if B., to the day of his dying, should rhyme on,
180   Heaping verses on verses and tomes upon tomes,
      He could ne'er reach the best point and vigor of Holmes.
      His are just the fine hands, too, to weave you a lyric
      Full of fancy, fun, feeling, or spiced with satiric
      In a measure so kindly, you doubt if the toes
185   That are trodden upon are your own or your foes'.

      "There is Lowell, who 's striving Parnassus to climb
      With a whole bale of *isms* tied together with rhyme,

He might get on alone, spite of brambles and boulders,
But he can't with that bundle he has on his shoulders,
190 The top of the hill he will ne'er come nigh reaching
Till he learns the distinction 'twixt singing and preaching;
His lyre has some chords that would ring pretty well,
But he 'd rather by half make a drum of the shell,
And rattle away till he 's old as Methusalem,[69]
195 At the head of a march to the last new Jerusalem.

·   ·   ·

"But what 's that? a mass-meeting? No, there come in lots
The American Bulwers, Disraelis, and Scotts,[70]
And in short the American everything elses,
200 Each charging the others with envies and jealousies;—
By the way, 't is a fact that displays what profusions
Of all kinds of greatness bless free institutions,
That while the Old World has produced barely eight
Of such poets as all men agree to call great,
205 And of other great characters hardly a score
(One might safely say less than that rather than more),
With you every year a whole crop is begotten,
They 're as much of a staple as corn is, or cotton;
Why, there 's scarcely a huddle of log-huts and shanties
210 That has not brought forth its own Miltons and Dantes;
I myself know ten Byrons, one Coleridge, three Shelleys,
Two Raphaels, six Titians (I think), one Apelles,[71]
Leonardos and Rubenses plenty as lichens,
One (but that one is plenty) American Dickens,
215 A whole flock of Lambs, any number of Tennysons,—
In short, if a man has the luck to have any sons,
He may feel pretty certain that one out of twain
Will be some very great person over again.

1848

from THE BIGLOW PAPERS:
THE PIOUS EDITOR'S CREED

I du believe in Freedom's cause,
    Ez fur away ez Payris is;
I love to see her stick her claws
    In them infarnal Phayrisees;
5   It 's wal enough agin a king
      To dror resolves an' triggers,—
But libbaty 's a kind o' thing
    Thet don't agree with niggers.

I du believe the people want
10   A tax on teas an' coffees,
Thet nothin' aint extravygunt,—
    Purvidin' I'm in office;
Fer I hev loved my country sence
    My eye-teeth filled their sockets,
15   An' Uncle Sam I reverence,
    Partic'larly his pockets.

I du believe in *any* plan
    O' levyin' the texes,
Ez long ez, like a lumberman,
20   I git jest wut I axes;
I go free-trade thru thick an' thin,
    Because it kind o' rouses
The folks to vote,—an' keeps us in
    Our quiet custom-houses.

25   I du believe it 's wise an' good
    To sen' out furrin missions,
Thet is, on sartin understood
    An' orthydox conditions;—
I mean nine thousan' dolls. per ann.,
30   Nine thousan' more fer outfit,
An' me to recommend a man
    The place 'ould jest about fit.

I du believe in special ways
    O' prayin' an' convartin';

35   The bread comes back in many days,
        An' buttered, tu, fer sartin;
    I mean in preyin' till one busts
        On wut the party chooses,
    An' in convartin' public trusts
40   To very privit uses.

    I du believe hard[72] coin the stuff
        Fer 'lectioneers to spout on;
    The people's ollers soft enough
        To make hard money out on;
45   Dear Uncle Sam pervides fer his,
        An' gives a good-sized junk to all,—
    I don't care *how* hard money is,
        Ez long ez mine 's paid punctooal.

    I du believe with all my soul
50   In the gret Press's freedom,
    To pint the people to the goal
        An' in the traces lead 'em;
    Palsied the arm thet forges yokes
        At my fat contracts squintin',
55   An' withered be the nose thet pokes
        Inter the gov'ment printin'!

    I du believe thet I should give
        Wut 's his'n unto Cæsar,[73]
    Fer it 's by him I move an' live,
60   Frum him my bread an' cheese air;
    I du believe thet all o' me
        Doth bear his superscription,—
    Will, conscience, honor, honesty,
        An' things o' thet description.

65   I du believe in prayer an' praise
        To him thet hez the grantin'
    O' jobs,—in every thin' thet pays,
        But most of all in CANTIN';
    This doth my cup with marcies fill,
70   This lays all thought o' sin to rest,—

    I *don't* believe in princerple,
      But oh, I *du* in interest.

    I du believe in bein' this
      Or thet, ez it may happen
75   One way or 't other hendiest is
      To ketch the people nappin';
    It aint by princerples nor men
      My preudunt course is steadied,—
    I scent wich pays the best, an' then
80   Go into it baldheaded.

    I du believe thet holdin' slaves
      Comes nat'ral to a Presidunt,[74]
    Let 'lone the rowdedow it saves
      To hev a wal-broke precedunt;
85   Fer any office, small or gret,
      I could n't ax with no face,
    'uthout I 'd ben, thru dry an' wet,
      Th' unrizzest kind o' doughface.[75]

    I du believe wutever trash
90   'll keep the people in blindness,—
    Thet we the Mexicuns can thrash
      Right inter brotherly kindness,
    Thet bombshells, grape, an' powder 'n' ball
      Air good-will's strongest magnets,
95   Thet peace, to make it stick at all,
      Must be druv in with bagnets.

    In short, I firmly du believe
      In Humbug generally,
    Fer it's a thing thet I perceive
100   To hev a solid vally;
    This heth my faithful shepherd ben,
      In pasturs sweet heth led me,
    An' this 'll keep the people green
      To feed ez they hev fed me.

               1848

THE DARKENED MIND[76]

The fire is burning clear and blithely,
Pleasantly whistles the winter wind;
We are about thee, thy friends and kindred,
On us all flickers the firelight kind;
5   There thou sittest in thy wonted corner
Lone and awful in thy darkened mind.

There thou sittest; now and then thou moanest;
Thou dost talk with what we cannot see,
Lookest at us with an eye so doubtful,
10 It doth put us very far from thee;
There thou sittest; we would fain be nigh thee,
But we know that it can never be.

We can touch thee, still we are no nearer;
Gather round thee, still thou art alone;
15 The wide chasm of reason is between us;
Thou confutest kindness with a moan;
We can speak to thee, and thou canst answer,
Like two prisoners through a wall of stone.

Hardest heart would call it very awful
20 When thou look'st at us and seest—oh, what?
If we move away, thou sittest gazing
With those vague eyes at the selfsame spot,
And thou mutterest, thy hands thou wringest,
Seeing something,—us thou seest not.

25 Strange it is that, in this open brightness,
Thou shouldst sit in such a narrow cell;
Strange it is that thou shouldst be so lonesome
Where those are who love thee all so well;
Not so much of thee is left among us
30 As the hum outliving the hushed bell.

1868

SONNET

On Being Asked for an Autograph
in Venice

Amid these fragments of heroic days
When thought met deed with mutual passion's leap,
There sits a Fame whose silent trump makes cheap
What short-lived rumor of ourselves we raise.
5   They had far other estimate of praise
Who stamped the signet of their souls so deep
In art and action, and whose memories keep
Their height like stars above our misty ways:
In this grave presence to record my name
10   Something within me hangs the head and shrinks.
Dull were the soul without some joy in fame;
Yet here to claim remembrance were, methinks,
Like him who, in the desert's awful frame,
Notches his cockney initials on the Sphinx.

                                        1875

THE BOSS[77]

Skilled to pull wires, he baffles Nature's hope,
Who sure intended him to stretch a rope.

                                        1886

IN A COPY OF OMAR KHAYYÁM

These pearls of thought in Persian gulfs were bred,
Each softly lucent as a rounded moon;
The diver Omar plucked them from their bed,
Fitzgerald strung them on an English thread.

5   Fit rosary for a queen, in shape and hue,
When Contemplation tells her pensive beads

Of mortal thoughts, forever old and new.
Fit for a queen? Why, surely then for you!

The moral? Where Doubt's eddies toss and twirl
10   Faith's slender shallop till her footing reel,
Plunge: if you find not peace beneath the whirl,
Groping, you may like Omar grasp a pearl.

                                                    1888

SCIENCE AND POETRY

He who first stretched his nerves of subtile wire
Over the land and through the sea-depths still,
Thought only of the flame-winged messenger
As a dull drudge that should encircle earth
5   With sordid messages of Trade, and tame
Blithe Ariel to a bagman. But the Muse
Not long will be defrauded. From her foe
Her misused wand she snatches; at a touch,
The Age of Wonder is renewed again,
10   And to our disenchanted day restores
The Shoes of Swiftness that give odds to Thought,
The Cloak that makes invisible;[78] and with these
I glide, an airy fire, from shore to shore,
Or from my Cambridge whisper to Cathay.

                                                    1888

WALT WHITMAN

(1819–1892)

The thirty-five years of Whitman's life leading up to the first edition of *Leaves of Grass* seem hardly to prepare for that momentous poetic event. Born on Long Island, he grew up in Brooklyn, where, after leaving public school at thirteen, he worked as a printer, as an itinerant schoolteacher, then as an editor and correspondent for various newspapers, churning out hack writing of every imaginable variety: reports, features, editorials, verse and pulp fiction, even a temperance novel. In 1848, he spent three months as an editor in New Orleans, where he is supposed to have undergone a transforming personal experience of some sort, returning in the guise of the rough and hearty "camerado" his later poems would celebrate. After seven more years in newspaper work and in business, he published privately the small first edition of *Leaves of Grass*, comprising a preface and twelve untitled poems. Over the next thirty-seven years, this work would grow and change continually with successive additions, deletions, revisions, and rearrangements of its contents. The second edition (1856) added twenty-one poems, as well as a letter of congratulation from Emerson and Whitman's acknowledgment. The third edition (1860), the first to be published commercially, added another 122 poems. The fourth (1867) included the separately published *Drum-Taps* (1865) and its *Sequel* (1866), poems arising from Whitman's voluntary service among the wounded in Washington military hospitals. The fifth edition (1871) annexed the separately printed "Passage to India" (1870). In 1873, having suffered a paralytic stroke, Whitman left Washington for Camden, New Jersey, where, except for brief trips to Colorado, Canada, and Boston, he would spend the rest of his days. More new poems expanded the sixth edition of *Leaves of Grass* (1876) to two volumes, with a new preface. The seventh (1881–82), adding twenty new poems to a completely reorganized table of contents, came out initially in Boston but was withdrawn under charges of indecency and reissued in Philadelphia. Following a second stroke, in 1888, Whitman published the eighth edition (1889), incorporating the poems and the preface from *November Boughs*, separately issued the year before. His final edition (1891–92), prepared on his deathbed, added still more poems, either new or previously published, and a new prose annex. In the last two decades of his life, Whitman also published several volumes of prose, including *Democratic Vistas* (1871), *Memoranda During the War* (1875), and *Specimen Days and Collect* (1882). The same years brought him increasing public attention, as a result of attacks upon his poetry, books written in his defense by American disciples, and the notice of such well-known writers in England as Dante Gabriel Rossetti and Algernon Charles Swinburne. Not until free verse became a common form of modern poetry, however, would his place in literary history be assured.

SONG OF MYSELF

1

I celebrate myself, and sing myself,
And what I assume you shall assume,
For every atom belonging to me as good belongs to you.

I loafe and invite my soul,
5   I lean and loafe at my ease observing a spear of summer grass.

My tongue, every atom of my blood, form'd from this soil,
    this air,
Born here of parents born here from parents the same, and
    their parents the same,
I, now thirty-seven years old in perfect health begin,
Hoping to cease not till death.

10   Creeds and schools in abeyance,
Retiring back a while sufficed at what they are, but never
    forgotten,
I harbor for good or bad, I permit to speak at every hazard,
Nature without check with original energy.

2

Houses and rooms are full of perfumes, the shelves are
    crowded with perfumes,
15   I breathe the fragrance myself and know it and like it,
The distillation would intoxicate me also, but I shall not let it.

The atmosphere is not a perfume, it has no taste of the
    distillation, it is odorless,
It is for my mouth forever, I am in love with it,
I will go to the bank by the wood and become undisguised
    and naked,
20   I am mad for it to be in contact with me.

The smoke of my own breath,
Echoes, ripples, buzz'd whispers, love-root, silk-thread, crotch
    and vine,
My respiration and inspiration, the beating of my heart, the
    passing of blood and air through my lungs,
The sniff of green leaves and dry leaves, and of the shore and
    dark-color'd sea-rocks, and of hay in the barn,
25   The sound of the belch'd words of my voice loos'd to the
    eddies of the wind,
A few light kisses, a few embraces, a reaching around of arms,
The play of shine and shade on the trees as the supple
    boughs wag,
The delight alone or in the rush of the streets, or along the
    fields and hill-sides,
The feeling of health, the full-noon trill, the song of me rising
    from bed and meeting the sun.

30   Have you reckon'd a thousand acres much? have you reckon'd
    the earth much?
Have you practis'd so long to learn to read?
Have you felt so proud to get at the meaning of poems?

Stop this day and night with me and you shall possess the
    origin of all poems,
You shall possess the good of the earth and sun, (there are
    millions of suns left,)
35   You shall no longer take things at second or third hand, nor
    look through the eyes of the dead, nor feed on the spectres
    in books,
You shall not look through my eyes either, nor take things
    from me,
You shall listen to all sides and filter them from your self.

3

I have heard what the talkers were talking, the talk of the
    beginning and the end,
But I do not talk of the beginning or the end.

40   There was never any more inception than there is now,
Nor any more youth or age than there is now,
And will never be any more perfection than there is now,
Nor any more heaven or hell than there is now.

Urge and urge and urge,
45   Always the procreant urge of the world.

Out of the dimness opposite equals advance, always substance
    and increase, always sex,
Always a knit of identity, always distinction, always a breed of
    life.

To elaborate is no avail, learn'd and unlearn'd feel that it is so.

Sure as the most certain sure, plumb in the uprights, well
    entretied,[79] braced in the beams,
50   Stout as a horse, affectionate, haughty, electrical,
I and this mystery here we stand.

Clear and sweet is my soul, and clear and sweet is all that is
    not my soul.

Lack one lacks both, and the unseen is proved by the seen,
Till that becomes unseen and receives proof in its turn.

55   Showing the best and dividing it from the worst age vexes age,
Knowing the perfect fitness and equanimity of things, while
    they discuss I am silent, and go bathe and admire myself.

Welcome is every organ and attribute of me, and of any man
    hearty and clean,
Not an inch nor a particle of an inch is vile, and none shall be
    less familiar than the rest.

I am satisfied—I see, dance, laugh, sing;
60   As the hugging and loving bed-fellow sleeps at my side
         through the night, and withdraws at the peep of the day
         with stealthy tread,
Leaving me baskets cover'd with white towels swelling the
         house with their plenty,
Shall I postpone my acceptation and realization and scream at
         my eyes,
That they turn from gazing after and down the road,
And forthwith cipher and show to me a cent,
65   Exactly the value of one and exactly the value of two, and
         which is ahead?

                    4

Trippers and askers surround me,
People I meet, the effect upon me of my early life or the ward
         and city I live in, or the nation,
The latest dates, discoveries, inventions, societies, authors old
         and new,
My dinner, dress, associates, looks, compliments, dues,
70   The real or fancied indifference of some man or woman I love,
The sickness of one of my folks or of myself, or ill-doing or
         loss or lack of money, or depressions or exaltations,
Battles, the horrors of fratricidal war, the fever of doubtful
         news, the fitful events;
These come to me days and nights and go from me again,
But they are not the Me myself.

75   Apart from the pulling and hauling stands what I am,
Stands amused, complacent, compassionating, idle, unitary,
Looks down, is erect, or bends an arm on an impalpable
         certain rest,
Looking with side-curved head curious what will come next,
Both in and out of the game and watching and wondering
         at it.

80   Backward I see in my own days where I sweated through fog
         with linguists and contenders,
I have no mockings or arguments, I witness and wait.

5

I believe in you my soul, the other I am must not abase itself
   to you,
And you must not be abased to the other.

Loafe with me on the grass, loose the stop from your throat,
85   Not words, not music or rhyme I want, not custom or lecture,
   not even the best,
Only the lull I like, the hum of your valvèd voice.

I mind how once we lay such a transparent summer morning,
How you settled your head athwart my hips and gently turn'd
   over upon me,
And parted the shirt from my bosom-bone, and plunged your
   tongue to my bare-stript heart,
90   And reach'd till you felt my beard, and reach'd till you held
   my feet.

Swiftly arose and spread around me the peace and knowledge
   that pass all the argument of the earth,
And I know that the hand of God is the promise of my own,
And I know that the spirit of God is the brother of my own,
And that all the men ever born are also my brothers, and the
   women my sisters and lovers,
95   And that a kelson[80] of the creation is love,
And limitless are leaves stiff or drooping in the fields,
And brown ants in the little wells beneath them,
And mossy scabs of the worm fence, heap'd stones, elder,
   mullein and poke-weed.

6

A child said *What is the grass?* fetching it to me with full
   hands;
100   How could I answer the child? I do not know what it is any
   more than he.

I guess it must be the flag of my disposition, out of hopeful
   green stuff woven.

Or I guess it is the handkerchief of the Lord,
A scented gift and remembrancer designedly dropt,
Bearing the owner's name someway in the corners, that we
    may see and remark, and say *Whose?*

105   Or I guess the grass is itself a child, the produced babe of the
    vegetation.

Or I guess it is a uniform hieroglyphic,
And it means, Sprouting alike in broad zones and narrow
    zones,
Growing among black folks as among white,
Kanuck, Tuckahoe, Congressman, Cuff,[81] I give them the
    same, I receive them the same.

110   And now it seems to me the beautiful uncut hair of graves.

Tenderly will I use you curling grass,
It may be you transpire from the breasts of young men,
It may be if I had known them I would have loved them,
It may be you are from old people, or from offspring taken
    soon out of their mothers' laps,
115   And here you are the mothers' laps.

This grass is very dark to be from the white heads of old
    mothers,
Darker than the colorless beards of old men,
Dark to come from under the faint red roofs of mouths.

O I perceive after all so many uttering tongues,
120   And I perceive they do not come from the roofs of mouths for
    nothing.

I wish I could translate the hints about the dead young men
    and women,
And the hints about old men and mothers, and the offspring
    taken soon out of their laps.

What do you think has become of the young and old men?
And what do you think has become of the women and
    children?

125 They are alive and well somewhere,
The smallest sprout shows there is really no death,
And if ever there was it led forward life, and does not wait at
    the end to arrest it,
And ceas'd the moment life appear'd.

All goes onward and outward, nothing collapses,
130 And to die is different from what any one supposed, and
    luckier.

               7

Has any one supposed it lucky to be born?
I hasten to inform him or her it is just as lucky to die, and I
    know it.

I pass death with the dying and birth with the new-wash'd
    babe, and am not contain'd between my hat and boots,
And peruse manifold objects, no two alike and every one
    good,
135 The earth good and the stars good, and their adjuncts all
    good.

I am not an earth nor an adjunct of an earth,
I am the mate and companion of people, all just as immortal
    and fathomless as myself,
(They do not know how immortal, but I know.)

Every kind for itself and its own, for me mine male and
    female,
140 For me those that have been boys and that love women,
For me the man that is proud and feels how it stings to be
    slighted,
For me the sweet-heart and the old maid, for me mothers and
    the mothers of mothers,
For me lips that have smiled, eyes that have shed tears,
For me children and the begetters of children.

145 Undrape! you are not guilty to me, nor stale nor discarded,
I see through the broadcloth and gingham whether or no,

And am around, tenacious, acquisitive, tireless, and cannot be
    shaken away.

8

The little one sleeps in its cradle,
I lift the gauze and look a long time, and silently brush away
    flies with my hand.

150   The youngster and the red-faced girl turn aside up the bushy
        hill,
    I peeringly view them from the top.

The suicide sprawls on the bloody floor of the bedroom,
I witness the corpse with its dabbled hair, I note where the
    pistol has fallen.

The blab of the pave, tires of carts, sluff of boot-soles, talk of
    the promenaders,
155   The heavy omnibus, the driver with his interrogating thumb,
        the clank of the shod horses on the granite floor,
    The snow-sleighs, clinking, shouted jokes, pelts of snow-balls,
    The hurrahs for popular favorites, the fury of rous'd mobs,
    The flap of the curtain'd litter, a sick man inside borne to the
        hospital,
    The meeting of enemies, the sudden oath, the blows and fall,
160   The excited crowd, the policeman with his star quickly
        working his passage to the centre of the crowd,
    The impassive stones that receive and return so many echoes,
    What groans of over-fed or half-starv'd who fall sunstruck or
        in fits,
    What exclamations of women taken suddenly who hurry home
        and give birth to babes,
    What living and buried speech is always vibrating here, what
        howls restrain'd by decorum,
165   Arrests of criminals, slights, adulterous offers made,
        acceptances, rejections with convex lips,
    I mind them or the show or resonance of them—I come and I
        depart.

9

The big doors of the country barn stand open and ready,
The dried grass of the harvest-time loads the slow-drawn
    wagon,
The clear light plays on the brown gray and green intertinged,
170   The armfuls are pack'd to the sagging mow.

I am there, I help, I came stretch'd atop of the load,
I felt its soft jolts, one leg reclined on the other,
I jump from the cross-beams and seize the clover and timothy,
And roll head over heels and tangle my hair full of wisps.

10

175   Alone far in the wilds and mountains I hunt,
Wandering amazed at my own lightness and glee,
In the late afternoon choosing a safe spot to pass the night,
Kindling a fire and broiling the fresh-kill'd game,
Falling asleep on the gather'd leaves with my dog and gun by
    my side.

180   The Yankee clipper is under her sky-sails, she cuts the sparkle
    and scud,
My eyes settle the land, I bend at her prow or shout joyously
    from the deck.

The boatmen and clam-diggers arose early and stopt for me,
I tuck'd my trowser-ends in my boots and went and had a
    good time;
You should have been with us that day round the chowder-
    kettle.

185   I saw the marriage of the trapper in the open air in the far
    west, the bride was a red girl,
Her father and his friends sat near cross-legged and dumbly
    smoking, they had moccasins to their feet and large thick
    blankets hanging from their shoulders,
On a bank lounged the trapper, he was drest mostly in skins,

his luxuriant beard and curls protected his neck, he held his
bride by the hand,
She had long eyelashes, her head was bare, her coarse straight
locks descended upon her voluptuous limbs and reach'd to
her feet.

The runaway slave came to my house and stopt outside,
190 I heard his motions crackling the twigs of the woodpile,
Through the swung half-door of the kitchen I saw him limpsy
and weak,
And went where he sat on a log and led him in and assured
him,
And brought water and fill'd a tub for his sweated body and
bruis'd feet,
And gave him a room that enter'd from my own, and gave
him some coarse clean clothes,
195 And remember perfectly well his revolving eyes and his
awkwardness,
And remember putting plasters on the galls of his neck and
ankles;
He staid with me a week before he was recuperated and pass'd
north,
I had him sit next me at table, my fire-lock lean'd in the
corner.

11

Twenty-eight young men bathe by the shore,
200 Twenty-eight young men and all so friendly;
Twenty-eight years of womanly life and all so lonesome.

She owns the fine house by the rise of the bank,
She hides handsome and richly drest aft the blinds of the
window.

Which of the young men does she like the best?
205 Ah the homeliest of them is beautiful to her.

Where are you off to, lady? for I see you,
You splash in the water there, yet stay stock still in your
room.

Dancing and laughing along the beach came the twenty-ninth
    bather,
The rest did not see her, but she saw them and loved them.

210   The beards of the young men glisten'd with wet, it ran from
    their long hair,
Little streams pass'd all over their bodies.

An unseen hand also pass'd over their bodies,
It descended tremblingly from their temples and ribs.

The young men float on their backs, their white bellies bulge
    to the sun, they do not ask who seizes fast to them,
215   They do not know who puffs and declines with pendant and
    bending arch,
They do not think whom they souse with spray.

12

The butcher-boy puts off his killing-clothes, or sharpens his
    knife at the stall in the market,
I loiter enjoying his repartee and his shuffle and break-down.

Blacksmiths with grimed and hairy chests environ the anvil,
220   Each has his main-sledge, they are all out, there is a great heat
    in the fire.

From the cinder-strew'd threshold I follow their movements,
The lithe sheer of their waists plays even with their massive
    arms,
Overhand the hammers swing, overhand so slow, overhand so
    sure,
They do not hasten, each man hits in his place.

13

225   The negro holds firmly the reins of his four horses, the block
    swags underneath on its tied-over chain,
The negro that drives the long dray of the stone-yard, steady
    and tall he stands pois'd on one leg on the string-piece,

His blue shirt exposes his ample neck and breast and loosens
    over his hip-band,
His glance is calm and commanding, he tosses the slouch of
    his hat away from his forehead,
The sun falls on his crispy hair and mustache, falls on the
    black of his polish'd and perfect limbs.

230   I behold the picturesque giant and love him, and I do not stop
    there,
I go with the team also.

In me the caresser of life wherever moving, backward as well
    as forward sluing,
To niches aside and junior bending, not a person or object
    missing,
Absorbing all to myself and for this song.

235   Oxen that rattle the yoke and chain or halt in the leafy shade,
    what is that you express in your eyes?
It seems to me more than all the print I have read in my life.

My tread scares the wood-drake and wood-duck on my distant
    and day-long ramble,
They rise together, they slowly circle around.

I believe in those wing'd purposes,
240   And acknowledge red, yellow, white, playing within me,
And consider green and violet and the tufted crown
    intentional,
And do not call the tortoise unworthy because she is not
    something else,
And the jay in the woods never studied the gamut, yet trills
    pretty well to me,
And the look of the bay mare shames silliness out of me.

14

245   The wild gander leads his flock through the cool night,
Ya-honk he says, and sounds it down to me like an invitation,
The pert may suppose it meaningless, but I listening close,
Find its purpose and place up there toward the wintry sky.

The sharp-hoof'd moose of the north, the cat on the house-sill
    the chickadee, the prairie-dog,
250   The litter of the grunting sow as they tug at her teats,
The brood of the turkey-hen and she with her half-spread
    wings,
I see in them and myself the same old law.

The press of my foot to the earth springs a hundred affections,
They scorn the best I can do to relate them.

255   I am enamour'd of growing out-doors,
Of men that live among cattle or taste of the ocean or woods,
Of the builders and steerers of ships and the wielders of axes
    and mauls, and the drivers of horses,
I can eat and sleep with them week in and week out.

What is commonest, cheapest, nearest, easiest, is Me,
260   Me going in for my chances, spending for vast returns,
Adorning myself to bestow myself on the first that will
    take me,
Not asking the sky to come down to my good will,
Scattering it freely forever.

15

The pure contralto sings in the organ loft,
265   The carpenter dresses his plank, the tongue of his foreplane
    whistles its wild ascending lisp,
The married and unmarried children ride home to their
    Thanksgiving dinner,
The pilot seizes the king-pin,[82] he heaves down with a
    strong arm,
The mate stands braced in the whale-boat, lance and harpoon
    are ready,
The duck-shooter walks by silent and cautious stretches,
270   The deacons are ordain'd with cross'd hands at the altar,
The spinning-girl retreats and advances to the hum of the big
    wheel,
The farmer stops by the bars as he walks on a First-day loafe[83]
    and looks at the oats and rye,
The lunatic is carried at last to the asylum a confirm'd case,

(He will never sleep any more as he did in the cot in his
    mother's bed-room;)

275   The jour printer[84] with gray head and gaunt jaws works at his
    case,

He turns his quid of tobacco while his eyes blurr with the
    manuscript;

The malform'd limbs are tied to the surgeon's table,

What is removed drops horribly in a pail;

The quadroon girl is sold at the auction-stand, the drunkard
    nods by the bar-room stove,

280   The machinist rolls up his sleeves, the policeman travels his
    beat, the gate-keeper marks who pass,

The young fellow drives the express-wagon, (I love him,
    though I do not know him;)

The half-breed straps on his light boots to compete in the race,

The western turkey-shooting draws old and young, some lean
    on their rifles, some sit on logs,

Out from the crowd steps the marksman, takes his position,
    levels his piece;

285   The groups of newly-come immigrants cover the wharf or
    levee,

As the woolly-pates hoe in the sugar-field, the overseer views
    them from his saddle,

The bugle calls in the ball-room, the gentlemen run for their
    partners, the dancers bow to each other,

The youth lies awake in the cedar-roof'd garret and harks to
    the musical rain,

The Wolverine sets traps on the creek that helps fill the Huron,

290   The squaw wrapt in her yellow-hemm'd cloth is offering
    moccasins and bead-bags for sale,

The connoisseur peers along the exhibition-gallery with half-
    shut eyes bent sideways,

As the deck-hands make fast the steamboat the plank is
    thrown for the shore-going passengers,

The young sister holds out the skein while the elder sister
    winds it off in a ball, and stops now and then for the knots,

The one-year wife is recovering and happy having a week ago
    borne her first child,

295   The clean-hair'd Yankee girl works with her sewing-machine
    or in the factory or mill,

The paving-man leans on his two-handed rammer, the

reporter's lead flies swiftly over the note-book, the sign-
painter is lettering with blue and gold,

The canal boy trots on the tow-path, the book-keeper counts
at his desk, the shoemaker waxes his thread,

The conductor beats time for the band and all the performers
follow him,

The child is baptized, the convert is making his first
professions,

300   The regatta is spread on the bay, the race is begun, (how the
white sails sparkle!)

The drover watching his drove sings out to them that would
stray,

The pedler sweats with his pack on his back, (the purchaser
higgling about the odd cent;)

The bride unrumples her white dress, the minute-hand of the
clock moves slowly,

The opium-eater reclines with rigid head and just-open'd lips,

305   The prostitute draggles her shawl, her bonnet bobs on her
tipsy and pimpled neck,

The crowd laugh at her blackguard oaths, the men jeer and
wink to each other,

(Miserable! I do not laugh at your oaths nor jeer you;)

The President holding a cabinet council is surrounded by the
great Secretaries,

On the piazza walk three matrons stately and friendly with
twined arms,

310   The crew of the fish-smack pack repeated layers of halibut in
the hold,

The Missourian crosses the plains toting his wares and his
cattle,

As the fare-collector goes through the train he gives notice by
the jingling of loose change,

The floor-men are laying the floor, the tinners are tinning the
roof, the masons are calling for mortar,

In single file each shouldering his hod pass onward the
laborers;

315   Seasons pursuing each other the indescribable crowd is
gather'd, it is the fourth of Seventh-month, (with salutes of
cannon and small arms!)

Seasons pursuing each other the plougher ploughs, the mower
mows, and the winter-grain falls in the ground;

Off on the lakes the pike-fisher watches and waits by the hole
    in the frozen surface,
The stumps stand thick round the clearing, the squatter strikes
    deep with his axe,
Flatboatmen make fast towards dusk near the cotton-wood or
    pecan-trees,
320   Coon-seekers go through the regions of the Red river or
    through those drain'd by the Tennessee, or through those of
    the Arkansas,
Torches shine in the dark that hangs on the Chattahooche or
    Altamahaw,[85]
Patriarchs sit at supper with sons and grandsons and great-
    grandsons around them,
In walls of adobie, in canvas tents, rest hunters and trappers
    after their day's sport,
The city sleeps and the country sleeps,
325   The living sleep for their time, the dead sleep for their time,
The old husband sleeps by his wife and the young husband
    sleeps by his wife;
And these tend inward to me, and I tend outward to them,
And such as it is to be of these more or less I am,
And of these one and all I weave the song of myself.

16

330   I am of old and young, of the foolish as much as the wise,
Regardless of others, ever regardful of others,
Maternal as well as paternal, a child as well as a man,
Stuff'd with the stuff that is coarse and stuff'd with the stuff
    that is fine,
One of the Nation of many nations, the smallest the same and
    the largest the same,
335   A Southerner soon as a Northerner, a planter nonchalant and
    hospitable down by the Oconee I live,
A Yankee bound my own way ready for trade, my joints the
    limberest joints on earth and the sternest joints on earth,
A Kentuckian walking the vale of the Elkhorn in my deer-skin
    leggings, a Louisianian or Georgian,
A boatman over lakes or bays or along coasts, a Hoosier,
    Badger, Buckeye;

At home on Kanadian snow-shoes or up in the bush, or with
    fishermen off Newfoundland,
340 At home in the fleet of ice-boats, sailing with the rest and
    tacking,
At home on the hills of Vermont or in the woods of Maine, or
    the Texan ranch,
Comrade of Californians, comrade of free North-Westerners,
    (loving their big proportions,)
Comrade of raftsmen and coalmen, comrade of all who shake
    hands and welcome to drink and meat,
A learner with the simplest, a teacher of the thoughtfullest,
345 A novice beginning yet experient of myriads of seasons,
Of every hue and caste am I, of every rank and religion,
A farmer, mechanic, artist, gentleman, sailor, quaker,
Prisoner, fancy-man, rowdy, lawyer, physician, priest.

I resist any thing better than my own diversity,
350 Breathe the air but leave plenty after me,
And am not stuck up, and am in my place.

(The moth and the fish-eggs are in their place,
The bright suns I see and the dark suns I cannot see are in
    their place,
The palpable is in its place and the impalpable is in its place.)

17

355 These are really the thoughts of all men in all ages and lands,
    they are not original with me,
If they are not yours as much as mine they are nothing, or
    next to nothing,
If they are not the riddle and the untying of the riddle they are
    nothing,
If they are not just as close as they are distant they are
    nothing.

This is the grass that grows wherever the land is and the
    water is,
360 This the common air that bathes the globe.

18

With music strong I come, with my cornets and my drums,
I play not marches for accepted victors only, I play marches
    for conquer'd and slain persons.

Have you heard that it was good to gain the day?
I also say it is good to fall, battles are lost in the same spirit in
    which they are won.

365   I beat and pound for the dead,
I blow through my embouchures my loudest and gayest for
    them.

Vivas to those who have fail'd!
And to those whose war-vessels sank in the sea!
And to those themselves who sank in the sea!
370   And to all generals that lost engagements, and all overcome
    heroes!
And the numberless unknown heroes equal to the greatest
    heroes known!

19

This is the meal equally set, this the meat for natural hunger,
It is for the wicked just the same as the righteous, I make
    appointments with all,
I will not have a single person slighted or left away,
375   The kept-woman, sponger, thief, are hereby invited,
The heavy-lipp'd slave is invited, the venerealee[86] is invited;
There shall be no difference between them and the rest.

This is the press of a bashful hand, this the float and odor of
    hair,
This the touch of my lips to yours, this the murmur of
    yearning,
380   This the far-off depth and height reflecting my own face,
This the thoughtful merge of myself, and the outlet again.

                •

Do you guess I have some intricate purpose?
Well I have, for the Fourth-month showers have, and the mica
    on the side of a rock has.

Do you take it I would astonish?
385   Does the daylight astonish? does the early redstart twittering
    through the woods?
Do I astonish more than they?

This hour I tell things in confidence,
I might not tell everybody, but I will tell you.

    20

Who goes there? hankering, gross, mystical, nude;
390   How is it I extract strength from the beef I eat?

What is a man anyhow? what am I? what are you?

All I mark as my own you shall offset it with your own,
Else it were time lost listening to me.

I do not snivel that snivel the world over,
395   That months are vacuums and the ground but wallow and
    filth.

Whimpering and truckling fold with powders[87] for invalids,
    conformity goes to the fourth-remov'd,
I wear my hat as I please indoors or out.

Why should I pray? why should I venerate and be
    ceremonious?

Having pried through the strata, analyzed to a hair, counsel'd
    with doctors and calculated close,
400   I find no sweeter fat than sticks to my own bones.

In all people I see myself, none more and not one a barley-
    corn less,
And the good or bad I say of myself I say of them.

·

I know I am solid and sound,
To me the converging objects of the universe perpetually flow,
405   All are written to me, and I must get what the writing means.

I know I am deathless,
I know this orbit of mine cannot be swept by a carpenter's
    compass,
I know I shall not pass like a child's carlacue[88] cut with a
    burnt stick at night.

I know I am august,
410   I do not trouble my spirit to vindicate itself or be understood,
I see that the elementary laws never apologize,
(I reckon I behave no prouder than the level I plant my house
    by, after all.)

I exist as I am, that is enough,
If no other in the world be aware I sit content,
415   And if each and all be aware I sit content.

One world is aware and by far the largest to me, and that is
    myself,
And whether I come to my own to-day or in ten thousand or
    ten million years,
I can cheerfully take it now, or with equal cheerfulness I can
    wait.

My foothold is tenon'd and mortis'd in granite,
420   I laugh at what you call dissolution,
And I know the amplitude of time.

21

I am the poet of the Body and I am the poet of the Soul,
The pleasures of heaven are with me and the pains of hell are
    with me,
The first I graft and increase upon myself, the latter I translate
    into a new tongue.

•

425 I am the poet of the woman the same as the man,
And I say it is as great to be a woman as to be a man,
And I say there is nothing greater than the mother of men.

I chant the chant of dilation or pride,
We have had ducking and deprecating about enough,
430 I show that size is only development.

Have you outstript the rest? are you the President?
It is a trifle, they will more than arrive there every one, and
still pass on.

I am he that walks with the tender and growing night,
I call to the earth and sea half-held by the night.

435 Press close bare-bosom'd night—press close magnetic
nourishing night!
Night of south winds—night of the large few stars!
Still nodding night—mad naked summer night.

Smile O voluptuous cool-breath'd earth!
Earth of the slumbering and liquid trees!
440 Earth of departed sunset—earth of the mountains misty-topt!
Earth of the vitreous pour of the full moon just tinged with
blue!
Earth of shine and dark mottling the tide of the river!
Earth of the limpid gray of clouds brighter and clearer for my
sake!
Far-swooping elbow'd earth—rich apple-blossom'd earth!
445 Smile, for your lover comes.

Prodigal, you have given me love—therefore I to you give
love!
O unspeakable passionate love.

22

You sea! I resign myself to you also—I guess what you mean,
I behold from the beach your crooked inviting fingers,
450 I believe you refuse to go back without feeling of me,

We must have a turn together, I undress, hurry me out of sight
    of the land,
Cushion me soft, rock me in billowy drowse,
Dash me with amorous wet, I can repay you.

Sea of stretch'd ground-swells,
455   Sea breathing broad and convulsive breaths,
Sea of the brine of life and of unshovell'd yet always-ready
    graves,
Howler and scooper of storms, capricious and dainty sea,
I am integral with you, I too am of one phase and of all
    phases.

Partaker of influx and efflux I, extoller of hate and
    conciliation,
460   Extoller of amies and those that sleep in each others' arms.

I am he attesting sympathy,
(Shall I make my list of things in the house and skip the house
    that supports them?)
I am not the poet of goodness only, I do not decline to be the
    poet of wickedness also.

What blurt is this about virtue and about vice?
465   Evil propels me and reform of evil propels me, I stand
    indifferent,
My gait is no fault-finder's or rejecter's gait,
I moisten the roots of all that has grown.

Did you fear some scrofula out of the unflagging pregnancy?
Did you guess the celestial laws are yet to be work'd over and
    rectified?

470   I find one side a balance and the antipodal side a balance,
Soft doctrine as steady help as stable doctrine,
Thoughts and deeds of the present our rouse and early start.

This minute that comes to me over the past decillions,
There is no better than it and now.

•

475 What behaved well in the past or behaves well to-day is not
  such a wonder,
 The wonder is always and always how there can be a mean
  man or an infidel.

23

 Endless unfolding of words of ages!
 And mine a word of the modern, the word En-Masse.

 A word of the faith that never balks,
480 Here or henceforward it is all the same to me, I accept Time
  absolutely.

 It alone is without flaw, it alone rounds and completes all,
 That mystic baffling wonder alone completes all.

 I accept Reality and dare not question it,
 Materialism first and last imbuing.

485 Hurrah for positive science! long live exact demonstration!
 Fetch stonecrop mixt with cedar and branches of lilac,
 This is the lexicographer, this the chemist, this made a
  grammar of the old cartouches,
 These mariners put the ship through dangerous unknown seas,
 This is the geologist, this works with the scalpel, and this is a
  mathematician.

490 Gentlemen, to you the first honors always!
 Your facts are useful, and yet they are not my dwelling,
 I but enter by them to an area of my dwelling.

 Less the reminders of properties told my words,
 And more the reminders they of life untold, and of freedom
  and extrication,
495 And make short account of neuters and geldings, and favor
  men and women fully equipt,
 And beat the gong of revolt, and stop with fugitives and them
  that plot and conspire.

24

Walt Whitman, a kosmos, of Manhattan the son,
Turbulent, fleshy, sensual, eating, drinking and breeding,
No sentimentalist, no stander above men and women or apart
    from them,
500   No more modest than immodest.

Unscrew the locks from the doors!
Unscrew the doors themselves from their jambs!

Whoever degrades another degrades me,
And whatever is done or said returns at last to me.

505   Through me the afflatus surging and surging, through me the
    current and index.

I speak the pass-word primeval, I give the sign of democracy,
By God! I will accept nothing which all cannot have their
    counterpart of on the same terms.

Through me many long dumb voices,
Voices of the interminable generations of prisoners and slaves,
510   Voices of the diseas'd and despairing and of thieves and
    dwarfs,
Voices of cycles of preparation and accretion,
And of the threads that connect the stars, and of wombs and
    of the father-stuff,
And of the rights of them the others are down upon,
Of the deform'd, trivial, flat, foolish, despised,
515   Fog in the air, beetles rolling balls of dung.
Through me forbidden voices,
Voices of sexes and lusts, voices veil'd and I remove the veil,
Voices indecent by me clarified and transfigur'd.

I do not press my fingers across my mouth,
520   I keep as delicate around the bowels as around the head and
    heart,
Copulation is no more rank to me than death is.
I believe in the flesh and the appetites,

Seeing, hearing, feeling, are miracles, and each part and tag of
    me is a miracle.

Divine am I inside and out, and I make holy whatever I touch
    or am touch'd from,
525 The scent of these arm-pits aroma finer than prayer,
This head more than churches, bibles, and all the creeds.

If I worship one thing more than another it shall be the spread
    of my own body, or any part of it,
Translucent mould of me it shall be you!
Shaded ledges and rests it shall be you!
530 Firm masculine colter it shall be you!
Whatever goes to the tilth of me it shall be you!
You my rich blood! your milky stream pale strippings of my
    life!
Breast that presses against other breasts it shall be you!
My brain it shall be your occult convolutions!
535 Root of wash'd sweet-flag! timorous pond-snipe! nest of
    guarded duplicate eggs! it shall be you!
Mix'd tussled hay of head, beard, brawn, it shall be you!
Trickling sap of maple, fibre of manly wheat, it shall be you!
Sun so generous it shall be you!
Vapors lighting and shading my face it shall be you!
540 You sweaty brooks and dews it shall be you!
Winds whose soft-tickling genitals rub against me it shall
    be you!
Broad muscular fields, branches of live oak, loving lounger in
    my winding paths, it shall be you!
Hands I have taken, face I have kiss'd, mortal I have ever
    touch'd, it shall be you.

I dote on myself, there is that lot of me and all so luscious,
545 Each moment and whatever happens thrills me with joy,
I cannot tell how my ankles bend, nor whence the cause of my
    faintest wish,

Nor the cause of the friendship I emit, nor the cause of the
    friendship I take again.

That I walk up my stoop, I pause to consider if it really be,
A morning-glory at my window satisfies me more than the
    metaphysics of books.

550   To behold the day-break!
The little light fades the immense and diaphanous shadows,
The air tastes good to my palate.

Hefts of the moving world at innocent gambols silently rising,
    freshly exuding,
Scooting obliquely high and low.

555   Something I cannot see puts upward libidinous prongs,
Seas of bright juice suffuse heaven.

The earth by the sky staid with, the daily close of their
    junction,
The heav'd challenge from the east that moment over my
    head,
The mocking taunt, See then whether you shall be master!

25

560   Dazzling and tremendous how quick the sun-rise would
    kill me,
If I could not now and always send sun-rise out of me.

We also ascend dazzling and tremendous as the sun,
We found our own O my soul in the calm and cool of the
    daybreak.

My voice goes after what my eyes cannot reach,
565   With the twirl of my tongue I encompass worlds and volumes
    of worlds.

Speech is the twin of my vision, it is unequal to measure itself,
It provokes me forever, it says sarcastically,
Walt you contain enough, why don't you let it out then?

Come now I will not be tantalized, you conceive too much of
    articulation,

570   Do you not know O speech how the buds beneath you are
            folded?
        Waiting in gloom, protected by frost,
        The dirt receding before my prophetical screams,
        I underlying causes to balance them at last,
        My knowledge my live parts, it keeping tally with the meaning
            of all things,
575   Happiness, (which whoever hears me let him or her set out in
            search of this day.)

        My final merit I refuse you, I refuse putting from me what I
            really am,
        Encompass worlds, but never try to encompass me,
        I crowd your sleekest and best by simply looking toward you.

        Writing and talk do not prove me,
580   I carry the plenum of proof and every thing else in my face,
        With the hush of my lips I wholly confound the skeptic.

        26

        Now I will do nothing but listen,
        To accrue what I hear into this song, to let sounds contribute
            toward it.

        I hear bravuras of birds, bustle of growing wheat, gossip of
            flames, clack of sticks cooking my meals,
585   I hear the sound I love, the sound of the human voice,
        I hear all sounds running together, combined, fused or
            following,
        Sounds of the city and sounds out of the city, sounds of the
            day and night,
        Talkative young ones to those that like them, the loud laugh
            of work-people at their meals,
        The angry base of disjointed friendship, the faint tones of the
            sick,
590   The judge with hands tight to the desk, his pallid lips
            pronouncing a death-sentence,
        The heave'e'yo of stevedores unlading ships by the wharves,
            the refrain of the anchor-lifters,
        The ring of alarm-bells, the cry of fire, the whirr of swift-

streaking engines and hose-carts with premonitory tinkles
and color'd lights,
The steam-whistle, the solid roll of the train of approaching
cars,
The slow march play'd at the head of the association marching
two and two,
595   (They go to guard some corpse, the flag-tops are draped with
black muslin.)

I hear the violoncello, ('tis the young man's heart's complaint,)
I hear the key'd cornet, it glides quickly in through my ears,
It shakes mad-sweet pangs through my belly and breast.

I hear the chorus, it is a grand opera,
600   Ah this indeed is music—this suits me.

A tenor large and fresh as the creation fills me,
The orbic flex of his mouth is pouring and filling me full.

I hear the train'd soprano (what work with hers is this?)
The orchestra whirls me wider than Uranus flies,
605   It wrenches such ardors from me I did not know I possess'd
them,
It sails me, I dab with bare feet, they are lick'd by the indolent
waves,
I am cut by bitter and angry hail, I lose my breath,
Steep'd amid honey'd morphine, my windpipe throttled in
fakes of death,
At length let up again to feel the puzzle of puzzles,
610   And that we call Being.

27

To be in any form, what is that?
(Round and round we go, all of us, and ever come back
thither,)
If nothing lay more develop'd the quahaug in its callous shell
were enough.

Mine is no callous shell,
615   I have instant conductors all over me whether I pass or stop,
They seize every object and lead it harmlessly through me.

I merely stir, press, feel with my fingers, and am happy,
To touch my person to some one else's is about as much as I
    can stand.

28

Is this then a touch? quivering me to a new identity,
620   Flames and ether making a rush for my veins,
Treacherous tip of me reaching and crowding to help them,
My flesh and blood playing out lightning to strike what is
    hardly different from myself,
On all sides prurient provokers stiffening my limbs,
Straining the udder of my heart for its withheld drip,
625   Behaving licentious toward me, taking no denial,
Depriving me of my best as for a purpose,
Unbuttoning my clothes, holding me by the bare waist,
Deluding my confusion with the calm of the sunlight and
    pasture-fields,
Immodestly sliding the fellow-senses away,
630   They bribed to swap off with touch and go and graze at the
    edges of me,
No consideration, no regard for my draining strength or my
    anger,
Fetching the rest of the herd around to enjoy them a while,
Then all uniting to stand on a headland and worry me.

The sentries desert every other part of me,
635   They have left me helpless to a red marauder,
They all come to the headland to witness and assist against
    me.

I am given up by traitors,
I talk wildly, I have lost my wits, I and nobody else am the
    greatest traitor,
I went myself first to the headland, my own hands carried me
    there.

·

640 You villain touch! what are you doing? my breath is tight in
       its throat,
     Unclench your floodgates, you are too much for me.

       29

     Blind loving wrestling touch, sheath'd hooded sharp-tooth'd
       touch!
     Did it make you ache so, leaving me?

     Parting track'd by arriving, perpetual payment of perpetual
       loan,
645 Rich showering rain, and recompense richer afterward.

     Sprouts take and accumulate, stand by the curb prolific and
       vital,
     Landscapes projected masculine, full-sized and golden.

       30

     All truths wait in all things,
     They neither hasten their own delivery nor resist it,
650 They do not need the obstetric forceps of the surgeon,
     The insignificant is as big to me as any,
     (What is less or more than a touch?)

     Logic and sermons never convince,
     The damp of the night drives deeper into my soul.

655 (Only what proves itself to every man and woman is so,
     Only what nobody denies is so.)

     A minute and a drop of me settle my brain,
     I believe the soggy clods shall become lovers and lamps,
     And a compend of compends is the meat of a man or woman,
660 And a summit and flower there is the feeling they have for
       each other,
     And they are to branch boundlessly out of that lesson until it
       becomes omnific,
     And until one and all shall delight us, and we them.

31

I believe a leaf of grass is no less than the journey-work of the
    stars,
And the pismire is equally perfect, and a grain of sand, and
    the egg of the wren,
665 And the tree-toad is a chef-d'œuvre for the highest,
And the running blackberry would adorn the parlors of
    heaven,
And the narrowest hinge in my hand puts to scorn all
    machinery,
And the cow crunching with depress'd head surpasses any
    statue,
And a mouse is miracle enough to stagger sextillions of
    infidels.

670 I find I incorporate gneiss, coal, long-threaded moss, fruits,
    grains, esculent roots,
And am stucco'd with quadrupeds and birds all over,
And have distanced what is behind me for good reasons,
But call any thing back again when I desire it.

In vain the speeding or shyness,
675 In vain the plutonic rocks send their old heat against my
    approach,
In vain the mastodon retreats beneath its own powder'd bones,
In vain objects stand leagues off and assume manifold shapes,
In vain the ocean settling in hollows and the great monsters
    lying low,
In vain the buzzard houses herself with the sky,
680 In vain the snake slides through the creepers and logs,
In vain the elk takes to the inner passes of the woods,
In vain the razor-bill'd auk sails far north to Labrador,
I follow quickly, I ascend to the nest in the fissure of the cliff.

32

I think I could turn, and live with animals, they are so placid
    and self-contain'd,
685 I stand and look at them long and long.

They do not sweat and whine about their condition,
They do not lie awake in the dark and weep for their sins,
They do not make me sick discussing their duty to God,
Not one is dissatisfied, not one is demented with the mania of
    owning things,
690   Not one kneels to another, nor to his kind that lived
    thousands of years ago,
Not one is respectable or unhappy over the whole earth.

So they show their relations to me and I accept them,
They bring me tokens of myself, they evince them plainly in
    their possession.

I wonder where they get those tokens,
695   Did I pass that way huge times ago and negligently drop
    them?
Myself moving forward then and now and forever,
Gathering and showing more always and with velocity,
Infinite and omnigenous,[89] and the like of these among them,
Not too exclusive toward the reachers of my remembrancers,
700   Picking out here one that I love, and now go with him on
    brotherly terms.

A gigantic beauty of a stallion, fresh and responsive to my
    caresses,
Head high in the forehead, wide between the ears,
Limbs glossy and supple, tail dusting the ground,
Eyes full of sparkling wickedness, ears finely cut, flexibly
    moving.

705   His nostrils dilate as my heels embrace him,
His well-built limbs tremble with pleasure as we race around
    and return.

I but use you a minute, then I resign you, stallion,
Why do I need your paces when I myself out-gallop them?
Even as I stand or sit passing faster than you.

33

710 Space and Time! now I see it is true, what I guessed at,
 What I guess'd when I loaf'd on the grass,
 What I guess'd while I lay alone in my bed,
 And again as I walk'd the beach under the paling stars of the
  morning.

 My ties and ballasts leave me, my elbows rest in sea-gaps,
715 I skirt sierras, my palms cover continents,
 I am afoot with my vision.

 By the city's quadrangular houses—in log huts, camping with
  lumbermen,
 Along the ruts of the turnpike, along the dry gulch and rivulet
  bed,
 Weeding my onion-patch or hoeing rows of carrots and
  parsnips, crossing savannas, trailing in forests,
720 Prospecting, gold-digging, girdling the trees of a new purchase,
 Scorch'd ankle-deep by the hot sand, hauling my boat down
  the shallow river,
 Where the panther walks to and fro on a limb overhead,
  where the buck turns furiously at the hunter,
 Where the rattlesnake suns his flabby length on a rock, where
  the otter is feeding on fish,
 Where the alligator in his tough pimples sleeps by the bayou,
725 Where the black bear is searching for roots or honey, where
  the beaver pats the mud with his paddle-shaped tail;
 Over the growing sugar, over the yellow-flower'd cotton plant,
  over the rice in its low moist field,
 Over the sharp-peak'd farm house, with its scallop'd scum and
  slender shoots from the gutters,
 Over the western persimmon, over the long-leav'd corn, over
  the delicate blue-flower flax,
 Over the white and brown buckwheat, a hummer and buzzer
  there with the rest,
730 Over the dusky green of the rye as it ripples and shades in the
  breeze;
 Scaling mountains, pulling myself cautiously up, holding on by
  low scragged limbs,

Walking the path worn in the grass and beat through the
leaves of the brush,

Where the quail is whistling betwixt the woods and the
wheat-lot,

Where the bat flies in the Seventh-month eve, where the great
gold-bug drops through the dark,

735 Where the brook puts out of the roots of the old tree and
flows to the meadow,

Where cattle stand and shake away flies with the tremulous
shuddering of their hides,

Where the cheese-cloth hangs in the kitchen, where andirons
straddle the hearth-slab, where cobwebs fall in festoons
from the rafters;

Where trip-hammers crash, where the press is whirling its
cylinders,

Wherever the human heart beats with terrible throes under its
ribs,

740 Where the pear-shaped balloon is floating aloft, (floating in it
myself and looking composedly down,)

Where the life-car⁹⁰ is drawn on the slip-noose, where the heat
hatches pale-green eggs in the dented sand,

Where the she-whale swims with her calf and never forsakes it,

Where the steam-ship trails hind-ways its long pennant of
smoke,

Where the fin of the shark cuts like a black chip out of the
water,

745 Where the half-burn'd brig is riding on unknown currents,

Where shells grow to her slimy deck, where the dead are
corrupting below;

Where the dense-starr'd flag is borne at the head of the
regiments,

Approaching Manhattan up by the long-stretching island,

Under Niagara, the cataract falling like a veil over my
countenance,

750 Upon a door-step, upon the horse-block of hard wood outside,

Upon the race-course, or enjoying picnics or jigs or a good
game of base-ball,

At he-festivals, with blackguard gibes, ironical license, bull-
dances,⁹¹ drinking, laughter,

At the cider-mill tasting the sweets of the brown mash, sucking
the juice through a straw,

At apple-peelings wanting kisses for all the red fruit I find,
755 At musters, beach-parties, friendly bees, huskings, house-
        raisings;
Where the mocking-bird sounds his delicious gurgles, cackles,
        screams, weeps,
Where the hay-rick stands in the barn-yard, where the dry-
        stalks are scatter'd, where the brood-cow waits in the
        hovel,
Where the bull advances to do his masculine work, where the
        stud to the mare, where the cock is treading the hen,
Where the heifers browse, where geese nip their food with
        short jerks,
760 Where sun-down shadows lengthen over the limitless and
        lonesome prairie,
Where herds of buffalo make a crawling spread of the square
        miles far and near,
Where the humming-bird shimmers, where the neck of the
        long-lived swan is curving and winding,
Where the laughing-gull scoots by the shore, where she laughs
        her near-human laugh,
Where bee-hives range on a gray bench in the garden half hid
        by the high weeds,
765 Where band-neck'd partridges roost in a ring on the ground
        with their heads out,
Where burial coaches enter the arch'd gates of a cemetery,
Where winter wolves bark amid wastes of snow and icicled
        trees,
Where the yellow-crown'd heron comes to the edge of the
        marsh at night and feeds upon small crabs,
Where the splash of swimmers and divers cools the warm
        noon,
770 Where the katy-did works her chromatic reed on the walnut-
        tree over the well,
Through patches of citrons and cucumbers with silver-wired
        leaves,
Through the salt-lick or orange glade, or under conical firs,
Through the gymnasium, through the curtain'd saloon,
        through the office or public hall;
Pleas'd with the native and pleas'd with the foreign, pleas'd
        with the new and old,
775 Pleas'd with the homely woman as well as the handsome,

Pleas'd with the quakeress as she puts off her bonnet and talks
    melodiously,
Pleas'd with the tune of the choir of the whitewash'd church,
Pleas'd with the earnest words of the sweating Methodist
    preacher, impress'd seriously at the camp-meeting;
Looking in at the shop-windows of Broadway the whole
    forenoon, flatting the flesh of my nose on the thick plate-
    glass,
780   Wandering the same afternoon with my face turn'd up to the
    clouds, or down a lane or along the beach,
My right and left arms round the sides of two friends, and I in
    the middle;
Coming home with the silent and dark-cheek'd bush-boy,
    (behind me he rides at the drape[92] of the day,)
Far from the settlements studying the print of animals' feet, or
    the moccasin print,
By the cot in the hospital reaching lemonade to a feverish
    patient,
785   Nigh the coffin'd corpse when all is still, examining with a
    candle;
Voyaging to every port to dicker and adventure,
Hurrying with the modern crowd as eager and fickle as any,
Hot toward one I hate, ready in my madness to knife him,
Solitary at midnight in my back yard, my thoughts gone from
    me a long while,
790   Walking the old hills of Judæa with the beautiful gentle God
    by my side,
Speeding through space, speeding through heaven and the
    stars,
Speeding amid the seven satellites and the broad ring, and the
    diameter of eighty thousand miles,
Speeding with tail'd meteors, throwing fire-balls like the rest,
Carrying the crescent child that carries its own full mother in
    its belly,
795   Storming, enjoying, planning, loving, cautioning,
Backing and filling, appearing and disappearing,
I tread day and night such roads.

I visit the orchards of spheres and look at the product,
And look at quintillions ripen'd and look at quintillions green.

•

800   I fly those flights of a fluid and swallowing soul,
       My course runs below the soundings of plummets.

       I help myself to material and immaterial,
       No guard can shut me off, no law prevent me.

       I anchor my ship for a little while only,
805   My messengers continually cruise away or bring their returns
          to me.

       I go hunting polar furs and the seal, leaping chasms with a
          pike-pointed staff, clinging to topples[93] of brittle and blue.

       I ascend to the foretruck,
       I take my place late at night in the crow's-nest,
       We sail the arctic sea, it is plenty light enough,
810   Through the clear atmosphere I stretch around on the
          wonderful beauty,
       The enormous masses of ice pass me and I pass them, the
          scenery is plain in all directions,
       The white-topt mountains show in the distance, I fling out my
          fancies toward them,
       We are approaching some great battle-field in which we are
          soon to be engaged,
       We pass the colossal outposts of the encampment, we pass
          with still feet and caution,
815   Or we are entering by the suburbs some vast and ruin'd city,
       The blocks and fallen architecture more than all the living
          cities of the globe.

       I am a free companion, I bivouac by invading watchfires,
       I turn the bridegroom out of bed and stay with the bride
          myself, I tighten her all night to my thighs and lips.

       My voice is the wife's voice, the screech by the rail of the
          stairs,
820   They fetch my man's body up dripping and drown'd.

       I understand the large hearts of heroes,
       The courage of present times and all times,

How the skipper saw the crowded and rudderless wreck of the
    steamship, and Death chasing it up and down the storm,
How he knuckled tight and gave not back an inch, and was
    faithful of days and faithful of nights,
825   And chalk'd in large letters on a board, *Be of good cheer, we
    will not desert you;*
How he follow'd with them and tack'd with them three days
    and would not give it up,
How he saved the drifting company at last,
How the lank loose-gown'd women look'd when boated from
    the side of their prepared graves,
How the silent old-faced infants and the lifted sick, and the
    sharp-lipp'd unshaved men;
830   All this I swallow, it tastes good, I like it well, it becomes
    mine,
I am the man, I suffer'd, I was there.

The disdain and calmness of martyrs,
The mother of old, condemn'd for a witch, burnt with dry
    wood, her children gazing on,
The hounded slave that flags in the race, leans by the fence,
    blowing, cover'd with sweat,
835   The twinges that sting like needles his legs and neck, the
    murderous buckshot and the bullets,
All these I feel or am.

I am the hounded slave, I wince at the bite of the dogs,
Hell and despair are upon me, crack and again crack the
    marksmen,
I clutch the rails of the fence, my gore dribs, thinn'd with the
    ooze of my skin,
840   I fall on the weeds and stones,
The riders spur their unwilling horses, haul close,
Taunt my dizzy ears and beat me violently over the head with
    whip-stocks.

Agonies are one of my changes of garments,
I do not ask the wounded person how he feels, I myself
    become the wounded person,
845   My hurts turn livid upon me as I lean on a cane and observe.

I am the mash'd fireman with breast-bone broken,
Tumbling walls buried me in their debris,
Heat and smoke I inspired, I heard the yelling shouts of my
    comrades,
I heard the distant click of their picks and shovels,
850   They have clear'd the beams away, they tenderly lift me forth.

I lie in the night air in my red shirt, the pervading hush is for
    my sake,
Painless after all I lie exhausted but not so unhappy,
White and beautiful are the faces around me, the heads are
    bared of their fire-caps,
The kneeling crowd fades with the light of the torches.

855   Distant and dead resuscitate,
They show as the dial or move as the hands of me, I am the
    clock myself.

I am an old artillerist, I tell of my fort's bombardment,
I am there again.

Again the long roll of the drummers,
860   Again the attacking cannon, mortars,
Again to my listening ears the cannon responsive.

I take part, I see and hear the whole,
The cries, curses, roar, the plaudits for well-aim'd shots,
The ambulanza[94] slowly passing trailing its red drip,
865   Workmen searching after damages, making indispensable
    repairs,
The fall of grenades through the rent roof, the fan-shaped
    explosion,
The whizz of limbs, heads, stone, wood, iron, high in the air.

Again gurgles the mouth of my dying general, he furiously
    waves with his hand,
He gasps through the clot *Mind not me—mind—the
entrenchments.*

34

870   Now I tell what I knew in Texas in my early youth,
      (I tell not the fall of Alamo,
      Not one escaped to tell the fall of Alamo,
      The hundred and fifty are dumb yet at Alamo,)
      'Tis the tale of the murder in cold blood of four hundred and
          twelve young men.

875   Retreating they had form'd in a hollow square with their
          baggage for breastworks,
      Nine hundred lives out of the surrounding enemy's, nine times
          their number, was the price they took in advance,
      Their colonel was wounded and their ammunition gone,
      They treated for an honorable capitulation, receiv'd writing
          and seal, gave up their arms and march'd back prisoners
          of war.

      They were the glory of the race of rangers,
880   Matchless with horse, rifle, song, supper, courtship,
      Large, turbulent, generous, handsome, proud, and affectionate,
      Bearded, sunburnt, drest in the free costume of hunters,
      Not a single one over thirty years of age.

      The second First-day morning they were brought out in squads
          and massacred, it was beautiful early summer.
885   The work commenced about five o'clock and was over by
          eight.

      None obey'd the command to kneel,
      Some made a mad and helpless rush, some stood stark and
          straight,
      A few fell at once, shot in the temple or heart, the living and
          dead lay together,
      The maim'd and mangled dug in the dirt, the new-comers saw
          them there,
890   Some half-kill'd attempted to crawl away,
      These were dispatch'd with bayonets or batter'd with the
          blunts of muskets,

A youth not seventeen years old seiz'd his assassin till two
    more came to release him,
The three were all torn and cover'd with the boy's blood.

At eleven o'clock began the burning of the bodies;
895   That is the tale of the murder of the four hundred and twelve
    young men.

35

Would you hear of an old-time sea-fight?
Would you learn who won by the light of the moon and stars?
List to the yarn, as my grandmother's father the sailor told it
    to me.

Our foe was no skulk in his ship I tell you, (said he,)
900   His was the surly English pluck, and there is no tougher or
    truer, and never was, and never will be;
Along the lower'd eve he came horribly raking us.

We closed with him, the yards entangled, the cannon touch'd,
My captain lash'd fast with his own hands.

We had receiv'd some eighteen pound shots under the water,
905   On our lower-gun-deck two large pieces had burst at the first
    fire, killing all around and blowing up overhead.

Fighting at sun-down, fighting at dark,
Ten o'clock at night, the full moon well up, our leaks on the
    gain, and five feet of water reported,
The master-at-arms loosing the prisoners confined in the after-
    hold to give them a chance for themselves.

The transit to and from the magazine is now stopt by the
    sentinels,
910   They see so many strange faces they do not know whom to
    trust.

Our frigate takes fire,
The other asks if we demand quarter?
If our colors are struck and the fighting done?

Now I laugh content, for I hear the voice of my little captain,
915   *We have not struck,* he composedly cries, *we have just begun
our part of the fighting.*

Only three guns are in use,
One is directed by the captain himself against the enemy's
main-mast,
Two well serv'd with grape and canister silence his musketry
and clear his decks.

The tops alone second the fire of this little battery, especially
the main-top,
920   They hold out bravely during the whole of the action.

Not a moment's cease,
The leaks gain fast on the pumps, the fire eats toward the
powder-magazine.

One of the pumps has been shot away, it is generally thought
we are sinking.

Serene stands the little captain,
925   He is not hurried, his voice is neither high nor low,
His eyes give more light to us than our battle-lanterns.

Toward twelve there in the beams of the moon they surrender
to us.

36

Stretch'd and still lies the midnight,
Two great hulls motionless on the breast of the darkness,
930   Our vessel riddled and slowly sinking, preparations to pass to
the one we have conquer'd,
The captain on the quarter-deck coldly giving his orders
through a countenance white as a sheet,
Near by the corpse of the child that serv'd in the cabin,
The dead face of an old salt with long white hair and carefully
curl'd whiskers,
The flames spite of all that can be done flickering aloft and
below,

935   The husky voices of the two or three officers yet fit for duty,
        Formless stacks of bodies and bodies by themselves, dabs of
             flesh upon the masts and spars,
        Cut of cordage, dangle of rigging, slight shock of the soothe of
             waves,
        Black and impassive guns, litter of power-parcels, strong scent,
        A few large stars overhead, silent and mournful shining,
940   Delicate sniffs of sea-breeze, smells of sedgy grass and fields by
             the shore, death-messages given in charge to survivors,
        The hiss of the surgeon's knife, the gnawing teeth of his saw,
        Wheeze, cluck, swash of falling blood, short wild scream, and
             long, dull, tapering groan,
        These so, these irretrievable.

        37

        You laggards there on guard! look to your arms!
945   In at the conquer'd doors they crowd! I am possess'd!
        Embody all presences outlaw'd or suffering,
        See myself in prison shaped like another man,
        And feel the dull unintermitted pain.

        For me the keepers of convicts shoulder their carbines and
             keep watch,
950   It is I let out in the morning and barr'd at night.

        Not a mutineer walks handcuff'd to jail but I am handcuff'd
             to him and walk by his side,
        (I am less the jolly one there, and more the silent one with
             sweat on my twitching lips.)

        Not a youngster is taken for larceny but I go up too, and am
             tried and sentenced.

        Not a cholera patient lies at the last gasp but I also lie at the
             last gasp,
955   My face is ash-color'd, my sinews gnarl, away from me people
             retreat.

        Askers embody themselves in me and I am embodied in them,
        I project my hat, sit shame-faced, and beg.

38

Enough! enough! enough!
Somehow I have been stunn'd. Stand back!
960 Give me a little time beyond my cuff'd head, slumbers, dreams,
    gaping,
I discover myself on the verge of a usual mistake.

That I could forget the mockers and insults!
That I could forget the trickling tears and the blows of the
    bludgeons and hammers!
That I could look with a separate look on my own crucifixion
    and bloody crowning.

965 I remember now,
I resume the overstaid fraction,
The grave of rock multiplies what has been confided to it, or
    to any graves,
Corpses rise, gashes heal, fastenings roll from me.

I troop forth replenish'd with supreme power, one of an
    average unending procession,
970 Inland and sea-coast we go, and pass all boundary lines,
Our swift ordinances on their way over the whole earth,
The blossoms we wear in our hats the growth of thousands of
    years.

Eleves,[95] I salute you! come forward!
Continue your annotations, continue your questionings.

39

975 The friendly and flowing savage, who is he?
Is he waiting for civilization, or past it and mastering it?

Is he some Southwesterner rais'd out-doors? is he Kanadian?
Is he from the Mississippi country? Iowa, Oregon, California?
The mountains? prairie-life, bush-life? or sailor from the sea?

•

980 Wherever he goes men and women accept and desire him,
They desire he should like them, touch them, speak to them,
    stay with them.

Behavior lawless as snow-flakes, words simple as grass,
    uncomb'd head, laughter, and naiveté,
Slow-stepping feet, common features, common modes and
    emanations,
They descend in new forms from the tips of his fingers,
985 They are wafted with the odor of his body or breath, they fly
    out of the glance of his eyes.

40

Flaunt of the sunshine I need not your bask—lie over!
You light surfaces only, I force surfaces and depths also.

Earth! you seem to look for something at my hands,
Say, old top-knot,[96] what do you want?

990 Man or woman, I might tell how I like you, but cannot,
And might tell what it is in me and what it is in you, but
    cannot,
And might tell that pining I have, that pulse of my nights and
    days.

Behold, I do not give lectures or a little charity,
When I give I give myself.

995 You there, impotent, loose in the knees,
Open your scarf'd chops[97] till I blow grit within you,
Spread your palms and lift the flaps of your pockets,
I am not to be denied, I compel, I have stores plenty and to spare,
And any thing I have I bestow.

1000 I do not ask who you are, that is not important to me,
You can do nothing and be nothing but what I will infold you.

To cotton-field drudge or cleaner of privies I lean,
On his right cheek I put the family kiss,
And in my soul I swear I never will deny him.

•

1005 On women fit for conception I start bigger and nimbler babes,
  (This day I am jetting the stuff of far more arrogant republics.)

  To any one dying, thither I speed and twist the knob of the
    door,
  Turn the bed-clothes toward the foot of the bed,
  Let the physician and the priest go home.

1010 I seize the descending man and raise him with resistless will,
  O despairer, here is my neck,
  By God, you shall not go down! hang your whole weight
    upon me.

  I dilate you with tremendous breath, I buoy you up,
  Every room of the house do I fill with an arm'd force,
1015 Lovers of me, bafflers of graves.

  Sleep—I and they keep guard all night,
  Not doubt, not decease shall dare to lay finger upon you,
  I have embraced you, and henceforth possess you to myself,
  And when you rise in the morning you will find what I tell
    you is so.

   41

1020 I am he bringing help for the sick as they pant on their backs,
  And for strong upright men I bring yet more needed help.

  I heard what was said of the universe,
  Heard it and heard it of several thousand years;
  It is middling well as far as it goes—but is that all?

1025 Magnifying and applying come I,
  Outbidding at the start the old cautious hucksters,
  Taking myself the exact dimensions of Jehovah,
  Lithographing Kronos,[98] Zeus his son, and Hercules his
    grandson,
  Buying drafts of Osiris, Isis, Belus, Brahma, Buddha,
1030 In my portfolio placing Manito loose, Allah on a leaf, the
    crucifix engraved,

With Odin and the hideous-faced Mexitli and every idol and
    image,
Taking them all for what they are worth and not a cent more,
Admitting they were alive and did the work of their days,
(They bore mites as for unfledg'd birds who have now to rise
    and fly and sing for themselves,)
1035   Accepting the rough deific sketches to fill out better in myself,
    bestowing them freely on each man and woman I see,
Discovering as much or more in a framer framing a house,
Putting higher claims for him there with his roll'd-up sleeves
    driving the mallet and chisel,
Not objecting to special revelations, considering a curl of
    smoke or a hair on the back of my hand just as curious as
    any revelation,
Lads ahold of fire-engines and hook-and-ladder ropes no less
    to me than the gods of the antique wars,
1040   Minding their voices peal through the crash of destruction,
Their brawny limbs passing safe over charr'd laths, their white
    foreheads whole and unhurt out of the flames;
By the mechanic's wife with her babe at her nipple interceding
    for every person born,
Three scythes at harvest whizzing in a row from three lusty
    angels with shirts bagg'd out at their waists,
The snag-tooth'd hostler with red hair redeeming sins past and
    to come,
1045   Selling all he possesses, traveling on foot to fee lawyers for his
    brother and sit by him while he is tried for forgery;
What was strewn in the amplest strewing the square rod about
    me, and not filling the square rod then,
The bull and the bug never worshipp'd half enough,
Dung and dirt more admirable than was dream'd,
The supernatural of no account, myself waiting my time to be
    one of the supremes,
1050   The day getting ready for me when I shall do as much good as
    the best, and be as prodigious;
By my life-lumps! becoming already a creator,
Putting myself here and now to the ambush'd womb of the
    shadows.

42

A call in the midst of the crowd,
My own voice, orotund sweeping and final.

1055 Come my children,
Come my boys and girls, my women, household and intimates,
Now the performer launches his nerve, he has pass'd his
    prelude on the reeds within.

Easily written loose-finger'd chords—I feel the thrum of your
    climax and close.

My head slues round on my neck,
1060 Music rolls, but not from the organ,
Folks are around me, but they are no household of mine.

Ever the hard unsunk ground,
Ever the eaters and drinkers, ever the upward and downward
    sun, ever the air and the ceaseless tides,
Ever myself and my neighbors, refreshing, wicked, real,
1065 Ever the old inexplicable query, ever that thorn'd thumb, that
    breath of itches and thirsts,
Ever the vexer's *hoot! hoot!* till we find where the sly one
    hides and bring him forth,
Ever love, ever the sobbing liquid of life,
Ever the bandage under the chin, ever the trestles of death.

Here and there with dimes on the eyes walking,
1070 To feed the greed of the belly the brains liberally spooning,
Tickets buying, taking, selling, but in to the feast never once
    going,
Many sweating, ploughing, thrashing, and then the chaff for
    payment receiving,
A few idly owning, and they the wheat continually claiming.

This is the city and I am one of the citizens,
1075 Whatever interests the rest interests me, politics, wars, markets,
    newspapers, schools,
The mayor and councils, banks, tariffs, steamships, factories,
    stocks, stores, real estate and personal estate.

•

The little plentiful manikins skipping around in collars and
    tail'd coats,
I am aware who they are, (they are positively not worms or
    fleas,)
I acknowledge the duplicates of myself, the weakest and
    shallowest is deathless with me,
1080   What I do and the same waits for them,
Every thought that flounders in me the same flounders in them.

I know perfectly well my own egotism,
Know my omnivorous lines and must not write any less,
And would fetch you whoever you are flush with myself.

1085   Not words of routine this song of mine,
But abruptly to question, to leap beyond yet nearer bring;
This printed and bound book—but the printer and the
    printing-office boy?
The well-taken photographs—but your wife or friend close
    and solid in your arms?
The black ship mail'd with iron, her mighty guns in her turrets
    —but the pluck of the captain and engineers?
1090   In the houses the dishes and fare and furniture—but the host
    and hostess, and the look out of their eyes?
The sky up there—yet here or next door, or across the way?
The saints and sages in history—but you yourself?
Sermons, creeds, theology—but the fathomless human brain,
And what is reason? and what is love? and what is life?

43

1095   I do not despise you priests, all time, the world over,
My faith is the greatest of faiths and the least of faiths,
Enclosing worship ancient and modern and all between ancient
    and modern,
Believing I shall come again upon the earth after five thousand
    years,
Waiting responses from oracles, honoring the gods, saluting
    the sun,
1100   Making a fetich of the first rock or stump, powowing with
    sticks in the circle of obis,[99]

Helping the lama or brahmin as he trims the lamps of the
    idols,
Dancing yet through the streets in a phallic procession, rapt
    and austere in the woods a gymnosophist,
Drinking mead from the skull-cup, to Shastas[100] and Vedas
    admirant, minding the Koran,
Walking the teokallis,[101] spotted with gore from the stone and
    knife, beating the serpent-skin drum,
1105   Accepting the Gospels, accepting him that was crucified,
    knowing assuredly that he is divine,
To the mass kneeling or the puritan's prayer rising, or sitting
    patiently in a pew,
Ranting and frothing in my insane crisis, or waiting dead-like
    till my spirit arouses me,
Looking forth on pavement and land, or outside of pavement
    and land,
Belonging to the winders of the circuit of circuits.

1110   One of that centripetal and centrifugal gang I turn and talk
    like a man leaving charges before a journey.

Down-hearted doubters dull and excluded,
Frivolous, sullen, moping, angry, affected, dishearten'd,
    atheistical,
I know every one of you, I know the sea of torment, doubt,
    despair and unbelief.

How the flukes splash!
1115   How they contort rapid as lightning, with spasms and spouts
    of blood!

Be at peace bloody flukes of doubters and sullen mopers,
I take my place among you as much as among any,
The past is the push of you, me, all, precisely the same,
And what is yet untried and afterward is for you, me, all,
    precisely the same.

1120   I do not know what is untried and afterward,
    But I know it will in its turn prove sufficient, and cannot fail.

·

Each who passes is consider'd, each who stops is consider'd,
  not a single one can it fail.

It cannot fail the young man who died and was buried,
Nor the young woman who died and was put by his side,
1125 Nor the little child that peep'd in at the door, and then drew
  back and was never seen again,
Nor the old man who has lived without purpose, and feels it
  with bitterness worse than gall,
Nor him in the poor house tubercled by rum and the bad
  disorder,
Nor the numberless slaughter'd and wreck'd, nor the brutish
  koboo[102] call'd the ordure of humanity,
Nor the sacs merely floating with open mouths for food to
  slip in,
1130 Nor any thing in the earth, or down in the oldest graves of the
  earth,
Nor any thing in the myriads of spheres, nor the myriads of
  myriads that inhabit them,
Nor the present, nor the least wisp that is known.

    44

It is time to explain myself—let us stand up.

What is known I strip away,
1135 I launch all men and women forward with me into the
  Unknown.

The clock indicates the moment—but what does eternity
  indicate?

We have thus far exhausted trillions of winters and summers,
There are trillions ahead, and trillions ahead of them.

Births have brought us richness and variety,
1140 And other births will bring us richness and variety.

I do not call one greater and one smaller,
That which fills its period and place is equal to any.

Were mankind murderous or jealous upon you, my brother,
    my sister?
I am sorry for you, they are not murderous or jealous
    upon me,
1145   All has been gentle with me, I keep no account with
    lamentation,
(What have I to do with lamentation?)

I am an acme of things accomplish'd, and I an encloser of
    things to be.

My feet strike an apex of the apices of the stairs,
On every step bunches of ages, and larger bunches between the
    steps,
1150   All below duly travel'd, and still I mount and mount.

Rise after rise bow the phantoms behind me,
Afar down I see the huge first Nothing, I know I was even
    there,
I waited unseen and always, and slept through the lethargic
    mist,
And took my time, and took no hurt from the fetid carbon.

1155   Long I was hugg'd close—long and long.

Immense have been the preparations for me,
Faithful and friendly the arms that have help'd me.

Cycles ferried my cradle, rowing and rowing like cheerful
    boatmen,
For room to me stars kept aside in their own rings,
1160   They sent influences to look after what was to hold me.

Before I was born out of my mother generations guided me,
My embryo has never been torpid, nothing could overlay it.

For it the nebula cohered to an orb,
The long slow strata piled to rest it on,
1165   Vast vegetables gave it sustenance,
Monstrous sauroids[103] transported it in their mouths and
    deposited it with care.

All forces have been steadily employ'd to complete and
    delight me,
Now on this spot I stand with my robust soul.

45

O span of youth! ever-push'd elasticity!
1170   O manhood, balanced, florid and full.

My lovers suffocate me,
Crowding my lips, thick in the pores of my skin,
Jostling me through streets and public halls, coming naked to
    me at night,
Crying by day *Ahoy!* from the rocks of the river, swinging and
    chirping over my head,
1175   Calling my name from flower-beds, vines, tangled underbrush,
Lighting on every moment of my life,
Bussing my body with soft balsamic busses,
Noiselessly passing handfuls out of their hearts and giving
    them to be mine.

Old age superbly rising! O welcome, ineffable grace of dying
    days!

1180   Every condition promulges[104] not only itself, it promulges what
    grows after and out of itself,
And the dark hush promulges as much as any.

I open my scuttle at night and see the far-sprinkled systems,
And all I see multiplied as high as I can cipher edge but the
    rim of the farther systems.

Wider and wider they spread, expanding, always expanding,
1185   Outward and outward and forever outward.

My sun has his sun and round him obediently wheels,
He joins with his partners a group of superior circuit,
And greater sets follow, making specks of the greatest inside
    them.

•

There is no stoppage and never can be stoppage,
1190   If I, you, and the worlds, and all beneath or upon their
     surfaces, were this moment reduced back to a pallid float, it
     would not avail in the long run,
We should surely bring up again where we now stand,
And surely go as much farther, and then farther and farther.

A few quadrillions of eras, a few octillions of cubic leagues, do
     not hazard the span or make it impatient,
They are but parts, any thing is but a part.

1195   See ever so far, there is limitless space outside of that,
Count ever so much, there is limitless time around that.

My rendezvous is appointed, it is certain,
The Lord will be there and wait till I come on perfect terms,
The great Camerado, the lover true for whom I pine will be there.

46

1200   I know I have the best of time and space, and was never
     measured and never will be measured.

I tramp a perpetual journey, (come listen all!)
My signs are a rain-proof coat, good shoes, and a staff cut
     from the woods,
No friend of mine takes his ease in my chair,
I have no chair, no church, no philosophy,
1205   I lead no man to a dinner-table, library, exchange,
But each man and each woman of you I lead upon a knoll,
My left hand hooking you round the waist,
My right hand pointing to landscapes of continents and the
     public road.

Not I, not any one else can travel that road for you,
1210   You must travel it for yourself.

It is not far, it is within reach,
Perhaps you have been on it since you were born and did not
     know,
Perhaps it is everywhere on water and on land.

                 •

Shoulder your duds dear son, and I will mine, and let us
    hasten forth,
1215   Wonderful cities and free nations we shall fetch as we go.

If you tire, give me both burdens, and rest the chuff[105] of your
    hand on my hip,
And in due time you shall repay the same service to me,
For after we start we never lie by again.

This day before dawn I ascended a hill and look'd at the
    crowded heaven,
1220   And I said to my spirit *When we become the enfolders of*
    those orbs, and the pleasure and knowledge of every thing
    in them, shall we be fill'd and satisfied then?
And my spirit said *No, we but level that lift to pass and*
    continue beyond.

You are also asking me questions and I hear you,
I answer that I cannot answer, you must find out for yourself.

Sit a while dear son,
1225   Here are biscuits to eat and here is milk to drink,
But as soon as you sleep and renew yourself in sweet clothes, I
    kiss you with a good-by kiss and open the gate for your
    egress hence.

Long enough have you dream'd contemptible dreams,
Now I wash the gum from your eyes,
You must habit yourself to the dazzle of the light and of every
    moment of your life.

1230   Long have you timidly waded holding a plank by the shore,
Now I will you to be a bold swimmer,
To jump off in the midst of the sea, rise again, nod to me,
    shout, and laughingly dash with your hair.

47

I am the teacher of athletes,
He that by me spreads a wider breast than my own proves the
       width of my own,
1235   He most honors my style who learns under it to destroy the
       teacher.

The boy I love, the same becomes a man not through derived
       power, but in his own right,
Wicked rather than virtuous out of conformity or fear,
Fond of his sweetheart, relishing well his steak,
Unrequited love or a slight cutting him worse than sharp steel
       cuts,
1240   First-rate to ride, to fight, to hit the bull's eye, to sail a skiff,
       to sing a song or play on the banjo,
Preferring scars and the beard and faces pitted with small-pox
       over all latherers,
And those well-tann'd to those that keep out of the sun.

I teach straying from me, yet who can stray from me?
I follow you whoever you are from the present hour,
1245   My words itch at your ears till you understand them.

I do not say these things for a dollar or to fill up the time
       while I wait for a boat,
(It is you talking just as much as myself, I act as the tongue
       of you,
Tied in your mouth, in mine it begins to be loosen'd.)

I swear I will never again mention love or death inside a
       house,
1250   And I swear I will never translate myself at all, only to him or
       her who privately stays with me in the open air.

If you would understand me go to the heights or water-shore,
The nearest gnat is an explanation, and a drop or motion of
       waves a key,
The maul, the oar, the hand-saw, second my words.

                              •

No shutter'd room or school can commune with me,
1255   But roughs and little children better than they.

The young mechanic is closest to me, he knows me well,
The woodman that takes his axe and jug with him shall take
       me with him all day,
The farm-boy ploughing in the field feels good at the sound of
       my voice,
In vessels that sail my words sail, I go with fishermen and
       seamen and love them.

1260   The soldier camp'd or upon the march is mine,
On the night ere the pending battle many seek me, and I do
       not fail them,
On that solemn night (it may be their last) those that know me
       seek me.

My face rubs to the hunter's face when he lies down alone in
       his blanket,
The driver thinking of me does not mind the jolt of his wagon,
1265   The young mother and old mother comprehend me,
The girl and the wife rest the needle a moment and forget
       where they are,
They and all would resume what I have told them.

48

I have said that the soul is not more than the body,
And I have said that the body is not more than the soul,
1270   And nothing, not God, is greater to one than one's self is,
And whoever walks a furlong without sympathy walks to his
       own funeral drest in his shroud,
And I or you pocketless of a dime may purchase the pick of
       the earth,
And to glance with an eye or show a bean in its pod
       confounds the learning of all times,
And there is no trade or employment but the young man
       following it may become a hero,
1275   And there is no object so soft but it makes a hub for the
       wheel'd universe,

And I say to any man or woman, Let your soul stand cool and
composed before a million universes.

And I say to mankind, Be not curious about God,
For I who am curious about each am not curious about God,
(No array of terms can say how much I am at peace about
God and about death.)

1280   I hear and behold God in every object, yet understand God
not in the least,
Nor do I understand who there can be more wonderful than
myself.

Why should I wish to see God better than this day?
I see something of God each hour of the twenty-four, and each
moment then,
In the faces of men and women I see God, and in my own face
in the glass,
1285   I find letters from God dropt in the street, and every one is
sign'd by God's name,
And I leave them where they are, for I know that wheresoe'er
I go,
Others will punctually come for ever and ever.

49

And as to you Death, and you bitter hug of mortality, it is idle
to try to alarm me.

To his work without flinching the accoucheur[106] comes,
1290   I see the elder-hand pressing receiving supporting,
I recline by the sills of the exquisite flexible doors,
And mark the outlet, and mark the relief and escape.

And as to you Corpse I think you are good manure, but that
does not offend me,
I smell the white roses sweet-scented and growing,
1295   I reach to the leafy lips, I reach to the polish'd breasts of
melons.

And as to you Life I reckon you are the leavings of many
    deaths,
(No doubt I have died myself ten thousand times before.)

I hear you whispering there O stars of heaven,
O suns—O grass of graves—O perpetual transfers and
    promotions,
1300   If you do not say any thing how can I say any thing?

Of the turbid pool that lies in the autumn forest,
Of the moon that descends the steeps of the soughing twilight,
Toss, sparkles of day and dusk—toss on the black stems that
    decay in the muck,
Toss to the moaning gibberish of the dry limbs.

1305   I ascend from the moon, I ascend from the night,
I perceive that the ghastly glimmer is noonday sunbeams
    reflected,
And debouch to the steady and central from the offspring
    great or small.

50

There is that in me—I do not know what it is—but I know it
    is in me.

Wrench'd and sweaty —calm and cool then my body becomes,
1310   I sleep—I sleep long.

I do not know it—it is without name—it is a word unsaid,
It is not in any dictionary, utterance, symbol.

Something it swings on more than the earth I swing on,
To it the creation is the friend whose embracing awakes me.

1315   Perhaps I might tell more. Outlines! I plead for my brothers
    and sisters.

Do you see O my brothers and sisters?
It is not chaos or death—it is form, union, plan—it is eternal
    life—it is Happiness.

51

The past and present wilt—I have fill'd them, emptied them,
And proceed to fill my next fold of the future.

1320 Listener up there! what have you to confide to me?
Look in my face while I snuff the sidle of evening,
(Talk honestly, no one else hears you, and I stay only a minute
    longer.)

Do I contradict myself?
Very well then I contradict myself,
1325 (I am large, I contain multitudes.)

I concentrate toward them that are nigh, I wait on the door-
    slab.

Who has done his day's work? who will soonest be through
    with his supper?
Who wishes to walk with me?

Will you speak before I am gone? will you prove already too
    late?

52

1330 The spotted hawk swoops by and accuses me, he complains of
    my gab and my loitering.

I too am not a bit tamed, I too am untranslatable,
I sound my barbaric yawp over the roofs of the world.

The last scud of day holds back for me,
It flings my likeness after the rest and true as any on the
    shadow'd wilds,
1335 It coaxes me to the vapor and the dusk.

I depart as air, I shake my white locks at the runaway sun,
I effuse my flesh in eddies, and drift it in lacy jags.

·

I bequeath myself to the dirt to grow from the grass I love,
If you want me again look for me under your boot-soles.

1340 You will hardly know who I am or what I mean,
But I shall be good health to you nevertheless,
And filter and fibre your blood.

Failing to fetch me at first keep encouraged,
Missing me one place search another,
1345 I stop somewhere waiting for you.

                                           1855

CROSSING BROOKLYN FERRY

1

Flood-tide below me! I see you face to face!
Clouds of the west—sun there half an hour high—I see you
    also face to face.

Crowds of men and women attired in the usual costumes, how
    curious you are to me!
On the ferry-boats the hundreds and hundreds that cross,
    returning home, are more curious to me than you suppose,
5   And you that shall cross from shore to shore years hence are
    more to me, and more in my meditations, than you might
    suppose.

2

The impalpable sustenance of me from all things at all hours
    of the day,
The simple, compact, well-join'd scheme, myself disintegrated,
    every one disintegrated yet part of the scheme,
The similitudes of the past and those of the future,
The glories strung like beads on my smallest sights and
    hearings, on the walk in the street and the passage over the
    river,

10   The current rushing so swiftly and swimming with me far
            away,
        The others that are to follow me, the ties between me and
            them,
        The certainty of others, the life, love, sight, hearing of others.

        Others will enter the gates of the ferry and cross from shore to
            shore,
        Others will watch the run of the flood-tide,
15   Others will see the shipping of Manhattan north and west, and
            the heights of Brooklyn to the south and east,
        Others will see the islands large and small;
        Fifty years hence, others will see them as they cross, the sun
            half an hour high,
        A hundred years hence, or ever so many hundred years hence,
            others will see them,
        Will enjoy the sunset, the pouring-in of the flood-tide, the
            falling-back to the sea of the ebb-tide.

        3

20   It avails not, time nor place—distance avails not,
        I am with you, you men and women of a generation, or ever
            so many generations hence,
        Just as you feel when you look on the river and sky, so I felt,
        Just as any of you is one of a living crowd, I was one of a
            crowd,
        Just as you are refresh'd by the gladness of the river and the
            bright flow, I was refresh'd,
25   Just as you stand and lean on the rail, yet hurry with the swift
            current, I stood yet was hurried,
        Just as you look on the numberless masts of ships and the
            thickstemm'd pipes of steamboats, I look'd.

        I too many and many a time cross'd the river of old,
        Watched the Twelfth-month sea-gulls, saw them high in the air
            floating with motionless wings, oscillating their bodies,
        Saw how the glistening yellow lit up parts of their bodies and
            left the rest in strong shadow,
30   Saw the slow-wheeling circles and the gradual edging toward
            the south,

Saw the reflection of the summer sky in the water,
Had my eyes dazzled by the shimmering track of beams,
Look'd at the fine centrifugal spokes of light round the shape
    of my head in the sunlit water,
Look'd on the haze on the hills southward and south-
    westward,
35   Look'd on the vapor as it flew in fleeces tinged with violet,
Look'd toward the lower bay to notice the vessels arriving,
Saw their approach, saw aboard those that were near me,
Saw the white sails of schooners and sloops, saw the ships at
    anchor,
The sailors at work in the rigging or out astride the spars,
40   The round masts, the swinging motion of the hulls, the slender
    serpentine pennants,
The large and small steamers in motion, the pilots in their
    pilothouses,
The white wake left by the passage, the quick tremulous whirl
    of the wheels,
The flags of all nations, the falling of them at sunset,
The scallop-edged waves in the twilight, the ladled cups, the
    frolicsome crests and glistening,
45   The stretch afar growing dimmer and dimmer, the gray walls
    of the granite storehouses by the docks,
On the river the shadowy group, the big steam-tug closely
    flank'd on each side by the barges, the hay-boat, the belated
    lighter,
On the neighboring shore the fires from the foundry chimneys
    burning high and glaringly into the night,
Casting their flicker of black contrasted with wild red and
    yellow light over the tops of houses, and down into the
    clefts of streets.

4

These and all else were to me the same as they are to you,
50   I loved well those cities, loved well the stately and rapid river,
The men and women I saw were all near to me,
Others the same—others who look back on me because I
    look'd forward to them,
(The time will come, though I stop here to-day and to-night.)

Connection'- timelessness, eternity

5

What is it then between us?
55   What is the count of the scores or hundreds of years
         between us?

Whatever it is, it avails not—distance avails not, and place
    avails not,
I too lived, Brooklyn of ample hills was mine,
I too walk'd the streets of Manhattan island, and bathed in the
    waters around it,
I too felt the curious abrupt questionings stir within me,
60   In the day among crowds of people sometimes they came
         upon me,
In my walks home late at night or as I lay in my bed they
    came upon me,
I too had been struck from the float forever held in solution,
I too had receiv'd identity by my body,
That I was I knew was of my body, and what I should be I
    knew I should be of my body.

Eins berg ?

6

65   It is not upon you alone the dark patches fall,
The dark threw its patches down upon me also,
The best I had done seem'd to me blank and suspicious,
My great thoughts as I supposed them, were they not in reality
    meagre?
Nor is it you alone who know what it is to be evil,
70   I am he who knew what it was to be evil,
I too knitted the old knot of contrariety,
Blabb'd, blush'd, resented, lied, stole, grudg'd,
Had guile, anger, lust, hot wishes I dared not speak,
Was wayward, vain, greedy, shallow, sly, cowardly, malignant,
75   The wolf, the snake, the hog, not wanting in me,
The cheating look, the frivolous word, the adulterous wish,
    not wanting,
Refusals, hates, postponements, meanness, laziness, none of
    these wanting,
Was one with the rest, the days and haps of the rest,

Was call'd by my nighest name by clear loud voices of young
    men as they saw me approaching or passing,
80   Felt their arms on my neck as I stood, or the negligent leaning
    of their flesh against me as I sat,
Saw many I loved in the street or ferry-boat or public
    assembly, yet never told them a word,
Lived the same life with the rest, the same old laughing,
    gnawing, sleeping,
Play'd the part that still looks back on the actor or actress,
The same old role, the role that is what we make it, as great
    as we like,
85   Or as small as we like, or both great and small.

    7

Closer yet I approach you,
What thought you have of me now, I had as much of you—I
    laid in my stores in advance,
I consider'd long and seriously of you before you were born.

Who was to know what should come home to me?
90   Who knows but I am enjoying this?
Who knows, for all the distance, but I am as good as looking
    at you now, for all you cannot see me?

    8

Ah, what can ever be more stately and admirable to me than
    mast-hemm'd Manhattan?
River and sunset and scallop-edg'd waves of flood-tide?
The sea-gulls oscillating their bodies, the hay-boat in the
    twilight, and the belated lighter?

95   What gods can exceed these that clasp me by the hand, and
    with voices I love call me promptly and loudly by my
    nighest name as I approach?
What is more subtle than this which ties me to the woman or
    man that looks in my face?
Which fuses me into you now, and pours my meaning
    into you?

•

We understand then do we not? *I don't.*
What I promis'd without mentioning it, have you not
   accepted?
100   What the study could not teach—what the preaching could
   not accomplish'd is accomplish'd, is it not? *What is?*

   9   *playstime!*

Flow on, river! flow with the flood-tide, and ebb with the ebb-
   tide!
Frolic on, crested and scallop-edg'd waves!
Gorgeous clouds of the sunset! drench with your splendor me,
   or the men and women generations after me!
Cross from shore to shore, countless crowds of passengers!
105   Stand up, tall masts of Mannahatta! stand up, beautiful hills of
   Brooklyn!
Throb, baffled and curious brain! throw out questions and
   answers!
Suspend here and everywhere, eternal float of solution!
Gaze, loving and thirsting eyes, in the house or street or public
   assembly!
Sound out, voices of young men! loudly and musically call me
   by my nighest name!
110   Live, old life! play the part that looks back on the actor or
   actress!
Play the old role, the role that is great or small according as
   one makes it!
Consider, you who peruse me, whether I may not in unknown
   ways be looking upon you;
Be firm, rail over the river, to support those who lean idly, yet
   haste with the hasting current;
Fly on, sea-birds! fly sideways, or wheel in large circles high in
   the air;
115   Receive the summer sky, you water, and faithfully hold it till
   all down-cast eyes have time to take it from you!
Diverge, fine spokes of light, from the shape of my head, or
   any one's head, in the sunlit water!
Come on, ships from the lower bay! pass up or down, white-
   sail'd schooners, sloops, lighters!
Flaunt away, flags of all nations! be duly lower'd at sunset!
Burn high your fires, foundry chimneys! cast black shadows at

nightfall! cast red and yellow light over the tops of the
   houses!
120 Appearances, new or henceforth, indicate what you are,
You necessary film, continue to envelop the soul,
About my body for me, and your body for you, be hung our
   divinest aromas,
Thrive, cities—bring your freight, bring your shows, ample
   and sufficient rivers,
Expand, being than which none else is perhaps more spiritual,
125 Keep your places, objects than which none else is more lasting.

You have waited, you always wait, you dumb, beautiful
   ministers,
We receive you with free sense at last, and are insatiate
   henceforward,
Not you any more shall be able to foil us, or withhold
   yourselves from us,
We use you, and do not cast you aside—we plant you
   permanently within us,
130 We fathom you not—we love you—there is perfection in you
   also,
You furnish your parts toward eternity,
Great or small, you furnish your parts toward the soul.

                                             1856

OUT OF THE CRADLE ENDLESSLY ROCKING

Out of the cradle endlessly rocking,
Out of the mocking-bird's throat, the musical shuttle,
Out of the Ninth-month[107] midnight,
Over the sterile sands and the fields beyond, where the child
   leaving his bed wander'd alone, bareheaded, barefoot,
5 Down from the shower'd halo,
Up from the mystic play of shadows twining and twisting as if
   they were alive,
Out from the patches of briers and blackberries,
From the memories of the bird that chanted to me,
From your memories sad brother, from the fitful risings and
   fallings I heard,

10   From under that yellow half-moon late-risen and swollen as if
            with tears,
        From those beginning notes of yearning and love there in the
            mist,
        From the thousand responses of my heart never to cease,
        From the myriad thence-arous'd words,
        From the word stronger and more delicious than any,
15   From such as now they start the scene revisiting,
        As a flock, twittering, rising, or overhead passing,
        Borne hither, ere all eludes me, hurriedly,
        A man, yet by these tears a little boy again,
        Throwing myself on the sand, confronting the waves,
20   I, chanter of pains and joys, uniter of here and hereafter,
        Taking all hints to use them, but swiftly leaping beyond them,
        A reminiscence sing.

        Once Paumanok,[108]
        When the lilac-scent was in the air and Fifth-month grass was
            growing,
25   Up this seashore in some briers,
        Two feather'd guests from Alabama, two together,
        And their nest, and four light-green eggs spotted with brown,
        And every day the he-bird to and fro near at hand,
        And every day the she-bird crouch'd on her nest, silent, with
            bright eyes,
30   And every day I, a curious boy, never too close, never
            disturbing them,
        Cautiously peering, absorbing, translating.

        Shine! shine! shine!
        Pour down your warmth, great sun!
        While we bask, we two together.

35   *Two together!*
        Winds blow south, or winds blow north,
        Day come white, or night come black,
        Home, or rivers and mountains from home,
        Singing all time, minding no time,
40   *While we two keep together.*

                        •

Till of a sudden,
May-be kill'd, unknown to her mate,
One forenoon the she-bird crouch'd not on the nest,
Nor return'd that afternoon, nor the next,
45   Nor ever appear'd again.

And thenceforward all summer in the sound of the sea,
And at night under the full of the moon in calmer weather,
Over the hoarse surging of the sea,
Or flitting from brier to brier by day,
50   I saw, I heard at intervals the remaining one, the he-bird,
The solitary guest from Alabama.

Blow! blow! blow!
Blow up sea-winds along Paumanok's shore;
I wait and I wait till you blow my mate to me.

55   Yes, when the stars glisten'd,
All night long on the prong of a moss-scallop'd stake,
Down almost amid the slapping waves,
Sat the lone singer wonderful causing tears.

He call'd on his mate,
60   He pour'd forth the meanings which I of all men know.

Yes my brother I know,
The rest might not, but I have treasur'd every note,
For more than once dimly down to the beach gliding,
Silent, avoiding the moonbeams, blending myself with the
    shadows,
65   Recalling now the obscure shapes, the echoes, the sounds and
    sights after their sorts,
The white arms out in the breakers tirelessly tossing,
I, with bare feet, a child, the wind wafting my hair,
Listen'd long and long.

Listen'd to keep, to sing, now translating the notes,
70   Following you my brother.

Soothe! soothe! soothe!
Close on its wave soothes the wave behind,

And again another behind embracing and lapping, every one
   close,
But my love soothes not me, not me.

75 Low hangs the moon, it rose late,
It is lagging—O I think it is heavy with love, with love.

O madly the sea pushes upon the land,
With love, with love.

O night! do I not see my love fluttering out among the
   breakers?
80 What is that little black thing I see there in the white?

Loud! loud! loud!
Loud I call to you, my love!

High and clear I shoot my voice over the waves,
Surely you must know who is here, is here,
85 You must know who I am, my love.

Low-hanging moon!
What is that dusky spot in your brown yellow?
O it is the shape, the shape of my mate!
O moon do not keep her from me any longer.

90 Land! land! O land!
Whichever way I turn, O I think you could give me my mate
   back again if you only would,
For I am almost sure I see her dimly whichever way I look.

O rising stars!
Perhaps the one I want so much will rise, will rise with some
   of you.

95 O throat! O trembling throat!
Sound clearer through the atmosphere!
Pierce the woods, the earth,
Somewhere listening to catch you must be the one I want.

•

Shake out carols!
100   Solitary here, the night's carols!
Carols of lonesome love! death's carols!
Carols under that lagging, yellow, waning moon!
O under that moon where she droops almost down into
    the sea!
O reckless despairing carols.

105   But soft! sink low!
Soft! let me just murmur,
And do you wait a moment you husky-nois'd sea,
For somewhere I believe I heard my mate responding to me,
So faint, I must be still, be still to listen,
110   But not altogether still, for then she might not come
    immediately to me.

Hither my love!
Here I am! here!
With this just-sustain'd note, I announce myself to you,
This gentle call is for you my love, for you.

115   Do not be decoy'd elsewhere,
That is the whistle of the wind, it is not my voice,
That is the fluttering of the spray,
Those are the shadows of leaves.

O darkness! O in vain!
120   O I am very sick and sorrowful.

O brown halo in the sky near the moon, drooping upon the
    sea!
O troubled reflection in the sea!
O throat! O throbbing heart!
And I singing uselessly, uselessly all the night.

125   O past! O happy life! O songs of joy!
In the air, in the woods, over fields,
Loved! loved! loved! loved! loved!
But my mate no more, no more with me!
We two together no more.

130 The aria sinking,
     All else continuing, the stars shining,
     The winds blowing, the notes of the bird continuous echoing,
     On the sands of Paumanok's shore gray and rustling,
     The yellow half-moon enlarged, sagging down, drooping, the
          face of the sea almost touching,
135 The boy ecstatic, with his bare feet the waves, with his hair
          the atmosphere dallying,
     The love in the heart long pent, now loose, now at last
          tumultuously bursting,
     The aria's meaning, the ears, the soul, swiftly depositing,
     The strange tears down the cheeks coursing,
     The colloquy there, the trio, each uttering,
140 The undertone, the savage old mother incessantly crying,
     To the boy's soul's questions sullenly timing, some drown'd
          secret hissing,
     To the outsetting bard.

     Demon or bird! (said the boy's soul,)
     Is it indeed toward your mate you sing? or is it really to me?
145 For I, that was a child, my tongue's use sleeping, now I have
          heard you,
     Now in a moment I know what I am for, I awake,
     And already a thousand singers, a thousand songs, clearer,
          louder and more sorrowful than yours,
     A thousand warbling echoes have started to life within me,
          never to die.

     O you singer solitary, singing by yourself, projecting me,
150 O solitary me listening, never more shall I cease
          perpetuating you,
     Never more shall I escape, never more the reverberations,
     Never more the cries of unsatisfied love be absent from me,
     Never again leave me to be the peaceful child I was before
          what there in the night,
     By the sea under the yellow and sagging moon,
155 The messenger there arous'd, the fire, the sweet hell within,
     The unknown want, the destiny of me.

     O give me the clew! (it lurks in the night here somewhere,)
     O if I am to have so much, let me have more!

A word then, (for I will conquer it,)
160 The word final, superior to all,
Subtle, sent up—what is it?—I listen;
Are you whispering it, and have been all the time, you sea-
    waves?
Is that it from your liquid rims and wet sands?

Whereto answering, the sea,
165 Delaying not, hurrying not,
Whisper'd me through the night, and very plainly before
    daybreak,
Lisp'd to me the low and delicious word death,
And again death, death, death, death,
Hissing melodious, neither like the bird nor like my arous'd
    child's heart,
170 But edging near as privately for me rustling at my feet,
Creeping thence steadily up to my ears and laving me softly all
    over,
Death, death, death, death, death.

Which I do not forget,
But fuse the song of my dusky demon and brother,
175 That he sang to me in the moonlight on Paumanok's gray
    beach,
With the thousand responsive songs at random,
My own songs awaked from that hour,
And with them the key, the word up from the waves,
The word of the sweetest song and all songs,
180 That strong and delicious word which, creeping to my feet,
(Or like some old crone rocking the cradle, swathed in sweet
    garments, bending aside,)
The sea whisper'd me.

            1860

I SAW IN LOUISIANA A LIVE-OAK GROWING

I saw in Louisiana a live-oak growing,
All alone stood it and the moss hung down from the branches,
Without any companion it grew there uttering joyous leaves of
    dark green,
And its look, rude, unbending, lusty, made me think of myself,
But I wonder'd how it could utter joyous leaves standing alone
    there without its friend near, for I knew I could not,
And I broke off a twig with a certain number of leaves upon
    it, and twined around it a little moss,
And brought it away, and I have placed it in sight in my
    room,
It is not needed to remind me as of my own dear friends,
(For I believe lately I think of little else than of them,)
Yet it remains to me a curious token, it makes me think of
    manly love;
For all that, and though the live-oak glistens there in Louisiana
    solitary in a wide flat space,
Uttering joyous leaves all its life without a friend a lover near,
I know very well I could not.

                        1860

CAVALRY CROSSING A FORD

A line in long array where they wind betwixt green islands,
They take a serpentine course, their arms flash in the sun—
    hark to the musical clank,
Behold the silvery river, in it the splashing horses loitering stop
    to drink,
Behold the brown-faced men, each group, each person a
    picture, the negligent rest on the saddles,
Some emerge on the opposite bank, others are just entering the
    ford—while,
Scarlet and blue and snowy white,
The guidon flags flutter gayly in the wind.

                        1865

BEAT! BEAT! DRUMS!

Beat! beat! drums!—blow! bugles! blow!
Through the windows—through doors—burst like a ruthless
    force,
Into the solemn church, and scatter the congregation,
Into the school where the scholar is studying;
5 Leave not the bridegroom quiet—no happiness must he have
    now with his bride,
Nor the peaceful farmer any peace, ploughing his field or
    gathering his grain,
So fierce you whirr and pound you drums—so shrill you
    bugles blow.

Beat! beat! drums!—blow! bugles! blow!
Over the traffic of cities—over the rumble of wheels in the
    streets;
10 Are beds prepared for sleepers at night in the houses? no
    sleepers must sleep in those beds,
No bargainers' bargains by day—no brokers or speculators—
    would they continue?
Would the talkers be talking? would the singer attempt to
    sing?
Would the lawyer rise in the court to state his case before the
    judge?
Then rattle quicker, heavier drums—you bugles wilder blow.

15 Beat! beat! drums!—blow! bugles! blow!
Make no parley—stop for no expostulation,
Mind not the timid—mind not the weeper or prayer,
Mind not the old man beseeching the young man,
Let not the child's voice be heard, nor the mother's entreaties,
20 Make even the trestles to shake the dead where they lie
    awaiting the hearses,
So strong you thump O terrible drums—so loud you bugles
    blow.
            1865

AS I LAY WITH MY HEAD
IN YOUR LAP CAMERADO

As I lay with my head in your lap camerado,
The confession I made I resume, what I said to you and the
    open air I resume,
I know I am restless and make others so,
I know my works are weapons full of danger, full of death,
5 For I confront peace, security, and all the settled laws, to
    unsettle them,
I am more resolute because all have denied me than I could
    ever have been had all accepted me,
I heed not and have never heeded either experience, cautions,
    majorities, nor ridicule,
And the threat of what is call'd hell is little or nothing to me,
And the lure of what is call'd heaven is little or nothing to me;
10 Dear camerado! I confess I have urged you onward with me,
    and still urge you, without the least idea what is our
    destination,
Or whether we shall be victorious, or utterly quell'd and
    defeated.

1865

YEARS OF THE MODERN

Years of the modern! years of the unperform'd!
Your horizon rises, I see it parting away for more august
    dramas,
I see not America only, not only Liberty's nation but other
    nations preparing,
I see tremendous entrances and exits, new combinations, the
    solidarity of races,
5 I see that force advancing with irresistible power on the
    world's stage,
(Have the old forces, the old wars, played their parts? are the
    acts suitable to them closed?)
I see Freedom, completely arm'd and victorious and very
    haughty, with Law on one side and Peace on the other,
A stupendous trio all issuing forth against the idea of caste;

What historic denouements are these we so rapidly approach?
10 I see men marching and countermarching by swift millions,
I see the frontiers and boundaries of the old aristocracies
    broken,
I see the landmarks of European kings removed,
I see this day the People beginning their landmarks, (all others
    give way;)
Never were such sharp questions ask'd as this day,
15 Never was average man, his soul, more energetic, more like
    a God,
Lo, how he urges and urges, leaving the masses no rest!
His daring foot is on land and sea everywhere, he colonizes the
    Pacific, the archipelagoes,
With the steamship, the electric telegraph, the newspaper, the
    wholesale engines of war,
With these and the world-spreading factories he interlinks all
    geography, all lands;
20 What whispers are these O lands, running ahead of you,
    passing under the seas?
Are all nations communing? is there going to be but one heart
    to the globe?
Is humanity forming en-masse? for lo, tyrants tremble, crowns
    grow dim,
The earth, restive, confronts a new era, perhaps a general
    divine war,
No one knows what will happen next, such portents fill the
    days and nights;
25 Years prophetical! the space ahead as I walk, as I vainly try to
    pierce it, is full of phantoms,
Unborn deeds, things soon to be, project their shapes
    around me,
This incredible rush and heat, this strange ecstatic fever of
    dreams O years!
Your dreams O years, how they penetrate through me! (I
    know not whether I sleep or wake;)
The perform'd America and Europe grow dim, retiring in
    shadow behind me,
30 The unperform'd, more gigantic than ever, advance, advance
    upon me.

                1865

WHEN LILACS LAST IN THE DOORYARD BLOOM'D

1   *Lincoln*

When lilacs last in the dooryard bloom'd
And the great star early droop'd in the western sky in the
    night,
I mourn'd, and yet shall mourn with ever-returning spring.

Ever-returning spring, trinity sure to me you bring,
5 Lilac blooming perennial and drooping star in the west,
And thought of him I love.

2

O powerful western fallen star!
O shades of night—O moody, tearful night!
O great star disappear'd—O the black murk that hides the
    star!
10 O cruel hands that hold me powerless—O helpless soul of me!
O harsh surrounding cloud that will not free my soul.

3

In the dooryard fronting an old farm-house near the white-
    wash'd palings,
Stands the lilac-bush tall-growing with heart-shaped leaves of
    rich green,
With many a pointed blossom rising delicate, with the perfume
    strong I love,
15 With every leaf a miracle—and from this bush in the
    dooryard,
With delicate-color'd blossoms and heart-shaped leaves of rich
    green,
A sprig with its flower I break.

4

In the swamp in secluded recesses,
A shy and hidden bird is warbling a song.

                •

20 Solitary the thrush,
The hermit withdrawn to himself, avoiding the settlements,
Sings by himself a song.

Song of the bleeding throat,
Death's outlet song of life, (for well dear brother I know,
25 If thou wast not granted to sing thou would'st surely die.)

5

Over the breast of the spring, the land, amid cities,
Amid lanes and through old woods, where lately the violets
    peep'd from the ground, spotting the gray debris,
Amid the grass in the fields each side of the lanes, passing the
    endless grass,
Passing the yellow-spear'd wheat, every grain from its shroud
    in the dark-brown fields uprisen,
30 Passing the apple-tree blows of white and pink in the orchards,
Carrying a corpse to where it shall rest in the grave,
Night and day journeys a coffin.

6

Coffin that passes through lanes and streets,
Through day and night with the great cloud darkening the
    land,
35 With the pomp of the inloop'd flags with the cities draped in
    black,
With the show of the States themselves as of crape-veil'd
    women standing,
With processions long and winding and the flambeaus of the
    night,
With the countless torches lit, with the silent sea of faces and
    the unbared heads,
With the waiting depot, the arriving coffin, and the sombre
    faces,
40 With dirges through the night, with the thousand voices rising
    strong and solemn,
With all the mournful voices of the dirges pour'd around the
    coffin,

The dim-lit churches and the shuddering organs—where amid
these you journey,
With the tolling tolling bells' perpetual clang,
Here, coffin that slowly passes,
45   I give you my sprig of lilac.

7

(Nor for you, for one alone,
Blossoms and branches green to coffins all I bring,
For fresh as the morning, thus would I chant a song for you O
sane and sacred death.

All over bouquets of roses,
50   O death, I cover you over with roses and early lilies,
But mostly and now the lilac that blooms the first,   *not*
Copious I break, I break the sprigs from the bushes,   *the*
With loaded arms I come, pouring for you,   *last*
For you and the coffins all of you O death.)

8

55   O western orb sailing the heaven,
Now I know what you must have meant as a month since I
walk'd,
As I walk'd in silence the transparent shadowy night,
As I saw you had something to tell as you bent to me night
after night,
As you droop'd from the sky low down as if to my side,
(while the other stars all look'd on,)
60   As we wander'd together the solemn night, (for something I
know not what kept me from sleep,)
As the night advanced, and I saw on the rim of the west how
full you were of woe,
As I stood on the rising ground in the breeze in the cool
transparent night,
As my soul in its trouble dissatisfied sank, as where you
sad orb,
Concluded, dropt in the night, and was gone.

9

65 Sing on there in the swamp,
O singer bashful and tender, I hear your notes, I hear your
call,
I hear, I come presently, I understand you,
But a moment I linger, for the lustrous star has detain'd me,
The star my departing comrade holds and detains me.

10

70 O how shall I warble myself for the dead one there I loved?
And how shall I deck my song for the large sweet soul that
has gone?
And what shall my perfume be for the grave of him I love?
Sea-winds blown from east and west,
Blown from the Eastern sea and blown from the Western sea,
till there on the prairies meeting,
75 These and with these and the breath of my chant,
I'll perfume the grave of him I love.

11

O what shall I hang on the chamber walls?
And what shall the pictures be that I hang on the walls,
To adorn the burial-house of him I love?

80 Pictures of growing spring and farms and homes,
With the Fourth-month eve at sundown, and the gray smoke
lucid and bright,
With floods of the yellow gold of the gorgeous, indolent,
sinking sun, burning, expanding the air,
With the fresh sweet herbage under foot, and the pale green
leaves of the trees prolific,
In the distance the flowing glaze, the breast of the river, with a
winddapple here and there,
85 With ranging hills on the banks, with many a line against the
sky, and shadows,
And the city at hand with dwellings so dense, and stacks of
chimneys,

And all the scenes of life and the workshops, and the workmen
  homeward returning.

12

Lo, body and soul—this land,
My own Manhattan with spires, and the sparkling and
  hurrying tides, and the ships,
90 The varied and ample land, the South and the North in the
  light, Ohio's shores and flashing Missouri,
And ever the far-spreading prairies cover'd with grass and
  corn.

Lo, the most excellent sun so calm and haughty,
The violet and purple morn with just-felt breezes,
The gentle soft-born measureless light,
95 The miracle spreading bathing all, the fulfill'd noon,
The coming eve delicious, the welcome night and the stars,
Over my cities shining all, enveloping man and land.

13

Sing on, sing on you gray-brown bird,
Sing from the swamps, the recesses, pour your chant from the
  bushes,
100 Limitless out of the dusk, out of the cedars and pines.

Sing on dearest brother, warble your reedy song,
Loud human song, with voice of uttermost woe.

O liquid and free and tender!
O wild and loose to my soul—O wondrous singer!
105 You only I hear—yet the star holds me, (but will soon depart,)
Yet the lilac with mastering odor holds me.

14

Now while I sat in the day and look'd forth,
In the close of the day with its light and the fields of spring,
  and the farmers preparing their crops,

In the large unconscious scenery of my land with its lakes and
    forests,
110 In the heavenly aerial beauty, (after the perturb'd winds and
    the storms,)
Under the arching heavens of the afternoon swift passing, and
    the voices of children and women,
The many-moving sea-tides, and I saw the ships how they
    sail'd,
And the summer approaching with richness, and the fields all
    busy with labor,
And the infinite separate houses, how they all went on, each
    with its meals and minutia of daily usages,
115 And the streets how their throbbings throbb'd, and the cities
    pent—lo, then and there,
Falling upon them all and among them all, enveloping me with
    the rest,
Appear'd the cloud, appear'd the long black trail,
And I knew death, its thought, and the sacred knowledge of
    death.

Then with the knowledge of death as walking one side of me,
120 And the thought of death close-walking the other side of me,
And I in the middle as with companions, and as holding the
    hands of companions,
I fled forth to the hiding receiving night that talks not,
Down to the shores of the water, the path by the swamp in
    the dimness,
To the solemn shadowy cedars and ghostly pines so still.

125 And the singer so shy to the rest receiv'd me,
The gray-brown bird I know receiv'd us comrades three,
And he sang the carol of death, and a verse for him I love.

From deep secluded recesses,
From the fragrant cedars and the ghostly pines so still,
130 Came the carol of the bird.

And the charm of the carol rapt me,
As I held as if by their hands my comrades in the night,
And the voice of my spirit tallied the song of the bird.

Come lovely and soothing death,
135   Undulate round the world, serenely arriving, arriving,
In the day, in the night, to all, to each,
Sooner or later delicate death.

Prais'd be the fathomless universe,
For life and joy, and for objects and knowledge curious,
140   And for love, sweet love—but praise! praise! praise!
For the sure-enwinding arms of cool-enfolding death.

Dark mother always gliding near with soft feet,
Have none chanted for thee a chant of fullest welcome?
Then I chant it for thee, I glorify thee above all,
145   I bring thee a song that when thou must indeed come, come
        unfalteringly.

Approach strong deliveress,
When it is so, when thou hast taken them I joyously sing the
        dead,
Lost in the loving floating ocean of thee,
Laved in the flood of thy bliss O death.

150   From me to thee glad serenades,
Dances for thee I propose saluting thee, adornments and
        feastings for thee,
And the sights of the open landscape and the high-spread sky
        are fitting,
And life and the fields, and the huge and thoughtful night.

The night in silence under many a star,
155   The ocean shore and the husky whispering wave whose voice I
        know,
And the soul turning to thee O vast and well-veil'd death,
And the body gratefully nestling close to thee.

Over the tree-tops I float thee a song,
Over the rising and sinking waves, over the myriad fields and
        the prairies wide,
160   Over the dense-pack'd cities all and the teeming wharves and
        ways,
I float this carol with joy, with joy to thee O death.

15

To the tally of my soul,
Loud and strong kept up the gray-brown bird.
With pure deliberate notes spreading filling the night.

165 Loud in the pines and cedars dim,
Clear in the freshness moist and the swamp-perfume,
And I with my comrades there in the night.

While my sight that was bound in my eyes unclosed,
As to long panoramas of visions.

170 And I saw askant the armies,
I saw as in noiseless dreams hundreds of battle-flags,
Borne through the smoke of the battles and pierc'd with
   missiles I saw them,
And carried hither and yon through the smoke, and torn and
   bloody,
And at last but a few shreds left on the staffs, (and all in
   silence,)
175 And the staffs all splinter'd and broken.

I saw battle-corpses, myriads of them,
And the white skeletons of young men, I saw them,
I saw the debris and debris of all the slain soldiers of the war,
But I saw they were not as was thought,
180 They themselves were fully at rest, they suffer'd not,
The living remain'd and suffer'd, the mother suffer'd,
And the wife and the child and the musing comrade suffer'd,
And the armies that remain'd suffer'd.

16

Passing the visions, passing the night,
185 Passing, unloosing the hold of my comrades' hands,
Passing the song of the hermit bird and the tallying song of my
   soul,
Victorious song, death's outlet song, yet varying ever-altering
   song,

As low and wailing, yet clear the notes, rising and falling,
    flooding the night,
Sadly sinking and fainting, as warning and warning, and yet
    again bursting with joy,
190 Covering the earth and filling the spread of the heaven,
As that powerful psalm in the night I heard from recesses,
Passing, I leave thee lilac with heart-shaped leaves,
I leave thee there in the door-yard, blooming, returning with
    spring.

I cease from my song for thee,
195 From my gaze on thee in the west, fronting the west,
    communing with thee,
O comrade lustrous with silver face in the night.

Yet each to keep and all, retrievements out of the night,
The song, the wondrous chant of the gray-brown bird,
And the tallying chant, the echo arous'd in my soul,
200 With the lustrous and drooping star with the countenance full
    of woe,
With the holders holding my hand nearing the call of the bird,
Comrades mine and I in the midst, and their memory ever to
    keep, for the dead I loved so well,
For the sweetest, wisest soul of all my days and lands—and
    this for his dear sake,
Lilac and star and bird twined with the chant of my soul,
205 There in the fragrant pines and the cedars dusk and dim.

                                                    1867

A NOISELESS PATIENT SPIDER

A noiseless patient spider,
I mark'd where on a little promontory it stood isolated,
Mark'd how to explore the vacant vast surrounding,
It launch'd forth filament, filament, filament, out of itself,
5   Ever unreeling them, ever tirelessly speeding them.

And you O my soul where you stand,
Surrounded, detached, in measureless oceans of space,

Ceaselessly musing, venturing, throwing, seeking the spheres to
    connect them,
Till the bridge you will need be form'd, till the ductile anchor
    hold,
10 Till the gossamer thread you fling catch somewhere, O my
    soul.
                    1868

PASSAGE TO INDIA

1

Singing my days,
Singing the great achievements of the present,
Singing the strong light works of engineers,
Our modern wonders, (the antique ponderous Seven outvied,)[109]
5   In the Old World the east the Suez canal,
The New by its mighty railroad spann'd,
The seas inlaid with eloquent gentle wires;
Yet first to sound, and ever sound, the cry with thee O soul,
The Past! the Past! the Past!

10 The Past—the dark unfathom'd retrospect!
The teeming gulf—the sleepers and the shadows!
The past—the infinite greatness of the past!
For what is the present after all but a growth out of the past?
(As a projectile form'd, impell'd, passing a certain line, still
    keeps on,
15 So the present, utterly form'd, impell'd by the past.)

2

Passage O soul to India!
Eclaircise[110] the myths Asiatic, the primitive fables.

Not you alone proud truths of the world,
Nor you alone ye facts of modern science,
20 But myths and fables of eld, Asia's, Africa's fables,
The far-darting beams of the spirit, the unloos'd dreams,

The deep diving bibles and legends,
The daring plots of the poets, the elder religions;
O you temples fairer than lilies pour'd over by the rising sun!
25 O you fables spurning the known, eluding the hold of the
        known, mounting to heaven!
You lofty and dazzling towers, pinnacled, red as roses,
        burnish'd with gold!
Towers of fables immortal fashion'd from mortal dreams!
You too I welcome and fully the same as the rest!
You too with joy I sing.

30 Passage to India!
Lo, soul, seest thou not God's purpose from the first?
The earth to be spann'd, connected by network,
The races, neighbors, to marry and be given in marriage,
The oceans to be cross'd, the distant brought near,
35 The lands to be welded together.

A worship new I sing,
You captains, voyagers, explorers, yours,
You engineers, you architects, machinists, yours,
You, not for trade or transportation only,
40 But in God's name, and for thy sake O soul.

                3

Passage to India!
Lo soul for thee of tableaus twain,
I see in one the Suez canal initiated, open'd,
I see the procession of steamships, the Empress Eugenie's[111]
        leading the van,
45 I mark from on deck the strange landscape, the pure sky, the
        level sand in the distance,
I pass swiftly the picturesque groups, the workmen gather'd,
The gigantic dredging machines.

In one again, different, (yet thine, all thine, O soul, the same,)
I see over my own continent the Pacific railroad surmounting
        every barrier,
50 I see continual trains of cars winding along the Platte carrying
        freight and passengers,

I hear the locomotives rushing and roaring, and the shrill
    steam-whistle,
I hear the echoes reverberate through the grandest scenery in
    the world,
I cross the Laramie plains, I note the rocks in grotesque
    shapes, the buttes,
I see the plentiful larkspur and wild onions, the barren,
    colorless, sage-deserts,
55   I see in glimpses afar or towering immediately above me the
    great mountains, I see the Wind river and the Wahsatch[112]
    mountains,
I see the Monument mountain and the Eagle's Nest, I pass the
    Promontory, I ascend the Nevadas,
I scan the noble Elk mountain and wind around its base,
I see the Humboldt range, I thread the valley and cross the
    river,
I see the clear waters of lake Tahoe, I see forests of majestic
    pines,
60   Or crossing the great desert, the alkaline plains, I behold
    enchanting mirages of waters and meadows,
Marking through these and after all, in duplicate slender lines,
Bridging the three or four thousand miles of land travel,
Tying the Eastern to the Western sea,
The road between Europe and Asia.

65   (Ah Genoese thy dream! thy dream!
Centuries after thou art laid in thy grave,
The shore thou foundest verifies thy dream.)

        4

Passage to India!
Struggles of many a captain, tales of many a sailor dead,
70   Over my mood stealing and spreading they come,
Like clouds and cloudlets in the unreach'd sky.

Along all history, down the slopes,
As a rivulet running, sinking now, and now again to the
    surface rising,
A ceaseless thought, a varied train—lo, soul, to thee, thy sight,
    they rise,

75   The plans, the voyages again, the expeditions;
     Again Vasco de Gama[113] sails forth,
     Again the knowledge gain'd, the mariner's compass,
     Lands found and nations born, thou born America,
     For purpose vast, man's long probation fill'd,
80   Thou rondure of the world at last accomplish'd.

               5

     O vast Rondure, swimming in space,
     Cover'd all over with visible power and beauty,
     Alternate light and day and the teeming spiritual darkness,
     Unspeakable high processions of sun and moon and countless
          stars above,
85   Below, the manifold grass and waters, animals, mountains,
          trees,
     With inscrutable purpose, some hidden prophetic intention,
     Now first it seems my thought begins to span thee.

     Down from the gardens of Asia descending radiating,
     Adam and Eve appear, then their myriad progeny after them,
90   Wandering, yearning, curious, with restless explorations,
     With questionings, baffled, formless, feverish, with never-happy
          hearts,
     With that sad incessant refrain, *Wherefore unsatisfied soul?*
     and *Whither O mocking life?*

     Ah who shall soothe these feverish children?
     Who justify these restless explorations?
95   Who speak the secret of impassive earth?
     Who bind it to us? what is this separate Nature so unnatural?
     What is this earth to our affections? (unloving earth, without a
          throb to answer ours,
     Cold earth, the place of graves.)

     Yet soul be sure the first intent remains, and shall be
          carried out,
100 Perhaps even now the time has arrived.
                         •

After the seas are all cross'd, (as they seem already cross'd,)
After the great captains and engineers have accomplish'd their
   work,
After the noble inventors, after the scientists, the chemist, the
   geologist, ethnologist,
Finally shall come the poet worthy of that name,
105   The true son of God shall come singing his songs.

Then not your deeds only O voyagers, O scientists and
   inventors, shall be justified,
All these hearts as of fretted children shall be sooth'd,
All affection shall be fully responded to, the secret shall be
   told,
All these separations and gaps shall be taken up and hook'd
   and link'd together,
110   The whole earth, this cold, impassive, voiceless earth, shall be
   completely justified,
Trinitas divine shall be gloriously accomplish'd and compacted
   by the true son of God, the poet,
(He shall indeed pass the straits and conquer the mountains,
He shall double the cape of Good Hope to some purpose,)
Nature and Man shall be disjoin'd and diffused no more,
115   The true son of God shall absolutely fuse them.

          6

Year at whose wide-flung door I sing!
Year of the purpose accomplish'd!
Year of the marriage of continents, climates and oceans!
(No mere doge of Venice now wedding the Adriatic,)
120   I see O year in you the vast terraqueous globe given and
   giving all,
Europe to Asia, Africa join'd, and they to the New World,
The lands, geographies, dancing before you, holding a festival
   garland,
As brides and bridegrooms hand in hand.

Passage to India!
125   Cooling airs from Caucasus, far, soothing cradle of man,
The river Euphrates flowing, the past lit up again.

                    •

Lo soul, the retrospect brought forward,
The old, most populous, wealthiest of earth's lands,
The streams of the Indus and the Ganges and their many
    affluents,
130 (I my shores of America walking to-day behold, resuming all,)
The tale of Alexander on his warlike marches suddenly dying,
On one side China and on the other Persia and Arabia,
To the south the great seas and the bay of Bengal,
The flowing literatures, tremendous epics, religions, castes,
135 Old occult Brahma interminably far back, the tender and
    junior Buddha,
Central and southern empires and all their belongings,
    possessors,
The wars of Tamerlane, the reign of Aurungzebe,
The traders, rulers, explorers, Moslems, Venetians, Byzantium,
    the Arabs, Portuguese,
The first traveler famous yet, Marco Polo, Batouta the Moor,[114]
140 Doubts to be solv'd, the map incognita, blanks to be fill'd,
The foot of man unstay'd, the hands never at rest,
Thyself O soul that will not brook a challenge.

The mediæval navigators rise before me,
The world of 1492, with its awaken'd enterprise,
145 Something swelling in humanity now like the sap of the earth
    in spring,
The sunset splendor of chivalry declining.

And who art thou sad shade?
Gigantic, visionary, thyself a visionary,
With majestic limbs and pious beaming eyes,
150 Spreading around with every look of thine a golden world,
Enhuing it with gorgeous hues.

As the chief histrion,[115]
Down to the footlights walks in some great scena,
Dominating the rest I see the Admiral himself,
155 (History's type of courage, action, faith,)
Behold him sail from Palos leading his little fleet,
His voyage behold, his return, his great fame,
His misfortunes, calumniators, behold him a prisoner, chain'd,
Behold his dejection, poverty, death.

•

160   (Curious in time I stand, noting the efforts of heroes,
      Is the deferment long? bitter the slander, poverty, death?
      Lies the seed unreck'd for centuries in the ground? lo, to God's
        due occasion,
      Uprising in the night, it sprouts, blooms,
      And fills the earth with use and beauty.)

      7

165   Passage indeed O soul to primal thought,
      Not lands and seas alone, thy own clear freshness,
      The young maturity of brood and bloom,
      To realms of budding bibles.

      O soul, repressless, I with thee and thou with me,
170   Thy circumnavigation of the world begin,
      Of man, the voyage of his mind's return,
      To reason's early paradise,
      Back, back to wisdom's birth, to innocent intuitions,
      Again with fair creation.

      8

175   O we can wait no longer,
      We too take ship O soul,
      Joyous we too launch out on trackless seas,
      Fearless for unknown shores on waves of ecstasy to sail,
      Amid the wafting winds, (thou pressing me to thee, I thee to
        me, O soul,)
180   Caroling free, singing our song of God,
      Chanting our chant of pleasant exploration.

      With laugh and many a kiss,
      (Let others deprecate, let others weep for sin, remorse,
        humiliation,)
      O soul thou pleasest me, I thee.
185   Ah more than any priest O soul we too believe in God,
      But with the mystery of God we dare not dally.

      O soul thou pleasest me, I thee,
      Sailing these seas or on the hills, or waking in the night,

Thoughts, silent thoughts, of Time and Space and Death, like
    waters flowing,
190   Bear me indeed as through the regions infinite,
Whose air I breathe, whose ripples hear, lave me all over,
Bathe me O God in thee, mounting to thee,
I and my soul to range in range of thee.

O Thou transcendent,
195   Nameless, the fibre and the breath,
Light of the light, shedding forth universes, thou centre of
    them,
Thou mightier centre of the true, the good, the loving,
Thou moral, spiritual fountain—affection's source—thou
    reservoir,
(O pensive soul of me—O thirst unsatisfied—waitest not
    there?
200   Waitest not haply for us somewhere there the Comrade
    perfect?)
Thou pulse—thou motive of the stars, suns, systems,
That, circling, move in order, safe, harmonious,
Athwart the shapeless vastnesses of space,
How should I think, how breathe a single breath, how speak,
    if out of myself,
205   I could not launch, to those, superior universes?

Swiftly I shrivel at the thought of God,
At Nature and its wonders, Time and Space and Death,
But that I, turning, call to thee O soul, thou actual Me,
And lo, thou gently masterest the orbs,
210   Thou matest Time, smilest content at Death,
And fillest, swellest full the vastnesses of Space.

Greater than stars or suns,
Bounding O soul thou journeyest forth;
What love than thine and ours could wider amplify?
215   What aspirations, wishes, outvie thine and ours O soul?
What dreams of the ideal? what plans of purity, perfection,
    strength?
What cheerful willingness for others' sake to give up all?
For others' sake to suffer all?

·

Reckoning ahead O soul, when thou, the time achiev'd,
220   The seas all cross'd, weather'd the capes, the voyage done,
Surrounded, copest, frontest God, yieldest, the aim attain'd,
As fill'd with friendship, love complete, the Elder Brother
    found,
The Younger melts in fondness in his arms.

9

Passage to more than India!
225   Are thy wings plumed indeed for such far flights?
O soul, voyagest thou indeed on voyages like those?
Disportest thou on waters such as those?
Soundest below the Sanscrit and the Vedas?
Then have thy bent unleash'd.

230   Passage to you, your shores, ye aged fierce enigmas!
Passage to you, to mastership of you, ye strangling problems!
You, strew'd with the wrecks of skeletons, that, living, never
    reach'd you.

Passage to more than India!
O secret of the earth and sky!
235   Of you O waters of the sea! O winding creeks and rivers!
Of you O woods and fields! of you strong mountains of my
    land!
Of you O prairies! of you gray rocks!
O morning red! O clouds! O rain and snows!
O day and night, passage to you!

240   O sun and moon and all you stars! Sirius and Jupiter!
Passage to you!

Passage, immediate passage! the blood burns in my veins!
Away O soul! hoist instantly the anchor!
Cut the hawsers—haul out—shake out every sail!
245   Have we not stood here like trees in the ground long enough?
Have we not grovel'd here long enough, eating and drinking
    like mere brutes?

Have we not darken'd and dazed ourselves with books long
    enough?

Sail forth—steer for the deep waters only,
Reckless O soul, exploring, I with thee, and thou with me,
250   For we are bound where mariner has not yet dared to go,
And we will risk the ship, ourselves and all.

O my brave soul!
O farther farther sail!
O daring joy, but safe! are they not all the seas of God?
255   O farther, farther, farther sail!
                1871

PRAYER OF COLUMBUS

A batter'd, wreck'd old man,
Thrown on this savage shore, far, far from home,
Pent by the sea and dark rebellious brows, twelve dreary
    months,
Sore, stiff with many toils, sicken'd and nigh to death,
5   I take my way along the island's edge,
Venting a heavy heart.

I am too full of woe!
Haply I may not live another day;
I cannot rest O God, I cannot eat or drink or sleep,
10   Till I put forth myself, my prayer, once more to Thee,
Breathe, bathe myself once more in Thee, commune with Thee,
Report myself once more to Thee.

Thou knowest my years entire, my life,
My long and crowded life of active work, not adoration
    merely;
15   Thou knowest the prayers and vigils of my youth,
Thou knowest my manhood's solemn and visionary
    meditations,

Thou knowest how before I commenced I devoted all to come
    to Thee,
Thou knowest I have in age ratified all those vows and strictly
    kept them,
Thou knowest I have not once lost nor faith nor ecstasy in
    Thee,
20   In shackles, prison'd, in disgrace, repining not,
Accepting all from Thee, as duly come from Thee.

All my emprises have been fill'd with Thee,
My speculations, plans, begun and carried on in thoughts of
    Thee,
Sailing the deep or journeying the land for Thee;
25   Intentions, purports, aspirations mine, leaving results to Thee.

O I am sure they really came from Thee,
The urge, the ardor, the unconquerable will,
The potent, felt, interior command, stronger than words,
A message from the Heavens whispering to me even in sleep,
30   These sped me on.

By me and these the work so far accomplish'd,
By me earth's elder cloy'd and stifled lands uncloy'd, unloos'd,
By me the hemispheres rounded and tied, the unknown to the
    known.

The end I know not, it is all in Thee,
35   Or small or great I know not—haply what broad fields, what
    lands,
Haply the brutish measureless human undergrowth I know,
Transplanted there may rise to stature, knowledge worthy
    Thee,
Haply the swords I know may there indeed be turn'd to
    reaping-tools.
Haply the lifeless cross I know Europe's dead cross, may bud
    and blossom there.

40   One effort more, my altar this bleak sand;
That thou O God my life hast lighted,
With ray of light, steady, ineffable, vouchsafed of Thee,

Light rare untellable, lighting the very light,
Beyond all signs, descriptions, languages;
45   For that O God, be it my latest word, here on my knees,
Old, poor, and paralyzed, I thank Thee.

My terminus near,
The clouds already closing in upon me,
The voyage balk'd, the course disputed, lost,
50   I yield my ships to Thee.

My hands, my limbs grow nerveless,
My brain feels rack'd, bewilder'd,
Let the old timbers part, I will not part,
I will cling fast to Thee, O God, though the waves buffet me,
55   Thee, Thee at least I know.

Is it the prophet's thought I speak, or am I raving?
What do I know of life? what of myself?
I know not even my own work past or present,
Dim ever-shifting guesses of it spread before me,
60   Of newer better worlds, their mighty parturition,
Mocking, perplexing me.

And these things I see suddenly, what mean they?
As if some miracle, some hand divine unseal'd my eyes,
Shadowy vast shapes smile through the air and sky,
65   And on the distant waves sail countless ships,
And anthems in new tongues I hear saluting me.

1874

TO A LOCOMOTIVE IN WINTER

Thee for my recitative,
Thee in the driving storm even as now, the snow, the winter-
day declining,
Thee in thy panoply, thy measur'd dual throbbing and thy
beat convulsive,
Thy black cylindric body, golden brass and silvery steel,

5 Thy ponderous side-bars, parallel and connecting rods,
   gyrating, shuttling at thy sides,
 Thy metrical, now swelling pant and roar, now tapering in the
   distance,
 Thy great protruding head-light fix'd in front,
 Thy long, pale, floating vapor-pennants, tinged with delicate
   purple,
 The dense and murky clouds out-belching from thy smoke-
   stack,
10 Thy knitted frame, thy springs and valves, the tremulous
   twinkle of thy wheels,
 Thy train of cars behind, obedient, merrily following,
 Through gale or calm, now swift, now slack, yet steadily
   careering;
 Type of the modern—emblem of motion and power—pulse of
   the continent,
 For once come serve the Muse and merge in verse, even as
   here I see thee,
15 With storm and buffeting gusts of wind and falling snow,
 By day thy warning ringing bell to sound its notes,
 By night thy silent signal lamps to swing.

 Fierce-throated beauty,
 Roll through my chant with all thy lawless music, thy swinging
   lamps at night,
20 Thy madly-whistled laughter, echoing, rumbling like an
   earthquake, rousing all,
 Law of thyself complete, thine own track firmly holding,
 (No sweetness debonair of tearful harp or glib piano thine,)
 Thy trills of shrieks by rocks and hills return'd,
 Launch'd o'er the prairies wide, across the lakes,
25 To the free skies unpent and glad and strong.

            1876

HERMAN MELVILLE

(1819–1891)

Melville is generally known as a novelist who wrote some poems at the end of his career. Since he wrote novels for only eleven years and poetry (including *Clarel*, one of the longest poems in the language) for over thirty, he is better thought of as a poet who wrote novels, early on, to make a living and quit when fiction no longer suited his purposes. He was born in New York City to Maria Gansevoort, the daughter of a Revolutionary War general, and Allan Melvill, a descendant of one member of the Boston Tea Party. When the bankruptcy and death of his father left his mother and seven siblings nearly destitute, Melville quit school and, after holding a series of jobs on land, signed on as cabin boy aboard a merchant vessel bound for Liverpool. The next five years he spent mostly at sea, initially as a whaleman in the Pacific and finally as an enlisted seaman on a U.S. man-of-war. On returning home in 1844, he began to write the novels that would quickly make him famous: *Typee* (1846), based on his sojourn in Nukuheva; *Omoo* (1847), on his adventures in Tahiti; *Redburn* (1849), on his early voyage to Liverpool; and *White-Jacket* (1850), on his naval service. In 1847, he married Elizabeth Shaw, the daughter of a Massachusetts Supreme Court chief justice then serving with the father-in-law of Oliver Wendell Holmes. By 1855, the Melvilles had four children, and he had written four enormously ambitious but decidedly unpopular narratives: *Mardi* (1849), a philosophical romance in a poetic style; *Moby-Dick* (1851), a metaphysical treatment of whaling; *Pierre, or The Ambiguities* (1852), a savage parody of popular novels; and *Israel Potter* (1855), an enigmatic fictional biography of a prisoner of war during the Revolution; as well as some fifteen stories, sketches, and reviews for the magazines. Exhausted by this furious rate of production, Melville refused an invitation from James Russell Lowell to contribute to the newly founded *Atlantic Monthly* and embarked on a long tour of Europe and the Holy Land. On his return, he published his last work of fiction, *The Confidence-Man* (1857), a philosophical satire on the problem of faith, which failed to sell. No longer able to support his family by writing, he tried lecturing on the lyceum circuit that was just then serving Emerson so well. When that failed and his efforts to secure a consular post proved fruitless, he took a job in New York as a customs inspector, a position he would hold for nineteen years.

In the meantime, he had turned his attention entirely to poetry. His first collection of poems, based on his Mediterranean travels, went unpublished. His second, *Battle-Pieces; or Aspects of the War* (1866), found a publisher but very little favor with either readers or reviewers. From then on, he published his poems privately: the two-volume *Clarel; a Poem and Pilgrimage in the Holy Land* (1876) with a subvention from his wife's uncle, *John Marr and Other Sailors* (1885) and *Timoleon Etc.* (1891) in tiny editions paid for out of an inheritance that had enabled him to retire from the customs service in 1885 and once again devote himself to writing. The papers left unpublished at his death included one completed collection of poems called "Weeds and Wildings, Chiefly; With a Rose or Two"; as well as at least two unfinished collections and the long story "Billy Budd," which had evolved from a prose headnote, like those in *John Marr*, to the poem "Billy in the Darbies."

IMMOLATED[116]

Children of my happier prime,
When One yet lived with me, and threw
Her rainbow over life and time,
Even Hope, my bride, and mother to you!
5   O, nurtured in sweet pastoral air,
And fed on flowers and light, and dew
Of morning meadows—spare, Ah, spare
Reproach; spare, and upbraid me not
That, yielding scarce to reckless mood
10   But jealous of your future lot,
I sealed you in a fate subdued.
Have I not saved you from the drear
Theft and ignoring which need be
The triumph of the insincere
15   Unanimous Mediocrity?
Rest therefore, free from all despite,
Snugged in the arms of comfortable night.

(1862)

THE PORTENT

(1859)

Hanging from the beam,
   Slowly swaying (such the law),
Gaunt the shadow on your green,
   Shenandoah!
5   The cut is on the crown
     (Lo, John Brown),
And the stabs shall heal no more.

Hidden in the cap
   Is the anguish none can draw;
10 So your future veils its face,
   Shenandoah!
But the streaming beard is shown
   (Weird John Brown),
The meteor of the war.

                1866

MISGIVINGS

(1860)

When ocean-clouds over inland hills
   Sweep storming in late autumn brown,
And horror the sodden valley fills,
   And the spire falls crashing in the town,
5   I muse upon my country's ills—
   The tempest bursting from the waste of Time
On the world's fairest hope linked with man's foulest crime.

Nature's dark side is heeded now—
   (Ah! optimist-cheer disheartened flown)—
10 A child may read the moody brow
   Of yon black mountain lone.
With shouts the torrents down the gorges go,
   And storms are formed behind the storm we feel:
The hemlock shakes in the rafter, the oak in the driving keel.

                1866

THE MARCH INTO VIRGINIA

Ending in the First Manassas
(July, 1861)

Did all the lets and bars appear
    To every just or larger end,
Whence should come the trust and cheer?
    Youth must its ignorant impulse lend—
5   Age finds place in the rear.
      All wars are boyish, and are fought by boys,
    The champions and enthusiasts of the state:
      Turbid ardors and vain joys
        Not barrenly abate—
10 Stimulants to the power mature,
      Preparatives of fate.

Who here forecasteth the event?
What heart but spurns at precedent
And warnings of the wise,
15 Contemned foreclosures of surprise?
The banners play, the bugles call,
The air is blue and prodigal.
    No berrying party, pleasure-wooed,
No picnic party in the May,
20 Ever went less loth than they
    Into that leafy neighborhood.
In Bacchic glee they file toward Fate,
Moloch's uninitiate;
Expectancy, and glad surmise
25 Of battle's unknown mysteries.
All they feel is this: 'tis glory,
A rapture sharp, though transitory,
Yet lasting in belaureled story.
So they gayly go to fight,
30 Chatting left and laughing right.

But some who this blithe mood present,
  As on in lightsome files they fare,

Shall die experienced ere three days be spent—
   Perish, enlightened by the vollied glare;
35   Or shame survive, and, like to adamant,
   Thy after shock, Manassas, share.

                        1866

THE TEMERAIRE[117]

(Supposed to Have Been Suggested
to an Englishman of the Old Order
by the Fight of the Monitor and Merrimac)

The gloomy hulls, in armor grim,
   Like clouds o'er moors have met,
And prove that oak, and iron, and man
   Are tough in fibre yet.

5   But Splendors wane. The sea-fight yields
      No front of old display;
The garniture, emblazonment,
      And heraldry all decay.

Towering afar in parting light,
10   The fleets like Albion's forelands shine—
The full-sailed fleets, the shrouded show
      Of Ships-of-the-Line.

      The fighting Temeraire,
         Built of a thousand trees,
15   Lunging out her lightnings,
         And beetling o'er the seas—
O Ship, how brave and rare,
   That fought so oft and well,
On open decks you manned the gun
20   Armorial.
What cheerings did you share,
   Impulsive in the van,

When down upon leagued France and
        Spain
25   We English ran—
    The freshet at your bowsprit
        Like the foam upon the can.
    Bickering, your colors
        Licked up the Spanish air,
30   You flapped with flames of battle-flags—
        Your challenge, Temeraire!
    The rear ones of our fleet
        They yearned to share your place,
    Still vying with the Victory
35   Throughout that earnest race—
    The Victory, whose Admiral,
        With orders nobly won,
    Shone in the globe of the battle glow—
        The angel in that sun.

40   Parallel in story,
        Lo, the stately pair,
    As late in grapple ranging,
        The foe between them there—
    When four great hulls lay tiered,
45   And the fiery tempest cleared,
    And your prizes twain appeared,
            Temeraire!

    But Trafalgar is over now,
        The quarter-deck undone;
50   The carved and castled navies fire
        Their evening-gun.
    O, Titan Temeraire,
        Your stern-lights fade away;
    Your bulwarks to the years must yield,
55   And heart-of-oak decay.
    A pigmy steam-tug tows you,
        Gigantic, to the shore—
    Dismantled of your guns and spars,
        And sweeping wings of war.

60   The rivets clinch the iron-clads,
            Men learn a deadlier lore;
        But Fame has nailed your battle-flags—
            Your ghost it sails before:
        O, the navies old and oaken,
65   O, the Temeraire no more!

                                            1866

A UTILITARIAN VIEW OF THE
MONITOR'S FIGHT

        Plain be the phrase, yet apt the verse,
            More ponderous than nimble;
        For since grimed War here laid aside
        His painted pomp, 'twould ill befit
5   Overmuch to ply
            The rhyme's barbaric cymbal.

        Hail to victory without the gaud
            Of glory; zeal that needs no fans
        Of banners; plain mechanic power
10   Plied cogently in War now placed—
                Where War belongs—
            Among the trades and artisans.

        Yet this was battle, and intense—
            Beyond the strife of fleets heroic;
15   Deadlier, closer, calm 'mid storm;
        No passion; all went on by crank,
                Pivot, and screw,
            And calculations of caloric.

        Needless to dwell; the story's known.
20   The ringing of those plates on plates
        Still ringeth round the world—
        The clangor of that blacksmiths' fray.
                The anvil-din
            Resounds this message from the Fates:

25   War shall yet be, and to the end;
          But war-paint shows the streaks of weather;
      War yet shall be, but warriors
      Are now but operatives; War's made
              Less grand than Peace,
30   And a singe runs through lace and feather.

                                                    1866

STONEWALL JACKSON

Mortally Wounded at Chancellorsville
(May, 1863)

      The Man who fiercest charged in fight,
          Whose sword and prayer were long—
                  Stonewall!
      Even him who stoutly stood for Wrong,
5   How can we praise? Yet coming days
          Shall not forget him with this song.

      Dead is the Man whose Cause is dead,
          Vainly he died and set his seal—
                  Stonewall!
10   Earnest in error, as we feel;
      True to the thing he deemed was due,
          True as John Brown or steel.

      Relentlessly he routed us;
          But *we* relent, for he is low—
15   Stonewall!
          Justly his fame we outlaw; so
      We drop a tear on the bold Virginian's bier,
          Because no wreath we owe.

                                        1866

STONEWALL JACKSON[118]

(Ascribed to a Virginian)

One man we claim of wrought renown
   Which not the North shall care to slur;
A Modern lived who sleeps in death,
   Calm as the marble Ancients are:
      'Tis he whose life, though a vapor's wreath,
       Was charged with the lightning's burning breath—
      Stonewall, stormer of the war.

But who shall hymn the Roman heart?
   A stoic he, but even more:
The iron will and lion thew
   Were strong to inflict as to endure:
Who like him could stand, or pursue?
His fate the fatalist followed through;
In all his great soul found to do
      Stonewall followed his star.

He followed his star on the Romney march
   Through the sleet to the wintry war;
And he followed it on when he bowed the grain—
   The Wind of the Shenandoah;
      At Gaines's Mill in the giants' strain—
      On the fierce forced stride to Manassas-plain,
      Where his sword with thunder was clothed again,
      Stonewall followed his star.

His star he followed athwart the flood
   To Potomac's Northern shore,
When midway wading, his host of braves
   "My Maryland!" loud did roar—
      To red Antietam's field of graves,
      Through mountain-passes, woods and waves,
      They followed their pagod with hymns and glaives,
      For Stonewall followed a star.

Back it led him to Marye's slope,
   Where the shock and the fame he bore;

And to green Moss-Neck it guided him—
35   Brief respite from throes of war:
        To the laurel glade by the Wilderness grim,
        Through climaxed victory naught shall dim,
        Even unto death it piloted him—
        Stonewall followed his star.

40 Its lead he followed in gentle ways
    Which never the valiant mar;
  A cap we sent him, bestarred, to replace
  The sun-scorched helm of war:
    A fillet he made of the shining lace
45   Childhood's laughing brow to grace—
        Not his was a goldsmith's star.

O, much of doubt in after days
    Shall cling, as now, to the war;
Of the right and the wrong they'll still debate,
50   Puzzled by Stonewall's star:
        "Fortune went with the North elate,"
        "Ay, but the South had Stonewall's weight,
        And he fell in the South's great war."

1866

THE HOUSE-TOP[119]

A Night Piece
(July, 1863)

No sleep. The sultriness pervades the air
And binds the brain—a dense oppression, such
As tawny tigers feel in matted shades,
Vexing their blood and making apt for ravage.
5 Beneath the stars the roofy desert spreads
Vacant as Libya. All is hushed near by.
Yet fitfully from far breaks a mixed surf
Of muffled sound, the Atheist roar of riot.
Yonder, where parching Sirius set in drought,
10 Balefully glares red Arson—there—and there.

Ships

The Town is taken by its rats—ship-rats
And rats of the wharves. All civil charms
And priestly spells which late held hearts in awe—
Fear-bound, subjected to a better sway
15 Than sway of self; these like a dream dissolve,
And man rebounds whole æons back in nature.
Hail to the low dull rumble, dull and dead,
And ponderous drag that jars the wall.
Wise Draco comes, deep in the midnight roll
20 Of black artillery; he comes, though late;
In code corroborating Calvin's creed[120]
And cynic tyrannies of honest kings;
He comes, nor parlies; and the Town, redeemed,
Gives thanks devout; nor, being thankful, heeds
25 The grimy slur on the Republic's faith implied,
Which holds that Man is naturally good,
And—more—is Nature's Roman, never to be scourged.

1866

THE COLLEGE COLONEL

He rides at their head;
    A crutch by his saddle just slants in view,
One slung arm is in splints, you see,
    Yet he guides his strong steed—how coldly too.

5   He brings his regiment home—
    Not as they filed two years before,
But a remnant half-tattered, and battered, and worn,
Like castaway sailors, who—stunned
        By the surf's loud roar,
10   Their mates dragged back and seen no more—
Again and again breast the surge,
    And at last crawl, spent, to shore.

A still rigidity and pale—
    An Indian aloofness lones his brow;
15 He has lived a thousand years

Compressed in battle's pains and prayers,
   Marches and watches slow.

There are welcoming shouts, and flags;
   Old men off hat to the Boy,
20 Wreaths from gay balconies fall at his feet,
   But to *him*—there comes alloy.

It is not that a leg is lost,
   It is not that an arm is maimed,
It is not that the fever has racked—
25   Self he has long disclaimed.

But all through the Seven Days' Fight,
   And deep in the Wilderness grim,
And in the field-hospital tent,
   And Petersburg crater, and dim
30 Lean brooding in Libby,[121] there came—
   Ah heaven!—what *truth* to him.

                     1866

THE MARTYR

Indicative of the Passion of the People
on the 15th Day of April, 1865

Good Friday was the day
   Of the prodigy and crime,
When they killed him in his pity,
   When they killed him in his prime
5 Of clemency and calm—
      When with yearning he was filled
      To redeem the evil-willed,
And, though conqueror, be kind;
   But they killed him in his kindness,
10   In their madness and their blindness,
And they killed him from behind.

There is sobbing of the strong,
   And a pall upon the land;
But the people in their weeping
15   Bare the iron hand;
Beware the People weeping
   When they bare the iron hand.

He lieth in his blood—
   The father in his face;
20 They have killed him, the Forgiver—
   The Avenger takes his place,
The Avenger wisely stern,
     Who in righteousness shall do
     What the heavens call him to,
25 And the parricides remand;
    For they killed him in his kindness,
    In their madness and their blindness,
And his blood is on their hand.

There is sobbing of the strong,
30   And a pall upon the land;
But the People in their weeping
        Bare the iron hand:
Beware the People weeping
   When they bare the iron hand.

                  1866

THE APPARITION

A Retrospect

Convulsions came; and, where the field
   Long slept in pastoral green,
A goblin-mountain was upheaved
(Sure the scared sense was all deceived),
5   Marl-glen and slag-ravine.

The unreserve of Ill was there,
   The clinkers in her last retreat;

But, ere the eye could take it in,
Or mind could comprehension win,
10   It sunk!—and at our feet.

So, then, Solidity's a crust—
    The core of fire below;
All may go well for many a year,
But who can think without a fear
15   Of horrors that happen so?

                                        1866

IRIS

    (1865)

When Sherman's March was over
    And June was green and bright,
She came among our mountains,
    A freak of new delight;
5   Provokingly our banner
        Salutes with Dixie's strain,—
Little rebel from Savannah,
        Three Colonels in her train.

Three bearded Puritan colonels:
10   But O her eyes, her mouth—
Magnolias in their languor
    And sorcery of the South.
High-handed rule of beauty,
    Are wars for man but vain?
15 Behold, three disenslavers
        Themselves embrace a chain!

But, loveliest invader,
    Out of Dixie did ye rove
By sallies of your raillery
20   To rally us, or move?
For under all your merriment
    There lurked a minor tone;

And of havoc we had tidings
   And a roof-tree overthrown.

25   Ah, nurtured in the trial—
       And ripened by the storm,
   Was your gaiety your courage,
       And levity its form?
   O'er your future's darkling waters,
30   O'er your past, a frozen tide,
   Like the petrel would you skim it,
       Like the glancing skater glide?

   But the ravisher has won her
       Who the wooers three did slight;
35   To his fastness he has borne her
       By the trail that leads thro' night.
   With Peace she came, the rainbow,
       And like a Bow did pass,
   The balsam-trees exhaling,
40   And tear-drops in the grass.

   Now laughed the leafage over
       Her pranks in woodland scene:
   Hath left us for the revel
       Deep in Paradise the green?
45   In truth we will believe it
       Under pines that sigh a balm,
   Though o'er thy stone be trailing
       Cypress-moss that drapes the palm.

                                        (1874)

THE ARCH[122]

           'Twas thereupon
   The Italian, as the eve drew on,
   Regained the gate, and hurried in
   As he would passionately win
5   Surcease to thought by rapid pace.

Eastward he bent, across the town,
Till in the Via Crucis¹²³ lone
An object there arrested him.
  With gallery which years deface,
10 Its bulk athwart the alley grim,
The arch named Ecce Homo threw;
The same, if child-like faith be true,
From which the Lamb of God was shown
By Pilate to the wolfish crew.
15 And Celio—in frame how prone
To kindle at that scene recalled—
Perturbed he stood, and heart-enthralled.
  No raptures which with saints prevail,
Nor trouble of compunction born
20 He felt, as there he seemed to scan
Aloft in spectral guise, the pale
Still face, the purple robe, and thorn;
And inly cried—*Behold the Man!*
Yon Man it is this burden lays:
25 Even he who in the pastoral hours,
Abroad in fields, and cheered by flowers,
Announced a heaven's unclouded days;
And, ah, with such persuasive lips—
Those lips now sealed while doom delays—
30 Won men to look for solace there;
But, crying out in death's eclipse,
When rainbow none his eyes might see,
Enlarged the margin for despair—
My God, my God, forsakest me?
35   Upbraider! we upbraid again;
Thee we upbraid; our pangs constrain
Pathos itself to cruelty.
Ere yet thy day no pledge was given
Of homes and mansions in the heaven—
40 Paternal homes reserved for us;
Heart hoped it not, but lived content—
Content with life's own discontent,
Nor deemed that fate ere swerved for us:
The natural law men let prevail;
45 Then reason disallowed the state

Of instinct's variance with fate.
But thou—ah, see, in rack how pale
Who did the world with throes convulse;
Behold him—yea—behold the Man
50   Who warranted if not began
The dream that drags out its repulse.
    Nor less[124] some cannot break from thee;
Thy love so locked is with thy lore,
They may not rend them and go free:
55   The head rejects; so much the more
The heart embraces—what? the love?
If true what priests avouch of thee,
The shark thou mad'st, yet claim'st the dove.
    Nature and thee in vain we search:
60   Well urged the Jews within the porch—
"How long wilt make us still to doubt?"
How long?—'Tis eighteen cycles now—
Enigma and evasion grow;
And shall we never find thee out?
65   What isolation lones thy state
That all we else know cannot mate
With what thou teachest? Nearing thee
All footing fails us; history
Shows there a gulf where bridge is none!
70   In lapse of unrecorded time,
Just after the apostles' prime,
What chance or craft might break it down?
Served this a purpose? By what art
Of conjuration might the heart
75   Of heavenly love, so sweet, so good,
Corrupt into the creeds malign,
Begetting strife's pernicious brood,
Which claimed for patron thee divine?
                Anew, anew,
80   For this thou bleedest, Anguished Face;
Yea, thou through ages to accrue,
Shalt the Medusa shield replace:
In beauty and in terror too
Shalt paralyze the nobler race—
85   Smite or suspend, perplex, deter—

Tortured, shalt prove a torturer.
Whatever ribald Future be,
Thee shall these heed, amaze their hearts with thee—
Thy white, thy red, thy fairness and thy tragedy.

                                                    1876

GUIDE AND GUARD[125]

Descending by the mountain-side
When crags give way to pastures wide,
And lower opening, ever new,
Glades, meadows, hamlets meet the view,
5   Which from above did coyly hide—
And with re-kindled breasts of spring
The robins through the orchard wing;
Excellent then—as *there* bestowed—
And true in charm the downward road.
10   Quite other spells an influence throw
Down going, down, to Jericho.
        Here first on path so evil-starred
Their guide they scan, and prize the guard.
        The guide, a Druze of Lebanon,
15   Was rumored for an Emir's son,
Or offspring of a lord undone
In Ibrahim's time.[126] Abrupt reverse
The princes in the East may know:
Lawgivers are outlaws at a blow,
20   And Crœsus dwindles in the purse.
Exiled, cut off, in friendless state,
The Druze maintained an air sedate;
Without the sacrifice of pride,
Sagacious still he earned his bread,
25   E'en managed to maintain the head,
Yes, lead men still, if but as guide
To pilgrims.
                Here his dress to mark:
A simple woolen cloak, with dark
30   Vertical stripes; a vest to suit;

White turban like snow-wreath; a boot
Exempt from spur; a sash of fair
White linen, long-fringed at the ends:
The garb of Lebanon. His mare
35 In keeping showed: the saddle plain:
Head-stall untassled, slender rein.
But nature made her rich amends
For art's default: full eye of flame
Tempered in softness, which became
40 Womanly sometimes, in desire
To be caressed; ears fine to know
Least intimation, catch a hint
As tinder takes the spark from flint
And steel. Veil-like her clear attire
45 Of silvery hair, with speckled show
Of grayish spots, and ample flow
Of milky mane. Much like a child
The Druze she'd follow, more than mild.
Not less, at need, what power she'd don,
50 Clothed with the thunderbolt would run
As conscious of the Emir's son
She bore; nor knew the hireling's lash,
Red rowel, or rebuke as rash.
Courteous her treatment. But deem not
55 This tokened a luxurious lot:
Her diet spare; sole stable, earth;
Beneath the burning sun she'd lie
With mane disheveled, whence her eye
Would flash across the fiery dearth,
60 As watching for that other queen,
Her mate, a beauteous Palmyrene,[127]
The pride of Tadmore's tented scene.
      Athwart the pommel-cloth coarse-spun
A long pipe lay, and longer gun,
65 With serviceable yataghan.
But prized above these arms of yore,
A new revolver bright he bore
Tucked in the belt, and oft would scan.
Accoutered thus, through desert-blight
70 Whose lord is the Amalekite,

And proffering or peace or war,
The swart Druze rode his silvery Zar.

Behind him, jogging two and two,
Came troopers six of tawny hue,
75   Bewrinkled veterans, and grave
As Carmel's prophets of the cave:[128]
Old Arab Bethlehemites, with guns
And spears of grandsires old. Weird ones,
Their robes like palls funereal hung
80   Down from the shoulder, one fold flung
In mufflement about the head,
And kept there by a fillet's braid.

Over this venerable troop
Went Belex doughty in command,
85   Erst of the Sultan's saucy troop
Which into death he did disband—
Politic Mahmoud—when that clan
By fair pretence, in festive way,
He trapped within the Artmedan—[129]
90   Of old, Byzantium's circus gay.
But Belex a sultana saved—
His senior, though by love enslaved,
Who fed upon the stripling's May—
Long since, for now his beard was gray;
95   Though goodly yet the features fine,
Firm chin, true lip, nose aquiline—
Type of the pure Osmanli breed.
But ah, equipments gone to seed—
Ah, shabby fate! his vesture's cloth
100   Hinted the Jew bazaar and moth:
The saddle, too, a cast-off one,
An Aga's erst, and late was sown
With seed-pearl in the seat: but now
All that, with tag-work,[130] all was gone—
105   The tag-work of wee bells in row
That made a small, snug, dulcet din
About the housings Damascene.[131]
But mark the bay: his twenty years

Still showed him pawing with his peers.
110 Pure desert air, doled diet pure,
Sleek tendance, brave result insure.
Ample his chest; small head, large eye—
How interrogative with soul—
Responsive too, his master by:
115 Trim hoof, and pace in strong control.
      Thy birth-day well they keep, thou Don,[132]
And well thy birth-day ode they sing;
Nor ill they named thee Solomon,
Prolific sire. Long live the king.

                      1876

BY THE JORDAN[133]

    Belex his flint adjusts and rights,
Sharp speaks unto his Bethlehemites;
Then, signaled by Djalea, through air
Surveys the further ridges bare.
5 Foreshortened 'gainst a long-sloped height
Beyond the wave whose wash of foam
Beats to the base of Moab home,
Seven furious horsemen fling their flight
Like eagles when they launching rush
10 To snatch the prey that hies to bush.
Dwarfed so these look, while yet afar
Descried. But trusting in their star,
Onward a space the party push;
But halt is called; the Druze rides on,
15 Bids Belex stand, and goes alone.
    Now, for the nonce, those speeders sink
Viewless behind the arborous brink.
Thereto the staid one rides—peers in—
Then waves a hand. They gain his side,
20 Meeting the river's rapid tide
Here sluicing through embowered ravine
Such as of yore was Midian's[134] screen
For rites impure. Facing, and near,
Across the waves which intervene,

25   In shade the robbers reappear:
      Swart, sinous men on silvery steeds—
      Abreast, save where the copse impedes.
      At halt, and mute, and in the van
      Confronting them, with lengthy gun
30   Athwart the knee, and hand thereon,
      Djalea waits. The mare and man
      Show like a stone equestrian
      Set up for homage. Over there
      'Twas hard for mounted men to move
35   Among the thickets interwove,
      Which dipped the stream and made a snare.
      But, undeterred, the riders press
      This way and that among the branches,
      Picking them lanes through each recess,
40   Till backward on their settling haunches
      The steeds withstand the slippery slope,
      While yet their outflung fore-feet grope;
      Then, like sword-push that ends in lunge,
      The slide becomes a weltering plunge:
45   The willows drip, the banks resound;
      They halloo, and with spray are crowned.
      The torrent, swelled by Lebanon rains,
      The spirited horses bravely stem,
      Snorting, half-blinded by their manes,
50   Nor let the current master them.
      As the rope-dancer on the hair
      Poises the long slim pole in air;
      Twirling their slender spears in pride,
      Each horseman in imperiled seat
55   Blends skill and grace with courage meet.
          Soon as they win the hither side,
      Like quicksilver to beach they glide,
      Dismounting, and essay the steep,
      The horses led by slackened rein:
60   Slippery foothold ill they keep.
      To help a grim one of the band
      Good Nehemiah with mickle strain
      Down reaches a decrepit hand:
      The sheik ignores it—bandit dun,
65   Foremost in stride as first in rank—
      Rejects it, and the knoll is won.

Challengingly he stares around,
Then stakes his spear upon the bank
As one reclaiming rightful ground.
70   Like otters when to land they go,
Riders and steeds how sleekly show.
    The first inquiring look they trace
Is gun by gun, as face by face:
Salute they yield, for arms they view
75   Inspire respect sincere and true.
    Meantime, while in their bearing shows
The thought which still their life attends,
And habit of encountering foes—
The thought that strangers scarce are friends—
80   What think the horses? Zar must needs
Be sociable; the robber steeds
She whinnies to; even fain would sway
Neck across neck in lovesome way.
Great Solomon, of rakish strain,
85   Trumpets—would be Don John again.
    The sheik, without a moment's doubt,
Djalea for captain singles out;
And, after parley brief, would fain
Handle that pistol of the guide,
90   The new revolver at his side.
The Druze assents, nor shows surprise.
Barrel, cap, screw, the Arab tries;
And ah, the contrast needs he own:
Alack, for his poor lance and gun,
95   Though heirlooms both: the piece in stock
Half honeycombed, with cumbrous lock;
The spear like some crusader's pole
Dropped long ago when death-damps stole
Over the knight in Richard's host,
100   Then left to warp by Acre lost:[135]
Dry rib of lance. But turning now
Upon his sweetheart, he was cheered:
Her eye he met, the violet-glow,
Peaked ear, the mane's redundant flow;
105   It heartened him, and round he veered;
Elate he shot a brigand glare:
I, Ishmael, have my desert mare!

                          1876

AFTERWARD

Seedsmen of old Saturn's land,
Love and peace went hand in hand,
   And sowed the Era Golden!

Golden time for man and mead:
5 Title none, nor title-deed,
   Nor any slave, nor Soldan.[136]

Venus burned both large and bright,
Honey-moon from night to night,
   Nor bride, nor groom waxed olden.

10 Big the tears, but ruddy ones,
Crushed from grapes in vats and tuns
   Of vineyards green and golden!

Sweet to sour did never sue,
None repented ardor true—
15   Those years did so embolden.

Glum Don Graveairs slunk in den:
Frankly roved the gods with men
   In gracious talk and golden.

Thrill it, cymbals of my rhyme,
20 Power was love, and love in prime,
   Nor revel to toil beholden.

Back, come back, good age, and reign,
Goodly age, and long remain—
   Saturnian Age, the Golden!

                  1876

ROLFE AND THE PALM[137]

         Whom weave ye in,
Ye vines, ye palms? whom now, Soolee?[138]
Lives yet your Indian Arcady?
His sunburnt face what Saxon shows—

5   His limbs all white as lilies be—
Where Eden, isled, impurpled glows
In old Mendanna's[139] sea?
Takes who the venture after me?
Who now adown the mountain dell
10   (Till mine, by human foot untrod—
Nor easy, like the steps to hell)
In panic leaps the appalling crag,
Alighting on the cloistral sod
Where strange Hesperian orchards drag,
15   Walled round by cliff and cascatelle—[140]
Arcades of Iris; and though lorn,
A truant ship-boy overworn,
Is hailed for a descended god?
Who sips the vernal cocoa's cream—
20   The nereids dimpling in the darkling stream?
For whom the gambol of the tricksy dream—
Even Puck's substantiated scene,
Yea, much as man might hope and more than heaven may mean?
And whom do priest and people sue,
25   In terms which pathos yet shall tone
When memory comes unto her own,
To dwell with them and ever find them true:
'Abide, for peace is here:
Behold, nor heat nor cold we fear,
30   Nor any dearth: one happy tide—
A dance, a garland of the year:
Abide!'
But who so feels the stars annoy,
Upbraiding him—how far astray!—
35   That he abjures the simple joy,
And hurries over the briny world away?
Renouncer! is it Adam's flight
Without compulsion or the sin?
And shall the vale avenge the slight
40   By haunting thee in hours thou yet shalt win?

1876

THE ISLAND[141]

"In waters where no charts avail,
Where only fin and spout ye see,
The lonely spout of hermit-whale,
God set that isle which haunteth me.
5   There clouds hang low, but yield no rain—
Forever hang, since wind is none
Or light; nor ship-boy's eye may gain
The smoke-wrapped peak, the inland one
Volcanic; this, within its shroud
10   Streaked black and red, burns unrevealed;
It burns by night—by day the cloud
Shows leaden all, and dull and sealed.
The beach is cinders. With the tide
Salt creek and ashy inlet bring
15   More loneness from the outer ring
Of ocean."
              Pause he made, and sighed.—
"But take the way across the marl,
A broken field of tumbled slabs
20   Like ice-cakes frozen in a snarl
After the break-up in a sound;
So win the thicket's upper ground
Where silence like a poniard stabs,
Since there the low throb of the sea
25   Not heard is, and the sea-fowl flee
Far off the shore, all the long day
Hunting the flying-fish their prey.
Haply in bush ye find a path:
Of man or beast it scarce may be;
30   And yet a wasted look it hath,
As it were traveled ceaselessly—
Century after century—
The rock in places much worn down
Like to some old, old kneeling-stone
35   Before a shrine. But naught's to see,
At least naught there was seen by me,
Of any moving, creeping one.
No berry do those thickets bear,
Nor many leaves. Yet even there,

40   Some sailor from the steerage den
      Put sick ashore—alas, by men
      Who weary of him thus abjure—
      The way may follow, in pursuit
      Of apples red—the homestead-fruit
45   He dreams of in his calenture.
      He drops, lost soul; but we go on—
      Advance, until in end be won
      The terraced orchard's mysteries,
      Which well do that imp-isle beseem;
50   Paved with jet blocks those terraces,
      The surface rubbed to unctuous gleam
      By something which has life, you feel:
      And yet, the shades but death reveal;
      For under cobwebbed cactus trees,
55   White by their trunks—what hulks be these
      Which, like old skulls of Anaks,[142] are
      Set round as in a Golgotha?
      But, list—a sound! Dull, dull it booms—
      Dull as the jar in vaulted tombs
60   When urns are shifted. With amaze
      Into the dim retreats ye gaze.
      Lo, 'tis the monstrous tortoise drear!
      Of huge humped arch, the ancient shell
      Is trenched with seams where lichens dwell,
65   Or some adhesive growth and sere:
      A lumpish languor marks the pace—
      A hideous, harmless look, with trace
      Of hopelessness; the eyes are dull
      As in the bog the dead black pool:
70   Penal his aspect; all is dragged,
      As he for more than years had lagged—
      A convict doomed to bide the place;
      A soul transformed—for earned disgrace
      Degraded, and from higher race.
75   Ye watch him—him so woe-begone:
      Searching, he creeps with laboring neck,
      Each crevice tries, and long may seek:
      Water he craves, where rain is none—
      Water within the parching zone,
80   Where only dews of midnight fall

And dribbling lodge in chinks of stone.
For meat the bitter tree is all—
The cactus, whose nipped fruit is shed
On those bleached skull-like hulks below,
85   Which, when by life inhabited,
Crept hither in last journey slow
After a hundred years of pain
And pilgrimage here to and fro,
For other hundred years to reign
90   In hollow of white armor so—
Then perish piecemeal. You advance:
Instant, more rapid than a glance,
Long neck and four legs are drawn in,
Letting the shell down with report
95   Upon the stone; so falls in court
The clattering buckler with a din.
There leave him, since for hours he'll keep
That feint of death.—But for the isle—
Much seems it like this barren steep:
100   As here, few there would think to smile."
     So, paraphrased in lines sincere
Which still similitude would win,
The sketch ran of that timoneer.
He ended, and how passive sate:
105   Nature's own look, which might recall
Dumb patience of mere animal,
Which better may abide life's fate
Than comprehend.
                      What may man know?
110   (Here pondered Clarel) let him rule—
Pull down, build up, creed, system, school,
And reason's endless battle wage,
Make and remake his verbiage—
But solve the world! Scarce that he'll do:
115   Too wild it is, too wonderful.
Since *this* world, then, can baffle so—
Our natural harbor—it were strange
If *that* alleged, which is afar,
Should not confound us when we range
120   In revery where its problems are.—

                                        1876

DIRGE

Stay, Death. Not mine the Christus-wand
Wherewith to charge thee and command:
I plead. Most gently hold the hand
Of her thou leadest far away;
5   Fear thou to let her naked feet
Tread ashes—but let mosses sweet
Her footing tempt, where'er ye stray.
Shun Orcus; win the moonlit land
Belulled—the silent meadows lone,
10   Where never any leaf is blown
From lily-stem in Azrael's hand.
There, till her love rejoin her lowly
(Pensive, a shade, but all her own)
On honey feed her, wild and holy;
15   Or trance her with thy choicest charm.
And if, ere yet the lover's free,
Some added dusk thy rule decree—
That shadow only let it be
Thrown in the moon-glade by the palm.

                                                    1876

VIA CRUCIS

Some leading thoroughfares of man
In wood-path, track, or trail began;
Though threading heart of proudest town,
They follow in controlling grade
5   A hint or dictate, nature's own,
By man, as by the brute, obeyed.

Within Jerusalem a lane,
Narrow, nor less an artery main
(Though little knoweth it of din),
10   In part suggests such origin.
The restoration or repair,
Successive through long ages there,

Of city upon city tumbled,
Might scarce divert that thoroughfare,
15   Whose hill abideth yet unhumbled
Above the valley-side it meets.
Pronounce its name, this natural street's:
The *Via Crucis*—even the way
Tradition claims to be the one
20   Trod on that Friday far away
By Him our pure exemplar shown.

'Tis Whitsun-tide. From paths without,
Through Stephen's gate—by many a vein
Convergent brought within this lane,
25   Ere sun-down shut the loiterer out—
As 'twere a frieze, behold the train!
Bowed water-carriers; Jews with staves,
Infirm gray monks; over-loaded slaves;
Turk soldiers—young, with home-sick eyes;
30   A Bey, bereaved through luxuries;
Strangers and exiles; Moslem dames
Long-veiled in monumental white,
Dumb from the mounds which memory claims;
A half-starved vagrant Edomite;
35   Sore-footed Arab girls, which toil
Depressed under heap of garden-spoil;
The patient ass with panniered urn;
Sour camels humped by heaven and man,
Whose languid necks through habit turn
40   For ease—for ease they hardly gain.
In varied forms of fate they wend—
Or man or animal, 'tis one:
Cross-bearers all, alike they tend
And follow, slowly follow on.

45   But, lagging after, who is he
Called early every hope to test,
And now, at close of rarer quest,
Finds so much more the heavier tree?
From slopes whence even Echo's gone,
50   Wending, he murmurs in low tone:

"They wire the world—far under sea
They talk; but never comes to me
A message from beneath the stone."

Dusked Olivet he leaves behind,
55   And, taking now a slender wynd,
Vanishes in the obscurer town.

                                    1876

EPILOGUE

If Luther's day expand to Darwin's year,
Shall that exclude the hope—foreclose the fear?

Unmoved by all the claims our times avow,
The ancient Sphinx still keeps the porch of shade;
5   And comes Despair, whom not her calm may cow,
And coldly on that adamantine brow
Scrawls undeterred his bitter pasquinade.
But Faith (who from the scrawl indignant turns)
With blood warm oozing from her wounded trust,
10   Inscribes even on her shards of broken urns
The sign o' the cross—*the spirit above the dust!*

Yea, ape and angel, strife and old debate—
The harps of heaven and dreary gongs of hell;
Science the feud can only aggravate—
15   No umpire she betwixt the chimes and knell:
The running battle of the star and clod
Shall run forever—if there be no God.

Degrees we know, unknown in days before;
The light is greater, hence the shadow more;
20   And tantalized and apprehensive Man
Appealing—Wherefore ripen us to pain?
Seems there the spokesman of dumb Nature's train.
But through such strange illusions have they passed
Who in life's pilgrimage have baffled striven—

25 Even death may prove unreal at the last,
    And stoics be astounded into heaven.

        Then keep thy heart, though yet but ill-resigned—
    Clarel, thy heart, the issues there but mind;
    That like the crocus budding through the snow—
30 That like a swimmer rising from the deep—
    That like a burning secret which doth go
    Even from the bosom that would hoard and keep;
    Emerge thou mayst from the last whelming sea,
    And prove that death but routs life into victory.

                                                    1876

TOM DEADLIGHT

    (1810)

During a tempest encountered homeward-bound from the Med-
iterranean, a grizzled petty-officer, one of the two captains of
the forecastle, dying at night in his hammock, swung in the *sick-
bay* under the tiered gun-decks of the British *Dreadnought,* 98,
wandering in his mind, though with glimpses of sanity, and start-
ing up at whiles, sings by snatches his good-bye and last injunc-
tions to two messmates, his watchers, one of whom fans the
fevered tar with the flap of his old sou'-wester. Some names and
phrases, with here and there a line, or part of one; these, in his
aberration, wrested into incoherency from their original connec-
tion and import, he involuntarily derives, as he does the measure,
from a famous old sea-ditty, whose cadences, long rife, and now
humming in the collapsing brain, attune the last flutterings of
distempered thought.

    Farewell and adieu to you noble hearties,—
        Farewell and adieu to you ladies of Spain,
    For I've received orders for to sail for the Deadman,[143]
        But hope with the grand fleet to see you again.

5   I have hove my ship to, with main-top-sail aback, boys;
        I have hove my ship to, for to strike soundings clear—

The black scud a'flying; but, by God's blessing, dam' me,
Right up the Channel for the Deadman I'll steer.

I have worried through the waters that are called the
Doldrums,
10   And growled at Sargasso that clogs while ye grope—
Blast my eyes, but the light-ship is hid by the mist, lads:—
Flying Dutchman—odds bobbs—off the Cape of Good
Hope!

But what's this I feel that is fanning my cheek, Matt?
The white goney's[144] wing?—how she rolls!—'t is the Cape!
15   Give my kit to the mess, Jock, for kin none is mine, none;
And tell *Holy Joe*[145] to avast with the crape.

Dead reckoning, says *Joe,* it won't do to go by;
But they doused all the glims, Matt, in sky t' other night.
Dead reckoning is good for to sail for the Deadman;
20   And Tom Deadlight he thinks it may reckon near right.

The signal!—it streams for the grand fleet to anchor.
The captains—the trumpets—the hullabaloo!
Stand by for blue-blazes,[146] and mind your shank-painters,[147]
For the Lord High Admiral, he's squinting at you!

25   But give me my *tot,* Matt, before I roll over;
Jock, let's have your flipper, it's good for to feel;
And don't sew me up without *baccy* in mouth, boys,
And don't blubber like lubbers when I turn up my keel.

                                                          1888

THE AEOLIAN HARP

At the Surf Inn

List the harp in window wailing
    Stirred by fitful gales from sea:
Shrieking up in mad crescendo—
    Dying down in plaintive key!

•

5   Listen: less a strain ideal
          Than Ariel's rendering of the Real.
       What that Real is, let hint
          A picture stamped in memory's mint.

       Braced well up, with beams aslant,
10   Betwixt the continents sails the *Phocion*,[148]
       To Baltimore bound from Alicant.[149]
       Blue breezy skies white fleeces fleck
       Over the chill blue white-capped ocean:
       From yard-arm comes—"Wreck ho, a wreck!"

15   Dismasted and adrift,
       Long time a thing forsaken;
       Overwashed by every wave
       Like the slumbering kraken;
       Heedless if the billow roar,
20   Oblivious of the lull,
       Leagues and leagues from shoal or shore,
       It swims—a levelled hull:
       Bulwarks gone—a shaven wreck,
       Nameless, and a grass-green deck.
25   A lumberman: perchance, in hold
       Prostrate pines with hemlocks rolled.

       It has drifted, waterlogged,
       Till by trailing weeds beclogged:
          Drifted, drifted, day by day,
30   Pilotless on pathless way.
       It has drifted till each plank
       Is oozy as the oyster-bank:
          Drifted, drifted, night by night,
          Craft that never shows a light;
35   Nor ever, to prevent worse knell,
       Tolls in fog the warning bell.

       From collision never shrinking,
       Drive what may through darksome smother;
       Saturate, but never sinking,
40   Fatal only to the *other!*
          Deadlier than the sunken reef

Since still the snare it shifteth,
— Torpid in dumb ambuscade
Waylayingly it drifteth.

45   O, the sailors—O, the sails!
O, the lost crews never heard of!
Well the harp of Ariel wails
Thoughts that tongue can tell no word of!

                                                1888

THE MALDIVE SHARK

About the Shark, phlegmatical one,
Pale sot of the Maldive sea,
The sleek little pilot-fish, azure and slim,
How alert in attendance be.
5   From his saw-pit[150] of mouth, from his charnel of maw
They have nothing of harm to dread,
But liquidly glide on his ghastly flank
Or before his Gorgonian head;
Or lurk in the port of serrated teeth
10   In white triple tiers of glittering gates,
And there find a haven when peril's abroad,
An asylum in jaws of the Fates!
They are friends; and friendly they guide him to prey,
Yet never partake of the treat—
15   Eyes and brains to the dotard lethargic and dull,
Pale ravener of horrible meat.

                                                1888

THE BERG

(A Dream)

I saw a ship of martial build
(Her standards set, her brave apparel on)
Directed as by madness mere
Against a stolid iceberg steer,

5   Nor budge it, though the infatuate ship went down.
       The impact made huge ice-cubes fall
       Sullen, in tons that crashed the deck;
       But that one avalanche was all—
       No other movement save the foundering wreck.

10   Along the spurs of ridges pale,
       Not any slenderest shaft and frail,
       A prism over glass-green gorges lone,
       Toppled; or lace of traceries fine,
       Nor pendant drops in grot or mine
15   Were jarred, when the stunned ship went down.
       Nor sole the gulls in cloud that wheeled
       Circling one snow-flanked peak afar,
       But nearer fowl the floes that skimmed
       And crystal beaches, felt no jar.
20   No thrill transmitted stirred the lock
       Of jack-straw needle-ice at base;
       Towers undermined by waves—the block
       Atilt impending—kept their place.
       Seals, dozing sleek on sliddery ledges
25   Slipt never, when by loftier edges
       Through very inertia overthrown,
       The impetuous ship in bafflement went down.

       Hard Berg (methought), so cold, so vast,
       With mortal damps self-overcast;
30   Exhaling still thy dankish breath—
       Adrift dissolving, bound for death;
       Though lumpish thou, a lumbering one—
       A lumbering lubbard loitering slow,
       Impingers rue thee and go down,
35   Sounding thy precipice below,
       Nor stir the slimy slug that sprawls
       Along thy dead indifference of walls.

                                    1888

THE ENVIABLE ISLES

Through storms you reach them and from storms are free.
 Afar descried, the foremost drear in hue,
But, nearer, green; and, on the marge, the sea
 Makes thunder low and mist of rainbowed dew.

5 But, inland, where the sleep that folds the hills
A dreamier sleep, the trance of God, instills—
 On uplands hazed, in wandering airs aswoon,
Slow-swaying palms salute love's cypress tree
 Adown in vale where pebbly runlets croon
10 A song to lull all sorrow and all glee.

Sweet-fern and moss in many a glade are here,
 Where, strown in flocks, what cheek-flushed myriads lie
Dimpling in dream—unconscious slumberers mere,
 While billows endless round the beaches die.

            1888

PEBBLES

I

Though the Clerk of the Weather insist,
 And lay down the weather-law,
Pintado and gannet they wist
That the winds blow whither they list
5 In tempest or flaw.

II

Old are the creeds, but stale the schools,
 Revamped as the mode may veer,
But Orm from the schools to the beaches strays,
And, finding a Conch hoar with time, he delays
10 And reverent lifts it to ear.
That Voice, pitched in far monotone,
 Shall it swerve? shall it deviate ever?

The Seas have inspired it, and Truth—
   Truth, varying from sameness never.

III

In hollows of the liquid hills
   Where the long Blue Ridges run,
The flattery of no echo thrills,
   For echo the seas have none;
Nor aught that gives man back man's strain—
The hope of his heart, the dream in his brain.

IV

On ocean where the embattled fleets repair,
Man, suffering inflictor, sails on sufferance there.

V

Implacable I, the old implacable Sea:
   Implacable most when most I smile serene—
Pleased, not appeased, by myriad wrecks in me.

VI

Curled in the comb of yon billow Andean,
   Is it the Dragon's heaven-challenging crest?[151]
Elemental mad ramping of ravening waters—
   Yet Christ on the Mount,[152] and the dove in her nest!

VII

Healed of my hurt, I laud the inhuman Sea—
Yea, bless the Angels Four[153] that there convene;
For healed I am even by their pitiless breath
Distilled in wholesome dew named rosmarine.

1888

AFTER THE PLEASURE PARTY

Lines traced under an image of Amor[154] threatening

> *Fear me, virgin whosoever*
> *Taking pride from love exempt,*
> *Fear me, slighted. Never, never*
> *Brave me, nor my fury tempt:*
> 5   *Downy wings, but wroth they beat*
> *Tempest even in reason's seat.*

Behind the house the upland falls
With many an odorous tree—
White marbles gleaming through green halls,
10   Terrace by terrace, down and down,
And meets the starlit Mediterranean Sea.

'Tis Paradise. In such an hour
Some pangs that rend might take release.
Nor less perturbed who keeps this bower
15   Of balm, nor finds balsamic peace?
From whom the passionate words in vent[155]
After long revery's discontent?

Tired of the homeless deep,
Look how their flight yon hurrying billows urge,
20   Hitherward but to reap
Passive repulse from the iron-bound verge!
Insensate, can they never know
'Tis mad to wreck the impulsion so?

An art of memory[156] is, they tell:
25   But to forget! forget the glade
Wherein Fate sprung Love's ambuscade,
To flout pale years of cloistral life
And flush me in this sensuous strife.
'Tis Vesta struck with Sappho's smart.
30   No fable her delirious leap:
With more of cause in desperate heart,
Myself could take it—but to sleep!

Now first I feel, what all may ween,
That soon or late, if faded e'en,
35 One's sex asserts itself. Desire,
The dear desire through love to sway,
Is like the Geysers that aspire—
Through cold obstruction win their fervid way.
But baffled here—to take disdain,
40 To feel rule's instinct, yet not reign;
To dote, to come to this drear shame—
Hence the winged blaze that sweeps my soul
Like prairie fires that spurn control,
Where withering weeds incense the flame.

45 And kept I long heaven's watch for this,
Contemning love, for this, even this?
O terrace chill in Northern air,
O reaching ranging tube I placed
Against yon skies, and fable chased
50 Till, fool, I hailed for sister there
Starred Cassiopea in Golden Chair.
In dream I throned me, nor I saw
In cell the idiot crowned with straw.

And yet, ah yet scarce ill I reigned,
55 Through self-illusion self-sustained,
When now—enlightened, undeceived—
What gain I barrenly bereaved!
Than this can be yet lower decline—
Envy and spleen, can these be mine?

60 The peasant girl demure that trod
Beside our wheels that climbed the way,
And bore along a blossoming rod
That looked the sceptre of May-day—
On her—to fire this petty hell,
65 His softened glance how moistly fell!
The cheat! on briars her buds were strung;
And wiles peeped forth from mien how meek.
The innocent bare-foot! young, so young!
To girls, strong man's a novice weak.

70   To tell such beads! And more remain,
        Sad rosary of belittling pain.

        When after lunch and sallies gay,
        Like the Decameron folk we lay
        In sylvan groups; and I—let be!
75   O, dreams he, can he dream that one
        Because not roseate feels no sun?
        The plain lone bramble thrills with Spring
        As much as vines that grapes shall bring.

        Me now fair studies charm no more.
80   Shall great thoughts writ, or high themes sung
        Damask wan cheeks—unlock his arm
        About some radiant ninny flung?
        How glad with all my starry lore,
        I'd buy the veriest wanton's rose
85   Would but my bee therein repose.

        Could I remake me! or set free
        This sexless bound in sex, then plunge
        Deeper than Sappho, in a lunge
        Piercing Pan's paramount mystery!
90   For, Nature, in no shallow surge
        Against thee either sex may urge,
        Why hast thou made us but in halves—
        Co-relatives? This makes us slaves.
        If these co-relatives never meet
95   Self-hood itself seems incomplete.
        And such the dicing of blind fate
        Few matching halves here meet and mate.
        What Cosmic jest or Anarch blunder
        The human integral clove asunder
100   And shied the fractions through life's gate?

        Ye stars that long your votary knew
        Rapt in her vigil, see me here!
        Whither is gone the spell ye threw
        When rose before me Cassiopea?
105   Usurped on by love's stronger reign—
        But lo, your very selves do wane:

Light breaks—truth breaks! Silvered no more,
But chilled by dawn that brings the gale
Shivers yon bramble above the vale,
110 And disillusion opens all the shore.

One knows not if Urania yet
The pleasure-party may forget;
Or whether she lived down the strain
Of turbulent heart and rebel brain;
115 For Amor so resents a slight,
And her's had been such haught disdain,
He long may wreak his boyish spite,
And boy-like, little reck the pain.

One knows not, no. But late in Rome
120 (For queens discrowned a congruous home)
Entering Albani's porch[157] she stood
Fixed by an antique pagan stone
Colossal carved. No anchorite seer,
Not Thomas a Kempis, monk austere,
125 Religious more are in their tone;
Yet far, how far from Christian heart
That form august of heathen Art.
Swayed by its influence, long she stood,
Till surged emotion seething down,
130 She rallied and this mood she won:

Languid in frame for me,
To-day by Mary's convent shrine,
Touched by her picture's moving plea
In that poor nerveless hour of mine,
135 I mused—A wanderer still must grieve.
Half I resolved to kneel and believe,
Believe and submit, the veil take on.
But thee, armed Virgin![158] less benign,
Thee now I invoke, thou mightier one.
140 Helmeted woman—if such term
Befit thee, far from strife
Of that which makes the sexual feud
And clogs the aspirant life—
O self-reliant, strong and free,

145   Thou in whom power and peace unite,
        Transcender! raise me up to thee,
        Raise me and arm me!

                       Fond appeal.
        For never passion peace shall bring,
150   Nor Art inanimate for long
        Inspire. Nothing may help or heal
        While Amor incensed remembers wrong.
        Vindictive, not himself he'll spare;
        For scope to give his vengeance play
155   Himself he'll blaspheme and betray.

        Then for Urania, virgins everywhere,
        O pray! Example take too, and have care.

                                         1891

THE NIGHT-MARCH

With banners furled, and clarions mute,
    An army passes in the night;
And beaming spears and helms salute
    The dark with bright.

5   In silence deep the legions stream,
    With open ranks, in order true;
Over boundless plains they stream and gleam—
    No chief in view!

Afar, in twinkling distance lost,
10   (So legends tell) he lonely wends
And back through all that shining host
    His mandate sends.
                    1891

ART

In placid hours well-pleased we dream
Of many a brave unbodied scheme.
But form to lend, pulsed life create,
What unlike things must meet and mate:
A flame to melt—a wind to freeze;
Sad patience—joyous energies;
Humility—yet pride and scorn;
Instinct and study; love and hate;
Audacity—reverence. These must mate,
And fuse with Jacob's[159] mystic heart,
To wrestle with the angel—Art.

1891

HERBA SANTA[160]

I

After long wars when comes release
Not olive wands proclaiming peace
　　An import dearer share
Than stems of Herba Santa hazed
　　In autumn's Indian air.
Of moods they breathe that care disarm,
They pledge us lenitive and calm.

II

Shall code or creed a lure afford
To win all selves to Love's accord?
When Love ordained a supper divine
　　For the wide world of man,
What bickerings o'er his gracious wine!
　　Then strange new feuds began.

Effectual more in lowlier way,
　　Pacific Herb, thy sensuous plea
The bristling clans of Adam sway

At least to fellowship in thee!
Before thine altar tribal flags are furled,
Fain woulds't thou make one hearthstone of the world.

III

20 To scythe, to sceptre, pen and hod—
        Yea, sodden laborers dumb;
    To brains overplied, to feet that plod,
    In solace of the *Truce of God*[161]
        The Calumet has come!

IV

25 Ah for the world ere Raleigh's[162] find
        Never that knew this suasive balm
    That helps when Gilead's fails to heal,
        Helps by an interserted charm.

    Insinuous thou that through the nerve
30   Windest the soul, and so canst win
        Some from repinings, some from sin,
    The Church's aim thou dost subserve.

    The ruffled fag fordone with care
        And brooding, Gold would ease this pain:
35 Him soothest thou and smoothest down
    Till some content return again.

    Even ruffians feel thy influence breed
        Saint Martin's summer[163] in the mind,
    They feel this last evangel plead,
40 As did the first, apart from creed,
        Be peaceful, man—be kind!

V

    Rejected once on higher plain,
    O Love supreme, to come again
        Can this be thine?

45   Again to come, and win us too
          In likeness of a weed
      That as a god didst vainly woo,
          As man more vainly bleed?

          VI

      Forbear, my soul! and in thine Eastern chamber[164]
50   Rehearse the dream that brings the long release:
      Through jasmine sweet and talismanic amber
          Inhaling Herba Santa in the passive Pipe of Peace.

                                                    1891

      IN A BYE-CANAL

      A swoon of noon, a trance of tide,
      The hushed siesta brooding wide
          Like calms far off Peru;
      No floating wayfarer in sight,
5   Dumb noon, and haunted like the night
          When Jael the wiled one slew.

      A languid impulse from the oar
      Plied by my indolent gondolier
      Tinkles against a palace hoar,
10   And, hark, response I hear!
      A lattice clicks; and lo, I see
      Between the slats, mute summoning me,
      What loveliest eyes of scintillation,
      What basilisk glance of conjuration!

15   Fronted I have, part taken the span
      Of portents in nature and peril in man.
      I have swum—I have been
      Twixt the whale's black flukes and the white shark's fin;
      The enemy's desert have wandered in,
20   And there have turned, have turned and scanned,
      Following me how noiselessly,

Envy and Slander, lepers hand in hand.
All this. But at the latticed eye—
"Hey! Gondolier, you sleep, my man;
25   Wake up!" And, shooting by, we ran;
The while I mused, This, surely now,
Confutes the Naturalists, allow!
Sirens, true sirens verily be,
Sirens, waylayers in the sea.

30   Well, wooed by these same deadly misses,
Is it shame to run?
No! flee them did divine Ulysses,
    Brave, wise, and Venus' son.

1891

THE ATTIC LANDSCAPE

Tourist, spare the avid glance
    That greedy roves the sight to see:
Little here of "Old Romance,"
    Or Picturesque of Tivoli.

5   No flushful tint the sense to warm—
Pure outline pale, a linear charm.
The clear-cut hills carved temples face,
Respond, and share their sculptural grace.

'Tis Art and Nature lodged together,
10   Sister by sister, cheek to cheek;
Such Art, such Nature, and such weather
    The All-in-All seems here a Greek.

1891

THE PARTHENON

I

SEEN ALOFT FROM AFAR

Estranged in site,
Aerial gleaming, warmly white,
You look a suncloud motionless
In noon of day divine;
5   Your beauty charmed enhancement takes
In Art's long after-shine.

II

NEARER VIEWED

Like Lais, fairest of her kind,
In subtlety your form's defined—
The cornice curved, each shaft inclined,
10 While yet, to eyes that do but revel
And take the sweeping view,
Erect this seems, and that a level,
To line and plummet true.

Spinoza gazes; and in mind
15 Dreams that one architect designed
Lais—and you!

III

THE FRIEZE

What happy musings genial went
With airiest touch the chisel lent
To frisk and curvet light
20 Of horses gay—their riders grave—
Contrasting so in action brave
With virgins meekly bright,
Clear filing on in even tone
With pitcher each, one after one
25 Like water-fowl in flight.

IV

THE LAST TILE

When the last marble tile was laid
The winds died down on all the seas;
    Hushed were the birds, and swooned the glade;
    Ictinus sat; Aspasia said
30 "Hist!—Art's meridian, Pericles!"

                                    1891

IN THE DESERT

Never Pharaoh's Night,[165]
Whereof the Hebrew wizards croon,
Did so the Theban flamens[166] try
As me this veritable Noon.

5   Like blank ocean in blue calm
    Undulates the ethereal frame;
    In one flowing oriflamme
    God flings his fiery standard out.

    Battling with the Emirs fierce
10 Napoleon a great victory won,[167]
    Through and through his sword did pierce;
    But, bayonetted by this sun
    His gunners drop beneath the gun.

    Holy, holy, holy Light!
15 Immaterial incandescence,
    Of God the effluence of the essence,[168]
    Shekinah intolerably bright!

                                    1891

THE LITTLE GOOD FELLOWS

Make way, make way, give leave to rove
Under your orchard as above;
A yearly welcome if ye love!
And all who loved us alway throve.

5   Love for love. For ever we
When some unfriended man we see
Lifeless under forest-eaves,
Cover him with buds and leaves;
And charge the chipmunk, mouse, and mole—
10   Molest not this poor human soul!

Then let us never on green floor
Where your paths wind round about,
Keep to the middle in misdoubt,
Shy and aloof, unsure of ye;
15   But come like grass to stones on moor,
Wherever mortals be.

But toss your caps, O maids and men,
Snow-bound long in farm-house pen:
We chase Old Winter back to den.
20   See our red waistcoats! Alive be then—
Alive to the bridal-favors when
They blossom your orchards every Spring,
And cock-robin curves on a bridegroom's wing!

(?)

THE CHIPMUNK

Heart of autumn!
   Weather meet,
Like to sherbert
   Cool and sweet.

5   Stock-still I stand,
   And *him* I see

Prying, peeping
　　From Beech-tree;
Crickling, crackling
10　　Gleefully!
But, affrighted
　　By wee sound,
Presto! vanish—
　　Whither bound?

15　So did Baby,
　　Crowing mirth
E'en as startled
By some inkling
　　Touching Earth,
20　Flit (and whither?)
　　From our hearth!

(?)

TIME'S BETRAYAL

The tapping of a mature maple for the syrup, however recklessly
done, does not necessarily kill it. No; since being an aboriginal
child of Nature, it is doubtless blest with a constitution enabling
it to withstand a good deal of hard usage. But systematically to
bleed the immature trunk, though some sugar-makers, detected
in the act on ground not their own, aver that it does the sylvan
younker a deal of good, can hardly contribute to the tree's am-
plest development or insure patriarchal long life to it. Certain it
is, that in some young maples the annual tapping would seem
to make precocious the autumnal ripening or change of the leaf.
And such premature change would seem strikingly to enhance
the splendor of the tints.

Someone, whose morals need mending,
Sallies forth like the pillaging bee;
He waylays the syrup ascending
In anyone's saccharine tree;
5　So lacking in conscience indeed,
So reckless what life he makes bleed,

That to get at the juices, his staple,
The desirable sweets of the Spring,
He poignards a shapely young maple,
10   In my second-growth coppice—its King.
Assassin! secure in a crime never seen,
The underwood dense, e'en his victim a screen,
So be. But the murder will out,
        Never doubt, never doubt:
15   In season the leafage will tell,
        Turning red ere the rime
Yet, in turning, all beauty excel
        For a time, for a time!

Small thanks to the scamp. But, in vision, to me
20   A goddess mild pointing the glorified tree,
"So they change who die early, some bards who life render:
Keats, stabbed by the Muses, his garland's a splendor!"

                                                    (1889)

ROSARY BEADS

1

THE ACCEPTED TIME

Adore the Roses; nor delay
        Until the rose-fane[169] fall,
Or ever their censers cease to sway:
        "To-day!" the rose-priests call.

2

WITHOUT PRICE

5   Have the Roses. Needs no pelf
        The blooms to buy,
Nor any rose-bed to thyself
        Thy skill to try:
But live up to the Rose's light,
10   Thy meat shall turn to roses red,
        Thy bread to roses white.

3

GRAIN BY GRAIN

Grain by grain the Desert drifts
Against the Garden-Land:
Hedge well thy Roses, head the stealth
15   Of ever-creeping Land.

(1889)

THE RUSTY MAN

(By a Soured One)

In La Mancha he[170] mopeth,
    With beard thin and dusty;
He doteth and mopeth
    In library fusty—
5   'Mong his old folios gropeth:
    Cites obsolete saws
    Of chivalry's laws—
    Be the wronged one's knight:
    Die, but do right.
10   So he rusts and musts,
    While each grocer green
Thriveth apace with the fulsome face
    Of a fool serene.

(?)

CAMOENS[171]

1

(BEFORE)

Restless, restless, craving rest,
Forever must I fan this fire,
Forever in flame on flame aspire?
Yea, for the God demands thy best.
5   The world with endless beauty teems,

And thought evokes new worlds of dreams:
Then hunt the flying herds of themes.
And fan, yet fan thy fervid fire
Until the crucibled ore shall show
10   That fire can purge, as well as glow.
In ordered ardor nobly strong,
Flame to the height of ancient song.

CAMOENS IN THE HOSPITAL

    2
    (AFTER)

What now avails the pageant verse,
Trophies and arms with music borne?
15   Base is the world; and some rehearse
How noblest meet ignoble scorn.
Vain now the ardor, vain thy fire,
Delirium mere, unsound desire:
Fate's knife hath ripped the chorded lyre.
20   Exhausted by the exacting lay,
Thou dost but fall a surer prey
To wile and guile ill understood;
While they who work them, fair in face,
Still keep their strength in prudent place,
25   And claim they worthier run life's race,
Serving high God with useful good.

                                    (?)

FRUIT AND FLOWER PAINTER

She dens in a garret
    As void as a drum;
In lieu of plum-pudding—
    She paints the plum!

5   No use in my grieving,
                The shops I must suit:
            Broken hearts are but potsherds—
                Paint flowers and fruit!

How whistles her garret,
10   A seine for the snows:
She hums *Si fortuna*,[172]
          And—paints the rose!

          December is howling,
              But feign it a flute:
15   Help on the deceiving—
              Paint flowers and fruit!

                                        (?)

IN SHARDS THE SYLVAN VASES LIE

In shards the sylvan vases lie,
Their links of dance undone;
And brambles wither by thy brim,
Choked Fountain of the Sun!
5   The spider in the laurel spins,
The weed exiles the flower,
And, flung to kiln, Apollo's bust
Makes lime for Mammon's tower.

                                        (?)

TO——

Ah, wherefore, lonely, to and fro
Flittest like the shades that go
Pale wandering by the weedy stream?
We, like they, are but a dream:
5   Then dreams, and less, our miseries be;
Yea, fear and sorrow, pain, despair
Are but phantoms. But what plea
Avails here? phantoms having power
To make the heart quake and the spirit cower.

                                        (?)

PONTOOSUCE[173]

Crowning a bluff where gleams the lake below,
Some pillared pines in well-spaced order stand
And like an open temple show.
And here in best of seasons bland,
5   Autumnal noon-tide, I look out
From dusk arcades on sunshine all about.

Beyond the Lake, in upland cheer
Fields, pastoral fields and barns appear,
They skirt the hills where lonely roads
10   Revealed in links thro' tiers of woods
Wind up to indistinct abodes
And faery-peopled neighborhoods;
While further fainter mountains keep
Hazed in romance impenetrably deep.

15   Look, corn in stacks, on many a farm,
And orchards ripe in languorous charm,
As dreamy Nature, feeling sure
Of all her genial labor done,
And the last mellow fruitage won,
20   Would idle out her term mature;
Reposing like a thing reclined
In kinship with man's meditative mind.

For me, within the brown arcade—
Rich life, methought; sweet here in shade
25   And pleasant abroad in air!—But, nay,
A counter thought intrusive played,
A thought as old as thought itself,
And who shall lay it on the shelf!—
I felt the beauty bless the day
30   In opulence of autumn's dower;
But evanescence will not stay!
A year ago was such an hour,
As this, which but foreruns the blast
Shall sweep these live leaves to the dead leaves past.

•

35   All dies!—

              I stood in revery long.
      Then, to forget death's ancient wrong,
      I turned me in the deep arcade,
      And there by chance in lateral glade
40   I saw low tawny mounds in lines
      Relics of trunks of stately pines
      Ranked erst in colonnades where, lo!
      Erect succeeding pillars show!

              All dies! and not alone
45   The aspiring trees and men and grass;
      The poet's forms of beauty pass,
      And noblest deeds they are undone.
      Even truth itself decays, and lo,
      From truth's sad ashes fraud and falsehood grow.

50   All dies!

      The workman dies, and after him, the work;
      Like to these pines whose graves I trace,
      Statue and statuary fall upon their face:
      In very amaranths the worm doth lurk,
55   Even stars, Chaldæans say, have left their place.
      Andes and Apalachee[174] tell
      Of havoc ere our Adam fell,
      And present Nature as a moss doth show
      On the ruins of the Nature of the æons of long ago.

60   But look—and hark!

              Adown the glade,
      Where light and shadow sport at will,
      Who cometh vocal, and arrayed
      As in the first pale tints of morn—
65   So pure, rose-clear, and fresh and chill!
      Some ground-pine sprigs her brow adorn,
      The earthy rootlets tangled clinging.
      Over tufts of moss which dead things made,
      Under vital twigs which danced or swayed,
70   Along she floats, and lightly singing:

                         •

"Dies, all dies!
The grass it dies, but in vernal rain
Up it springs and it lives again;
Over and over, again and again
75   It lives, it dies and it lives again.
Who sighs that all dies?
Summer and winter, and pleasure and pain
And everything everywhere in God's reign,
They end, and anon they begin again:
80   Wane and wax, wax and wane:
Over and over and over amain
End, ever end, and begin again—
End, ever end, and forever and ever begin again!"

She ceased, and nearer slid, and hung
85   In dewy guise; then softlier sung:
"Since light and shade are equal set
And all revolves, nor more ye know;
Ah, why should tears the pale cheek fret
For aught that waneth here below.
90   Let go, let go!"

With that, her warm lips thrilled me through,
She kissed me, while her chaplet cold
Its rootlets brushed against my brow,
With all their humid clinging mould.
95   She vanished, leaving fragrant breath
And warmth and chill of wedded life and death.

(?)

BILLY IN THE DARBIES[175]

Good of the Chaplain to enter Lone Bay[176]
And down on his marrow-bones here and pray
For the likes just o' me, Billy Budd.—But look:
Through the port comes the moon-shine astray!
5   It tips the guard's cutlass and silvers this nook;
But 'twill die in the dawning of Billy's last day.
A jewel-block[177] they'll make of me tomorrow,

Pendant pearl from the yard-arm-end
Like the ear-drop I gave to Bristol Molly—
10   O, 'tis me, not the sentence they'll suspend.
Ay, Ay, all is up; and I must up too
Early in the morning, aloft from alow.
On an empty stomach, now, never it would do.
They'll give me a nibble—bit o' biscuit ere I go.
15   Sure, a messmate will reach me the last parting cup;
But, turning heads away from the hoist and the belay,
Heaven knows who will have the running of me up!
No pipe to those halyards.—But aren't it all sham?
A blur's in my eyes; it is dreaming that I am.
20   A hatchet to my hawser? All adrift to go?
The drum roll to grog, and Billy never know?
But Donald he has promised to stand by the plank;
So I'll shake a friendly hand ere I sink.
But—no! It is dead then I'll be, come to think.—
25   I remember Taff the Welshman when he sank.
And his cheek it was like the budding pink[.]
But me they'll lash in hammock, drop me deep.
Fathoms down, fathoms down, how I'll dream fast asleep.
I feel it stealing now. Sentry, are you there?
30   Just ease these darbies at the wrist, and roll me over fair,
I am sleepy, and the oozy weeds about me twist.

(1886–91)

FREDERICK GODDARD TUCKERMAN

(1821–1873)

Named for a relative who had once traveled in Switzerland with Wordsworth, Tuckerman was born into a prominent Boston family and reared in comfort on Beacon Hill. Private schooling took him, in 1837, to Harvard, where he came under the influence of his Greek tutor, Jones Very. Although circumstances, perhaps an illness, caused him shortly to withdraw from the College, he returned to the Law School a year later and took his degree in 1842. Admitted to the Massachusetts bar in 1844, he practiced law for only a short time before a legacy from his father enabled him to retire and devote himself to botany, astronomy, and poetry, his preferred occupations. In 1847, he married Hannah Lucinda Jones and removed with her to Greenfield, Massachusetts, there to live in semi-seclusion for the rest of his days. Following the death of an infant daughter in 1848, Hannah bore their first son. In 1851, Tuckerman made a literary tour of England. A year after the birth of his second son, in 1853, he returned to England as the guest of Tennyson, who, on parting, gave him the manuscript of "Locksley Hall." At about this time, Tuckerman's poems began to appear in the magazines. In 1857, after giving birth to a daughter, Hannah died, triggering the grief and religious questionings recorded in his five series of sonnets. When his only collection of poems appeared, privately printed, in 1860, he sent copies to Bryant, Emerson, Longfellow, and Very, whose opinions he valued and all of whom responded warmly to the volume. Three years later, the collection was published in England, perhaps at Tennyson's urging. This edition, along with the appearance of two of the poems in American magazines, led to commercial publication of the volume in Boston, in 1864 and again in 1869. Otherwise, Tuckerman published nothing more, although such now-esteemed poems as "The Cricket" were written after 1869, the year his first son died. At the time of his own death, from heart disease, he was all but forgotten and remained so until the 1930s, when reprintings of the sonnets and first printings of "The Cricket" brought him to critical notice. His complete poems appeared only in 1965.

SONNETS: FIRST SERIES

I

Sometimes, when winding slow by brook and bower,
Beating the idle grass,—of what avail,
I ask, are these dim fancies, cares and fears?
What though from every bank I drew a flower,—
5   Bloodroot, king orchis, or the pearlwort pale,—
And set it in my verse with thoughtful tears?
What would it count though I should sing my death
And muse and mourn with as poetic breath
As in damp garden walks the autumn gale
10   Sighs o'er the fallen floriage? What avail
Is the swan's voice if all the hearers fail?
Or his great flight that no eye gathereth
In the blending blue? And yet depending so,
God were not God, whom knowledge cannot know.

II

15   Wherefore, with this belief held like a blade,
Gathering my strength and purpose still and slow,
I wait, resolved to carry it to the heart
Of that dark doubt in one collected blow,
And stand at guard with spirit undismayed:
20   Nor fear the Opposer's anger, arms or art,
When from a hiding near behold him start
With a fresh weapon of my weakness made
And goad me with myself, and urge the attack
While I strike short and still give back and back
25   While the foe rages. Then from that disgrace
He points to where they sit that have won the race,
Laurel on laurel wreathing face o'er face,
And leaves me lower still, for, ranked in place,

III

And borne with theirs, my proudest thoughts do seem
30   Bald at the best and dim: a barren gleam
Among the immortal stars, and faint and brief

As northlight flitting in the dreary north.
What have thy dreams, a vague prospective worth?
An import imminent? or dost thou deem
35 Thy life so fair that thou wouldst set it forth
Before the day? or art thou wise in grief,
Has fruitful sorrow swept thee with her wing?
Today I heard a sweet voice carolling
In the woodlot paths, with laugh and careless cry
40 Leading her happy mates: apart I stepped,
And while the laugh and song went lightly by,
In the wild bushes I sat down and wept.

IV

Nor looks that backward life so bare to me,
My later youth, and ways I've wandered through,
45 But touched with innocent grace, the purring bee
O'er the maple log, the white-heaped cherry tree
That hummed all day in the sun, the April blue;
Yet hardly now one ray the Forward hath
To show where sorrow rests and rest begins,
50 Although I check my feet nor walk to wrath
Through days of crime, and grosser shadowings
Of evil done in the dark, but fearfully
Mid unfulfilled yet unrelinquished sins
That hedge me in and press about my path
55 Like purple poison flowers of stramony
With their dull opiate breath and dragon wings.

V

And so the day drops by, the horizon draws
The fading sun and we stand struck in grief,
Failing to find our haven of relief,
60 Wide of the way, nor sure to turn or pause,
And weep to view how fast the splendor wanes
And scarcely heed that yet some share remains
Of the red afterlight, some time to mark,
Some space between the sundown and the dark;
65 But not for him those golden calms succeed
Who while the day is high and glory reigns

Sees it go by, as the dim pampas plain,
Hoary with salt and gray with bitter weed,
Sees the vault blacken, feels the dark wind strain,
70   Hears the dry thunder roll, and knows no rain.

VI

Not sometimes, but to him that heeds the whole
And in the Ample reads his personal page,
Laboring to reconcile, content, assuage
The vexed conditions of his heritage,
75   Forever waits an angel at the goal.
And ills seem but as food for spirits sage,
And grief becomes a dark apparelage,
The weed and wearing of the sacred soul.
Might I but count, but here, one watchlight spark!
80   But vain, O vain this turning for the light,
Vain as a groping hand to rend the dark—
I call, entangled in the night, a night
Of wind and voices, but the gusty roll
Is vague, nor comes their cheer of pilotage.

VII

85   Dank fens of cedar, hemlock branches gray
With trees and trail of mosses, wringing-wet,
Beds of the black pitchpine in dead leaves set
Whose wasted red has wasted to white away,
Remnants of rain and droppings of decay,
90   Why hold ye so my heart, nor dimly let
Through your deep leaves the light of yesterday,
The faded glimmer of a sunshine set?
Is it that in your darkness, shut from strife,
The bread of tears becomes the bread of life?
95   Far from the roar of day, beneath your boughs
Fresh griefs beat tranquilly, and loves and vows
Grow green in your gray shadows, dearer far
Even than all lovely lights and roses are?

VIII

As when down some broad river dropping, we
100   Day after day behold the assuming shores
Sink and grow dim, as the great watercourse
Pushes his banks apart and seeks the sea:
Benches of pines, high shelf and balcony,
To flats of willow and low sycamores
105   Subsiding, till where'er the wave we see,
Himself is his horizon utterly.
So fades the portion of our early world,
Still on the ambit hangs the purple air;
Yet while we lean to read the secret there,
110   The stream that by green shoresides plashed and purled
Expands: the mountains melt to vapors rare,
And life alone circles out flat and bare.

IX

Yet wear we on, the deep light disallowed
That lit our youth; in years no longer young
115   We wander silently, and brood among
Dead graves, and tease the sunbreak and the cloud
For import: were it not better yet to fly,
To follow those that go before the throng,
Reasoning from stone to star, and easily
120   Exampling this existence? Or shall I—
Who yield slow reverence where I cannot see
And gather gleams where'er by chance or choice
My footsteps draw, though brokenly dispensed—
Come into light at last? or suddenly
125   Struck to the knees like Saul,[178] one arm against
The overbearing brightness, hear a voice?

X

An upper chamber in a darkened house,
Where, ere his footsteps reached ripe manhood's brink,
Terror and anguish were his lot to drink;
130   I cannot rid the thought nor hold it close

But dimly dream upon that man alone:
Now though the autumn clouds most softly pass,
The cricket chides beneath the doorstep stone
And greener than the season grows the grass.
135   Nor can I drop my lids nor shade my brows,
But there he stands beside the lifted sash;
And with a swooning of the heart, I think
Where the black shingles slope to meet the boughs
And, shattered on the roof like smallest snows,
140   The tiny petals of the mountain ash.

XI

What profits it to me, though here allowed
Life, sunlight, leisure, if they fail to urge
Me to due motion or myself to merge
With the onward stream, too humble, or too proud?
145   That find myself not with the popular surge
Washed off and on, or up to higher reefs
Flung with the foremost when the rolling crowd
Hoists like a wave, nor strong to speak aloud.
But standing here, gazing on mine own griefs,
150   Dark household woe, and wounds that bleed and smart,
With still lips and an outcry in the heart,
Or on from day to day I coldly creep
By summer farms and fields, by stream and steep,
Dull, and like one exhausted with deep sleep.

XII

155   Tall stately plants with spikes and forks of gold
Crowd every slope: my heart repeats its cry,
A cry for strength, for strength and victory:
The will to strive, the courage overbold
That would have moved me once to turn indeed
160   And level with the dust each lordly weed.
But now I weep upon my wayside walks
And sigh for those fair days, when glorying
I stood a boy amid the mullein-stalks
And wished myself like him the Lion King:[179]

165 There, where his shield shed arrows and his helm
Rang like a bell beaten with axe and brand,
He pushed the battle backward, realm on realm
Fallen in the swordswing of his stormy hand.

XIII

As one who walks and weeps by alien brine
170 And hears the heavy land-wash break, so I,
Apart from friends, remote in misery,
But brood on pain and find in heaven no sign:
The lights are strange, and bitter voices by.
So the doomed sailor, left alone to die,
175 Looks sadly seaward at the day's decline
And hears his parting comrades' jeers and scoffs
Or sees through mists that hinder and deform
The dewy stars of home, sees Regulus shine
With a hot flicker through the murky damp
180 And setting Sirius twitch and twinge like a lamp
Slung to the masthead in a night of storm
Of lonely vessel laboring in the troughs.

XIV

Not proud of station, nor in worldly pelf
Immoderately rich, nor rudely gay:
185 Gentle he was and generous in a way,
And with a wise direction ruled himself.
Blest Nature spread his table every day,
And so he lived, to all the blasts that woo
Responsible, as yon long locust spray
190 That waves and washes in the windy blue.
Nor wanted he a power to reach and reap
From hardest things a consequence and use,
And yet this friend of mine, in one small hour
Fell from himself, and was content to weep
195 For eyes love-dark, red lips, and cheeks in hues
Not red, but rose-dim like the jacinth flower.

XV

And she, her beauty never made her cold,
Young-Oread-like beside the green hill crest
And blissfully obeying Love's behest,
200 She turned to him as to a god of old,
Her smitten soul with its full strength and spring
Retaliating his love: unto that breast,
Ere scarce the arms dared open to infold,
She gave herself as but a little thing.
205 And now, to impulse cold, to passion dead,
With the wild grief of unperfected years,
He kissed her hands, her mouth, her hair, her head,
Gathered her close and closer to drink up
The odour of her beauty, then in tears
210 As for a world, gave from his lips the cup.

XVI

Yet Nature, where the thunder leaves its trace
On the high hemlock pine or sandstone bank,
Hating all shock of hue or contrast rank,
With some consenting color heals the place,
215 Or o'er it draws her mosses green and dank:
So gentle Time will bring with tender craft
Another day, and other greens ingraft
On the dead soil so fire-burned now and blank.
What we have had, we hold, and cannot sink
220 Remembrance: patience cometh from above;
And now he breathes apart to daily drink
In tears the bitter ashes of his love,
Yet precious rich, and a diviner draught
Than Agria[180] or Artemisia[181] drank.

XVII

225 All men, the preacher saith, whate'er or whence
Their increase walking through this world has been,
Both those that gather out, or after glean,
Or hold in simple fee[182] of harvests dense,
Though but perhaps a flowerless barren green,

230 Barren with spots of sorrel, knot grass, spurge:
Yet to one end their differing paths converge
And all must render answer, here or hence.
Lo! Death is at the doors, he crieth, with blows,
But what to him unto whose feverish sense
235 The stars tick audibly, and the wind's low surge
In the pine, attended, tolls and throngs and grows
On the dread ear, a thunder too profound
For bearing, a Niagara of sound!

XVIII

Perchance his own small field some charge demands:
240 So full the eternal choral sobs and swells,
But clear away the weeds, although there lurk
Within the weeds a few dim asphodels,
Flowers of a former day, how fair, how fair!
And yet behold them not, but to the work,
245 Before the short light darken, set thy hands:
Nor over the surface dip with easy share,
But beam-deep, plough and plunge your parallels,[183]
Breaking in clod and flower, that so may spring
From the deep grain a goodlier growth and kind,
250 Unstirred of heats that blast, of frosts that bind,
Nor swept aside ere the seed catch, by wing
Of casual shower nor any chance of wind.

XIX

Yet vain, perhaps, the fruits our care applaud:
If the Forefate decree the harvest fat
255 Why should we mind this thing or matter that,
To sift the seed and blow the chaff abroad?
But doubt not so the Giver to defraud
Who will accuse thy labor: spend, nor slack
Of thy best strength and sweetness too, till God
260 With a full hand and flowing pay thee back.
Behold, on rolling zone and zodiac
The spray and scatter of his bounty flung,
And what canst thou, to whom no hands belong
To hasten by one hour the morning's birth?

265   Or stay one planet at his circle hung,
        In the great flight of stars across the earth?

        xx

        Still craves the spirit: never Nature solves
        That yearning which with her first breath began,
        And in its blinder instinct still devolves
270   On god or pagod, Manada[184] or man,
        Or lower yet, brute service, apes and wolves.
        By Borneo's surf the bare barbarian
        Still to the sands beneath him bows to pray:
        Give Greek his god, the Bheel[185] his devil sway
275   And what remains to me, who count no odds
        Between such Lord and him I saw today,
        The farmer mounted on his market load,
        Bundles of wool and locks of upland hay,
        The son of toil that his own works bestrode,
280   And him, Ophion,[186] earliest of the gods?

        xxi

        O Father, God! to whom in happier days
        My father bade me cry when troubles fall,
        Again I come before thy tribunal
        Too faint for prayer and all too blind for praise,
285   Yet owning never through life's dim career
        The eye that would not see and reckless ear:
        Against my head no more thy tempests call;
        Refreshing that wild sorrow of the heart
        And those fierce tears, another morning raise
290   Upon this vision now so dimmed and swoln:
        Guide me as once unto thy feet to flee
        Claiming no price of labor, place, or part,
        And only seek before thy footstool fall'n
        Tears in mine eyes, to lift these hands of me.

        xxii

295   The morning comes, not slow with reddening gold,
        But wildly driven with windy shower and sway

As if the wind would blow the dark away:
Voices of wail, of misery multifold,
Wake with the light and its harsh glare obey.
300 And yet I walk betimes this day of spring,
Still my own private portion reckoning,
Not to compute, though every tear be told.
O might I on the gale my sorrow fling!
But sweep, sweep on, wild blast; who bids thee stay?
305 Across the stormy headlands shriek and sing
And, earlier than the daytime bring the day
To pouring eyes half-quenched with watery sight,
And breaking hearts that hate the morning light.

XXIII

Shall I not see her? yes: for one has seen
310 Her in her beauty since we called her dead,
One like herself, a fair young mother led
By her own lot to feel compassion keen;
And unto her last night my Anna came
And sat within her arms and spoke her name
315 While the old smile, she said, like starlight gleamed,
And like herself in fair young bloom, she said,
Only the white more white, the red more red,
And fainter than the mist her pressure seemed.
And words there were, though vague yet beautiful,
320 Which she who heard them could not tell to me;
It is enough: my Anna did not flee
To grief or fear, nor lies in slumber dull.

XXIV

Perhaps a dream: yet surely truth has beamed
Oft from the gate of dreams upon the brain
325 As on yon mountain dark with thunder-rain,
Today through cloudy clefts the glory streamed.
Why do men doubt, and balance, and disdain
Where she, the gentler spirit, seeks to skim
Light from the vague, though thick the shadows swim,
330 Still counting what she may not all explain—
Not to be lost, or lightly disesteemed

Though cloudy of shape it seem, and meaning dim?
Did Manoah's wife[187] doubt ere she showed to him
The angel standing in the golden grain?
335   Had Deborah fear? or was that vision vain
That Actia, Arlotte, and Mandané[188] dreamed?

XXV

By this low fire I often sit to woo
Memory to bring the days forever done,
And call the mountains where our love begun
340   And the dear happy woodlands dipped in dew,
And pore upon the landscape like a book
But cannot find her: or there rise to me
Gardens and groves in light and shadow outspread;
Or on a headland far away I see
345   Men marching slow in orderly review,
And bayonets flash as, wheeling from the sun,
Rank after rank give fire: or sad, I look
On miles of moonlit brine, with many a bed
Of wave weed heaving. There the wet sands shine
350   And just awash, the low reef lifts its line.

XXVI

For Nature daily through her grand design
Breathes contradiction where she seems most clear,
For I have held of her the gift to hear
And felt indeed endowed of sense divine
355   When I have found by guarded insight fine,
Cold April flowers in the green end of June,
And thought myself possessed of Nature's ear
When by the lonely mill-brook into mine,
Seated on slab or trunk asunder sawn,
360   The night-hawk blew his horn at summer noon;
And in the rainy midnight I have heard
The ground sparrow's long twitter from the pine,
And the catbird's silver song, the wakeful bird
That to the lighted window sings for dawn.

XXVII

365 So to the mind long brooding but on it
A haunting theme for anger, joy, or tears,
With ardent eyes, not what we think appears;
But hunted home, behold! its opposite.
Worn sorrow breaking in disastrous mirth,
370 And wild tears wept of laughter, like the drops
Shook by the trampling thunder to the earth;
And each seems either, or but a counterfeit
Of that it would dissemble: hopes are fears
And love is woe: nor here the discord stops;
375 But through all human life runs the account,
Born into pain and ending bitterly—
Yet sweet perchance, betweentime, like a fount
That rises salt and freshens to the sea.

XXVIII

Not the round natural world, not the deep mind,
380 The reconcilement holds: the blue abyss
Collects it not; our arrows sink amiss
And but in Him may we our import find.
The agony to know, the grief, the bliss
Of toil, is vain and vain: clots of the sod
385 Gathered in heat and haste and flung behind
To blind ourselves and others, what but this
Still grasping dust and sowing toward the wind?
No more thy meaning seek, thine anguish plead.
But leaving straining thought and stammering word,
390 Across the barren azure pass to God:
Shooting the void in silence like a bird,
A bird that shuts his wings for better speed.

1860

INFATUATION

'Tis his one hope: all else that round his life
So fairly circles, scarce he numbers now.
The pride of name, a lot with blessings rife,
Determined friends, great gifts that him endow,
5   Are shrunk to nothing in a woman's smile.
Counsel, reproof, entreaty, all are lost
Like windy waters which their strength exhaust,
And leave no impress; worldly lips revile
With sneer and stinging gibe, but idly by,
10   Unfelt, unheard, the impatient arrows fly:
Careless, he joins a parasitic train,
Fops, fools and flatterers whom her arts enchain,
Nor counts aught base that may to her pertain.
Immersed in love, or what he deems is such,
15   The present exigence he looks to please,
Nor seeks beyond, but only strives to clutch
That which will goad his heart but ne'er can ease:
As the drenched sailor, wrecked in Indian seas,
To some low reef of wounding coral clings
20   Mid slav'ry weed and drift and ocean scurf;
Yet heedeth not companionship of these,
But strains his quivering grasp and stoutly swings,
Despite of lifting swell and flinging surf.

                                          1860

RHOTRUDA

In the golden reign of Charlemaign the king,
The three and thirtieth year, or thereabout,
Young Eginardus, bred about the court,
(Left mother-naked at a postern door),
5   Had thence by slow degrees ascended up:
First page, then pensioner, lastly the king's knight
And secretary; but held these steps for naught
Save as they led him to the Princess' feet,
Eldest and loveliest of the regal three:
10   Most gracious too, and liable to love.

For Bertha was betrothed, and she, the third,
Giselia, would not look upon a man.
So, bending his whole heart unto this end,
He watched and waited, trusting to stir to fire
15 The indolent interest in those large eyes,
And feel the languid hands beat in his own,
Ere the new spring; and well he played his part,
Slipping no chance to bribe or brush aside
All that would stand between him and the light,
20 Making fast foes in sooth, but feeble friends.
But what cared he, who had read of ladies' love,
And how young Launcelot gained his Guinivere,
A foundling too, or of uncertain strain?[189]
And when one morning, coming from the bath,
25 He crossed the Princess on the palace stair,
And kissed her there in her sweet disarray,
Nor met the death he dreamed of in her eyes,
He knew himself a hero of old romance,
Not seconding, but surpassing what had been.

30 And so they loved, if that tumultuous pain
Be love,—disquietude of deep delight,
And sharpest sadness: nor though he knew her heart
His very own,—gained on the instant too,
And like a waterfall that at one leap
35 Plunges from pines to palms, shattered at once
To wreaths of mist and broken spray-bows bright,—
He loved not less, nor wearied of her smile;
Yet through the daytime held aloof and strange
His walk, mingling with knightly mirth and game,
40 Solicitous but to avoid alone
Aught that might make against him in her mind;
Yet strong in this, that, let the world have end,
He had pledged his own, and held Rhotruda's troth.

But Love, who had led these lovers thus along,
45 Played them a trick one windy night and cold:
For Eginardus, as his wont had been,
Crossing the quadrangle, and under dark,
No faint moonshine, nor sign of any star,
Seeking the Princess' door, such welcome found,

50   The knight forgot his prudence in his love;
      For lying at her feet, her hands in his,
      And telling tales of knightship and emprise,
      And ringing war; while up the smooth white arm
      His fingers slid insatiable of touch,
55   The night grew old: yet of the hero-deeds
      That he had seen he spoke, and bitter blows
      Where all the land seemed driven into dust
      Beneath fair Pavia's wall, where Loup beat down
      The Langobard,[190] and Charlemaign laid on,
60   Cleaving horse and rider;—then, for dusty drought
      Of the fierce tale, he drew her lips to his,
      And silence locked the lovers fast and long,
      Till the great bell crashed One into their dream.

      The castle-bell! and Eginard not away!
65   With tremulous haste she led him to the door,
      When, lo! the courtyard white with fallen snow,
      While clear the night hung over it with stars.
      A dozen steps, scarce that, to his own door:
      A dozen steps? a gulf impassable!
70   What to be done? Their secret must not lie
      Bare to the sneering eye with the first light;
      She could not have his footsteps at her door!
      Discovery and destruction were at hand:
      And, with the thought they kissed, and kissed again;
75   When suddenly the lady, bending, drew
      Her lover towards her half-unwillingly,
      And on her shoulders fairly took him there,
      Who held his breath to lighten all his weight,—
      And lightly carried him the courtyard's length
80   To his own door; then, like a frightened hare,
      Fled back in her own tracks unto her bower,
      To pant awhile, and rest that all was safe.

      But Charlemaign the king, who had risen by night
      To look upon memorials,[191] or at ease
85   To read and sign an ordinance of the realm,—
      The Cunigosteura or Fanolehen[192]
      For tithing corn, so to confirm the same
      And stamp it with the pommel of his sword,—

Hearing their voices in the court below,
90   Looked from his window and beheld the pair.

Angry the king, yet laughing half to view
The strangeness and vagary of the feat:
Laughing indeed! with twenty minds to call
From his inner bed chamber the Forty[193] forth,
95   Who watched all night beside their monarch's bed
With naked swords and torches in their hands,
And test this lover's-knot with steel and fire;
But with a thought,—tomorrow yet will serve
To greet these mummers,—softly the window closed,
100   And so went back to his corn-tax again.

But with the morn the king a meeting called
Of all his lords, courtiers and kindred too,
And squire and dame, in the great Audience Hall
Gathered, where sat the king, with the high crown
105   Upon his brow, beneath a drapery
That fell around him like a cataract!
With flecks of color crossed and cancellate;
And over this, like trees about a stream,
Rich carven-work, heavy with wreath and rose,
110   Palm and palmirah,[194] fruit and frondage, hung.

And more the high Hall held of rare and strange,
For on the king's right hand Leoena[195] bowed
In cloudlike marble, and beside her crouched
The tongueless lioness: on the other side,
115   And poising this, the second Sappho stood,—
Young Erexcea,[196] with her head discrowned,
The anadema[197] on the horn of her lyre;
And by the walls there hung in sequence long,
Merlin himself, and Uterpendragon,
120   With all their mighty deeds, down to the day
When all the world seemed lost in wreck and rout,
A wrath of crashing steeds and men; and, in
The broken battle, fighting hopelessly,
King Arthur with the ten wounds on his head.[198]
125   But not to gaze on these, appeared the peers.
Stern looked the king, and, when the court was met,

The lady and her lover in the midst,—
Spoke to his lords, demanding them of this:
What merits he, the servant of the king,
130   Forgetful of his place, his trust, his oath,
Who, for his own bad end, to hide his fault,
Makes use of her, a Princess of the realm,
As of a mule? a beast of burden! borne
Upon her shoulders through the winter's night
135   And wind and snow? "Death!" said the angry lords;
And knight and squire and minion murmured, "Death!"
Not one discordant voice: but Charlemaign,
Though to his foes a circulating sword,
Yet, as a king, mild, gracious, exorable,
140   Blest in his children too, with but one born
To vex his flesh like an ingrowing nail,
Looked kindly on the trembling pair, and said:
"Yes, Eginardus, well hast thou deserved
Death for this thing, for, hadst thou loved her so,
145   Thou shouldst have sought her Father's will in this,—
Protector and disposer of his child,—
And asked her hand of him, her lord and thine.
Thy life is forfeit here, but take it, thou!
Take even two lives for this forfeit one;
150   And thy fair portress,—wed her; honor God,
Love one another, and obey the king."

Thus far the legend; but of Rhotrude's smile,
Or of the lords' applause, as truly they
Would have applauded their first judgment too,
155   We nothing learn: yet still the story lives,
Shines like a light across those dark old days,
Wonderful glimpse of woman's wit and love,
And worthy to be chronicled with hers
Who to her lover dear threw down her hair,
160   When all the garden glanced with angry blades![199]
Or like a picture framed in battle-pikes
And bristling swords, it hangs before our view:—
The palace court white with the fallen snow,
The good king leaning out into the night,
165   And Rhotrude bearing Eginard on her back.

1860

AS SOMETIMES IN A GROVE

As sometimes in a grove at morning chime,
    To hit his humor,
The poet lies alone and trifles time,—
    A slow consumer:
5   While terebinthine tears the dark greens shed,
    Balsamic grument,[200]
And pinestraws fall into his breast, or spread
    A sere red strewment:[201]

As come dark motions of the memory,
10   Which no denial
Can wholly chase away; nor may we see,
    In faint espial,
The features of that doubt we brood upon
    With dull persistence,
15 As in broad noon our recollections run
    To pre-existence;

As when a man, lost on a prairie plain
    When day is fleeting,
Looks on the glory, and then turns again,
20   His steps repeating,
And knows not if he draws his comrades nigher,
    Nor where their camp is,
Yet turns once more to view those walls of fire
    And chrysolampis:[202]

25 So idleness, and phantasy, and fear,
    As with dim grandeur
The night comes crowned, seem his who wanders here
    In rhyme a ranger;
Seem his, who once has seen his morning go,
30   Nor dreamed it mattered,
Mysterious Noon, and, when the night comes, lo,
    A life well-scattered

Is all behind, and howling wastes before:
    O that some warmer
35 Imagination might those deeps explore,

And turn informer.
In the old track we paddle on, and way,
    Nor can forego it;
Or up behind that horseman of the day,
40   A modern poet,

We mount, uncertain where we may arrive
    Or what we trust to,
Unknowing where indeed our friend may drive
    His Pegasus to:
45 Now reining daintily by stream and sward
    In managed canter,
Now plunging on, through brick and beam and board,
    Like a Levanter!

Yet ever running on the earth his course,
50   And sometimes into,
Chasing false fire, we fare from bad to worse;
    With such a din too—
As this that now awakes your grief and ire,
    Reader or rider
55 Of halting verse; till in the Muse's mire
    We sink beside her.

O in this day of light, must he then lie
    In darkness Stygian,
Who for his friend may choose Philosophy,
60   Reason, Religion?
And find, though late, that creeds of good men prove
    No form or fable,
But stand on God's broad justice, and his love
    Unalterable?

65 Must he then fail because his youth went wide?
    O hard endeavor
To gather grain from the marred mountain side;
    Or to dissever
The lip from its old draught: we tilt the cup,
70   And drug reflection,
Or juggle with the soul, and so patch up
    A peace or paction;[203]

Would carry heaven with half our sins on board
    Or blending thickly
75 Earth's grosser sweet with that, to our reward
    Would mount up quickly;
Ready to find, when this had dimmed and shrunk,
    A more divine land,
And lightly, as a sailor climbs a trunk
80   In some dark pineland.

Truly a treasure in a hollow tree
    Is golden honey,
Breathing of mountain dew, clean fragrancy,
    And uplands sunny;
85 But who, amid a thousand men or youth,
    Landward or seabred,
Would choose his honey bitter in the mouth
    With bark and beebread?

No! though the wish to join that harping choir
90   May oft assail us,
We scarce shall find vague doubt, or half desire
    Will aught avail us;
Nor fullest trust that firmest faith can get,
    Dark fear supplanting;
95 There may be blue and better blue, and yet
    Our part be wanting.

Alas! the bosom sin that haunts the breast
    We pet and pension;
Or let the foolish deed still co-exist
100   With fair intention.
From some temptation, where we did not dare,
    We turn regretful;
And so the devil finds his empty snare?
    Not by a netful!

105 O conscience, coward conscience! teasing so
    Priest, lawyer, statist,
Thou art a cheat, and may be likened to
    Least things or greatest:
A rocking stone poised on a lonely tower

110   In pastures hilly,
        Or like an anther of that garden-flower,
            The tiger-lily,

        Stirred at a breath, or stern to break and check
            All winds of heaven;
115   While toward some devil's dance we crane the neck
            And sigh unshriven;
        Or lightly follow where our leaders go
            With pipe and tambour,
        Chafing our follies till they fragrant grow,
120   And like rubbed amber.

        Yet, for these things, not godlike seems the creed
            To crush the creature,
        Nor Christly sure; but shows it like indeed
            A pulpit preacher,
125   To fling a pebble in a pond and roar
            "There! sink or swim, stone,
        Get safe to land with all your ballast, or
            Black fire and brimstone!"

        Ah, in a world with joy and sorrow torn,
130   No life is sweeter
        Than his, just starting in his journey's morn;
            And seems it bitter
        To give up all things for the pilgrim's staff
            And garment scanty;
135   The moonlight walk, the dream, the dance, the laugh,
            And fair Rhodanthe.

        And must it be, when but to him, in truth,
            Whom it concerneth,
        The spirit speaks? Yet to the tender tooth
140   The tongue still turneth.
        And he, who proudly walks through life, and hears
            Paean and plaudit,
        Looks ever to the end with doubts and fears,
            And that last audit.

145 But, as we sometimes see before the dawn,
     With motion gentle,
   Across the lifeless landscape softly drawn
     A misty mantle:
   Up from the river to the bluffs away,
150   The low land blurring,
   All dim and still, and in the broken gray
     Some faint stars stirring:

   So, when the shadow falls across our eyes,
     And interveneth
155 A veil 'twixt us and all we know and prize;
     Then, in the zenith,
   May heaven's lone lights not pass in wreaths obscure,
     But still sojourning
   Amid the cloud, appoint us to the pure
160   And perfect morning.

   And even here,—when stretching wide our hands,
     Longing and leaning
   To find, 'mid jarring claims and fierce demands,
     Our strength and meaning:
165 Though troubled to its depths the spirit heaves,
     Though dim despairing,—
   Shall we not find Life's mesh of wreck and leaves
     Pale pearls insnaring?

   Yes,—as the waters cast upon the land
170   Loose dulse and laver,
   And where the sea beats in, befringe the sand
     With wild sea-slaver,—
   For currents lift the laden and the light,
     Groundswell and breaker;
175 Not weedy trash alone, but corallite,[204]
     Jasper, and nacre.

   And though at times the tempter sacks our souls,
     And fiends usurp us,
   Let us still press for right, as ocean rolls,

180   With power and purpose,
Returning still, though backward flung and foiled,
    To higher station,
So to work out, distained and sorely soiled,
    Our own salvation.

185   Nor following Folly's lamp, nor Learning's lore,
    But, humbly falling
Before our Father and our Friend, implore
    Our gift and calling:
Outside the vineyard we have wandered long
190   In storm and winter;
O guide the grasping hands, the footsteps wrong,
    And bid us enter

Ere the day draw to dark: nor heave and prize
    With strength unable,
195   Nor range a world for wisdom's fruit that lies
    On our own table.
So shall we find each movement an advance,
    Each hour momentous,
If but in our own place and circumstance,
200   Thou, God, content us.

               1860

CORALIE

Pale water flowers
That quiver in the quick turn of the brook,
    And thou, dim nook,—
Dimmer in twilight,—call again to me
5   Visions of life and glory that were ours
When first she led me here, young Coralie.

No longer blest:
Yet standing here in silence, may not we
    Fancy or feign

10   That little flowers do fall about thy rest
       In silver mist and tender-dropping rain,
       And that thy world is peace, loved Coralie?

       Our friendships flee—
       And, darkening all things with her mighty shade,
15   Comes Misery:
       No longer look the faces that we see
       With the old eyes, and Woe itself shall fade,
       Nor even this be left us, Coralie!

       Feelings and fears,
20   That once were ours, have perished in the mould,
          And grief is cold:
       Hearts may be dead to grief, and if our tears
       Are failing or forgetful, there will be
       Mourners about thy bed, lost Coralie.

25   The brook-flowers shine,
       And a faint song the falling water has,
          But not for thee;
       The dull night weepeth, and the sorrowing pine
       Drops his dead hair upon thy young grave grass,
30   My Coralie! my Coralie!

                    ———————

       I took from its glass a flower
       To lay on her grave with dull accusing tears;
       But the heart of the flower fell out as I handled the rose,
       And my heart is shattered, and soon will wither away.

35   I watch the changing shadows,
       And the patch of windy sunshine upon the hill,
       And the long blue woods; and a grief no tongue can tell
       Breaks at my eyes in drops of bitter rain.

       I hear her baby wagon,
40   And the little wheels go over my heart:
       O when will the light of the darkened house return?
       O when will she come who made the hills so fair?

I sit by the parlor window
When twilight darkens, and winds get cold without;
45   But the blessed feet no more come up the walk,
And my little girl and I cry softly together.

1860

THE CRICKET

I

The humming bee purrs softly o'er his flower;
    From lawn and thicket
The dogday locust singeth in the sun
    From hour to hour:
5   Each has his bard, and thou, ere day be done,
        Shalt have no wrong.
So bright that murmur mid the insect crowd,
Muffled and lost in bottom-grass, or loud
        By pale and picket:
10   Shall I not take to help me in my song
        A little cooing cricket?

II

The afternoon is sleepy; let us lie
Beneath these branches whilst the burdened brook,
Muttering and moaning to himself, goes by;
15   And mark our minstrel's carol whilst we look
Toward the faint horizon swooning blue.
        Or in a garden bower,
Trellised and trammeled with deep drapery
        Of hanging green,
20   Light glimmering through—
There let the dull hop be,
Let bloom, with poppy's dark refreshing flower:
Let the dead fragrance round our temples beat.
Stunning the sense to slumber, whilst between
25   The falling water and fluttering wind
        Mingle and meet,

Murmur and mix,
No few faint pipings from the glades behind,
  Or alder-thicks:[205]
30 But louder as the day declines,
From tingling tassel, blade, and sheath,
Rising from nets of river vines,
    Winrows and ricks,
    Above, beneath,
35   At every breath,
At hand, around, illimitably
Rising and falling like the sea,
    Acres of cricks!

III

Dear to the child who hears thy rustling voice
40 Cease at his footstep, though he hears thee still,
Cease and resume with vibrance crisp and shrill,
Thou sittest in the sunshine to rejoice.
Night lover too; bringer of all things dark
And rest and silence; yet thou bringest to me
45 Always that burthen of the unresting Sea,
The moaning cliffs, the low rocks blackly stark;
These upland inland fields no more I view,
But the long flat seaside beach, the wild seamew,
  And the overturning wave!
50 Thou bringest too, dim accents from the grave
To him who walketh when the day is dim,
Dreaming of those who dream no more of him,
With edged remembrances of joy and pain;
And heyday looks and laughter come again:
55 Forms that in happy sunshine lie and leap,
With faces where but now a gap must be,
Renunciations, and partitions deep
And perfect tears, and crowning vacancy!
And to thy poet at the twilight's hush,
60 No chirping touch of lips with laugh and blush,
But wringing arms, hearts wild with love and woe,
Closed eyes, and kisses that would not let go!

IV

So wert thou loved in that old graceful time
   When Greece was fair,
65   While god and hero hearkened to thy chime;
      Softly astir
Where the long grasses fringed Caÿster's[206] lip;
Long-drawn, with glimmering sails of swan and ship,
   And ship and swan;
70   Or where
   Reedy Eurotas[207] ran.
Did that low warble teach thy tender flute,
   Xenaphyle,[208]
Its breathings mild? say! did the grasshopper
75   Sit golden in thy purple hair
      O Psammathe?[209]
      Or wert thou mute,
Grieving for Pan amid the alders there?
And by the water and along the hill
80   That thirsty tinkle in the herbage still,
Though the lost forest wailed to horns of Arcady?

V

Like the Enchanter old—[210]
Who sought mid the dead water's weeds and scum
For evil growths beneath the moonbeam cold,
85   Or mandrake or dorcynium;
And touched the leaf that opened both his ears,
So that articulate voices now he hears
In cry of beast, or bird, or insect's hum,—
Might I but find thy knowledge in thy song!
90   That twittering tongue,
Ancient as light, returning like the years.
      So might I be,
Unwise to sing, thy true interpreter
Through denser stillness and in sounder dark,
95   Than ere thy notes have pierced to harrow me.
      So might I stir
      The world to hark
      To thee my lord and lawgiver,

And cease my quest:
100   Content to bring thy wisdom to the world;
Content to gain at last some low applause,
        Now low, now lost
Like thine from mossy stone, amid the stems and straws,
        Or garden gravemound tricked and dressed—
105   Powdered and pearled
        By stealing frost—
In dusky rainbow beauty of euphorbias![211]
For larger would be less indeed, and like
The ceaseless simmer in the summer grass
110   To him who toileth in the windy field,
        Or where the sunbeams strike,
Naught in innumerable numerousness.
        So might I much possess,
        So much must yield;
115   But failing this, the dell and grassy dike,
The water and the waste shall still be dear,
And all the pleasant plots and places
        Where thou hast sung, and I have hung
        To ignorantly hear.
120   Then Cricket, sing thy song! or answer mine!
Thine whispers blame, but mine has naught but praises.
It matters not. Behold! the autumn goes,
        The shadow grows,
The moments take hold of eternity;
125   Even while we stop to wrangle or repine
        Our lives are gone—
        Like thinnest mist,
Like yon escaping color in the tree;
Rejoice! rejoice! whilst yet the hours exist—
130   Rejoice or mourn, and let the world swing on
Unmoved by cricket song of thee or me.

                                        (c. 1870)

EMILY DICKINSON

(1830–1886)

Emily Dickinson experienced inside her head as much as Napoléon did outside his. She lived her entire life in the house where she was born, in Amherst, Massachusetts, all but her last eight years under the shadow of her father, Edward Dickinson, a prominent lawyer, sometime state legislator and United States congressman, and the treasurer of Amherst College, which his father had founded. Outwardly at least, that paternal dominance appears to have been absolute. When Emily's older brother, William Austin, married a friend of hers and planned to leave Amherst, Edward persuaded the couple to build a house next door and eventually arranged for his son to replace him as college treasurer. Like Emily, her younger sister, Lavinia, remained at home unmarried, and there are stories of the father's having forbade at least one of Emily's intended engagements.

Behind this facade of parental control and filial obedience, however, family life was anything but regular. Austin's marriage foundered early, and for years he maintained a sexual liaison with a friend of Lavinia's, in the Dickinson house, apparently with the full knowledge of both daughters. Emily almost never visited her brother's home, next door, declined to accompany her parents to church, and, from her mid-twenties on, secluded herself increasingly in her room, where she wrote poems that, had he known about either one, would have disturbed her father no less than Austin's carnal recreations.

Emily's early life foreshadows none of these deviances. After public school, she attended Amherst Academy for two years, then Mount Holyoke Female Seminary for one, 1847–48. Her letters from this time show her a lively, witty, gregarious, socially adroit young woman, unusual, if at all, only in her bubbling loquacity. In the early 1850s, however, her life underwent a radical change, roughly coincident with two events that would resurface, somewhat enigmatically, in her later poems and letters. The first was the early death of a young clerk in her father's law office who had encouraged her early attempts at verse. The second was the departure for San Francisco of a married clergyman whom she had met in Philadelphia and with whom she had conceived some sort of personal attachment. Whatever the causes, she began, around 1854, to sever all immediate relations with the world outside her room and to write the nearly two thousand poems that have since been attributed to her.

From that time on, she communicated with others almost entirely by letters, often interspersed with poems, and by notes in verse. Among her correspondents, two of the most notable were Samuel Bowles, editor of the *Springfield Republican,* whom she met in 1858 and to whom she sent at least fifty poems in the (mistaken) hope that he would find one suitable to print; and Thomas Wentworth Higginson, literary editor of the *Atlantic Monthly,* from whom she sought advice, only to sidestep it when it came and then ask for more.

When her father died, in 1874, and her mother declined into invalidism shortly thereafter, she became head of the household, discharging all the domestic duties that position entailed. In 1882, her mother died, leaving her and Lavinia alone together until Emily herself died, of liver disease, four years later.

Among her sister's effects, Lavinia found some fifteen hundred manuscript poems, some in finished form carefully bound in fascicles, some in revised drafts, some in first drafts on scraps of paper. This unearthing began a publishing history so vexed by editorial interference, family rivalry, and belated discoveries that the canon remains uncertain and may never be fixed. Between 1890 and 1945 there appeared seven successive collections of new poems, all of them more or less "improved" by the editors, some of them found later to lack a discoverable source in manuscript and therefore of doubtful attribution, many of them of unknown date. In 1955, Thomas H. Johnson prepared a variorum edition of 1,775 poems and fragments, arranged under the numbers employed below.

49

I never lost as much but twice,
And that was in the sod.
Twice have I stood a beggar
Before the door of God!

5   Angels—twice descending
Reimbursed my store—

Burglar! Banker—Father!
I am poor once more!

                    (1858)

95

My nosegays are for Captives—
Dim—long expectant eyes,
Fingers denied the plucking,
Patient till Paradise.

5   To such, if they should whisper
Of morning and the moor,
They bear no other errand,
And I, no other prayer.

                    (1858)

77

I never hear the word "escape"
Without a quicker blood,
A sudden expectation,
A flying attitude!

5   I never hear of prisons broad
By soldiers battered down,
But I tug childish at my bars
Only to fail again!

                    (1859)

89

Some things that fly there be—
Birds—Hours—the Bumblebee—
Of these no Elegy.

Some things that stay there be—
5   Grief—Hills—Eternity—
Nor this behooveth me.

There are that resting, rise.
Can I expound the skies?
How still the Riddle lies!

(1859)

135

Water, is taught by thirst.
Land—by the Oceans passed.
Transport—by throe—
Peace—by its battles told—
5 Love, by Memorial Mold—[212]
Birds, by the Snow.

(1859)

185

"Faith" is a fine invention
When Gentlemen can *see*—
But *Microscopes* are prudent
In an Emergency.

(1860)

211

Come slowly—Eden!
Lips unused to Thee—
Bashful—sip thy Jessamines—
As the fainting Bee—

5 Reaching late his flower,
Round her chamber hums—
Counts his nectars—
Enters—and is lost in Balms.

(1860)

213

Did the Harebell loose her girdle
To the lover Bee
Would the Bee the Harebell *hallow*
Much as formerly?

5   Did the "Paradise"—persuaded—
Yield her moat of pearl—
Would the Eden *be* an Eden,
Or the Earl—an *Earl?*

(1860)

243

I've known a Heaven, like a Tent—
To wrap its shining Yards—
Pluck up its stakes, and disappear—
Without the sound of Boards
5   Or Rip of Nail—Or Carpenter—
But just the miles of Stare—
That signalize a Show's Retreat—
In North America—

No Trace—no Figment of the Thing
10 That dazzled, Yesterday,
No Ring—no Marvel—
Men, and Feats—
Dissolved as utterly—
As Bird's far Navigation
15 Discloses just a Hue—
A plash of Oars, a Gaiety—
Then swallowed up, of View.

(1861)

249

Wild Nights—Wild Nights!
Were I with thee

Wild Nights should be
Our luxury!

5   Futile—the Winds—
To a Heart in port—
Done with the Compass—
Done with the Chart!

Rowing in Eden—
10   Ah, the Sea!
Might I but moor—Tonight—
In Thee!

                    (1861)

          257

Delight is as the flight—
Or in the Ratio of it,
As the Schools would say—
The Rainbow's way—
5   A Skein
Flung colored, after Rain,
Would suit as bright,
Except that flight
Were Aliment—

10   "If it would last"
I asked the East,
When that Bent Stripe
Struck up my childish
Firmament—
15   And I, for glee,
Took Rainbows, as the common way,
And empty Skies
The Eccentricity—

And so with Lives—
20   And so with Butterflies—
Seen magic—through the fright
That they will cheat the sight—

And Dower latitudes far on—
Some sudden morn—
25   Our portion—in the fashion—
Done—
                    (1861)

            258

There's a certain Slant of light,
Winter Afternoons—
That oppresses, like the Heft
Of Cathedral Tunes—

5   Heavenly Hurt, it gives us—
We can find no scar,
But internal difference,
Where the Meanings, are—

None may teach it—Any—
10   'Tis the Seal Despair—[213]
An imperial affliction
Sent us of the Air—

When it comes, the Landscape listens—
Shadows—hold their breath—
15   When it goes, 'tis like the Distance
On the look of Death—
                    (1861)

            281

'Tis so appalling—it exhilarates—
So over Horror, it half Captivates—
The Soul stares after it, secure—
A Sepulchre, fears frost, no more—

5   To scan a Ghost, is faint—
But grappling, conquers it—

How easy, Torment, now—
Suspense kept sawing so—

The Truth, is Bald, and Cold—
10 But that will hold—
If any are not sure—
We show them—prayer—
But we, who know,
Stop hoping, now—

15 Looking at Death, is Dying—
Just let go the Breath—
And not the pillow at your Cheek
So Slumbereth—

Others, Can wrestle—
20 Yours, is done—
And so of Woe, bleak dreaded—come,
It sets the Fright at liberty—
And Terror's free—
Gay, Ghastly, Holiday!

(1861)

290

Of Bronze—and Blaze—
The North—Tonight—
So adequate—it forms—
So preconcerted with itself—
5   So distant—to alarms—
An Unconcern so sovereign
To Universe, or me—
Infects my simple spirit
With Taints of Majesty—
10 Till I take vaster attitudes—
And strut upon my stem—
Disdaining Men, and Oxygen,
For Arrogance of them—

My Splendors, are Menagerie—
15 But their Completeless Show
Will entertain the Centuries
When I, am long ago,
An Island in dishonored Grass—
Whom none but Beetles—know.

(1861)

301

I reason, Earth is short—
And Anguish—absolute—
And many hurt,
But, what of that?

5   I reason, we could die—
The best Vitality
Cannot excel Decay,
But, what of that?

I reason, that in Heaven—
10 Somehow, it will be even—
Some new Equation, given—
But, what of that?

(1862)

307

The One who could repeat the Summer day—
Were greater than itself—though He
Minutest of Mankind should be—

And He—could reproduce the Sun—
5   At period of going down—
The Lingering—and the Stain—I mean—

When Orient have been outgrown—
And Occident—become Unknown—
His Name—remain—

(1862)

315

He fumbles at your Soul
As Players at the Keys
Before they drop full Music on—
He stuns you by degrees—
5   Prepares your brittle Nature
For the Ethereal Blow
By fainter Hammers—further heard—
Then nearer—Then so slow
Your Breath has time to straighten—
10   Your Brain—to bubble Cool—
Deals—One—imperial—Thunderbolt—
That scalps your naked Soul—

When Winds take Forests in their Paws—
The Universe—is still—

                        (1862)

326

I cannot dance upon my Toes—
No Man instructed me—
But oftentimes, among my mind,
A Glee possesseth me,

5   That had I Ballet knowledge—
Would put itself abroad
In Pirouette to blanch a Troupe—
Or lay a Prima,²¹⁴ mad,

And though I had no Gown of Gauze—
10   No Ringlet, to my Hair,
Nor hopped to Audiences—like Birds,
One Claw upon the Air,

Nor tossed my shape in Eider Balls,
Nor rolled on wheels of snow
15   Till I was out of sight, in sound,
The House encore me so—

Nor any know I know the Art
I mention—easy—Here—
Nor any Placard boast me—
20   It's full as Opera—

(1862)

328

A Bird came down the Walk—
He did not know I saw—
He bit an Angleworm in halves
And ate the fellow, raw,

5   And then he drank a Dew
From a convenient Grass—
And then hopped sidewise to the Wall
To let a Beetle pass—

He glanced with rapid eyes
10   That hurried all around—
They looked like frightened Beads, I thought—
He stirred his Velvet Head

Like one in danger, Cautious,
I offered him a Crumb
15   And he unrolled his feathers
And rowed him softer home—

Than Oars divide the Ocean,
Too silver for a seam—
Or Butterflies, off Banks of Noon
20   Leap, plashless as they swim.

(1862)

338

I know that He exists.
Somewhere—in Silence—
He has hid his rare life
From our gross eyes.

5   'Tis an instant's play.
'Tis a fond Ambush—
Just to make Bliss
Earn her own surprise!

But—should the play
10   Prove piercing earnest—
Should the glee—glaze—
In Death's—stiff—stare—

Would not the fun
Look too expensive!
15   Would not the jest—
Have crawled too far!

                    (1862)

357

God is a distant—stately Lover—
Woos, as He states us—by His Son—
Verily, a Vicarious Courtship—
"Miles", and "Priscilla", were such an One—[215]

5   But, lest the Soul—like fair "Priscilla"
Choose the Envoy—and spurn the Groom—
Vouches, with hyperbolic archness—
"Miles", and "John Alden" were Synonym—

                              (1862)

410

The first Day's Night had come—
And grateful that a thing
So terrible—had been endured—
I told my Soul to sing—

5   She said her Strings were snapt—
Her Bow—to Atoms blown—
And so to mend her—gave me work
Until another Morn—

And then—a Day as huge
10   As Yesterdays in pairs,
Unrolled its horror in my face—
Until it blocked my eyes—

My Brain—begun to laugh—
I mumbled—like a fool—
15   And tho' 'tis Years ago—that Day—
My Brain keeps giggling—still.

And Something's odd—within—
That person that I was—
And this One—do not feel the same—
20   Could it be Madness—this?

(1862)

414

'Twas like a Maelstrom, with a notch,
That nearer, every Day,
Kept narrowing its boiling Wheel
Until the Agony

5   Toyed coolly with the final inch
Of your delirious Hem—
And you dropt, lost,
When something broke—
And let you from a Dream—

10   As if a Goblin with a Gauge—
        Kept measuring the Hours—
        Until you felt your Second
        Weigh, helpless, in his Paws—

        And not a Sinew—stirred—could help,
15   And sense was setting numb—
        When God—remembered—and the Fiend
        Let go, then, Overcome—

        As if your Sentence stood—pronounced—
        And you were frozen led
20   From Dungeon's luxury of Doubt
        To Gibbets, and the Dead—

        And when the Film had stitched your eyes
        A Creature gasped "Reprieve"!
        Which Anguish was the utterest—then—
25   To perish, or to live?

                                    (1862)

        435

        Much Madness is divinest Sense—
        To a discerning Eye—
        Much Sense—the starkest Madness—
        'Tis the Majority
5   In this, as All, prevail—
        Assent—and you are sane—
        Demur—you're straightway dangerous—
        And handled with a Chain—

                                    (1862)

        448

        This was a Poet—It is That
        Distills amazing sense
        From ordinary Meanings—
        And Attar so immense

5   From the familiar species
       That perished by the Door—
       We wonder it was not Ourselves
       Arrested it—before—

       Of Pictures, the Discloser—
10   The Poet—it is He—
       Entitles Us—by Contrast—
       To ceaseless Poverty—

       Of Portion—so unconscious—
       The Robbing—could not harm—
15   Himself—to Him—a Fortune—
       Exterior—to Time—

                          (1862)

       501

       This World is not Conclusion.
       A Species stands beyond—
       Invisible, as Music—
       But positive, as Sound—
5   It beckons, and it baffles—
       Philosophy—don't know—
       And through a Riddle, at the last—
       Sagacity, must go—
       To guess it, puzzles scholars—
10   To gain it, Men have borne
       Contempt of Generations
       And Crucifixion, shown—
       Faith slips—and laughs, and rallies—
       Blushes, if any see—
15   Plucks at a twig of Evidence—
       And asks a Vane, the way—
       Much Gesture, from the Pulpit—
       Strong Hallelujahs roll—
       Narcotics cannot still the Tooth
20   That nibbles at the soul—

                          (1862)

502

At least—to pray—is left—is left—
Oh Jesus—in the Air—
I know not which thy chamber is—
I'm knocking—everywhere—

5   Thou settest Earthquake in the South—
And Maelstrom, in the Sea—
Say, Jesus Christ of Nazareth—
Hast thou no Arm for Me?

(1862)

506

He touched me, so I live to know
That such a day, permitted so,
I groped upon his breast—
It was a boundless place to me
5   And silenced, as the awful sea
Puts minor streams to rest.

And now, I'm different from before,
As if I breathed superior air—
Or brushed a Royal Gown—
10   My feet, too, that had wandered so—
My Gypsy face—transfigured now—
To tenderer Renown—

Into this Port, if I might come,
Rebecca,[216] to Jerusalem,
15   Would not so ravished turn—
Nor Persian, baffled at her shrine
Lift such a Crucifixal sign
To her imperial Sun.[217]

(1862)

519

'Twas warm—at first—like Us—
Until there crept upon
A Chill—like frost upon a Glass—
Till all the scene—be gone.

5   The Forehead copied Stone—
The Fingers grew too cold
To ache—and like a Skater's Brook—
The busy eyes—congealed—

It straightened—that was all—
10   It crowded Cold to Cold—
It multiplied indifference—
As Pride were all it could—

And even when with Cords—
'Twas lowered, like a Weight—
15   It made no Signal, nor demurred,
But dropped like Adamant.

                              (1862)

547

I've seen a Dying Eye
Run round and round a Room—
In search of Something—as it seemed—
Then Cloudier become—
5   And then—obscure with Fog—
And then—be soldered down
Without disclosing what it be
'Twere blessed to have seen—

                            (1862)

556

The Brain, within its Groove
Runs evenly—and true—

But let a Splinter swerve—
'Twere easier for You—

5   To put a Current back—
When Floods have slit the Hills—
And scooped a Turnpike for Themselves—
And trodden out the Mills—

(1862)

577

If I may have it, when it's dead,
I'll be contented—so—
If just as soon as Breath is out
It shall belong to me—

5   Until they lock it in the Grave,
'Tis Bliss I cannot weigh—
For tho' they lock Thee in the Grave,
Myself—can own the key—

Think of it Lover! I and Thee
10   Permitted—face to face to be—
After a Life—a Death—We'll say—
For Death was That—
And this—is Thee—

I'll tell Thee All—how Bald it grew—
15   How Midnight felt, at first—to me—
How all the Clocks stopped in the World—
And Sunshine pinched me—'Twas so cold—

Then how the Grief got sleepy—some—
As if my Soul were deaf and dumb—
20   Just making signs—across—to Thee—
That this way—thou could'st notice me—

I'll tell you how I tried to keep
A smile, to show you, when this Deep
All Waded—We look back for Play,
25   At those Old Times—in Calvary.

Forgive me, if the Grave come slow—
For Coveting to look at Thee—
Forgive me, if to stroke thy frost
Outvisions Paradise!

(1862)

599

There is a pain—so utter—
It swallows substance up—
Then covers the Abyss with Trance—
So Memory can step
5   Around—across—upon it—
As one within a Swoon—
Goes safely—where an open eye—
Would drop Him—Bone by Bone.

(1862)

606

The Trees like Tassels—hit—and swung—
There seemed to rise a Tune
From Miniature Creatures
Accompanying the Sun—

5   Far Psalteries of Summer—
Enamoring the Ear
They never yet did satisfy—
Remotest—when most fair

The Sun shone whole at intervals—
10   Then Half—then utter hid—
As if Himself were optional
And had Estates of Cloud

Sufficient to enfold Him
Eternally from view—

15 Except it were a whim of His
To let the Orchards grow—

A Bird sat careless on the fence—
One gossipped in the Lane
On silver matters charmed a Snake
20 Just winding round a Stone—

Bright Flowers slit a Calyx
And soared upon a Stem
Like Hindered Flags—Sweet hoisted—
With Spices—in the Hem—

25 'Twas more—I cannot mention—
How mean—to those that see—
Vandyke's[218] Delineation
Of Nature's—Summer Day!

(1862)

612

It would have starved a Gnat—
To live so small as I—
And yet I was a living Child—
With Food's necessity

5 Upon me—like a Claw—
I could no more remove
Than I could coax a Leech away—
Or make a Dragon—move—

Nor like the Gnat—had I—
10 The privilege to fly
And seek a Dinner for myself—
How mightier He—than I—

Nor like Himself—the Art
Upon the Window Pane

15   To gad my little Being out—
        And not begin—again—

                                (1862)

                613

        They shut me up in Prose—
        As when a little Girl
        They put me in the Closet—
        Because they liked me "still"—

5   Still! Could themself have peeped—
        And seen my Brain—go round—
        They might as wise have lodged a Bird
        For Treason—in the Pound—

        Himself has but to will
10   And easy as a Star
        Abolish his Captivity—
        And laugh—No more have I—

                                (1862)

                622

        To know just how He suffered—would be dear—
        To know if any Human eyes were near
        To whom He could entrust His wavering gaze—
        Until it settled broad—on Paradise—

5   To know if He was patient—part content—
        Was Dying as He thought—or different—
        Was it a pleasant Day to die—
        And did the Sunshine face His way—

        What was His furthest mind—Of Home—or God—
10   Or what the Distant say—
        At news that He ceased Human Nature
        Such a Day—

And Wishes—Had He Any—
Just His Sigh—Accented—
15 Had been legible—to Me—
And was He Confident until
Ill fluttered out—in Everlasting Well—

And if He spoke—What name was Best—
What last
20 What One broke off with
At the Drowsiest—

Was He afraid—or tranquil—
Might He know
How Conscious Consciousness—could grow—
25 Till Love that was—and Love too best to be—
Meet—and the Junction be Eternity

                                    (1862)

    629

I watched the Moon around the House
Until upon a Pane—
She stopped—a Traveller's privilege—for Rest—
And there upon

5   I gazed—as at a stranger—
The Lady in the Town
Doth think no incivility
To lift her Glass—upon—

But never Stranger justified
10 The Curiosity
Like Mine—for not a Foot—nor Hand—
Nor Formula—had she—

But like a Head—a Guillotine
Slid carelessly away—
15 Did independent, Amber—
Sustain her in the sky—

Or like a Stemless Flower—
Upheld in rolling Air
By finer Gravitations—
20   Than bind Philosopher—

No Hunger—had she—nor an Inn—
Her Toilette—to suffice—
Nor Avocation—nor Concern
For little Mysteries

25   As harass us—like Life—and Death—
And Afterwards—or Nay—
But seemed engrossed to Absolute—
With shining—and the Sky—

The privilege to scrutinize
30   Was scarce upon my Eyes
When, with a Silver practise—
She vaulted out of Gaze—

And next—I met her on a Cloud—
Myself too far below
35   To follow her superior Road—
Or its advantage—Blue—

(1862)

632

The Brain—is wider than the Sky—
For—put them side by side—
The one the other will contain
With ease—and You—beside—

5   The Brain is deeper than the sea—
For—hold them—Blue to Blue—
The one the other will absorb—
As Sponges—Buckets—do—

The Brain is just the weight of God—
10   For—Heft them—Pound for Pound—

And they will differ—if they do—
As Syllable from Sound—

(1862)

640

I cannot live with You—
It would be Life—
And Life is over there—
Behind the Shelf

5   The Sexton keeps the Key to—
Putting up
Our Life—His Porcelain—
Like a Cup—

Discarded of the Housewife—
10   Quaint—or Broke—
A newer Sevres pleases—
Old Ones crack—

I could not die—with You—
For One must wait
15   To shut the Other's Gaze down—
You—could not—

And I—Could I stand by
And see You—freeze—
Without my Right of Frost—
20   Death's privilege?

Nor could I rise—with You—
Because Your Face
Would put out Jesus'—
That New Grace

25   Glow plain—and foreign
On my homesick Eye—
Except that You than He
Shone closer by—

They'd judge Us—How—
30   For You—served Heaven—You know,
Or sought to—
I could not—

Because You saturated Sight—
And I had no more Eyes
35   For sordid excellence
As Paradise

And were You lost, I would be—
Though My Name
Rang loudest
40   On the Heavenly fame—

And were You—saved—
And I—condemned to be
Where You were not—
That self—were Hell to Me—

45   So We must meet apart—
You there—I—here—
With just the Door ajar
That Oceans are—and Prayer—
And that White Sustenance—
50   Despair—

           (1862)

      652

A Prison gets to be a friend—
Between its Ponderous face
And Ours—a Kinsmanship express—
And in its narrow Eyes—

5   We come to look with gratitude
For the appointed Beam
It deal us—stated as our food—
And hungered for—the same—

We learn to know the Planks—
10 That answer to Our feet—
So miserable a sound—at first—
Nor ever now—so sweet—

As plashing in the Pools—
When Memory was a Boy—
15 But a Demurer Circuit—
A Geometric Joy—

The Posture of the Key
That interrupt the Day
To Our Endeavor—Not so real
20 The Cheek of Liberty—

As this Phantasm Steel—
Whose features—Day and Night—
Are present to us—as Our Own—
And as escapeless—quite—

25 The narrow Round—the Stint—
The slow exchange of Hope—
For something passiver—Content
Too steep for looking up—

The Liberty we knew
30 Avoided—like a Dream—
Too wide for any Night but Heaven—
If That—indeed—redeem—

(1862)

656

The name—of it—is "Autumn"—
The hue—of it—is Blood—
An Artery—upon the Hill—
A Vein—along the Road—

5 Great Globules—in the Alleys—
And Oh, the Shower of Stain—

When Winds—upset the Basin—
And spill the Scarlet Rain—

It sprinkles Bonnets—far below—
10   It gathers ruddy Pools—
Then—eddies like a Rose—away—
Upon Vermilion Wheels—

(1862)

657

I dwell in Possibility—
A fairer House than Prose—
More numerous of Windows—
Superior—for Doors—

5   Of Chambers as the Cedars—
Impregnable of Eye—
And for an Everlasting Roof
The Gambrels of the Sky—

Of Visitors—the fairest—
10   For Occupation—This—
The spreading wide my narrow Hands
To gather Paradise—

(1862)

670

One need not be a Chamber—to be Haunted—
One need not be a House—
The Brain has Corridors—surpassing
Material Place—

5   Far safer, of a Midnight Meeting
External Ghost
Than its interior Confronting—
That Cooler Host.

Far safer, through an Abbey gallop,
10   The Stones a'chase—
Than Unarmed, one's a'self encounter—
In lonesome Place—

Ourself behind ourself, concealed—
Should startle most—
15   Assassin hid in our Apartment
Be Horror's least.

The Body—borrows a Revolver—
He bolts the Door—
O'erlooking a superior spectre—
20   Or More—

(1862)

754

My Life had stood—a Loaded Gun—
In Corners—till a Day
The Owner passed—identified—
And carried Me away—

5   And now We roam in Sovereign Woods—
And now We hunt the Doe—
And every time I speak for Him—
The Mountains straight reply—

And do I smile, such cordial light
10   Upon the Valley glow—
It is as a Vesuvian face
Had let its pleasure through—

And when at Night—Our good Day done—
I guard My Master's Head—
15   'Tis better than the Eider-Duck's
Deep Pillow—to have shared—

To foe of His—I'm deadly foe—
None stir the second time—

On whom I lay a Yellow Eye—
20   Or an emphatic Thumb—

Though I than He—may longer live
He longer must—than I—
For I have but the power to kill,
Without—the power to die—

(1862)

1053

It was a quiet way—
He asked if I was his—
I made no answer of the Tongue
But answer of the Eyes—
5   And then He bore me on
Before this mortal noise
With swiftness, as of Chariots
And distance, as of Wheels.
This World did drop away
10   As Acres from the feet
Of one that leaneth from Balloon
Upon an Ether street.
The Gulf behind was not,
The Continents were new—
15   Eternity it was before
Eternity was due.
No Seasons were to us—
It was not Night nor Morn—
But Sunrise stopped upon the place
20   And fastened it in Dawn.

(1862)

1712

A Pit—but Heaven over it—
And Heaven beside, and Heaven abroad,

And yet a Pit—
With Heaven over it.

5   To stir would be to slip—
To look would be to drop—
To dream—to sap the Prop
That holds my chances up.
Ah! Pit! With Heaven over it!

10 The depth is all my thought—
I dare not ask my feet—
'Twould start us where we sit
So straight you'd scarce suspect
It was a Pit—with fathoms under it—
15 Its Circuit just the same.
Seed—summer—tomb—
Whose Doom to whom?

                              (1862)

        525

I think the Hemlock likes to stand
Upon a Marge of Snow—
It suits his own Austerity—
And satisfies an awe

5   That men, must slake in Wilderness—
And in the Desert—cloy—
An instinct for the Hoar, the Bald—
Lapland's—necessity—

The Hemlock's nature thrives—on cold—
10 The Gnash of Northern winds
Is sweetest nutriment—to him—
His best Norwegian Wines—

To satin Races—he is nought—
But Children on the Don,

15   Beneath his Tabernacles, play,
        And Dnieper Wrestlers, run.
                                        (1863)

        665

        Dropped into the Ether Acre—
        Wearing the Sod Gown—
        Bonnet of Everlasting Laces—
        Brooch—frozen on—

5   Horses of Blonde—and Coach of Silver—
        Baggage a strapped Pearl—
        Journey of Down—and Whip of Diamond—
        Riding to meet the Earl—
                                        (1863)

        709

        Publication—is the Auction
        Of the Mind of Man—
        Poverty—be justifying
        For so foul a thing

5   Possibly—but We—would rather
        From Our Garret go
        White—Unto the White Creator—
        Than invest—Our Snow—

        Thought belong to Him who gave it—
10   Then—to Him Who bear
        Its Corporeal illustration—Sell
        The Royal Air—

        In the Parcel—Be the Merchant
        Of the Heavenly Grace—
15   But reduce no Human Spirit
        To Disgrace of Price—
                                        (1863)

771

None can experience stint
Who Bounty—have not known—
The fact of Famine—could not be
Except for Fact of Corn—

5   Want—is a meagre Art
Acquired by Reverse—
The Poverty that was not Wealth—
Cannot be Indigence.

(1863)

812

A Light exists in Spring
Not present on the Year
At any other period—
When March is scarcely here

5   A Color stands abroad
On Solitary Fields
That Science cannot overtake
But Human Nature feels.

It waits upon the Lawn,
10   It shows the furthest Tree
Upon the furthest Slope you know
It almost speaks to you.

Then as Horizons step
Or Noons report away
15   Without the Formula of sound
It passes and we stay—

A quality of loss
Affecting our Content
As Trade had suddenly encroached
20   Upon a Sacrament.

(1864)

824

The Wind begun to rock the Grass
With threatening Tunes and low—
He threw a Menace at the Earth—
A Menace at the Sky.

5   The Leaves unhooked themselves from Trees—
And started all abroad
The Dust did scoop itself like Hands
And threw away the Road.

The Wagons quickened on the Streets
10   The Thunder hurried slow—
The Lightning showed a Yellow Beak
And then a livid Claw.

The Birds put up the Bars to Nests—
The Cattle fled to Barns—
15   There came one drop of Giant Rain
And then as if the Hands

That held the Dams had parted hold
The Waters Wrecked the Sky,
But overlooked my Father's House—
20   Just quartering a Tree—

                                        (1864)

854

Banish Air from Air—
Divide Light if you dare—
They'll meet
While Cubes in a Drop
5   Or Pellets of Shape
Fit
Films cannot annul
Odors return whole
Force Flame
10   And with a Blonde push

Over your impotence
Flits Steam.

(1864)

915

Faith—is the Pierless Bridge
Supporting what We see
Unto the Scene that We do not—
Too slender for the eye

5   It bears the Soul as bold
As it were rocked in Steel
With Arms of Steel at either side—
It joins—behind the Veil

To what, could We presume
10   The Bridge would cease to be
To Our far, vacillating Feet
A first Necessity.

(1864)

925

Struck, was I, not yet by Lightning—
Lightning—lets away
Power to perceive His Process
With Vitality.

5   Maimed—was I—yet not by Venture—
Stone of stolid Boy—
Nor a Sportsman's Peradventure—
Who mine Enemy?

Robbed—was I—intact to Bandit—
10   All my Mansion torn—
Sun—withdrawn to Recognition—
Furthest shining—done—

Yet was not the foe—of any—
Not the smallest Bird
15   In the nearest Orchard dwelling
Be of Me—afraid.

Most—I love the Cause that slew Me.
Often as I die
Its beloved Recognition
20   Holds a Sun on Me—

Best—at Setting—as is Nature's—
Neither witnessed Rise
Till the infinite Aurora
In the other's eyes.

(1864)

949

Under the Light, yet under,
Under the Grass and the Dirt,
Under the Beetle's Cellar
Under the Clover's Root,

5   Further than Arm could stretch
Were it Giant long,
Further than Sunshine could
Were the Day Year long,

Over the Light, yet over,
10   Over the Arc of the Bird—
Over the Comet's chimney—
Over the Cubit's Head,

Further than Guess can gallop
Further than Riddle ride—
15   Oh for a Disc to the Distance
Between Ourselves and the Dead!

(1864)

959

A loss of something ever felt I—
The first that I could recollect
Bereft I was—of what I knew not
Too young that any should suspect

5   A Mourner walked among the children
I notwithstanding went about
As one bemoaning a Dominion
Itself the only Prince cast out—

Elder, Today, a session wiser
10 And fainter, too, as Wiseness is—
I find myself still softly searching
For my Delinquent Palaces—

And a Suspicion, like a Finger
Touches my Forehead now and then
15 That I am looking oppositely
For the site of the Kingdom of Heaven—

                                (1864)

997

Crumbling is not an instant's Act
A fundamental pause
Dilapidation's processes
Are organized Decays.

5   'Tis first a Cobweb on the Soul
A Cuticle of Dust
A Borer in the Axis
An Elemental Rust—

Ruin is formal—Devil's work
10 Consecutive and slow—

Fail in an instant, no man did
Slipping—is Crash's law.

(1865)

1056

There is a Zone whose even Years
No Solstice interrupt—
Whose Sun constructs perpetual Noon
Whose perfect Seasons wait—

5   Whose Summer set in Summer, till
The Centuries of June
And Centuries of August cease
And Consciousness—is Noon.

(1865)

1090

I am afraid to own a Body—
I am afraid to own a Soul—
Profound—precarious Property—
Possession, not optional—

5   Double Estate—entailed at pleasure
Upon an unsuspecting Heir—
Duke in a moment of Deathlessness
And God, for a Frontier.

(1866)

1128

These are the Nights that Beetles love—
From Eminence remote
Drives ponderous perpendicular
His figure intimate
5   The terror of the Children
The merriment of men

Depositing his Thunder
He hoists abroad again—
A Bomb upon the Ceiling
10   Is an improving thing—
It keeps the nerves progressive
Conjecture flourishing—
Too dear the Summer evening
Without discreet alarm—
15   Supplied by Entomology
With its remaining charm—

(1868)

1173

The Lightning is a yellow Fork
From Tables in the sky
By inadvertent fingers dropt
The awful Cutlery

5   Of mansions never quite disclosed
And never quite concealed
The Apparatus of the Dark
To ignorance revealed.

(1870)

1235

Like Rain it sounded till it curved
And then I knew 'twas Wind—
It walked as wet as any Wave
But swept as dry as sand—
5   When it had pushed itself away
To some remotest Plain
A coming as of Hosts was heard
That was indeed the Rain—
It filled the Wells, it pleased the Pools
10   It warbled in the Road—
It pulled the spigot from the Hills
And let the Floods abroad—

It loosened acres, lifted seas
The sites of Centres stirred
15   Then like Elijah rode away
Upon a Wheel of Cloud.[219]

(1872)

1247

To pile like Thunder to its close
Then crumble grand away
While Everything created hid
This—would be Poetry—

5   Or Love—the two coeval come—
We both and neither prove—
Experience either and consume—
For None see God and live—

(1873)

1311

This dirty—little—Heart
Is freely mine.
I won it with a Bun—
A Freckled shrine—

5   But eligibly fair
To him who sees
The Visage of the Soul
And not the knees.

(1874)

1331

Wonder—is not precisely Knowing
And not precisely Knowing not—
A beautiful but bleak condition
He has not lived who has not felt—

5 Suspense—is his maturer Sister—
   Whether Adult Delight is Pain
   Or of itself a new misgiving—
   This is the Gnat that mangles men—

                                    (1874)

      1575

   The Bat is dun, with wrinkled Wings—
   Like fallow Article—
   And not a song pervade his Lips—
   Or none perceptible.

5 His small Umbrella quaintly halved
   Describing in the Air
   An Arc alike inscrutable
   Elate Philosopher.

   Deputed from what Firmament—
10 Of what Astute Abode—
   Empowered with what Malignity
   Auspiciously withheld—

   To his adroit Creator
   Ascribe no less the praise—
15 Beneficent, believe me,
   His Eccentricities—

                                    (1876)

      1400

   What mystery pervades a well!
   That water lives so far—
   A neighbor from another world
   Residing in a jar

5 Whose limit none have ever seen,
   But just his lid of glass—

Like looking every time you please
In an abyss's face!

The grass does not appear afraid,
10 I often wonder he
Can stand so close and look so bold
At what is awe to me.

Related somehow they may be,
The sedge stands next the sea—
15 Where he is floorless
And does no timidity betray

But nature is a stranger yet;
The ones that cite her most
Have never passed her haunted house,
20 Nor simplified her ghost.

To pity those that know her not
Is helped by the regret
That those who know her, know her less
The nearer her they get.

                    (1877)

1433

How brittle are the Piers
On which our Faith doth tread—
No Bridge below doth totter so—
Yet none hath such a Crowd.

5 It is as old as God—
Indeed—'twas built by him—
He sent his Son to test the Plank,
And he pronounced it firm.

                    (1878)

1445

Death is the supple Suitor
That wins at last—
It is a stealthy Wooing
Conducted first
By pallid innuendoes
And dim approach
But brave at last with Bugles
And a bisected Coach
It bears away in triumph
To Troth unknown
And Kindred as responsive
As Porcelain.

(1878)

1527

Oh give it Motion—deck it sweet
With Artery and Vein—
Upon its fastened Lips lay words—
Affiance it again
To that Pink stranger we call Dust—
Acquainted more with that
Than with this horizontal one
That will not lift its Hat—

(1881)

1542

Come show thy Durham Breast
To her who loves thee best,
Delicious Robin—
And if it be not me
At least within my Tree
Do the avowing—
Thy Nuptial so minute
Perhaps is more astute
Than vaster suing—

10   For so to soar away
      Is our propensity
      The Day ensuing—
                          (1882)

      1551

      Those—dying then,
      Knew where they went—
      They went to God's Right Hand—
      That Hand is amputated now
5   And God cannot be found—

      The abdication of Belief
      Makes the Behavior small—
      Better an ignis fatuus
      Than no illume at all—
                          (1882)

      1670

      In Winter in my Room
      I came upon a Worm—
      Pink, lank and warm—
      But as he was a worm
5   And worms presume
      Not quite with him at home—
      Secured him by a string
      To something neighboring
      And went along.

10   A Trifle afterward
      A thing occurred
      I'd not believe it if I heard
      But state with creeping blood—
      A snake with mottles rare
15   Surveyed my chamber floor
      In feature as the worm before

But ringed with power—
The very string with which
I tied him—too
20   When he was mean and new
That string was there—

I shrank—"How fair you are"!
Propitiation's claw—
"Afraid," he hissed
25   "Of me"?
"No cordiality"—
He fathomed me—
Then to a Rhythm *Slim*
Secreted in his Form
30   As Patterns swim
Projected him.

That time I flew
Both eyes his way
Lest he pursue
35   Nor ever ceased to run
Till in a distant Town
Towns on from mine
I set me down
This was a dream.

                 (?)

1718

Drowning is not so pitiful
As the attempt to rise.
Three times, 'tis said, a sinking man
Comes up to face the skies,
5   And then declines forever
To that abhorred abode,
Where hope and he part company—
For he is grasped of God.
The Maker's cordial visage,

10   However good to see,
        Is shunned, we must admit it,
        Like an adversity.

                        (?)

        1751

        There comes an hour when begging stops,
        When the long interceding lips
        Perceive their prayer is vain.
        "Thou shalt not" is a kinder sword
5   Than from a disappointing God
        "Disciple, call again."

                        (?)

SARAH MORGAN BRYAN PIATT

(1836–1919)

Named for her grandfather Morgan Bryan, who, with his brother-in-law Daniel Boone, first settled Kentucky, Sarah Morgan Bryan was born in Lexington. When she was seven, her mother died, leaving her to be reared by various friends and relatives, including an aunt with whom she lived while completing her studies at Henry Female College in New Castle. Her first poems, published in southern newspapers, had already earned her a local reputation by the time she met and married John James Piatt, an editor at the *Louisville Journal* and the co-author with his friend William Dean Howells of a volume of poems. The Piatts moved to Washington, D.C., he to take up the first in a series of government posts, in the Treasury Department, she to bear the first of their seven children, three of whom would not survive infancy. Together, the couple produced the first of their verse collaborations, *The Nests at Washington* (1864). Moving to North Bend, Ohio, in 1867, John divided his time between editorial work on Cincinnati newspapers and his post as librarian of the U.S. House of Representatives, while Sarah turned out six volumes of her own poems: *A Voyage to the Fortunate Isles* (1874), *That New World* (1877), *Poems in Company with Children* (1877), *A Woman's Poems* (1878), *Dramatic Persons and Moods* (1880), and *A Book About Baby* (1882). In 1882, John was appointed U.S. consul at Cork, Ireland, a position he would hold until 1895. During those years, Sarah associated with such well-known English writers as Edmund Gosse, Austin Dobson, and Alice Meynell and earned a following among British critics with ten more books of poetry: *An Irish Garland* (1884), *The Children Out of-Doors* (with her husband, 1885), *In Primrose Time* (1886), *Select Poems* (1886), *Songs and Satires* (1886), *Child's World Ballads* (1887), *The Witch in the Glass* (1889), *An Irish Wildflower, Etc.* (1891), *An Enchanted Castle* (1893), and a two-volume collected *Poems* (1894)—all published both in Britain and the United States. In 1895, the Piatts returned to North Bend, where he resumed his editorial work for the *Cincinnati Enquirer*, and she published one last book of poems, *Child's World Ballads: Second Series* (1895). When her husband died, in 1917, she removed to her son's home in Caldwell, New Jersey, for the remainder of her life.

THE PALACE-BURNER

A Picture in a Newspaper[220]

She has been burning palaces. "To see
    The sparks look pretty in the wind?" Well, yes—
And something more. But women brave as she
    Leave much for cowards, such as I, to guess.

5   But this is old, so old that everything
    Is ashes here—the woman and the rest.
Two years are—oh! so long. Now you may bring
    Some newer pictures. You like this one best?

You wish that you had lived in Paris then?—
10   You would have loved to burn a palace, too?
But they had guns in France, and Christian men
    Shot wicked little Communists like you.

You would have burned the palace?—Just because
    You did not live in it yourself! Oh! why
15   Have I not taught you to respect the laws?
    You would have burned the palace—would not *I*?

Would I? Go to your play. Would I, indeed?
    I? Does the boy not know my soul to be
Languid and worldly, with a dainty need
20   For light and music? Yet he questions me.

Can he have seen my soul more near than I?
    Ah! in the dusk and distance sweet she seems,
With lips to kiss away a baby's cry,
    Hands fit for flowers, and eyes for tears and dreams.

25   Can he have seen my soul? And could she wear
    Such utter life upon a dying face:
Such unappealing, beautiful despair:
    Such garments—soon to be a shroud—with grace?

Has she a charm so calm that it could breathe
30   In damp, low places till some frightened hour;

Then start, like a fair, subtle snake, and wreathe
   A stinging poison with a shadowy power?

Would *I* burn palaces? The child has seen
   In this fierce creature of the Commune here,
35   So bright with bitterness and so serene,
   A being finer than my soul, I fear.

                                        1874

A DOUBT

It is subtle, and weary, and wide;
It measures the world at my side;
   It touches the stars and the sun;
It creeps with the dew to my feet;
5   It broods on the blossoms, and none,
Because of its brooding, are sweet;
It slides as a snake in the grass,
Whenever, wherever I pass.

It is blown to the South with the bird;
10 At the North, through the snow, it is heard;
   With the moon from the chasms of night
It rises, forlorn and afraid;
   If I turn to the left or the right
I can not forget or evade;
15 When it shakes at my sleep as a dream,
If I shudder, it stifles my scream.

It smiles from the cradle; it lies
On the dust of the grave, and it cries
   In the winds and the waters; it slips
20 In the flush of the leaf to the ground;
   It troubles the kiss at my lips;
It lends to my laughter a sound;
It makes of the picture but paint;
It unhaloes the brow of the saint.

25   The ermine and crown of the king,
      The sword of the soldier, the ring
          Of the bride, and the robe of the priest,
      The gods in their prisons of stone,
          The angels that sang in the East—
30   Yea, the cross of my Lord, it has known;
      And wings there are none that can fly
      From its shadow with me, till I die!

                                                    1874

THIS WORLD

      Why do we love her?—that she gave us birth?
      How can we thank her for ourselves? Are we,
      The pale, weak children of her old age, worth
          The light that shows——there is a mirror. See!

5   Why do we love her? In her withering days,
          Careless or frozen-hearted, half-asleep,
      She leaves us to our fierce and foolish plays,
          Nor kisses off the after-tears we weep.

      She lets us follow our own childish cries,
10   And find strange playmates; lets our baby hands
      Reach for the red glare in the tiger's eyes,
          Or the fair snake—the rainbow of the sands.

      She lets us climb, through deadly dews and vines,
          After illusive birds that nurse no song,
15   Or die for some faint wreath of snow, that shines
          On those great heights where gods alone belong.

      Still let us love her for her lovely years.
          Yet beautiful with moonlight beauty, she
      Now wonders vaguely, through forlornest tears,
20   How far away her morning's sun may be.

      Still let us love her. She is sad and blind,
          And with wan arms forever reaching back,

Into the dreadful dark of Space, to find
    Her radiant footsteps—that have left no track.

25 Still let us love her, though, indeed, she seems
    To give to our small wants small heed at best.
Let her sit muffled in her ancient dream,
    With souls of her first children at her breast.

Better she brood, with wide unshadowed eyes,
30   On phantom Hebrews under phantom palms,
With phantom roses flushed, and phantom skies
    Brooding above them full of Bible calms;

Better she help the young Egyptian make
    His play-house pyramid with her fancy's hands,
35 Or teach his Memnon's pulseless heart to ache
    With hollow music in forgotten sands;

Better, in vanished temples, watch the Greek
    Carve his divine white toys; better she hold
The Roman's savage sword and hear the shriek,
40   Than feel the silence through the silken fold;

For Antony's dusk queen[221] to lift the snake,
    For Brutus' wife[222] the shining death of fire—
Yea, all were better than to sit and take
    Dull honey from To-day and never tire.

45 So let us love her, our poor Mother yet,
    For songs, for pictures that her sons have made;
Aye, let us love her more if she forget—
    To think of us would make her shrink, afraid!

1874

IN HER PRISON

Watched with the cruel watching of the stars
Barred by the powers of darkness with their bars:

Oh! those that see me see as far as space,
And these that hold me circle every place.

5   My feet are tangled in the chains of Time,
My hands cannot take hold on air and climb.

And I am dumb—because the heavens are high,
And who can hope to scale them with a cry?

The floor is gray with mould on which I tread,
10   Dust gathers in the silence overhead.

With bitter bread and water hardly sweet
My jailer mocks me, saying: "Drink and eat."

Yet somewhere there are carpets soft and rare,
And lights and laughter in the world—somewhere?

15   And somewhere there are golden cups of wine,
And snowy cakes where combs of honey shine.

Through other lips I taste the wine, and touch
Through other feet the carpets—that is much.

I see through other eyes the lights, and hear
20   The laughter clearly, not with mine own ear.

My grating gathers me a drop of dew;
Some piteous blossom sends its sweetness through.

Some tender bird, far on a sunny tree,
Breaks his wild song and gives one half to me.

25   The palace music leaves the palace guest,
And falls to dreaming here upon my breast.

Yet, spite of all, sometimes my Prison shakes
With the great yearning of a heart that aches.

Oh! that its lonesome roof would fall to-night,
30   And show me for an instant—something White!

1877

ANSWERING A CHILD

But if I should ask the king?—
    He could if he would? Ah, no.
Though he took from his hand the ring,
    Though he took from his head the crown—
5   In the dust I should lay them down.

If I sat at a fairy's feet?—
    A fairy could if she would?
(Oh, the fairy-faith is sweet!)
    Though she gave me her wand and her wings,
10   To me they were pitiful things.

Ask God?—He can if He will?—
    He is better than fairies or kings?
(Ask God?—He would whisper: "Be still.")
    Though He gave me each star I can see
15   Through my tears—it were nothing to me.

"He can do"———But He cannot undo
    The terrible darkened gate
Which the fire of His will went through,
    Leading the Dead away.
20   For the Past it is vain to pray!

1877

NO HELP

When will the flowers grow there? I cannot tell.
    Oh, many and many a rain will beat there first,
Stormy and dreary, such as never fell
    Save when the heart was breaking that had nursed
5   Something most dear a little while, and then
Murmured at giving God his own again.

The woods were full of violets, I know;
    And some wild sweet-briers grew so near the place:
Their time is not yet come. Dead leaves and snow
10   Must cover first the darling little face
From these wet eyes, forever fixed upon
Your last still cradle, O most precious one!

Is he not with his Father? So I trust.
    Is he not His? Was he not also mine?
15 His mother's empty arms yearn toward the dust.
    Heaven lies too high, the soul is too divine.
I wake at night and miss him from my breast,
And—human words can never say the rest.

Safe? But out of the world, out of my sight!
20   My way to him through utter darkness lies.
I am gone blind with weeping, and the light—
    If there be light—is shut inside the skies.
Think you, to give my bosom back his breath,
I would not kiss him from the peace called Death?

25 And do I want a little Angel? No,
    I want my Baby—with such piteous pain,
That were this bitter life thrice bitter, oh!
    I could not choose but take him back again.
God cannot help me, for God cannot break
30 His own dark Law—for my poor sorrow's sake.

                                                    1877

IN A QUEEN'S DOMAIN

Ah, my subject, the rose, I know,
    Will give me her breath and her blush;
And my subject, the lily, spread snow,
    If I pass, for my foot to crush.

5   My subjects, the lamb and the fawn,
    They hide their heads in my breast;
And my subject, the dove, coos on,
    Though my hand creep close to her nest.

But my subject, the bee, will sting;
10   And my subject, the thorn, will tear;
And my subject, the tiger, will spring
    At me, with a cry and a glare.

And my subject, the lion, will shake
    With his anger my loneliest lands;
15   And my subject, the snake (ah! the snake!)
    Will strike me dead in the sands!

                 1877

IF I HAD MADE THE WORLD

If I had made the world—ah me!
    I might have left some things undone!
But as to *him*—my boy, you see,
A pretty world this world would be,
5   I'd say, without George Washington!

Would I have made the Baby? Oh,
    There were no need of anything
Without the Baby, you must know!
————I'm a Republican, and so
10   I never would have made "the King."

I might have made the President—
    Had I known how to make him right!
————Columbus? Yes, if I had meant

To find a flowering continent
15   Already made for me, I might.

I would have made one poet too—
     Has God made more? ———Yes, I forgot,
There is no need of asking you;
You know as little as I do.
20   A poet is—well, who knows what?

And yet a poet is, my dear,
     A man who writes a book like this,
(There never *was* but one, I hear;)
     ———Yes, it is hard to spell S-h-a-k-e-s-p-e-a-r-e.
25   So, now, Good-night,—and here's a kiss.

You are not tired?—you want to know
     What else I would have made? Not much.
A few white lambs that would not grow;
Some violets that would stay; some snow
30   Not quite too cold for you to touch.

I'd not have taught my birds to fly;
     My deepest seas would not be deep!—
My highest mountains hardly high;
My deserts full of dates should lie—
35   But why will you not go to sleep?

I'd *not* have made the wind, because
     It's made of—nothing. Never mind.
Nor any white bears—they have claws;
(Nor "Science," no, nor "Nature's laws!")
40   Nor made the North Pole hard to find!

I'd *not* have made the monkeys—(then
     No one could ever prove to me
There ever was a season when
All these fine creatures we call men
45   Hung chattering in some tropic tree!)

Once more, Good-night. This time you hear?
   Please hear as well my morning call.
————Yes, first I'll tell you something queer:
If *I* had made the world, I fear—
50   I'd not have made the world at all!

                          1877

STONE FOR A STATUE

Leave what is white for whiter use.
   For such a purpose as your own
Would be a dreary jest, a harsh abuse,
   A bitter wrong to snowy stone.

5 Let the pure marble's silence hold
   Its unshaped gods, and do not break
Those hidden images divine and old,
   To-day, for one mean man's small sake!

                          1878

ARMY OF OCCUPATION

[At Arlington, Va., 1866.]

The summer blew its little drifts of sound—
   Tangled with wet leaf-shadows and the light
Small breath of scatter'd morning buds—around
The yellow path through which our footsteps wound.
5   Below, the Capitol rose, glittering, white,

There stretch'd a sleeping army. One by one,
   They took their places until thousands met;
No leader's stars flash'd on before, and none
Lean'd on his sword or stagger'd with his gun—
10   I wonder if their feet have rested yet!

They saw the dust, they join'd the moving mass,
   They answer'd the fierce music's cry for blood,

Then straggled here and lay down in the grass:—
　　Wear flowers for such, shores whence their feet did pass;
15　　　Sing tenderly, O river's haunted flood!

They had been sick, and worn, and weary, when
　　They stopp'd on this calm hill beneath the trees:
Yet if, in some red-clouded dawn, again
The country should be calling to her men,
20　　　Shall the reveillé not remember these?

Around them underneath the mid-day skies
　　The dreadful phantoms of the living walk,
And by low moons and darkness, with their cries—
The mothers, sisters, wives with faded eyes,
25　　　Who call still names amid their broken talk.

And there is one who comes alone and stands
　　At his dim fireless hearth—chill'd and oppress'd
By Something he has summon'd to his lands,
While the weird pallor of its many hands
30　　　Points to his rusted sword in his own breast!

　　　　　　　　　　　　　　　　　　　　　1878

A LESSON IN A PICTURE

So it is whispered here and there,
　　That you are rather pretty? Well?
(Here's matter for a bird of the air
　　To drop down from the dusk and tell.)
5　Let's have no lights, my child. Somehow,
The shadow suits your blushes now.

The blonde young man who called to-day
　　(He only rang to leave a book?—
Yes, and a flower or two, I say!)
10　　　Was handsome, look you. Will you look?
You did not know his eyes were fine?—
You did not? Can you look in mine?

What is it in this picture here,
    That you should suddenly watch it so?
15 A maiden leaning, half in fear,
    From her far casement; and, below,
In cap and plumes (or cap and bells?)
Some fairy tale her lover tells.

Suppose this lonesome night could be
20   Some night a thousand springs ago,
Dim round that tower; and you were she,
    And your shy friend her lover (Oh!)
And I—her mother! And suppose
I knew just why she wore that rose.

25 Do you think I'd kiss my girl, and say:
    "Make haste to bid the wedding guest,
And make the wedding garment gay,—
    You could not find in East or West
So brave a bridegroom; I rejoice
30 That you have made so sweet a choice"?

Or say, "To look forever fair,
    Just keep this turret moonlight wound
About your face; stay in mid-air;—
    Rope-ladders lead one to the ground,
35 Where all things take the touch of tears,
And nothing lasts a thousand years"?

1879

A PIQUE AT PARTING

Why, sir, as to that——I did not know it was time for the
    moon to rise.
    (So, the longest day of them all can end, if we will have
      patience with it.)
One woman can hardly care, I think, to remember another
    one's eyes,
    And——the bats are beginning to flit.
5   . . . . We hate one another? It may be true.

What else do you teach us to do?
Yea, verily, to love you.

My lords—and gentlemen—are you sure that after we love
quite all
There is in your noble selves to be loved, no time on our
hands will remain?
10 Why, an hour a day were enough for this. We may watch the
wild leaves fall
On the graves you forget. . . . . It is plain
That you were not pleased when she said——Just so;
Still, what do we want, after all, you know,
But room for a rose to grow?

15 You leave us the baby to kiss, perhaps; the bird in the cage to
sing;
The flower on the window, the fire on the hearth (and the
fires in the heart) to tend.
When the wandering hand that would reach somewhere has
become the Slave of the Ring,
You give us—an image to mend;
Then shut with a careless smile, the door—
20 (There's dew or frost on the path before;)
We are safe inside. What more?

If the baby should moan, or the bird sit hushed, or the flower
fade out—what then?
Ah? the old, old feud of mistress and maid would be left
though the sun went out?
You can number the stars and call them by names, and, as
men, you can wring from men
25 The world—for they own it, no doubt.
We, not being eagles, are doves? Why, yes,
We must hide in the leaves, I guess,
And coo down our loneliness.

God meant us for saints? Yes—in Heaven. Well, I, for one, am
content
30 To trust Him through darkness and space to the end—if an
end there shall be;

But, as to His meanings, I fancy I never knew quite what He
    meant.
And——why, what were you saying to me
Of the saints—or *that* saint? It is late;
The lilies look weird by the gate.
35   . . . . Ah, sir, as to that—we will wait.

              1880

HER WORD OF REPROACH

We must not quarrel, whatever we do;
    For if I was (but I was not!) wrong,
Here are the tears for it, here are the tears:—
    What else has a woman to offer you?
5 Love might not last for a thousand years,
    You know, though the stars should rise so long.

Oh you, you talk in a man's great way!—
    So, love would last though the stars should fall?
Why, yes. If it last to the grave, indeed,
10   After the grave last on it may.
But—in the grave? Will its dust take heed
    Of anything sweet—or the sweetest of all?

Ah, death is nothing! It may be so.
    Yet, granting at least that death is death
15 (Pray look at the rose, and hear the bird),
    Whatever it is—we must die to know!
Sometime we may long to say one word
    Together—and find we have no breath.

Ah me, how divine you are growing again!—
20   How coldly sure that the Heavens are sure,
Whither too lightly you always fly
    To hide from the passion of human pain.
Come, grieve that the Earth is not secure,
    For this one night—and forget the sky!

              1880

SAD SPRING-SONG

Blush and blow, blush and blow,
   Wind and wild-rose, if you will;
You are sweet enough, I know—
You are sweet enough, but, oh,
Lying lonely, lying low,
   There is something sweeter still.

Come and go, come and go,
   Suns of morning, moons of night;
You are fair enough, I know—
You are fair enough, but oh,
Hidden darkly, hidden low,
   Lies the light that gave you light.

1880

SIDNEY LANIER

(1842–1881)

The story of Lanier's life reads like a prospectus for *Gone With the Wind*. Born and raised in Macon, Georgia, amidst circumstances of cultured gentility, and possessed of rare musical gifts, he went from private schooling to Oglethorpe University, graduating at the top of his class, in 1860, with plans to continue his studies in Germany. At the outbreak of the Civil War, the romantic youth became a devoted Confederate and, joining the Macon Volunteers, marched into Virginia to participate in the Seven Days Battles, including the bloody attack on Malvern Hill. After further service as a mounted scout on the James River, he became a signal officer on a blockade runner, whose capture left him a prisoner for the last four months of the war. Returning to defeated, devastated Georgia, he spent the next eight years working wherever he could to support himself and, after 1867, his wife and four sons, deferring all the while both his musical ambitions and the urge to write poetry that had come upon him in prison. In the year of his marriage, he managed to publish a novel, *Tiger-Lilies*, based on his experiences in the war. By 1873, however, his financial situation had not improved, while his health had so deteriorated that he determined to devote what remained to him of life to music and poetry.

Far from focusing his energies, that commitment scattered them in all directions. Musical study led to a chair in the orchestra of the Peabody Institute in Baltimore, and to study in the history of music as a cultural force and a component of education. Lanier's pursuit of poetry led in succession to publications in *Lippincott's Magazine* (Philadelphia), to a commission to write the words to a cantata for the 1876 Centennial Exposition in Philadelphia, to English studies at the Peabody Institute, to a series of lectures under auspices of the Institute, and finally to an appointment in English at Johns Hopkins University. His lectures appeared in three collections: *The Science of English Verse* (1880), which sought to equate the laws of verse and music on the basis of metrical quantity (duration of sound) rather than quality (relative stress); *The English Novel* (1883), published after his death; and *Shakespere and His Forerunners*, published in 1902. In these last hectic years of life, Lanier's poetry also had to compete with a good deal of hack writing, including *Florida* (1876), a guidebook based on his travels in search of health, as well as four volumes of medieval history, legend, and balladry for boys. Three years after his death from tuberculosis in 1881, his wife edited a complete collection of his poems, which reappeared with additions in 1891 and 1906. His complete writings were published in 1945.

SONG FOR "THE JACQUERIE"[223]

     May the maiden,
     Violet-laden
Out of the violet sea,
     Comes and hovers
5   Over lovers,
Over thee, Marie, and me,
     Over me and thee.

     Day the stately,
     Sunken lately
10   Into the violet sea,
     Backward hovers
     Over lovers,
Over thee, Marie, and me,
     Over me and thee.

15   Night the holy,
     Sailing slowly
Over the violet sea,
     Stars uncovers
     Over lovers,
20   Stars for thee, Marie, and me,
     Stars for me and thee.

            1868

NIRVÂNA

Through seas of dreams and seas of phantasies,
Through seas of solitudes and vacancies,
And through my Self, the deepest of the seas,
        I strive to thee, Nirvâna.

5   Oh long ago the billow-flow of sense,
Aroused by passion's windy vehemence,
Upbore me out of depths to heights intense,
        But not to thee, Nirvâna.

By waves swept on, I learned to ride the waves.
10 I served my masters till I made them slaves.
I baffled Death by hiding in his graves,
        His watery graves, Nirvâna.

And once I clomb a mountain's stony crown
And stood, and smiled no smile and frowned no frown,
15 Nor ate, nor drank, nor slept, nor faltered down,
        Five days and nights, Nirvâna.

Sunrise and noon and sunset and strange night
And shadow of large clouds and faint starlight
And lonesome Terror stalking round the height,
20   I minded not, Nirvâna.

The silence ground my soul keen like a spear.
My bare thought, whetted as a sword, cut sheer
Through time and life and flesh and death, to clear
        My way unto Nirvâna.

25 I slew gross bodies of old ethnic hates
That stirred long race-wars betwixt States and States.
I stood and scorned these foolish dead debates,
        Calmly, calmly, Nirvâna.

I smote away the filmy base of Caste.
30 I thrust through antique blood and riches vast,
And all big claims of the pretentious Past
        That hindered my Nirvâna.

Then all fair types, of form and sound and hue,
Up-floated round my sense and charmed anew.
35 —I waved them back into the void blue:
          I love them not, Nirvâna.

And all outrageous ugliness of time,
Excess and Blasphemy and squinting Crime
Beset me, but I kept my calm sublime:
40   I hate them not, Nirvâna.

High on the topmost thrilling of the surge
I saw, afar, two hosts to battle urge.
The widows of the victors sang a dirge,
          But I wept not, Nirvâna.

45 I saw two lovers sitting on a star.
He kissed her lip, she kissed his battle-scar.
They quarrelled soon, and went two ways, afar.
          O Life! I laughed, Nirvâna.

And never a king but had some king above,
50 And never a law to right the wrongs of Love,
And ever a fangèd snake beneath a dove,
          Saw I on earth, Nirvâna.

But I, with kingship over kings, am free.
I love not, hate not: right and wrong agree:
55 And fangs of snakes and lures of doves to me
          Are vain, are vain, Nirvâna.

So by mine inner contemplation long,
By thoughts that need no speech nor oath nor song,
My spirit soars above the motley throng
60   Of days and nights, Nirvâna.

O Suns, O Rains, O Day and Night, O Chance,
O Time besprent with seven-hued circumstance,
I float above ye all into the trance
          That draws me nigh Nirvâna.

65 Gods of small worlds, ye little Deities
Of humble Heavens under my large skies,
And Governor-Spirits, all, I rise, I rise,
     I rise into Nirvâna.

The storms of Self below me rage and die.
70 On the still bosom of mine ecstasy,
A lotus on a lake of balm, I lie
     Forever in Nirvâna.

               1871

TO BEETHOVEN

In o'er-strict calyx lingering,
    Lay music's bud too long unblown,
Till thou, Beethoven, breathed the spring:
    Then bloomed the perfect rose of tone.

5 O Psalmist of the weak, the strong,
    O Troubadour of love and strife,
Co-Litanist of right and wrong,
    Sole Hymner of the whole of life,

I know not how, I care not why,—
10   Thy music sets my world at ease,
And melts my passion's mortal cry
    In satisfying symphonies.

It soothes my accusations sour
    'Gainst thoughts that fray the restless soul:
15 The stain of death; the pain of power;
    The lack of love 'twixt part and whole;

The yea-nay of Freewill and Fate,
    Whereof both cannot be, yet are;
The praise a poet wins too late
20   Who starves from earth into a star;

The lies that serve great parties well,
    While truths but give their Christ a cross;

The loves that send warm souls to hell,
    While cold-blood neuters take no loss;

25   Th' indifferent smile that nature's grace
      On Jesus, Judas, pours alike;
    Th' indifferent frown on nature's face
      When luminous lightnings strangely strike

    The sailor praying on his knees
30   And spare his mate that's cursing God;
    How babes and widows starve and freeze,
      Yet Nature will not stir a clod;

    Why Nature blinds us in each act
      Yet makes no law in mercy bend,
35   No pitfall from our feet retract,
      No storm cry out *Take shelter, friend;*

    Why snakes that crawl the earth should ply
      Rattles, that whoso hears may shun,
    While serpent lightnings in the sky,
40   But rattle when the deed is done;

    How truth can e'er be good for them
      That have not eyes to bear its strength,
    And yet how stern our lights condemn
      Delays that lend the darkness length;

45   To know all things, save knowingness;
      To grasp, yet loosen, feeling's rein;
    To waste no manhood on success;
      To look with pleasure upon pain;

    Though teased by small mixt social claims,
50   To lose no large simplicity,
    And midst of clear-seen crimes and shames
      To move with manly purity;

    To hold, with keen, yet loving eyes,
      Art's realm from Cleverness apart,

55   To know the Clever good and wise,
            Yet haunt the lonesome heights of Art;

        O Psalmist of the weak, the strong,
            O Troubadour of love and strife,
        Co-Litanist of right and wrong,
60   Sole Hymner of the whole of life,

        I know not how, I care not why,
            Thy music brings this broil at ease,
        And melts my passion's mortal cry
            In satisfying symphonies.

65   Yea, it forgives me all my sins,
            Fits life to love like rhyme to rhyme,
        And tunes the task each day begins
            By the last trumpet-note of Time.

                                        1877

TO RICHARD WAGNER

        "I saw a sky of stars that rolled in grime.
            All glory twinkled through some sweat of fight,
        From each tall chimney of the roaring time
            That shot his fire far up the sooty night
5   Mixt fuels—Labor's Right and Labor's Crime—
            Sent upward throb on throb of scarlet light
        Till huge hot blushes in the heavens blent
            With golden hues of Trade's high firmament.

        "Fierce burned the furnaces; yet all seemed well,
10   Hope dreamed rich music in the rattling mills.
        'Ye foundries, ye shall cast my church a bell,'
            Loud cried the Future from the farthest hills:
        'Ye groaning forces, crack me every shell
            Of customs, old constraints, and narrow ills;
15   Thou, lithe Invention, wake and pry and guess,
            Till thy deft mind invents me Happiness.'

"And I beheld high scaffoldings of creeds
　　Crumbling from round Religion's perfect Fane:
And a vast noise of rights, wrongs, powers, needs,
20　　　—Cries of new Faiths that called 'This Way is plain,'
—Grindings of upper against lower greeds—
　　—Fond sighs for old things, shouts for new,—did reign
Below that stream of golden fire that broke,
　　Mottled with red, above the seas of smoke.

25　"Hark! Gay fanfares from halls of old Romance
　　Strike through the clouds of clamor: who be these
That, paired in rich processional, advance
　　From darkness o'er the murk mad factories
Into yon flaming road, and sink, strange Ministrants
30　　　Sheer down to earth, with many minstrelsies
And motions fine, and mix about the scene
　　And fill the Time with forms of ancient mien?

"Bright ladies and brave knights of Fatherland;
　　Sad mariners, no harbor e'er may hold,
35　A swan soft floating tow'rds a magic strand;
　　Dim ghosts, of earth, air, water, fire, steel, gold,
Wind, grief, and love; a lewd and lurking band
　　Of Powers—dark Conspiracy, Cunning cold,
Gray Sorcery; magic cloaks and rings and rods;
40　　　Valkyries, heroes, Rhinemaids, giants, gods!

· · ·

"O Wagner, westward bring thy heavenly art,
　　No trifler thou: Siegfried and Wotan be
Names for big ballads of the modern heart.
　　Thine ears hear deeper than thine eyes can see.
45　Voice of the monstrous mill, the shouting mart,
　　Not less of airy cloud and wave and tree,
Thou, thou, if even to thyself unknown,
　　Hast power to say the Time in terms of tone."

1877

THE REVENGE OF HAMISH

It was three slim does and a ten-tined buck in the bracken lay;
    And all of a sudden the sinister smell of a man,
    Awaft on a wind-shift, wavered and ran
Down the hill-side and sifted along through the bracken and
    passed that way.

5   Then Nan got a-tremble at nostril; she was the daintiest doe;
    In the print of her velvet flank on the velvet fern
    She reared, and rounded her ears in turn.
Then the buck leapt up, and his head as a king's to a crown
    did go

Full high in the breeze, and he stood as if Death had the form
    of a deer;
10   And the two slim does long lazily stretching arose,
    For their day-dream slowlier came to a close,
Till they woke and were still, breath-bound with waiting and
    wonder and fear.

Then Alan the huntsman sprang over the hillock, the hounds
    shot by,
    The does and the ten-tined buck made a marvellous bound,
15   The hounds swept after with never a sound,
But Alan loud winded his horn in sign that the quarry was
    nigh.

For at dawn of that day proud Maclean of Lochbuy to the
    hunt had waxed wild,
    And he cursed at old Alan till Alan fared off with the
    hounds
For to drive him the deer to the lower glen-grounds:
20   "I will kill a red deer," quoth Maclean, "in the sight of the
    wife and the child."

So gayly he paced with the wife and the child to his chosen
    stand;
    But he hurried tall Hamish the henchman ahead: "Go
    turn,"—
Cried Maclean—"if the deer seek to cross to the burn,

Do thou turn them to me: nor fail, lest thy back be red as thy
    hand."

25   Now hard-fortuned Hamish, half blown of his breath with the
        height of the hill,
    Was white in the face when the ten-tined buck and the does
    Drew leaping to burn-ward; huskily rose
His shouts, and his nether lip twitched, and his legs were o'er-
    weak for his will.

So the deer darted lightly by Hamish and bounded away to the
    burn.
30   But Maclean never bating his watch tarried waiting below.
    Still Hamish hung heavy with fear for to go
All the space of an hour; then he went, and his face was
    greenish and stern,

And his eye sat back in the socket, and shrunken the eyeballs
    shone,
    As withdrawn from a vision of deeds it were shame to see.
35   "Now, now, grim henchman, what is 't with thee?"
Brake Maclean, and his wrath rose red as a beacon the wind
    hath upblown.

"Three does and a ten-tined buck made out," spoke Hamish,
    full mild,
    "And I ran for to turn, but my breath it was blown, and
        they passed;
    I was weak, for ye called ere I broke me my fast."
40   Cried Maclean: "Now a ten-tined buck in the sight of the wife
    and the child

I had killed if the gluttonous kern had not wrought me a
    snail's own wrong!"
    Then he sounded, and down came kinsmen and
    clansmen all:
    "Ten blows, for ten tine, on his back let fall,
And reckon no stroke if the blood follow not at the bite of
    the thong!"

45   So Hamish made bare, and took him his strokes; at the last he
            smiled.
        "Now I'll to the burn," quoth Maclean, "for it still may be,
        If a slimmer-paunched henchman will hurry with me,
        I shall kill me the ten-tined buck for a gift to the wife and the
            child!"

        Then the clansmen departed, by this path and that; and over
            the hill
50   Sped Maclean with an outward wrath for an inward shame;
        And that place of the lashing full quiet became;
        And the wife and the child stood sad; and bloody-backed
            Hamish sat still.

        But look! red Hamish has risen; quick about and about
            turns he.
        "There is none betwixt me and the crag-top!" he screams
            under breath.
55   Then, livid as Lazarus lately from death,
        He snatches the child from the mother, and clambers the crag
            toward the sea.

        Now the mother drops breath; she is dumb, and her heart goes
            dead for a space,
        Till the motherhood, mistress of death, shrieks, shrieks
            through the glen,
        And that place of the lashing is live with men,
60   And Maclean, and the gillie that told him, dash up in a
            desperate race.

        Not a breath's time for asking; an eye-glance reveals all the
            tale untold.
        They follow mad Hamish afar up the crag toward the sea,
        And the lady cries: "Clansmen, run for a fee!—
        Yon castle and lands to the two first hands that shall hook
            him and hold

65   Fast Hamish back from the brink!"—and ever she flies up the
            steep,
        And the clansmen pant, and they sweat, and they jostle and
            strain.

But, mother, 'tis vain; but, father, 'tis vain;
Stern Hamish stands bold on the brink, and dangles the child
 o'er the deep.

Now a faintness falls on the men that run, and they all stand
 still.
70 And the wife prays Hamish as if he were God, on her
 knees,
Crying: "Hamish! O Hamish! but please, but please
For to spare him!" and Hamish still dangles the child, with a
 wavering will.

On a sudden he turns; with a sea-hawk scream, and a gibe,
 and a song,
Cries: "So; I will spare ye the child if, in sight of ye all,
75 Ten blows on Maclean's bare back shall fall,
And ye reckon no stroke if the blood follow not at the bite of
 the thong!"

Then Maclean he set hardly his tooth to his lip that his tooth
 was red,
Breathed short for a space, said: "Nay, but it never shall be!
Let me hurl off the damnable hound in the sea!"
80 But the wife: "Can Hamish go fish us the child from the sea, if
 dead?

Say yea!—Let them lash *me*, Hamish?"—"Nay!"—"Husband,
 the lashing will heal;
But, oh, who will heal me the bonny sweet bairn in his
 grave?
Could ye cure me my heart with the death of a knave?
Quick! Love! I will bare thee—so—kneel!" Then Maclean
 'gan slowly to kneel

85 With never a word, till presently downward he jerked to the
 earth.
Then the henchman—he that smote Hamish—would
 tremble and lag;
"Strike, hard!" quoth Hamish, full stern, from the crag;
Then he struck him, and "One!" sang Hamish, and danced
 with the child in his mirth.

And no man spake beside Hamish; he counted each stroke
    with a song.
90   When the last stroke fell, then he moved him a pace down
      the height,
    And he held forth the child in the heartaching sight
Of the mother, and looked all pitiful grave, as repenting a
    wrong.

And there as the motherly arms stretched out with the
    thanksgiving prayer—
    And there as the mother crept up with a fearful swift pace,
95   Till her finger nigh felt of the bairnie's face—
In a flash fierce Hamish turned round and lifted the child in
    the air,

And sprang with the child in his arms from the horrible height
    in the sea,
    Shrill screeching, "Revenge!" in the wind-rush; and pallid
      Maclean,
    Age-feeble with anger and impotent pain,
100 Crawled up on the crag, and lay flat, and locked hold of dead
    roots of a tree—

And gazed hungrily o'er, and the blood from his back drip-
    dripped in the brine,
    And a sea-hawk flung down a skeleton fish as he flew,
    And the mother stared white on the waste of blue,
And the wind drove a cloud to seaward, and the sun began to
    shine.

1878

TO BAYARD TAYLOR

To range, deep-wrapt, along a heavenly height,
    O'erseeing all that man but undersees;
To loiter down lone alleys of delight,
    And hear the beating of the hearts of trees,
5   And think the thoughts that lilies speak in white
    By greenwood pools and pleasant passages;

With healthy dreams a-dream in flesh and soul,
    To pace, in mighty meditations drawn,
From out the forest to the open knoll
10   Where much thyme is, whence blissful leagues of lawn
Betwixt the fringing woods to southward roll
    By tender inclinations; mad with dawn,

Ablaze with fires that flame in silver dew
    When each small globe doth glass the morning-star,
15 Long ere the sun, sweet-smitten through and through
    With dappled revelations read afar,
Suffused with saintly ecstasies of blue
    As all the holy eastern heavens are,—

To fare thus fervid to what daily toil
20   Employs thy spirit in that larger Land
Where thou art gone; to strive, but not to moil
    In nothings that do mar the artist's hand,
Not drudge unriched, as grain rots back to soil,—
    No profit out of death,—going, yet still at stand,—

25 Giving what life is here in hand to-day
    For that that's in to-morrow's bush, perchance,—
Of this year's harvest none in the barn to lay,
    All sowed for next year's crop,—a dull advance
In curves that come but by another way
30   Back to the start,—a thriftless thrift of ants

Whose winter wastes their summer; O my Friend,
    Freely to range, to muse, to toil, is thine:
Thine, now, to watch with Homer sails that bend
    Unstained by Helen's beauty o'er the brine
35 Tow'rds some clean Troy no Hector need defend
    Nor flame devour; or, in some mild moon's shine,

Where amiabler winds the whistle heed,
    To sail with Shelley[224] o'er a bluer sea,
And mark Prometheus, from his fetters freed,
40   Pass with Deucalion over Italy,
While bursts the flame from out his eager reed
    Wild-stretching towards the West of destiny;

Or, prone with Plato, Shakspere and a throng
 Of bards beneath some plane-tree's cool eclipse
45 To gaze on glowing meads where, lingering long,
 Psyche's large Butterfly[225] her honey sips;
Or, mingling free in choirs of German song,
 To learn of Goethe's life from Goethe's lips;

These, these are thine, and we, who still are dead,
50 Do yearn—nay, not to kill thee back again
Into this charnel life, this lowlihead,[226]
 Not to the dark of sense, the blinking brain,
The hugged delusion drear, the hunger fed
 On husks of guess, the monarchy of pain,

55 The cross of love, the wrench of faith, the shame
 Of science that cannot prove proof is, the twist
Of blame for praise and bitter praise for blame,
 The silly stake and tether round the wrist
By fashion fixed, the virtue that doth claim
60 The gains of vice, the lofty mark that's missed

By all the mortal space 'twixt heaven and hell,
 The soul's sad growth o'er stationary friends
Who hear us from our height not well, not well,
 The slant of accident, the sudden bends
65 Of purpose tempered strong, the gambler's spell,
 The son's disgrace, the plan that e'er depends

On others' plots, the tricks that passion plays
 (I loving you, you him, he none at all),
The artist's pain—to walk his blood-stained ways,
70 A special soul, yet judged as general—
The endless grief of art, the sneer that says,
 The war, the wound, the groan, the funeral pall—

Not into these, bright spirit, do we yearn
 To bring thee back, but oh, to be, to be
75 Unbound of all these gyves, to stretch, to spurn
 The dark from off our dolorous lids, to see
Our spark, Conjecture, blaze and sunwise burn,
 And suddenly to stand again by thee!

Ah, not for us, not yet, by thee to stand:
80   For us, the fret, the dark, the thorn, the chill;
For us, to call across unto thy Land,
          "Friend, get thee to the ministrels' holy hill,
And kiss those brethren for us, mouth and hand,
          And make our duty to our master Will."[227]

1879

EDWIN ARLINGTON ROBINSON

(1869–1935)

From the moment he discovered his literary calling, at twenty, until he died correcting the proofs for *King Jasper*, a half century later, Robinson did virtually nothing but write poetry. Descended through his mother from the seventeenth-century Massachusetts poet Anne Bradstreet, Robinson was born in Head Tide, Maine, and reared in the town of Gardiner, where he finished high school in 1888. Three years later, he entered Harvard as a special student but soon withdrew to aid his family, suddenly impoverished by the death of his father and by economic recession. In 1896, the year his mother died of diphtheria, he published at his own expense *The Torrent and the Night Before*, his first collection of poems. The next year, a much expanded version appeared under the title of *Children of the Night*, and Robinson moved to New York City. He lived there in poverty until *Captain Craig* (1902), the first of his long verse narratives, fell into the hands of President Theodore Roosevelt, who arranged for its republication (1905) and found the poet a job with the New York customs service. With the publication of *Town Down the River* (1910), dedicated to Roosevelt, Robinson came to popular and critical attention. In the next twenty-five years, he would publish sixteen more volumes of verse, including a dozen book-length narratives on medieval and contemporary themes, as well as two plays. For this work, he would be showered with honors, most notably three Pulitzer Prizes: in 1921 (the first ever awarded for poetry) for his *Collected Poems*, in 1924 for *The Man Who Died Twice*, and in 1927 for *Tristram*. Although his adherence to traditional forms of versification and structure have tended to marginalize him somewhat among the experimental Modernists, *Children of the Night* has been generally recognized as the beginning of a new era in American poetry.

WALT WHITMAN

The master-songs are ended, and the man
That sang them is a name. And so is God
A name; and so is love, and life, and death,
And everything.—But we, who are too blind

5   To read what we have written, or what faith
       Has written for us, do not understand:
       We only blink, and wonder.

       Last night it was the song that was the man,
       But now it is the man that is the song.
10   We do not hear him very much to-day;—
       His piercing and eternal cadence rings
       Too pure for us—too powerfully pure,
       Too lovingly triumphant, and too large;
       But there are some that hear him, and they know
15   That he shall sing to-morrow for all men.
       And that all time shall listen.

       The master-songs are ended?—Rather say
       No songs are ended that are ever sung,
       And that no names are dead names. When we write
20   Men's letters on proud marble or on sand,
       We write them there forever.
                                        1896

JOHN EVERELDOWN

       "Where are you going to-night, to-night,—
           Where are you going, John Evereldown?
       There's never the sign of a star in sight,
           Nor a lamp that's nearer than Tilbury Town.
5   Why do you stare as a dead man might?
       Where are you pointing away from the light?
       And where are you going to-night, to-night,—
           Where are you going, John Evereldown?"

       "Right through the forest, where none can see,
10   There's where I'm going, to Tilbury Town.
       The men are asleep,—or awake, may be,—
           But the women are calling John Evereldown.
       Ever and ever they call for me,
       And while they call can a man be free?

15 So right through the forest, where none can see,
  There's where I'm going, to Tilbury Town."

 "But why are you going so late, so late,—
  Why are you going, John Evereldown?
 Though the road be smooth and the way be straight
20 There are two long leagues to Tilbury Town.
 Come in by the fire, old man, and wait!
 Why do you chatter out there by the gate?
 And why are you going so late, so late,—
  Why are you going, John Evereldown?"

25 "I follow the women wherever they call,—
  That's why I'm going to Tilbury Town.
 God knows if I pray to be done with it all,
  But God is no friend to John Evereldown.
 So the clouds may come and the rain may fall,
30 The shadows may creep and the dead men crawl,—
 But I follow the women wherever they call,
  And that's why I'm going to Tilbury Town."

             1896

LUKE HAVERGAL

 Go to the western gate, Luke Havergal,
 There where the vines cling crimson on the wall,
 And in the twilight wait for what will come.
 The leaves will whisper there of her, and some,
5 Like flying words, will strike you as they fall;
 But go, and if you listen she will call.
 Go to the western gate, Luke Havergal—
 Luke Havergal.

 No, there is not a dawn in eastern skies
10 To rift the fiery night that's in your eyes;
 But there, where western glooms are gathering,
 The dark will end the dark, if anything:
 God slays Himself with every leaf that flies,
 And hell is more than half of paradise.

15   No, there is not a dawn in eastern skies—
      In eastern skies.

      Out of a grave I come to tell you this,
      Out of a grave I come to quench the kiss
      That flames upon your forehead with a glow
20   That blinds you to the way that you must go.
      Yes, there is yet one way to where she is,
      Bitter, but one that faith may never miss.
      Out of a grave I come to tell you this—
      To tell you this.

25   There is the western gate, Luke Havergal,
      There are the crimson leaves upon the wall.
      Go, for the winds are tearing them away,—
      Nor think to riddle the dead words they say,
      Nor any more to feel them as they fall;
30   But go, and if you trust her she will call.
      There is the western gate, Luke Havergal—
      Luke Havergal.

                         1896

THREE QUATRAINS

      I

As long as Fame's imperious music rings
    Will poets mock it with crowned words august;
And haggard men will clamber to be kings
    As long as Glory weighs itself in dust.

      II

5   Drink to the splendor of the unfulfilled,
        Nor shudder for the revels that are done:
     The wines that flushed Lucullus are all spilled,
        The strings that Nero fingered are all gone.

III

We cannot crown ourselves with everything,
    Nor can we coax the Fates for us to quarrel:
No matter what we are, or what we sing,
    Time finds a withered leaf in every laurel.

1896

THE HOUSE ON THE HILL

They are all gone away,
    The House is shut and still,
There is nothing more to say.

Through broken walls and gray
    The winds blow bleak and shrill:
They are all gone away.

Nor is there one to-day
    To speak them good or ill:
There is nothing more to say.

Why is it then we stray
    Around the sunken sill?
They are all gone away,

And our poor fancy-play
    For them is wasted skill:
There is nothing more to say.

There is ruin and decay
    In the House on the Hill:
They are all gone away,
There is nothing more to say.

1896

AARON STARK

Withal a meagre man was Aaron Stark,
Cursed and unkempt, shrewd, shrivelled, and morose.
A miser was he, with a miser's nose,
And eyes like little dollars in the dark.
5 His thin, pinched mouth was nothing but a mark;
And when he spoke there came like sullen blows
Through scattered fangs a few snarled words and close,
As if a cur were chary of its bark.

Glad for the murmur of his hard renown,
10 Year after year he shambled through the town,
A loveless exile moving with a staff;
And oftentimes there crept into his ears
A sound of alien pity, touched with tears,—
And then (and only then) did Aaron laugh.

                                                    1896

SONNET

Oh for a poet—for a beacon bright
To rift this changeless glimmer of dead gray;
To spirit back the Muses, long astray,
And flush Parnassus with a newer light;
5 To put these little sonnet-men to flight
Who fashion, in a shrewd mechanic way,
Songs without souls, that flicker for a day,
To vanish in irrevocable night.

What does it mean, this barren age of ours?
10 Here are the men, the women, and the flowers.
The seasons, and the sunset, as before.
What does it mean? Shall there not one arise
To wrench one banner from the western skies,
And mark it with his name forevermore?

                                                    1896

VERLAINE[228]

Why do you dig like long-clawed scavengers
To touch the covered corpse of him that fled
The uplands for the fens, and rioted
Like a sick satyr with doom's worshippers?
5   Come! let the grass grow there; and leave his verse
To tell the story of the life he led.
Let the man go: let the dead flesh be dead,
And let the worms be its biographers.

Song sloughs away the sin to find redress
10   In art's complete remembrance: nothing clings
For long but laurel to the stricken brow
That felt the Muse's finger; nothing less
Than hell's fulfilment of the end of things
Can blot the star that shines on Paris now.

1896

RICHARD CORY

Whenever Richard Cory went down town,
We people on the pavement looked at him:
He was a gentleman from sole to crown,
Clean favored, and imperially slim.

5   And he was always quietly arrayed,
And he was always human when he talked;
But still he fluttered pulses when he said,
"Good-morning," and he glittered when he walked.

And he was rich—yes, richer than a king—
10   And admirably schooled in every grace:
In fine, we thought that he was everything
To make us wish that we were in his place.

So on we worked, and waited for the light,
And went without the meat, and cursed the bread;

15   And Richard Cory, one calm summer night,
        Went home and put a bullet through his head.

                                                    1897

CLIFF KLINGENHAGEN

Cliff Klingenhagen had me in to dine
With him one day; and after soup and meat,
And all the other things there were to eat,
Cliff took two glasses and filled one with wine
5   And one with wormwood. Then, without a sign
For me to choose at all, he took the draught
Of bitterness himself, and lightly quaffed
It off, and said the other one was mine.

And when I asked him what the deuce he meant
10 By doing that, he only looked at me
And smiled, and said it was a way of his.
And though I know the fellow, I have spent
Long time a-wondering when I shall be
As happy as Cliff Klingenhagen is.

                                                    1897

REUBEN BRIGHT

Because he was a butcher and thereby
Did earn an honest living (and did right),
I would not have you think that Reuben Bright
Was any more a brute than you or I:
5   For when they told him that his wife must die,
He stared at them, and shook with grief and fright,
And cried like a great baby half that night,
And made the women cry to see him cry.

And after she was dead, and he had paid
10 The singers and the sexton and the rest,
He packed a lot of things that she had made

Most mournfully away in an old chest
Of hers, and put some chopped-up cedar boughs
In with them, and tore down the slaughter house.

1897

THE TAVERN

Whenever I go by there nowadays
And look at the rank weeds and the strange grass,
The torn blue curtains and the broken glass,
I seem to be afraid of the old place;
And something stiffens up and down my face,
For all the world as if I saw the ghost
Of old Ham Amory, the murdered host,
With his dead eyes turned on me all aglaze.

The Tavern has a story, but no man
Can tell us what it is. We only know
That once long after midnight, years ago,
A stranger galloped up from Tilbury Town,
Who brushed, and scared, and all but overran
That skirt-crazed reprobate, John Evereldown.

1897

from OCTAVES

XV

We lack the courage to be where we are:—
We love too much to travel on old roads,
To triumph on old fields; we love too much
To consecrate the magic of dead things,
And yieldingly to linger by long walls
Of ruin, where the ruinous moonlight
That sheds a lying glory on old stones
Befriends us with a wizard's enmity.

XIX

Nor jewelled phrase nor mere mellifluous rhyme
10   Reverberates aright, or ever shall,
One cadence of that infinite plain-song
Which is itself all music. Stronger notes
Than any that have ever touched the world
Must ring to tell it—ring like hammer-blows,
15   Right-echoed of a chime primordial,
On anvils, in the gleaming of God's forge.

XX

The prophet of dead words defeats himself:
Whoever would acknowledge and include
The foregleam and the glory of the real,
20   Must work with something else than pen and ink
And painful preparation: he must work
With unseen implements that have no names,
And he must win withal, to do that work,
Good fortitude, clean wisdom, and strong skill.

1897

EXPLANATORY NOTES

1. A mountain in a region of the Ecuadorian Andes plagued by earthquakes.
2. (Latin) "Whose cattle?"
3. The Kanawha River in West Virginia.
4. Patent cosmetics.
5. From "Magnes" (The Lodestone) by Claudian Claudianus, Roman poet of the fourth century A.D.: ". . . dark, dull, and common, it adorns neither the braided locks of kings nor the snowy necks of maidens; nor does it sparkle in the belts of warriors. But consider the marvellous properties of this unprepossessing stone and you will see that it has more value than gorgeous gems or the pearl that the Indian seeks amidst the kelp along the shores of the Red Sea."
6. This allusion, presumably familiar at the time, has lost all meaning except for that conferred by the ironic last line of the stanza.
7. Long known as a haven for outlaws—from the religious exiles who settled it; to the smugglers, privateers, and slavers who came to infest Newport; to the rebels who sought refuge in Tiverton during the Revolution—the colony was nevertheless called Rhodes's Island in its original charter.
8. John Adams (1735–1826) and the Marquis de Lafayette (1757–1834): major figures in the American Revolution. The episode recounted here took place during Lafayette's triumphal return visit to the United States in 1824–25.
9. A ceremonial hat carried under the arm.
10. From William Cowper's *The Task* (1785), Book 4, line 120.
11. His command of the Delphic oracle: access to prophecy.
12. Maitreya, a poet-prophet in the sacred Hindu text *Vishnu Purana*.
13. Legally entailed.
14. Respectively, a New Hampshire river and that state's tallest mountain (Mount Washington).
15. Judges 14.
16. Musketequid: Indian name for the Concord River in Massachusetts.
17. (Italian) "Mid-passage," from the opening line of Dante's *Inferno*.
18. Dante, *Inferno* 10.31–34.

19. The volume *Latinae epistolae*, published in Paris in 1759, includes a letter from one Brother Ilario, of the monastery of Corvo in the diocese of Luni, recounting this meeting with the poet.

20. En Gedi: a village on the shore of the Dead Sea (1 Samuel 24.1).

21. Basra: city in Iraq, called Bassorah in the *Arabian Nights*.

22. *Judenstrasse* (German): street of Jews.

23. (Hebrew) "Bitter"; here "bitterness" (Exodus 15.23).

24. (Greek) "[Let them] be cursed, [for] the Lord is come" (1 Corinthians 22).

25. John Winthrop (1588–1649), first governor of the Massachusetts Bay colony.

26. Thomas Morton (1590?–1647), English adventurer and author of the *New English Canaan* (1637); he vexed the Plymouth colony by trading guns and liquor with the Indians for furs and by the impious behavior of his companions at their outlaw settlement called Merry Mount.

27. Presumably without benefit of clergy.

28. Deuteronomy 32.32–33, as interpreted by John Milton in *Paradise Lost*, Book X, lines 547–72.

29. Sodom and Gomorrah (Genesis 19).

30. Singular form of Abruzzi, a wild region of the Apennine Mountains, in Italy.

31. Hashish.

32. From Swabia.

33. (Arabic) *Shaitan*: satanic.

34. In "The Tale of the Third Calender" (or "Kalendar") from the *Arabian Nights*.

35. Winged steed on which Muhammad rode to the heavens.

36. Fishing ground on the Gulf of Saint Lawrence, in Canada.

37. Kansas residence of John Brown (1800–1859) and the location of skirmishes between his fellow abolitionists and local pro-slavery forces.

38. In Book VIII of Virgil's *Aeneid*, the Etrurian (Tuscan) King Mezentius punishes his captive foes by chaining them to corpses.

39. Genesis 37.25.

40. Eden.

41. Castor and Pollux.

42. (French) "Concealed."

43. Fernan Mendes Pinto: sixteenth-century Portuguese adventurer whose narrative *Peregrinaçao* (published 1614) earned him the name "Prince of Liars."

44. Suffused with scoria.

45. The constellation Leo in the zodiac.

46. Railroad tunnel in the Berkshire Mountains of Massachusetts, completed in 1875, after twenty-four years of work.

47. John Cumming (1807–1881) and William Miller (1782–1849), self-styled prophets of the millennium.

48. Genesis 3.15.

49. Acts 2.

50. (Latin) "Such is life."

51. Punkatasset Hill, in Concord, Massachusetts.

52. Billerica, Massachusetts.

53. Rufus Wilmot Griswold (1815–1857), editor of *The Poets and Poetry of America* (1842).

54. *In loco disipis* (Latin) means "indulge in trifling" (Horace, *Odes* 4, 12, 48). *Locofoco* was the name given to the anti-slavery faction of the Democratic party, to which Bryant belonged.

55. The fictional speaker here is Apollo, whom Greek myth associates closely with the oracle at Delphi. The workings of the oracle entailed the placement of a golden tripod over the mouth of a deep cave. On the tripod sat Pythia, the priestess of Apollo, who translated the exhalations of the cave into oracles, with the help, if necessary, of an attendant poet.

56. Taillefer, the troubadour who sang as he led the Norman army into battle at Hastings in 1066.

57. The question (Latin) "Whether this be your son's cloak?" (Genesis 37.32) is here addressed to George Fox (1624–1691), founder of the Society of Friends, or Quakers, of which Whittier was a lifelong member.

58. Castalia's.

59. Cornelius Mathews (1817–1889), New York author, editor, and Poe's sometime associate; he had no part in Poe's attacks on Longfellow in the *New York Evening Mirror* (1845).

60. William Collins (1721–1759) and Thomas Gray (1716–1771), English poets of the so-called Graveyard School.

61. Attempts to imitate Classical patterns of longer and shorter syllables with the relatively stressed syllables typical of English, as in Longfellow's *Evangeline*.

62. Alexander Pope translated Homer's *Iliad* (1715–20) and *Odyssey* (1725–26).

63. Another name for Homer.

64. Again, Homer.

65. Johann Strauss (1825–1899), Austrian composer of waltzes.

66. Thomas Campbell (1777–1844), English poet.

67. In Part II of Holmes's metrical essay called "Poetry."

68. Poem (1846) by Edward George Bulwer-Lytton (1803–1873).

69.   Methuselah (Genesis 5.21–27).
70.   Benjamin Disraeli (1804–1881) and Sir Walter Scott (1771–1832), English novelists.
71.   Greek painter in the court of Alexander the Great.
72.   With commodity value equal to its face value; as opposed to paper money, greenbacks.
73.   Matthew 22.21.
74.   While eight of the first eleven presidents (including Washington, Jefferson, and Jackson) were personally involved in the slave economy, Lowell probably had in mind here James K. Polk, the sitting president when these words were written.
75.   (Slang) An unprincipled politician, ready to put on any face.
76.   Lowell's subject here is his mentally ill mother.
77.   Head of an urban political machine.
78.   Two of the four magic gifts conferred upon the hero of the nursery tale "Jack the Giant Killer."
79.   In carpentry: cross-braced.
80.   Keelson.
81.   (Slang) A black American.
82.   An extended hand spoke on a ship's wheel.
83.   Quaker name for Sunday and Whitman's coinage from the verb "loaf."
84.   A journeyman in that trade.
85.   (Chatahoochee) Rivers in Louisiana.
86.   Whitman's coinage: syphilitic.
87.   Paper envelope containing a medical prescription.
88.   Curlicue.
89.   Of all sorts.
90.   A device for rescuing passengers from sinking ships.
91.   All-male dances derived from American Indian ceremonies.
92.   Close.
93.   Whitman's coinage: chunks of ice that have toppled down the slope.
94.   *Ambulancia* (Spanish): ambulance.
95.   (French) Disciples.
96.   (Slang) American Indian.
97.   (Slang) Wrinkled lips.
98.   Kronos is Cronus, the Titan, called Saturn in Roman mythology. The other less familiar names on this list are Belus, a legendary king of Assyria; and Mexitli, the Aztec god of war.
99.   *Obi*: an African form of sorcery carried to the New World by slaves.
100.   Shastras: sacred Hindu texts.
101.   Aztec temples.
102.   A Sumatran from the region of Palembang.

103. Saurians.
104. Broadcasts.
105. Heel.
106. (French) A male midwife.
107. Quaker term for September.
108. Indian name for Long Island, New York.
109. Superseded.
110. Whitman's coinage: make clear, translate.
111. The French ship *L'Aigle*, on which the wife of Napoléon III led the naval procession at the opening ceremonies, November 17, 1869.
112. Wasatch.
113. Vasco da Gama.
114. Ibn Battuta (1303–1377) recorded his lifelong travels in Asia and Africa.
115. *Histrio* (Latin): actor.
116. Preparing to leave his home in Pittsfield, Massachusetts, for New York City in 1862, Melville reviewed all the poems he had written to date, recopied those he wished to save, and burned the rest.
117. At the National Gallery in London, in 1857, Melville saw J.M.W. Turner's painting of H.M.S. *Temeraire,* which had fought alongside Admiral Horatio Nelson's *Victory* at the battle of Trafalgar (here pronounced Tráfalgár), being towed by a steam tug down the Thames to a shipyard to be dismantled.
118. The proper names in this poem all denote Civil War battles in which the Confederate general Thomas J. Jackson participated.
119. In the summer of 1863, mobs rioted in New York City, attacking black citizens and burning down a home for African-American orphans, to protest conscription into the Union army.
120. The doctrine of John Calvin (1509–1564) asserting the natural depravity of humans.
121. A Confederate prison. The preceding names denote Civil War battles.
122. In this excerpt from *Clarel,* Celio, an Italian visitor to the city of Jerusalem, contemplates the arch called Ecce Homo (Latin: "Behold the man!"), where Pontius Pilate presented Jesus to the multitude for judgment (John 19.5).
123. (Latin) "Way of the Cross"—another name for the Via Dolorosa (Latin: "Sorrowful Way"), along which Jesus passed to his crucifixion.
124. Still.
125. In this canto, the narrator describes the Druze (Druse) guide Djalea and Belex, the guard commander, who together lead Clarel and his companions (including Nehemiah) on their tour of the Holy Land.

126. Ibrahim Pasha, Egyptian commander of Syria (1832–1841).
127. From Palmyra, called Tadmor in the Bible (1 Kings 9.18).
128. 1 Kings 18.
129. In 1826, Mahmoud II, sultan of Turkey, slaughtered the rebellious Janisseries in Et Meidan square, Constantinople.
130. Ornamentation.
131. Inlaid with threads of gold or silver.
132. Belex's horse, Solomon, which the narrator here and elsewhere refers to as Don John (Don Juan).
133. In this excerpt, the traveling party encounters a band of Arabs who may be robbers.
134. The Midianite (Numbers 25.6–8).
135. King Richard I of England, called the Lion-Hearted, captured the city of Acre in 1191, during the Third Crusade.
136. Sultan.
137. In this excerpt, Rolfe, one of Clarel's fellow tourists, recalls his youthful adventures in Polynesia.
138. The fictional name of Rolfe's island paradise.
139. Alvaro Mendaña de Neyra, sixteenth-century Spanish navigator who discovered and named the Marquesas Islands.
140. (French) Small waterfall.
141. Here, another of Clarel's companions, an old sea captain, recalls an altogether different sort of Pacific island, presumably one of the Galápagos.
142. Numbers 13.33.
143. Dodman's Point, a prominent landmark for ships homeward bound to Plymouth, England.
144. Albatross.
145. Ship's chaplain.
146. Hell.
147. Short ropes or chains for securing an anchor when not in use.
148. Athenian general and envoy, fourth century B.C.
149. Alicante, Spain.
150. An excavation over which large logs were laid to be cut lengthwise into planks by two sawyers, one on the log and the other in the pit below.
151. John Milton, *Paradise Lost*, Book 7, lines 214–15.
152. Where Christ preached to the multitudes (Matthew 5); also Calvary (Luke 23.33), where he was crucified.
153. Revelation 7.1–3.
154. A personification of love: Cupid.
155. Erupt.

156. An *ars memoria* (Latin), on the model of Ovid's *Ars amatoria* (The Art of Love) or various writings under such titles as *Ars moriendi* (The Art of Death), *Ars poetica* (The Art of Poetry), etc.

157. The Villa Albani in Rome, noted for its collection of antique statuary.

158. Athene.

159. Genesis 32.22–32.

160. (Spanish) "Holy Weed."

161. An eleventh-century edict, issued by the Church and ratified by European nations, forbidding war during the period between Lent and Advent each year or in the days surrounding holy festivals. The ban was seldom observed.

162. Sir Walter Raleigh (1554–1618), credited with introducing tobacco into England.

163. Indian summer.

164. Smoking room.

165. Exodus 10.21–29.

166. Priests of Thebes on the upper Nile.

167. At the Battle of the Pyramids, July 1798, when the French defeated the Mamluke army.

168. John Milton, *Paradise Lost*, Book 3, lines 1–6.

169. Rose temple.

170. Don Quixote.

171. Luis de Camoëns (1524 or 1525–1580) wrote *The Lusiads*, Portugal's great national epic, but died in poverty.

172. (Latin) *Si fortuna juvat*: "If fortune smiles."

173. Pontoosuc: a lake near Melville's home in Pittsfield, Massachussets.

174. Apparently, the bay in northern Florida; but more likely, given the context, Melville's shorthand for the Appalachian Mountains.

175. Manacles.

176. Ship's brig.

177. One of the pulleys that hang like earrings from the ends of topsail yards on a square-rigged ship.

178. Acts 9.

179. Richard I of England (reigned 1189–99).

180. The significance of this allusion, like those to Leoena and Erexcea in "Rhotruda" and to Xenaphyle in "The Cricket," is its utter obscurity. Whereas such allusions in Bryant, Longfellow, or Whittier would have been familiar to their intended readers, Tuckerman's, like those of many Modernist poets, seem to hold meaning for the poet alone.

181. Either the queen of Halicarnasus, who fought alongside Xerxes against the Greeks at the naval battle of Salamis (480 B.C.), or else the fourth-century queen of Caria, who married her brother Mausolus and grieved inconsolably after his death.

182. Fee simple.

183. Share, beam, and parallels are all parts of a plow.

184. (Spanish) Herd or flock: here, "animal."

185. Bel: the principal deity of Babylonia (Isaiah 46.1).

186. One of the Titans, identified in Christian tradition with Satan.

187. The mother of Samson (Judges 13.2–25).

188. The mothers, respectively, of Caesar Augustus, William the Conqueror, and Cyrus the Great.

189. "Too," here, seems to refer solely to Eginardus and to mean "in addition," rather than "as well," since Launcelot and Guinevere were both the children of kings.

190. In 774, Charlemagne conquered the city of Pavia, crushing the Lombard supremacy.

191. Trophies.

192. Tribes under the sway of Charlemagne.

193. This allusion is obscure. Charlemagne's attendants were called The Twelve; while The Forty (*Les Quarante*) are the members of the French Academy.

194. Palmyra, a kind of palm tree.

195. The allusion is obscure.

196. Apparently a dishonored female poet ("second Sappho . . . discrowned"). The allusion, however, is obscure.

197. Crown of laurel.

198. The tapestry depicts the legend of King Arthur from the time of Merlin's association with Arthur's father, Uther Pendragon, to the death of Arthur in the battle of Camlan.

199. Apparently an allusion to the German folktale "Rapunzel," in which the heroine, imprisoned in a tower by a witch, lets down her hair so that her lover can climb up to her. If so, the "angry blades" may be the thorn bushes at the base of the tower, onto which the prince leaps, blinding himself.

200. Tuckerman's coinage, from "grume": a viscous, sticky material, like tree sap.

201. That which is scattered.

202. (Greek) "Glittering with gold."

203. Agreement, truce.

204. Skeleton of the coral polyp.

205. Thickets.

206. River in Asia Minor, site of the ancient city of Ephesus.

207. Peloponnesian river, the ancient site of Sparta.
208. The allusion is obscure.
209. One of Apollo's lovers, the mother of Linus.
210. Tiresias.
211. Poinsettias.
212. Likeness of someone deceased.
213. Revelation 8.
214. Prima ballerina.
215. The story is told in Longfellow's poem *The Courtship of Miles Standish*.
216. Genesis 24.64.
217. An oblique allusion, perhaps, to the election of Esther by the Persian king Ahasuerus and her part in the ("crucifixal") hanging of Haman (Esther 2–7).
218. Sir Anthony Van Dyck (1599–1641), Flemish painter.
219. 2 Kings 2.
220. Illustration of a Communarde in the Paris uprising of 1871.
221. Cleopatra.
222. Portia.
223. Lanier's long-planned but never-finished romance on the uprising of French peasants in 1358, as recounted by Jean Froissart in his late-fourteenth-century *Chronicles*.
224. Percy Bysshe Shelley (1792–1822), English poet and author of *Prometheus Unbound*, drowned when his sailboat was overtaken by a storm.
225. In works of art, Psyche is often portrayed as a maiden with the wings of a butterfly.
226. Humble condition.
227. Shakespeare.
228. Paul Verlaine (1844–1896), French poet.

FOR THE BEST IN PAPERBACKS, LOOK FOR THE

In every corner of the world, on every subject under the sun, Penguin represents quality and variety—the very best in publishing today.

For complete information about books available from Penguin—including Penguin Classics, Penguin Compass, and Puffins—and how to order them, write to us at the appropriate address below. Please note that for copyright reasons the selection of books varies from country to country.

In the United States: Please write to *Penguin Group (USA), P.O. Box 12289 Dept. B, Newark, New Jersey 07101-5289* or call 1-800-788-6262.

In the United Kingdom: Please write to *Dept. EP, Penguin Books Ltd, Bath Road, Harmondsworth, West Drayton, Middlesex UB7 0DA.*

In Canada: Please write to *Penguin Books Canada Ltd, 10 Alcorn Avenue, Suite 300, Toronto, Ontario M4V 3B2.*

In Australia: Please write to *Penguin Books Australia Ltd, P.O. Box 257, Ringwood, Victoria 3134.*

In New Zealand: Please write to *Penguin Books (NZ) Ltd, Private Bag 102902, North Shore Mail Centre, Auckland 10.*

In India: Please write to *Penguin Books India Pvt Ltd, 11 Panchsheel Shopping Centre, Panchsheel Park, New Delhi 110 017.*

In the Netherlands: Please write to *Penguin Books Netherlands bv, Postbus 3507, NL-1001 AH Amsterdam.*

In Germany: Please write to *Penguin Books Deutschland GmbH, Metzlerstrasse 26, 60594 Frankfurt am Main.*

In Spain: Please write to *Penguin Books S. A., Bravo Murillo 19, 1° B, 28015 Madrid.*

In Italy: Please write to *Penguin Italia s.r.l., Via Benedetto Croce 2, 20094 Corsico, Milano.*

In France: Please write to *Penguin France, Le Carré Wilson, 62 rue Benjamin Baillaud, 31500 Toulouse.*

In Japan: Please write to *Penguin Books Japan Ltd, Kaneko Building, 2-3-25 Koraku, Bunkyo-Ku, Tokyo 112.*

In South Africa: Please write to *Penguin Books South Africa (Pty) Ltd, Private Bag X14, Parkview, 2122 Johannesburg.*